WRITING AND ANALYSIS IN THE LAW

SECOND EDITION

By

HELENE S. SHAPO
Professor of Law
Director of Legal Writing
Northwestern University School of Law

MARILYN R. WALTER
Professor of Law
Director of the Legal Writing Program
Brooklyn Law School

ELIZABETH FAJANS, Ph.D.
Writing Specialist
Brooklyn Law School

Westbury, New York
THE FOUNDATION PRESS, INC.
1991

Library of Congress Cataloging-in-Publication Data

Shapo, Helene S., 1938–
    Writing and analysis in the law / by Helene S. Shapo, Marilyn R.
Walter, Elizabeth Fajans.—2nd ed.
        p.   cm.
    Includes index.
    ISBN 0–88277–874–9
    1. Legal composition.   I. Walter, Marilyn R., 1943–
II. Fajans, Elizabeth.   III. Title.
KF250.S5   1991
808'.06643—dc20   90–28400

    S., W. & F.–Writing and Analysis 2nd Ed. FP
    2nd Reprint—1993

PREFACE

Many people find writing a difficult and frustrating process. As a result, they put off writing projects in the hope that they will eventually be struck by inspiration. Unfortunately, few professions, especially the legal profession, are willing to postpone business in anticipation of this happening.

This book is devoted, therefore, to taking control over the writing process away from chance and investing it in ourselves. We have tried to break the legal reasoning and writing process into manageable components to enable you to be conscious of that process and to be master of your thoughts and their expression. We hope this awareness of the writing process will also make you less anxious when writing and more satisfied with your work when finished.

Writing and Analysis in the Law is a collaborative effort. Decisions about the scope of the book and the focus of each chapter were made jointly. In addition, the authors edited each other's chapters extensively, making both substantive and stylistic contributions to each chapter. We have learned much from each other and hope the book confirms our belief in the benefits of editing and rewriting. Nonetheless, we would like to give proper acknowledgement to Helene Shapo as the primary author of chapters one, three, four, ten, and eleven, to Marilyn Walter as the primary author of chapters two, five, twelve, and fourteen, and to Elizabeth Fajans as the primary author of chapters six, seven, eight, nine, and thirteen.

*

v

ACKNOWLEDGEMENTS

We would like to acknowledge and thank our students. Their progress marks our success as teachers and their questions spur our own development. We would like to offer special thanks to those students and ex-students who have given us permission to use their work in this book: Robert Banozic, Dale Berson, Brian Blanchard, Robert M. Bornstein, Gail Cagney, Anthony T. Cartusciello, Abigail Chanis, Barbara Curry, Laura E. Ewall, Patricia Gennerich, Victor Gialleonardo, Rhonda Katz, Jane Levin, Kathleen Lewis, Philip J. Loree, Bruce E. Loren, Joseph Macaluso, Linda Mendelowitz-Alpert, Donna A. Mulcahy, Bonnie M. Murphy, Anthony Rothschild, Ann Ruben, Alice F. Rubin, Concettina Sacheli, Thomas Skinner, Leslie Soule, Abby Sternschein, Melissa Wynne, Roberta Wilensky, and Mona Zessimopoulos. Three research assistants from Northwestern University School of Law—Anne Meyer, Kevin Osborne, and Robert Sell—provided perceptive suggestions for many of our chapters for the first edition. Jim Groth was an invaluable editor for the second edition.

We are also indebted to our colleagues, from whom we have learned much. Professors Ursula Bentele, Neil Cohen, Will Hellerstein, Sara Robbins, and Jeff Stempel, faculty members at Brooklyn, and Professor George Grossman and especially Professor Marshall S. Shapo of Northwestern read various chapters for us and made valuable suggestions. Professors Jim Haddad and John Elson of the Northwestern faculty give their time every year to help teach appellate advocacy to the first-year class; their ideas have inevitably found their way into the final chapters of this book. Professor Cynthia Grant Bowman of Northwestern graciously provided us with the memorandum on which Appendix E is in large part based. Many legal writing instructors, past and present, and other colleagues have allowed us to base examples and exercises on problems they developed for their classes. We extend thanks to those from Brooklyn—Bob Begleiter, Stacy Caplow, Eve Cary, Martha Dietz, Mollie Falk, Philip Genty, Paul Green, Sharon Katz, Roseann MacKechnie, Kirsten Mishkin, Kate O'Neill, Pamela Perron, Susan Pouncey, Carrie Teitcher, Carol Ziegler—and to those from Northwestern—Marion Gray, Peter Humphrey, Mardell Nereim, and Judith Rosenbaum. Judith also did some valuable editing for us.

We would also like to express our gratitude to Brooklyn Law School and Northwestern University School of Law. These institutions not only gave us general encouragement, but also invested in our project by granting us research stipends.

Finally, Marilyn Walter and Elizabeth Fajans would like to thank their secretary, Alice Salome, for her efficiency and graciousness—even after interminable hours word processing, and Jeanne McHugh for her helpful assistance on the second edition. Similarly, Helene Shapo would like to thank Nancy Wagner and Cindy Seitz for their generous secretarial assistance and Cheryl Parker for her work on the second edition.

TABLE OF CONTENTS

TABLE OF CONTENTS

TABLE OF CONTENTS

TABLE OF CONTENTS

WRITING AND ANALYSIS IN THE LAW

*

Chapter One
Introduction to the Legal System and Legal Writing

I. The Primary Sources of Law

Students decide to come to law school for many good and diverse reasons. However, despite our numerous years teaching in law schools, we have never heard new students say they have come to law school because they like to write. Yet lawyers write all the time. They write to colleagues; they write to adversaries in a law suit; they write to third parties requesting favors or information; they write to judges. They write documents for many different purposes: to inform an adversary that a client is open to settlement but willing to litigate if pressed too hard; they write to persuade a court to rule in a client's favor. To be a good lawyer, you must be a good writer. And to be a good legal writer, you must have both a good understanding of law and a good grasp of principles of writing.

This book introduces you to the sources of authority with which a lawyer works and upon which a lawyer's writing revolves. It introduces you to legal analysis and some forms of legal writing. Finally, it tries to integrate those lawyerly enterprises with that which all good writing must demonstrate, namely, a clear sense of audience, purpose, organization, and paragraph and sentence structure.

When you were an undergraduate or graduate student, you probably read a variety of primary and secondary sources to get the information you needed to write papers. You may have relied

1

upon several secondary sources, such as books written by others about the topics of your papers. As a lawyer you will also use many different sources of information to acquire the necessary background information to analyze a legal question. A lawyer's most important sources of information, however, are primary sources.

Primary sources in law include both case law (judicial decisions) and enacted law (statutes, constitutions, and administrative regulations). These are the formal sources of enforceable legal rules in this country. Although you may not study administrative and constitutional law until the second or third year of law school, you will have to learn to use case law and statutory law throughout your first year and for almost all the writing that you do in your legal writing course. That is because in our legal system, analysis of a problem is controlled by enacted provisions, such as legislation, that regulate the subject matter of that problem and by the decisions of earlier cases that involved issues and facts similar to that problem. This year you will be learning how to find those legal authorities, how to use them, and how to write about them.

The first information you need concerns the origins of the primary authorities of the law. Because most of your first year classes emphasize case law, this introduction will begin with judicial decisions. You should be aware, however, that enacted law forms a significant part of the body of law in our country. You must always consult these sources first when you do research for a problem because constitutional provisions and statutes take precedence over case law. However, even when you find an applicable statute or constitutional provision, you must also determine whether any case law is relevant to the problem. Legal research entails searching for cases that have interpreted the particular statute or constitutional provision. When you find these cases, you analyze how they are relevant to your problem or explain why the cases are not relevant. When no statute or constitutional provision applies, then you must rely solely on earlier cases—the common law—on the subject.

The United States is a common law country, in that rules of law come from the written decisions of judges who hear and decide litigation. The common law is judge-made law. Judges are empowered by statute or by constitutional provision in every state and in our federal system to decide controversies between litigants. When a judge decides a case, the decision attains the status of law, and it becomes a precedent for future legal controversies that are similar. Our common law system, like the English system from which it came, is a system of precedent. In the simplest sense, precedents are just the decisions of judges in previous litigation. Those decisions, however, play a dual role. First, the decision resolves the litigation that is before the court. Second, if that decision is published, it becomes available for use by judges in later litigation. According to the doctrine of precedent, judges should resolve litigation according to the resolutions of all similar cases in the past.

Many factors in addition to similarity determine how a case is used as a precedent, and this book will introduce you to some of those factors. For example, the value of a decision is affected by the court that decided the case. The purpose of this introductory section is to explain where our law comes from and how a decision's value as a precedent is affected by the nature of the court that decided the case.

II. Structure of the Court System in the United States

A. The Vertical Structure of our Court System

Case law in the United States comes from litigation conducted in many court systems. Each state, as well as the District of Columbia and the federal government, has its own system of courts. Each is a separate jurisdiction. For our purposes, a jurisdiction is the area over which the courts of a particular judicial system are empowered to resolve disputes and thus to enforce their decisions. Jurisdiction is determined by a geographic area, like a state, and it can also be based upon subject matter. Subject matter jurisdiction is the authority of a court to resolve disputes in only a particular subject area of the law, such as criminal law.

The structure of the court system within each jurisdiction is a hierarchical one. Courts are organized along a vertical structure, and the position of a court within that structure has important consequences. Courts in which litigation begins are called courts of original jurisdiction. In many states, the lowest rung of the courts of original jurisdiction is occupied by a so-called court of inferior jurisdiction. This court has the power to hear only limited types of cases, such as misdemeanor cases or cases in which the amount of damages the complaining party (the plaintiff) demands from the party sued (the defendant) does not exceed a specified sum. These courts have various names, such as courts of common pleas or small claims courts. Other courts of inferior jurisdiction are limited to deciding cases about one particular subject matter, for example, juvenile or family law matters. Courts of inferior jurisdiction may be conducted informally. For example, the parties often represent themselves and the court does not follow the formal rules of evidence. The decisions of these courts are not published and they have no value as precedent to future litigants.

The next rung up from the courts of inferior jurisdiction is occupied by the trial courts. Litigation often begins at this level, and the trial courts are usually the courts in which the parties first litigated the cases that appear as appellate decisions in your case books. Trial courts are usually courts of general jurisdiction, that is, they may hear cases of all subject matters. Thus, a trial court may hear civil litigation, which is litigation between private parties who are designated as the plaintiff and the defendant. It may also hear criminal cases. Criminal litigation is brought by the state, which prosecutes the criminal charges against a defendant or defendants. There is no private party plaintiff in a criminal case.

A trial court is presided over by one judge. It is the particular province of the trial court to determine the facts of the case. The trier of fact, either judge or jury, "finds," that is, determines, the facts from the evidence at trial, the examination of witnesses, and the admissions of the parties. For example, one issue in a case may be the speed at which a vehicle was travelling. This fact may be disputed by the parties. The trial judge or the jury, if the question is put to a jury, will resolve the dispute and "find," for example, that a party traveled at 75 miles per hour. The court then decides the case by applying the applicable law to that fact.

Often the trial court judge will decide a case by procedures that preclude a trial. For example, one of the parties may bring a motion (a request to the court) for the court to take a particular action. Some types of motions, if granted, will result in a decision that eliminates the need for a trial. You will learn about those types of motions in your civil procedure course. If a case is not ended on a motion, and the parties do not voluntarily settle their dispute, then the case will go to trial.

The next step up the hierarchy of courts from the trial courts is occupied by the appellate courts. The party that has lost at the trial level, either by motion or after trial, may ask for review by a higher court. This review is known as an appeal. The party who appeals is usually called the appellant and the other party, the appellee. The appellate court determines whether the lower court committed any error significant enough to require that the decision be reversed or modified, or a new trial be granted.

Most states provide two levels of appellate courts. The first is an intermediate court of appeals. The second is the highest court of appeals and is usually known as the state's supreme court, although some states use other designations. Sometimes a jurisdiction's highest court is described as the court of last resort.

Generally, the intermediate appellate court hears appeals from the trial courts, and the supreme court hears appeals from the intermediate courts of appeals. In many states with intermediate courts of appeals, however, the supreme court must hear appeals for certain types of issues directly from the trial courts. There is no further appeal of the decisions of the court of last resort as to matters of state law.

Some states have no intermediate court of appeals. In those states, trial court decisions will be reviewed directly by the court of last resort. In either system, except for certain types of cases, the court of last resort need not hear every case for which an appeal has been requested. Rather, the court has discretion to choose which cases to hear.

In many states, the intermediate appellate level consists of more than one court. For example, the state may be geographically divided into appellate districts, with each district having its own court of appeals. That district will contain several trial courts, the appeals from which all go to the one court of appeals for that district. Each court of appeals is a co-equal, that is, each occupies the same rung on the court hierarchy as the others. The state will have only one court of last resort, however, and that court is superior to all other state courts.

An appeal is heard by more than one judge, and because the appeal should be heard by an odd number of judges, all appellate courts require three or more judges. The judges decide the case by voting and usually one of the judges from the majority writes the decision. A judge who disagrees with the majority may write his or her own opinion, called a dissenting opinion (or just a dissent). In addition, a judge who has voted with the majority as to the outcome of the case may write a separate opinion to express his or her differing views about certain aspects of the case. This decision is a concurring opinion ("concurring" because the judge concurred in the outcome of the case). The name of the judge who writes an opinion appears at the beginning of that opinion. Sometimes the opinion of the court does not bear the name of an author, but is designated a "per curiam" decision. This means a decision "by the court" and may be used for a shorter opinion on an issue about which there is general unanimity.

The procedure of an appeal differs from proceedings before a trial court. An appeal does not involve another trial before the panel of appellate judges. That is, the parties do not submit evidence or examine witnesses, nor does the court empanel a jury. Rather, the parties' lawyers argue to the appellate judges to persuade them that the court below did or did not commit an error or errors. Typically, this argument is made by means of written documents called appellate briefs that the attorneys submit to the court. The attorneys may also argue orally before the judges, although not all appeals involve oral argument. In addition, the appellate court reviews the record of the proceedings below.

Most state trial court decisions do not result in explanatory judicial opinions and so are not published, but the verdicts are recorded in the court files. Many, but not all, of the appellate decisions, however, are published in volumes called case reporters.

B. *The System of Courts: The Federal Courts*

We have explained the vertical system of courts and its hierarchy of higher and lower courts in terms of a state court system. In this country, we also have a system of federal courts that parallels the state courts. Federal courts are empowered by federal statutes and the constitution to hear certain types of cases. There is federal jurisdiction for cases that involve questions of federal law, such as federal statutory or administrative agency matters, cases in which the United States is a party, and cases that involve citizens of different states.

The trial courts within the federal system are called district courts. There is at least one United States District Court within each state. A district court's territorial jurisdiction is limited to the area of its district. A state with a small population and a low volume of litigation may have one district court and the entire state will comprise that district; for example, Rhode Island has one district court called the United States District Court for the District of Rhode Island. The volume of litigation in most states, however, requires more than one court in the state and thus the district is divided geographically. For example, Illinois is divided into three district courts: The United States District Court for the Northern District of Illinois, the United States District Court for the Southern District of Illinois, and the United States District Court for the Central District of Illinois.

Each intermediate appellate court in the federal system is called the United States Court of Appeals. For appellate court purposes, the United States is divided into thirteen circuits, so there are thirteen United States Courts of Appeals, eleven of which are identified by a number. Thus, the complete title of one court is The United States Court of Appeals for the First Circuit. The eleven numbered circuits are made up of a designated group of contiguous states (and also may include territories). The United States Court of Appeals for the Seventh Circuit, for example, is made up of the states of Illinois, Wisconsin, and Indiana. The other two courts of appeals are the United States Court of Appeals for the District of Columbia, and the United States Court of

Appeals for the Federal Circuit.[1] Appeals from the district courts within the area that makes up a circuit go to the court of appeals for that circuit. A case that was litigated in the United States District Court for the Northern District of Illinois, for example, would be appealed to the United States Court of Appeals for the Seventh Circuit.

The highest court in the federal system is the Supreme Court of the United States. This court hears cases from all the United States Courts of Appeals and, for certain issues, from district courts and from the highest courts of the state systems. The Supreme Court must hear certain types of cases and has discretion to hear other requests.[2]

III. The Development of the Law Through the Common Law Process

A. Precedent and Stare Decisis

The position of a court within the structure determines how its decisions are treated as precedent. Some precedents have greater authoritative value than others. In order to describe the weight of precedent, we must first discuss some important characteristics of the American system of precedent and its companion doctrine, stare decisis. That term is a shortened form of the phrase stare decisis et non quieta movere, which means "to stand by precedents and not to disturb settled points." In this country, stare decisis means that a court should follow the common law precedents. But the doctrine also means that a court must follow only those precedents that are binding authority.

Precedent becomes "binding authority" on a court if the precedent case was decided by that court or a higher court in the same jurisdiction. Cases decided by other courts, such as a court of another state, are persuasive authority only. When an authority is persuasive, the court deciding a dispute may take into account the decision in the precedent case, but it need not follow that decision. If precedents exist that are binding authority on the particular point of law, however, then those precedents constrain a judge to decide a pending case according to the principles laid down by the earlier decisions or to repudiate the decisions.

1. The United States Court of Appeals for the Federal Circuit hears certain specialized cases such as international trade and copyright cases.

2. The United States also has courts of limited jurisdiction, that is, courts that are competent to hear only specialized subject matters, such as tax courts. You will rarely read cases from these courts in your first year of law school and we will not include them in this discussion.

When you search for case authorities to help you answer the issue before you, you will search first for precedents that are binding on the court where the dispute will be decided because these cases provide the constraints within which you must analyze the problem. If the issue has never been litigated in the jurisdiction of the dispute (sometimes called a "case of first impression"), you should familiarize yourself with how courts in other jurisdictions have analyzed the problem. Precedents that are not binding on a court may nevertheless persuade the court to decide your case in a particular way.

Even if there is relevant case law in the jurisdiction in which your dispute will be litigated, you may still want to familiarize yourself with case law in other jurisdictions. This is especially so if those cases are factually similar, or well-reasoned, or particularly influential decisions.

B. Binding and Persuasive Authority

Because the United States is composed of many jurisdictions, including each of the states and the federal court system, it is important to determine which precedents a court in each jurisdiction must follow besides its own prior decisions.

1. State Courts

A state court must follow precedents from the higher courts in the state in matters of state law. Thus, a trial court must follow the precedents of the state's highest court. If the state court system includes a tier of intermediate appellate courts, as most state systems now do, the trial court must also follow the precedents of the intermediate courts of that state. Depending upon the rules of procedure of the jurisdiction, the trial court may be bound only by the intermediate court that has the authority to review its decisions, or it may be bound by the decisions of any of that state's intermediate courts of appeals that are not in conflict with the court that reviews its decisions. An intermediate appellate court must follow the decisions of the state's highest court, but it is not bound by the decisions of the other intermediate courts because those courts are not superior to it, although these decisions usually are very persuasive.

In addition, the state court is bound by the statutes of that state, as interpreted by its courts. The statutes of one state do not bind the decisions of the courts in another jurisdiction. If another state has a statute that is the same as, or has language similar to, the statute that controls your case, the interpretations given to that statute by the courts of the other state may be persuasive to the court of your state, but they are not binding on it. That is, the court may, but does not have to, follow the other state's interpretation of the statute.

If your case is not governed by either a statute or a judicial precedent from your jurisdiction, then look to precedents in other states. Those precedents are persuasive only. The courts of a state are not required to follow precedents from other states, but they will take those decisions into account in reaching their own decisions.

2. Federal Courts

The decisions of the Supreme Court of the United States are binding on all courts in all jurisdictions for matters of constitutional and other federal law. The decisions of the courts of appeals do not bind each other, even in cases in which the appellate court has interpreted a federal statute. For matters of federal law a court of appeals is bound only by its own decisions and those of the Supreme Court. A federal district court (the trial court) is bound by its own decisions, the decisions of the court of appeals of the circuit in which the district court is located, and the decisions of the Supreme Court. The district court is not bound by the decisions of any other district court, nor by the decisions of other federal courts of appeals. Again, as always, a court will take account of the decisions of other courts.

Questions of state law, either common law or statutory, often come to the federal courts in lawsuits between parties from different states. These actions are known as "diversity suits" because they are based on "diversity of citizenship." In diversity suits, the federal court must apply state law and thus follow the state courts' decisions on state substantive law questions. A detailed discussion of problems related to federalism, that is, the relationship between state courts and federal courts and state law and federal law, is beyond the scope of this introductory explanation.

3. Writing About Legal Authority

The common law and statutes of a jurisdiction are binding on future litigation within that jurisdiction. Thus, when you write an analysis of a legal problem you should always identify and explain that jurisdiction's law on the issue of the problem. Begin first with relevant statutes, if there are any, and the cases that interpret that statute. Explain relevant case law first from the highest court of the jurisdiction and then other reported decisions from that jurisdiction's lower courts.

If there is controlling law from the jurisdiction of the problem, you should not begin by writing about the law in other jurisdictions or with explanations from other sources such as hornbooks or a law dictionary.

Read the two examples below, which are introductory sentences to a discussion about a false imprisonment problem in the state of Kent. What is the difference between them? Which is the better way to begin the discussion?

> 1. In most states, the definition of false imprisonment requires that the defendant intend to confine the plaintiff within boundaries set by the defendant. Some other jurisdictions also require that the plaintiff be aware of the confinement.
>
> The definition of false imprisonment in Kent is "the intentional unlawful restraint of another against that person's will." Jones v. Smith.
>
> 2. In Kent, false imprisonment is "the intentional unlawful restraint of an individual's personal liberty or freedom of locomotion against that person's will." Orange v. Brass. A person need not use force to effect false imprisonment, but may restrain by words alone. Id. "Against that person's will" requires that the person be aware of the confinement. Jones v. Smith.

Example 1 incorrectly begins with the law of other states. Example 2 correctly begins by setting out the law of the jurisdiction of the problem.

C. Stare Decisis and Overruling Decisions

The standard definition of stare decisis implies that following precedent is mandatory and that precedent is binding authority within a particular jurisdiction. Yet the doctrine as applied in the United States does not produce rigid adherence to prior decisions. Instead, a court has freedom to overrule its previous decisions and thus decide a case by a rule different from the one it had previously adopted.[3] A court overrules its earlier decision by explicitly or implicitly deciding in a later case that it will no longer follow that previous decision.

One reason that a court may overrule a case is that the earlier decision has become outdated because of changed conditions. Other reasons are that the existing rule has produced undesirable results or that the prior decision was based on what is now recognized as poor reasoning. Sometimes a changed interpretation reflects a difference in the views of the present judges on the court as compared with those of the previous court.

When a court overrules a previous case, that change in the law has no effect on the parties to the litigation that produced the

---

3. A court cannot overrule the decision of a higher court, however. If a judge of a lower court were to refuse to follow the decision of a higher court, that judge's decision would no doubt be appealed.

prior decision, nor on other parties whose rights have been determined under that precedent. The results between those parties became final at the time of the last decision in those cases. Indeed, sometimes the change in the law will not affect the parties in the very case in which the court overrules the earlier decision and announces its changed rule. This result occurs when the court makes the new rule prospective, that is, applicable in future cases only.

Another means of overruling a judicial decision is by legislation. The legislature may change by statute a rule that came from a particular decision or a common law rule of long standing. This change in the law binds the courts within that jurisdiction.

A more literal interpretation of stare decisis would lead to a more rigid system of law than now exists in this country or would require frequent appeal to legislative bodies to correct by statute undesirable or outdated judicial decisions.

D. Holding and Dicta

A judge may decide to be bound by a precedent and to reach the same outcome in a case before the court when the causes of action are the same and the material facts are similar enough so that the reasoning of the earlier case applies. Even if there is such a similar case from a court that is binding on the judge's decision, however, that judge is bound only by the holding of the previous decision. This is another limitation on the binding force of precedents in addition to the limitation that arises from a judge's ability to overrule an earlier decision.

The holding of a case is the rule of law that comes from that decision. The holding can be defined as the judgment plus the material facts of the case.[4] Several other definitions of the holding exist.[5] But whichever definition is used, the holding of a case must include the court's decision as to the question that was actually before the court. That decision is a function of the important facts of that litigated case and the reasons that the court gave for deciding the issue as it did based on those facts. Thus, the holding is different from general principles of law or from definitions. If a court in a contract case says "a contract requires an offer and an acceptance," that is a principle that has come from many years of contract litigation, but it is not necessarily a statement of the decision in the particular contract case. The holding would be a statement like, "a seller offers goods to a

4. See G. Williams, Learning the Law 72 (8th ed. 1969).

5. See, e.g., E. Bodenheimer, J. Oakely & J. Love, An Introduction to the Anglo–American Legal System 85–88 (1980).

customer by advertising the goods and designating the price and quantity of the goods."

Formulating the holding of a case can be a difficult task and one that you will refine throughout your legal career. Part of the difficulty of isolating the holding lies in the need to decide first which facts were essential to the decision and then to describe those facts. If you include all or almost all of the facts of the precedent and describe the facts exactly as they were in the case, then the holding you derive will be very narrow; it will apply to almost no future cases because there may never be another case with such similar facts. For example, in a false imprisonment case, the plaintiff may have been kept in a corner of a room by a black and white bulldog that growled and showed its teeth. If you include each of these facts as necessary to the decision in this case, the decision will bind very few future courts because it will apply only to cases in which black and white bulldogs growled and showed their teeth.

If, however, you omit some facts and describe the relevant facts more broadly, then the holding will apply to a larger number of future cases whose facts come within that broader description. For example, you could say that a defendant is liable for false imprisonment if his dog growled at the plaintiff, and the plaintiff remained immobilized because he reasonably believed that the dog would bite him if he moved. In this example, the facts have been stated more generally; they will include more than the specific details of the case and cover a wider range of activity.

If you relate the facts even more generally, you could describe the dog as a household pet or a domestic animal that made noises at the plaintiff. The descriptions "household pet" and "domestic animal" and "noises" include more types of animals and behavior than do the descriptions "dog" and "growled." Often there may be more than one statement of the holding that is correct because it is difficult to determine how broadly to describe crucial facts. When you describe the facts too broadly your description will include facts that may raise considerations that are different from those that the court took into account when it made its decision. For example, the description "household pet" includes a white rabbit. And although a rabbit may cause fear in a person who hates rodents, the issue of whether that person's fear is reasonable raises questions about phobia that are different from considerations about a dog's ferocity.

Sometimes you cannot really determine the holding of a case until it has been interpreted by other courts. However, frequently common sense will take you a long way. Common sense will tell you that the fact that the defendant's dog was black and white should not be important to the decision in the false imprisonment example, but that the breed of dog could be important because of its size or ferocity. Common sense will also tell you that "household pet" is probably too broad a description for false imprisonment purposes because the term includes white rabbits and goldfish. Beyond that, you will acquire the added experience and judgment that will come with being a law student and lawyer.

Sometimes the court itself will announce its holding. You should not always accept that court's formulation, however. You must be sure that the judge has not stated the holding too broadly or too narrowly and that the principle the judge has articulated was actually required for the resolution of that case. For example, if the court deciding the hypothetical false imprisonment problem had written, "We therefore hold that the defendant's dog's growling at the plaintiff was sufficient to constitute false imprisonment," that court would have stated its holding too broadly. A literal application of this statement of the holding would permit liability if a person's dog growled at someone on the street. The statement must be read in conjunction with the facts of the case that the plaintiff was kept immobilized in the corner of a room.

The binding nature of a statute is somewhat different from that of a case. If the legal authority that you are applying is a statute, then the entire statute is binding authority, and all the statutory requirements must be satisfied. This is not always as simple as it sounds, however. As indicated earlier, there may be case law interpreting the statute that tells you how the statutory language must be satisfied. The statute may contain internal contradictions that a court may have reconciled, for example, or a court may have decided that the legislature meant an "or" instead of an "and" in part of the statute. These interpretations affect the manner in which the statutory language is binding.

There are many statements in a judicial decision that are not part of the holding and are not binding on later courts. These statements are called dicta. For example, the statement "but if the defendant's cat had trapped the plaintiff in the corner of the room, the defendant would not be liable," would not be part of the holding of the false imprisonment case we have hypothesized. This is so because the plaintiff was not trapped by a cat, and so that is not a material fact of the case. Therefore, dicta about a cat in an earlier case concerning a dog would not bind a judge who had to decide a later case in which a defendant's hissing cat had kept a plaintiff in a corner of a room.

Statements that are dicta are not always unimportant, however. Sometimes the dicta in a case become more important in later

years than the holding of the case. Dicta is analogous to persuasive authority in that the statements may be persuasive to a later
judge, but the judge is not bound to follow them.

When you write about judicial decisions, you will have to
describe the action that the court took by using a verb. For
example, you will be saying that the court said something, or held
something, or found something. You must be careful to use the
correct verb. It would be incorrect to say "the trial court held
that the defendant's car was traveling at ninety miles per hour" if
this sentence states a finding of fact by a court. In that case, the
sentence should be written, "the trial court found that the defendant's car was traveling at ninety miles per hour."

A sentence correctly describing the holding of this case might
be written, "the court held that the defendant was guilty of
reckless driving for driving ninety miles per hour in a forty-mile-
per-hour zone."

To describe a court's dicta, you should use a verb such as
"said," or "stated," or "explained." For example, the hypothetical
dicta used in the false imprisonment example, "but if the defendant's cat had trapped the plaintiff in the corner of the room, the
defendant would not be liable," should not be preceded by the
inaccurate statement "the court held," but by a statement such as
"the court said" or "the court hypothesized."

Read the case decision below. Then choose the best statement
of the holding from the five choices.

<u>In Re Gaunt</u>

Terse, J.

John Gaunt was having coffee with his nephew Felix. John
told Felix that he was giving him a gift of his gold watch, which
he kept in a safe deposit box in his bank. He said he would get
the watch for Felix the next time he went to the bank. John
died that night, without going to the bank. Felix has demanded
the watch be delivered over to him as his gift. The administrator
of John's estate is keeping the watch as part of the estate.

Felix's demand must be refused. A completed gift requires
first that the donor intend to give the gift, second, delivery of the
item of gift, and third, acceptance by the donee. Only then does
the intended donee have title to the item. John probably did
intend that Felix have the watch. The watch had been John's
grandfather's and Felix is the next male heir in that family. We
can assume that Felix would have accepted the watch. Senti-
ment aside, it is a valuable piece of jewelry. John, however,
never delivered the watch to Felix. If he had given him the key
to the safe deposit box, that may have been a constructive
delivery, effective to create a gift. As it is, without delivery,

John made only an unenforceable promise. A court will not enforce an uncompleted gift.

Which is the best statement of the holding in In re Gaunt?

    1. The court held that delivery of a key to a safe deposit box is a delivery of the item kept in the box because it is a constructive delivery.

    2. The court held that there are three requirements for a valid gift: intent to give, delivery, and acceptance.

    3. The court held that a decedent's jewelry remains part of his estate at death if he has not given it away during his life.

    4. The court held that a decedent had not made an effective gift of personal property during his life where he made an oral promise of the gift without delivery of the item to the intended donee.

    5. A court will not enforce an incomplete promise of a gift.

Sentence four is the best statement of the holding:

    1. Sentence 1 is a statement of dicta in In re Gaunt. John did not give the safe deposit key to Felix. The court used that fact as a hypothetical of what may have been a delivery for purposes of satisfying the requirements of a gift.

    2. Sentence 2 is the general rule of the three requirements for a gift which had been formulated before this case was litigated. Not all three were disputed in this case.

    3. Sentence 3 sounds as if it could be the holding, but it is really a general rule of property law that tells the result of the decision in this case.

    4. Sentence 4 is the holding that decides the question in this case of whether John Gaunt had given away the property during his lifetime if he had not delivered the watch to his nephew. If he had not, then John still owned the watch and the result described in Sentence Three occurs.

    5. Sentence 5 is a reason for the decision in the case.

The holding could be made broader or narrower by describing the intended item of gift differently. The gift could be described as

    1. property (which includes real and personal property)

    2. jewelry

    3. a gold watch

    4. a family heirloom

What differences might these descriptions make? Would you describe the parties involved as an uncle and nephew instead of a decedent and a donee?

Exercise 1–A

If your client is an attorney being sued by the beneficiary of a will for failing to have the will signed in the right place, how might you state the holding of Neptune v. Pluto, the case below?

Neptune v. Pluto

Venus, J.

In this suit, Jane Neptune has sued John Pluto for negligence. John Pluto, a notary public in Oz, wrote a will for Bill Mars and supervised the signing of the will. The state's statute requires three witnesses to the will. After Mars died, his will was declared invalid because only two people witnessed his will. Jane Neptune was Mars's only beneficiary. Because Mars's will was invalid, she could not take his property. Neptune, however, was not Pluto's client. Generally, only a client can sue a professional for negligence. Of course, Pluto was practicing law without a license. In any event, Pluto was clearly negligent in supervising the execution of the will and should be amenable to suit by the disappointed beneficiary.

––––––

Which is the best statement of the holding for your client?

1. A notary public who improperly executes a person's will can be sued by the beneficiary of the will who has lost her legacy because of the error.

2. A professional who improperly executes a person's will can be sued by the beneficiary of the will who has lost her legacy because of the error.

3. A notary public who practices law without a license and fails to have the proper number of witnesses to a customer's will can be sued by the beneficiary of the will who has lost her legacy because of the error.

Exercise 1–B

Beta v. Adam

Terse, J.

Beta has sued Adam, the owner of a restaurant, for false imprisonment. Adam believed that Beta was leaving without paying her bill. Beta in fact had left the money on her table. Adam told Beta that she could not leave until someone verified that she had paid. Adam took Beta's pocketbook in which Beta had her keys, money, credit cards, and her checkbook. The restaurant was very busy and understaffed. Beta stayed with Adam for twenty minutes until Adam found an employee to see if Beta had left the money on the table.

Although Adam never physically prevented Beta from leaving, and Beta could have walked out of the restaurant at any time, Adam is liable to Beta for falsely imprisoning her. A person falsely imprisons another by unlawfully confining her within fixed boundaries, if he acts intending to do so. Adam confined Beta in the restaurant by telling her she could not leave and by taking her purse. Confinement may be effected by duress, even duress that is not the product of threatening behavior. Beta could not leave the restaurant because she believed that she could have lost her pocketbook with its valuable contents if she did so. Thus, she was unlawfully confined. She acted reasonably by remaining in the restaurant until she recovered her possessions.

————

Which is the broadest formulation of the holding? The most narrow?

1. The defendant unlawfully confined the plaintiff by duress when he took an item from the plaintiff in order to have her remain on the premises.

2. The owner of a restaurant unlawfully confined his customer when he told her she could not leave and took her pocketbook away for twenty minutes until he could verify her payment of her bill.

3. A person falsely imprisons another by means of duress that does not involve physical force when he takes an item of value belonging to the other.

E. The Weight of Authority

Besides the judgments involved in determining the holding and the dicta of a case, and therefore which part of that case is binding, you must make other judgments in using precedents. For example, you must decide which of many relevant cases are most important to your problem and will have the most weight with the court deciding your own case. Several factors can determine the weight of an authority.

The precedents that are binding authority are of course the most important. Always begin your analysis with the cases on the same issue from the jurisdiction of your problem. Start with the cases from the highest court. In addition, the decisions of the courts within the jurisdiction, even if not binding (such as decisions of another court of appeals) generally will be the most persuasive authority to a court. As to the weight of authority of cases from all jurisdictions, the similarity of the facts between the precedent and your problem is important. The more similar the specific facts between the cases, the greater weight the precedent will have for your own problem.

Another important factor is the level of the court that decided the previous case. A case decided by a state's supreme court will be more authoritative than one decided by a lower state court. Language from the Supreme Court of the United States will often be given more weight than language from another court. This is so even if the Supreme Court case is not binding on the issue because it did not involve a federal or constitutional issue, or the language was dicta.

An opinion written by a particular judge may be important because of the excellent reputation of the judge. In addition, decisions from a particular court in a particular era may carry extra weight because of the membership of the court during those years. Exemplary are the New York Court of Appeals (the highest court in New York) during the time when Benjamin Cardozo was a member of the court and the California Supreme Court during the service of Justice Roger Traynor.

A case decided by a unanimous court or a nearly unanimous court may be more persuasive as a precedent than one in which the court was closely divided. And statements from concurring or dissenting opinions will usually not carry as much weight as statements from majority decisions, although exceptions exist.

Another factor to consider in evaluating the weight of a precedent is the year of the decision. If a case is old and the decision reflects policies or social conditions that are no longer as important as they once were, then the precedent will have little weight even if the facts of the case are very similar to your problem. If, however, the decision is based on reasoning that is still valid, the age of the case may not be important.

The courts in some states may favor decisions from states that are geographically close or have similar social or economic conditions that relate to the litigation. In addition, a decision that interprets a statute may be persuasive to another court in a case that involves a similar statute.

Very important is the depth and quality of the prior treatment of the relevant issue. A case in which the issue received the full attention of the previous court and was fully and articulately discussed will be more important than one in which the question received cursory attention. And well reasoned decisions with careful explanations will probably already have achieved deserved respect in the field.

No matter how many of these factors are present, however, a case from another jurisdiction is not binding on a court, and does not foreclose the decision of that issue.

IV. *Statutes and the Relationship Between Case Law and Statutes*

The preceding material in this introduction reflects the historic importance of case law to our legal system. You should be aware, however, that enacted law, especially statutory law, forms a greater part of the body of legal authority in our country than ever before. In fact, enacted law should be the first source in which you research a legal problem. In this section we will discuss enacted law in the form of statutory law and its characteristics and relationship with case law.

Statutes are enacted by legislative bodies that are constitutionally empowered to exercise the legislative function within a jurisdiction. The federal legislative body is the United States Congress. Each state has its own legislature and also has municipal and, perhaps, county forms of legislatures. In addition, state and federal administrative bodies may have limited legislative functions in that they are empowered to enact regulations concerning the subject matter of their administration. These regulations provide another form of enforceable law.

Enacted law, like case law, falls along a vertical hierarchy.[6] At the top of that hierarchy is the Constitution of the United States. Next are both federal statutes and treaties. Federal statutes, when enacted within the powers conferred by the Constitution, take precedence over statutes of other jurisdictions. Then come federal executive orders and administrative regulations, state constitutions (a constitution, however, is the highest authority within a state as long as it does not conflict with federal law), state statutes, state administrative regulations, and municipal enactments.

A jurisdiction's constitution and its statutes are the highest authority within that jurisdiction, and the courts are bound by them. A legislature may change the common law by passing legislation that changes the common law rule. That change then supersedes the old rule. A court cannot in turn overrule that legislative enactment. The legislature may also create new causes of action that were not available in the common law but which result from legislation such as worker's compensation laws and employment discrimination laws. A legislature may also enact a common law rule into statute; for example, many criminal statutes have codified what were previously common law crimes. Then the case law interpreting that common law rule may still be valid.

Because a jurisdiction's constitution is more authoritative than its statutes, the legislature may act only within its constitutional powers. Although a court cannot overrule legislation, that is, it cannot decide it will not follow the law imposed by the particular statute, a court may review a statute's validity. Legislation may be challenged in court on the ground that the legislature exceeded its constitutional powers. A reviewing court may then decide a statute is unconstitutional and is invalid.

6. This hierarchy is taken from E.A. Farnsworth, An Introduction to the Legal System of the United States 55–57 (1983).

Courts are constantly deciding statutory issues because statutes must be enforced and frequently must be enforced by litigation. A person's challenge to the constitutionality of a statute, for example, will usually arise during litigation in which the government attempts to enforce the statute against that person.

More often, however, a court must decide not the validity of the statute, but how to apply the statute. As a necessary step in this litigation, the court may have to interpret the meaning of the statutory language in order to apply and enforce it. By its nature, legislation is cast in general terms because it is law written in broad categories to affect future conduct rather than law written to decide a specific case. General legislative language must then be applied to individuals and to the particular controversy being litigated. Thus, a good portion of a court's work is deciding questions that involve the interpretation of statutes. The legislature could still have the last word. If it does not agree with the court's statutory interpretation, it can amend the statute. In reality, however, a legislature rarely follows the course of judicial interpretation of a statute and even more rarely reacts to judicial interpretation by amending the statute.

When you are writing about a problem that is controlled by a statute of that jurisdiction, you should always include an explanation of that statute's terms. The explanation usually should be at the beginning of your written analysis. Do not start writing about the problem as if the reader knows the statute's terms unless you have been instructed to do so.

Exercise 1–C

What is the difference between the two examples below? Which is the better introduction to a discussion of a statute?

1. Under the Wills Act of Kent, a person's will must be in writing, signed at the end by the person, and attested by two competent witnesses. Smith fulfilled all these requirements when he executed his will, even though he signed the will with his initials only.

2. Smith's will is valid because he fulfilled the three requirements under Kent law. He fulfilled the second requirement even though he used only his initials to sign the will.

V. Citation

One consequence of relying on legal authorities in your written work is that you also will be learning how to provide citations to those legal authorities. A writer who quotes from or borrows ideas from others or discusses and analyzes another's work must acknowledge those sources by proper citation. Not to do so is plagiarism.

Citation is important to all types of writing, but you probably will use more citations in your legal writing than you are accustomed to using. Because of the doctrine of precedent, lawyers analyzing a common law action constantly rely on case law to prove that the legal theory offered as the governing rule of law is valid and has been applied in similar situations. In a statutory action, lawyers quote and thus cite the statute that supplies the governing rule of law. They also use cases to help interpret what the statute means. Thus, a legal argument requires identifying the sources of the governing principles of law as well as analyzing what they mean. The writer must cite to those sources each time they are mentioned or relied upon. Lawyers also use secondary authority such as books and periodical articles, as support for their legal analysis. These sources also must be cited.

Legal citations tell the reader many things. As mentioned above, the presence of a citation tells the reader that the preceding text is based upon information from another source and is not original with the writer. A citation to a case also tells the reader that there is legal authority for the previous statement and where the reader can find that authority. A citation provides information that helps the reader evaluate the weight of the precedent. For example, the citation tells which court decided the case.

Most law schools and lawyers use a specialized citation form found in a book called A Uniform System of Citation, known as the Bluebook. Some lawyers adhere strictly to the requirements of the Bluebook, others make changes to suit their own practices or to comply with the rules of a particular court or agency. Most law schools require that students use Bluebook citation form in their writing.

Besides learning correct citation form, you should also become familiar with certain conventions of legal citation. In legal memoranda and briefs, which are typical law school writing assignments, you will put citations in the text right after the material for which they provide authority, rather than in footnotes. You should use citations to authority for direct quotations, for text that paraphrases the authority, and for text that is based on information in the authority, although not quoting or paraphrasing from it. Notice the citations in the following paragraph. See the Appendix for an explanation of the citation form.

> The law of battery in this state is adopted from the Restatement of Torts. Lion v. Tiger, 50 N.W.2d 10 (N.D. 1954). A person may be liable for battery if the person directly or indirectly causes a "harmful contact" with another's person, and the person intends to cause the contact. Id. at 12; Restatement (Second) of Torts § 13(b) (1977). Under

this definition, Smith will not be liable because she did not act with the required intent.

The first citation, to the case of <u>Lion v. Tiger</u>, supplies the authority for the statement about the state's law of battery. It tells you that the court that decided <u>Lion v. Tiger</u> is the court that adopted the Restatement definition. The second citation provides the source of the definitions. These sources are the case already cited (<u>Id</u>. means that the citation is the same as the previous one) and the Restatement of Torts.

Exercise 1-D

Where do citations belong in the following paragraphs? Why?

1. The test for determining whether a plaintiff is entitled to attorney's fees involves four factors: whether the litigation provided a public benefit, whether the plaintiff gained financially from the litigation, whether the plaintiff had a personal interest in the materials sought, and whether the government unreasonably withheld the materials. The factors usually have equal weight. However, if the government acted particularly unreasonably, the last criterion may be more important.

2. The Kent statute permits an unwitnessed will. This type of will is known as a holographic will. To be valid, a holographic will must be entirely written and dated by the testator. The courts have interpreted "dated" to mean month, day, and year.

Once you become accustomed to using legal citations, you will find that they can contribute to your legal writing style by keeping unnecessary information out of your text. For example, one common writing weakness of lawyers is to explain textually the information that is available in the citation, instead of using the citation to provide that information. Notice the differences in these three sentences:

1. In an old 1922 Massachusetts case, the Supreme Judicial Court held that the plaintiff must prove fraud in order to invalidate an antenuptial contract. <u>Wellington v. Rugg</u>, 243 Mass. 30, 136 N.E. 831 (1922).

2. In Massachusetts, a plaintiff must prove fraud in order to invalidate an antenuptial contract. <u>Wellington v. Rugg</u>, 243 Mass. 30, 136 N.E. 831 (1922).

3. Massachusetts is the only state that requires a plaintiff to prove fraud in order to invalidate an antenuptial contract, a rule that dates back to 1922. <u>See Wellington v. Rugg</u>, 243 Mass. 30, 136 N.E. 831 (1922).

The writer of sentence 1 has supplied two facts in the text that are provided in the citation, that the case was decided in 1922 and that the highest court in Massachusetts decided it. (If the citation does not specifically include the name of the court within the parenthesis and the court is not otherwise identifiable by the citation, the case was decided by the highest court of the state). Unless the writer had a particular reason to include those facts in the text, they are unnecessary, and the sentence is better written as in sentence 2. If the writer wanted to emphasize that the rule is an old one, sentence 3 provides more specific emphasis than sentence 1.

Although the examples may seem strange to you now, citation will become an important and familiar aspect of your writing about legal materials.

———

Exercise 1–E

1. You are doing research for a state law problem. Your research uncovers some cases similar to the case you are working on, which you are appealing to the intermediate appellate court of your state. These cases are from:

    a.   Another intermediate appellate court of the state

    b.   A diversity suit in a federal district court in the state, applying the state's law on that issue

    c.   The federal court of appeals for the circuit of your state in an appeal from a district court from a different state

    d.   A state trial court's judgment entered in a decision that was not published but which you know about

    e.   The highest court of the state

What weight would you assign to these authorities? Evaluate how important each is as a precedent.

2. Because the domiciles of the parties permit, you have decided to litigate an Illinois property law question in the United States District Court for the Northern District of Illinois. In which sources of primary law would you do your research? Why?

    a.   United States Supreme Court cases

    b.   Cases from the Illinois Supreme Court and intermediate appellate courts

    c.   Cases from the United States Court of Appeals for the Seventh Circuit

    d.   Cases from the other two United States district courts in Illinois

    e.   Property law cases from other states

Would there be any difference if your case is a contracts case and Illinois has adopted the Uniform Commercial Code?

3. You are doing research for a state law problem about the liability of owners of recreational land to people who use those premises. There are two questions involved, whether the land your client owns is recreational land, and if so, whether your client did not fulfill his legal duties.

How relevant are the following authorities to your analysis of this problem?

a. A newspaper article about accidents in parks

b. A statute of the state that limits the liability of owners of recreational land

c. The regulations of a state agency requiring safety features on recreational land that is open to the public

d. A brochure printed by the owner of the recreational land

e. Case law from the state's intermediate appellate courts interpreting the statutory term "recreational land"

f. Case law from the highest court of another state that has an almost identical statute. These cases interpret the term "recreational land"

g. A case from your state's appellate court that interprets the term "recreational area" in a different state statute about licensing for privately owned recreational areas

h. The notes of the drafters of a uniform act about liability of owners of recreational areas, an act that your state has adopted

Chapter Two
Analyzing Legal Authority:
Case Law

I. Introduction

In your first year of law school, you will be analyzing a case in two contexts. First, your professors may suggest that you "brief" (summarize) each case assigned for class. For this purpose, you consider each case in isolation, just trying to understand that particular case. In the second context, however, your concern is the impact that a case may have as precedent for your own problem case, often a hypothetical fact pattern. There, you analyze the relationship between cases. Your success in both of these contexts will depend to some extent on how carefully you identify the significant parts of a judicial decision.

II. Briefing a Case: Finding the Parts of a Judicial Decision

You brief a case to help you understand its significance. There are different methods of briefing a case and the following format is meant to be only an example. Your professors may suggest a format to you, or you may devise your own system by identifying what helps you in your classes. Whatever method you use, read through the case once to get a general idea of what it is about before you start your brief.

The typical components of a case brief are:

A. Facts

The facts describe the events between the parties that led to the litigation and tell how the case came before the court that is now deciding it. Include those facts that are relevant to the issue the court must decide and to the reasons for its decision. You will not know which facts are relevant until you know what the issue or issues are. For example, if the issue is whether a minor falsely represented himself as an adult for the purpose of fraudulently inducing a car salesman to contract with him, relevant facts would include the minor's written and oral statements about his age, his height and weight, and his manner of dress. These facts are relevant because they can help prove how the minor represented his age. However, the minor's eye color, the weather on the day the contract was signed, and the payment schedule in the contract would not be relevant to the issue of false representation.

In the fact section, you should also include the relevant background for the case. State who the plaintiff and defendant are, the basis for the plaintiff's suit, and the relief the plaintiff is seeking. Also include the procedural history, although you may put the procedural facts under a separate heading. Include any dispositive motions, such as a motion to dismiss for failure to state a claim. If the case is an appeal, state the lower court's decision, the grounds for that decision, and the party who appealed.

Often you will have to understand the procedural posture of a case in order to understand the court's decision. For example, if the appeal is from a successful motion to dismiss, then the appellate court will decide whether the plaintiff's pleadings stated a claim and whether the plaintiff should be permitted to continue the lawsuit. The court will not decide who should win the lawsuit if it continues.

B. Issue(s)

The issue is the question that the court must decide to resolve the dispute between the parties in the case before it. To find the issue, you have to identify the rule of law that governs the dispute and ask how it should apply to those facts. You usually write the issue for your case brief as a question that combines the rule of law with the material facts of the case, that is, those facts that raise the dispute. Although we use the word "issue" in the singular, there can be and often is more than one issue in a case.

C. Holding(s)

The holding, as was explained in Chapter One, is the court's decision on the question that was actually before it. The court may make a number of legal statements, but if they do not relate to the question actually before it, they are dicta. The holding provides the answer to the question asked in the issue statement. If there is more than one issue, there may be more than one holding.

D. Reasoning

The court's reasoning explains and supports the court's decision. For example, the court may have looked at two lines of authority and decided the case was more like one group of cases than another, or the court may have referred to a particular rule of law and decided that the policy justifying that rule was no longer valid, or the court may have concluded that the facts of this particular case required a new treatment. In any event, it is important to isolate the court's reasoning from the facts and the holding of the case.

E. Policy

Underlying legal decisions are the social policies or goals that the decision-maker wishes to further. When a court explicitly refers to those policies in a case, include that information in your case brief, since it will probably help you understand the court's decision.

Read the following case. A sample brief for the case is provided.

Jones v. Hadican
552 F.2d 249 (8th Cir. 1977).

Sylvester Jones appeals from the district court's dismissal of his complaint for lack of subject-matter jurisdiction. We affirm.

The facts underlying this controversy are undisputed. In 1976, appellant, then a citizen of Missouri, was convicted under a 14–count indictment for conspiracy to distribute heroin, distribution of heroin, use of a communications facility in furtherance of the distribution of heroin, and possession of heroin with intent to distribute, in violation of 21 U.S.C. §§ 841(a)(1), 843(b) and 846.

He was sentenced to 35 years imprisonment to be followed by an 11–year special parole term and fined $24,000. His conviction was affirmed on appeal. United States v. Jones, 545 F.2d 1112 (8th Cir. 1976). Appellant was represented at trial and on appeal by a court-appointed attorney, J. Martin Hadican, also a citizen of Missouri.

On November 2, 1976, appellant filed a civil complaint against Hadican in the [United States] District Court, charging Hadican with malpractice and seeking damages of $1,308,500. Appellant alleged jurisdiction by virtue of diversity of citizenship under 28 U.S.C.

§ 1332(a)(1). The District Court, sua sponte, dismissed the complaint for lack of diversity, holding that appellant's original domicile (Missouri) did not change when he was incarcerated in the Leavenworth Penitentiary [in Kansas]. The propriety of that holding is the central issue on appeal.

It has long been held that, for purposes of determining diversity of citizenship, the controlling consideration is the domicile of the individual. (citations omitted) With respect to the domicile of prisoners, the traditional rule is that a prisoner does not acquire a new domicile when he is incarcerated in a different state; instead, he retains the domicile he had prior to his incarceration. (citations omitted) This rule was based on the notion . . . that a change of domicile requires a voluntary act and that a domicile of a person cannot be changed by virtue of the legal and physical compulsion of imprisonment. Over the years, this rule has hardened into an irrebuttable presumption.

This irrebuttable presumption rule was rejected by the Sixth Circuit in Stifel v. Hopkins, 477 F.2d 1116 (6th Cir. 1973). In a thoughtful opinion, the court found that the rationale of enforced movement did not justify an irrebuttable presumption in all cases. Rather, the court held that the presumption could be rebutted by a prisoner who could show facts sufficient to indicate a bona fide intention to change his domicile to the place of his incarceration.

We are persuaded that the approach of Stifel v. Hopkins expresses the better view. While retaining the usually valid presumption that a prisoner retains his pre-incarceration domicile, it is sufficiently flexible to allow a prisoner to show truly exceptional circumstances which would justify a finding that he has acquired a new domicile at the place of his incarceration. Under the rule of Stifel v. Hopkins, however, a prisoner must still introduce more than "unsubstantiated declarations" to rebut the presumption that he retains his pre-incarceration domicile. Id. at 1126. [The prisoner's] complaint must allege facts sufficient to raise a substantial question about the prisoner's intention to acquire a new domicile.

Even giving a liberal interpretation to appellant's pro se complaint, he failed to allege facts sufficient to raise a substantial question as to domicile. The complaint merely alleged that his "legal residence" is Leavenworth, Kansas, that he is serving a long sentence, and that his marriage has "irrevocably deteriorated." There are no other facts in the District Court record or in appellant's brief on appeal which indicate a bona fide intention to change his domicile. Furthermore, appellant's complaint indicates that he continues to own certain "choice" real estate in Missouri and that his real estate business has not been terminated.

Because appellant failed to allege facts sufficient to create a substantial question that he intended to acquire a new domicile, the District Court properly determined that no diversity of citizenship existed. As no other basis for jurisdiction appears, the District Court order dismissing the complaint for lack of subject-matter jurisdiction is affirmed.[1]

Sample Brief of Jones v. Hadican

A. Facts:

—Plaintiff Sylvester Jones was living in Missouri when he was convicted of various crimes and sentenced to 35 years imprisonment. Jones was serving his sentence at the federal prison in Leavenworth, Kansas.

—Jones has attempted to sue his lawyer, J. Martin Hadican, for malpractice in the federal district court in Missouri, alleging jurisdiction based on diversity of citizenship. Hadican is a citizen of Missouri.

—Jones stated that his "legal residence" was Leavenworth, Kansas, and that although he is married, his marriage had "irrevocably deteriorated." Jones continued to own real estate in Missouri. His real estate business in Missouri continued.

—The district judge dismissed Jones's complaint on the grounds that Jones remained a citizen of Missouri, and, therefore, no diversity of citizenship existed. Jones appealed.

B. Issue(s):

1. For purposes of a federal district court's diversity jurisdiction, is a prisoner irrebuttably presumed to retain his pre-incarceration domicile?

2. If not, does a prisoner allege facts sufficient to raise a substantial question of his intention to change his domicile to the state of his incarceration if he alleges that intent but maintains property and a business in the state of his original domicile?

C. Holding(s):

1. A prisoner may rebut the presumption that he retains his pre-incarceration domicile.

2. A prisoner does not allege facts sufficient to raise a substantial question of his intent to change his domicile to the state of incarceration if he maintains property and a business in the state of his original domicile.

D. Reasoning:

—The court has subject matter jurisdiction under the diversity of citizenship statute, 28 U.S.C. § 1332(a)(1), if the parties to the litigation are citizens of different states. Jones's lawyer is a

---

1. All footnotes in the case are omitted.

citizen of Missouri. Jones was a citizen of Missouri before his incarceration.

—Under the traditional rule, a prisoner does not acquire a new domicile in the state in which he is incarcerated because he does not voluntarily move to the new state. This rule has become an irrebuttable presumption.

—The court rejects the traditional rule and adopts the reasoning of Stifel v. Hopkins, 477 F.2d 1116 (6th Cir. 1973). The Stifel court decided that the presumption could be rebutted by a prisoner who could show exceptional circumstances "indicating a bona fide intention to change his domicile to the place of his incarceration." This rule retains the usually valid presumption, yet provides flexibility for exceptional circumstances.

—The prisoner, however, must allege facts in his complaint which raise a substantial question about his intent to acquire a new domicile. Jones has not alleged sufficient facts to raise a substantial question as to domicile. Therefore, his domicile did not change.

E. Policy (this may be considered part of reasoning):

—To provide the flexibility to deal with exceptional circumstances, the irrebuttable presumption rule with regard to the domicile of a prisoner should be rejected, and a prisoner should be permitted to show a bona fide intention to change his domicile.

III. Using the Parts of a Judicial Decision

A. Reasoning by Analogy

Under the doctrine of precedent, judges decide cases according to principles laid down in earlier similar cases. Lawyers (and law students) who are working on a legal problem must find those earlier cases and analyze the impact that those cases will have on the decision in their own problem. Thus, lawyers are always comparing cases by drawing analogies and making distinctions between them. By comparing their problem to decided cases, lawyers decide how the decisions of previous cases apply to the new problem. If the cases resemble each other in important ways, such as by their relevant facts, then they are analogous and should also resemble each other in their outcome. Cases are analogous if they are alike in ways that are important to their outcome and if the differences between them are not enough to destroy that analogy.

Facts are not the only important element used to determine whether a case is analogous to your case. The issues the court dealt with must be the same or similar in important ways to the issues in your case. The court's reasoning must apply equally well to the facts in your case. And no policy can exist which would lead to a different result in your case.

If you decide, however, that the cases are different and that the decision in the precedent case should not control the outcome of your problem, you are "distinguishing" the cases. If you distinguish a prior case, you avoid its impact on your case and you restrict its application in future cases. You may distinguish a case by establishing that the differences in the facts require that the court apply a different rule. Or you may decide that the same rule should be applied, but that the facts in your case require a different outcome. Be careful, however, not to distinguish cases too easily. Each case will have some differences from other cases. The distinguishing facts you select must be significant.

By comparing and contrasting your problem with the precedents, you will be able to determine how well the rules of those cases fit your case. This in turn should enable you to predict the probable outcome of your own case. When you reason by analogy, though, you can only offer probable proof for your conclusions, not certainty. Your task is to assess all the possible applications of the relevant rules and to offer the best prediction of the outcome.

Although analogizing and distinguishing may sound like mechanical exercises, legal analysis is rarely analysis by rote. Comparing the similarities and contrasting the differences between cases is often a creative process and the ability to do this is one of the hallmarks of a skillful lawyer. You will become more sophisticated in this process as you gain experience.

B. Applying Precedent

1. Facts

When you brief a case, you concentrate on how the facts of that case are relevant to the issue in the case and the reasons for the court's holding. However, when you are considering the relationship between a precedent and your problem case, you view the facts somewhat differently. Now, you also try to determine if the facts in the two cases are basically analogous or distinguishable.

For example, one of the elements of the tort of intentional infliction of emotional distress is that the defendant's conduct must be outrageous. Suppose you were asked to analyze whether Olympia Department Store's conduct was outrageous if it made daily phone calls to a customer over a three month period in attempting to collect payment for a debt. In the jurisdiction of this problem, there may be no cases about the issue of outrageous conduct in which a store made phone calls to a customer. But there may be a case in which a department store sent daily letters to a customer over a three month period in attempting to collect a debt. In that case, the court had decided that the conduct was not outrageous on the grounds that a creditor could use reasonable, if annoying, methods to collect a debt, and that the letters fell within reasonable limits.

You may decide that the two cases resemble each other because three months of daily telephone calls are like three months of daily letters. Both are persistent communications from an outside source. You may, therefore, conclude that the cases are analogous and should resemble each other in result also. Under this reasoning, Olympia's conduct would not be characterized as outrageous.

On the other hand, you might argue that the cases are distinguishable because phone calls are a much more intrusive kind of communication than letters. Or you could distinguish the case if the basic facts were different, if, for example, the customer never actually owed the debt. Under this circumstance, the precedent would be distinguishable since the court's reasoning was premised on the existence of the underlying debt.

The facts of one case need not be identical to the facts of another case for the cases to be analogous. A case can be precedent for your problem when the facts are similar according to certain general classifications. For example, the relative bargaining strength of a party to a contract is one factor the courts will consider in deciding whether a contract is unconscionable (unfair and, therefore, unenforceable). Thus, an analogy could be drawn between a case in which the owner of a small gas station dealing with EXXON claimed a contract was unconscionable and a case in which a consumer dealing with General Motors claimed a contract was unconscionable. Both the station owner and the consumer could fit under the more general classification of vulnerable buyers in a weak bargaining position. Similarly, a rule for automobiles may apply equally to snowmobiles or even to mopeds, since all could be classified as motorized vehicles.

In applying precedent, as when briefing a case, you must first determine which facts are relevant to the issue that a court must decide and to the reasons for its decision.

Exercise 2–A

Read the following case. Identify the issue in the case and make a list of the facts that are relevant to a court's decision on that issue.

In Re Estate of Winter

The heirs of Robert Winter seek to void a contract for the sale of land Mr. Winter made three weeks before his death. They allege that Winter was mentally incompetent to make a contract at that time. In this state, a contract may be voidable on grounds of mental incompetence if, because of a person's mental illness, he was unable to reasonably understand the nature and consequences of the transaction in question. Since Winter was incompetent under this standard, the contract he made for the sale of land is voidable and will not be enforced.

Mr. Winter had a stroke in 1982. He suffered from a vascular disease which resulted in partial amputation of his foot. As a result of this amputation, he became unable to continue to operate his farm himself. In 1983, Mr. Winter's wife died. Since he was unable to take care of himself, he moved in with one of his daughters, Sandra Bright. Another one of his daughters testified that from that point on, Winter seemed to lose interest in everything. He stopped managing his own affairs. Mrs. Bright handled all of his finances. She balanced his checkbook, deposited his social security checks, and managed the farm.

As time went on, Mr. Winter became easily confused and lethargic, spending much of his time sitting in a chair, staring out of the window. A family friend testified that when Winter described the farm, he sometimes said it was 200 acres and sometimes said it was 2,000 acres. (The farm is 2,000 acres.) Dr. Crabtree, Winter's longtime physician, said that in his opinion, from March 1984 until he died, Winter was totally incompetent to handle any of his own affairs, including taking care of his own body.

In May 1984, while Mrs. Bright was out for the afternoon, Herbert Spencer paid Winter a visit. Mr. Spencer offered to buy the farm from Winter. Winter agreed and signed a contract for the sale of the farm to Spencer for what a local real estate agent said was far below its actual value. In addition, Winter did not reserve a right of way for himself and his family, creating a problem of access from the road to their other piece of property. Mr. Winter died three weeks after the sale of the farm.

The evidence suggests that at the time of the contract, Winter was unable to understand the nature and consequences of the transaction of the sale of land. He did not appear to have a clear idea of the number of acres in question. The price he received was below the fair market value of the property. He failed to reserve an important right of access for himself. His physician testified that he was incompetent to handle his own affairs. His daughter had, in fact, been taking care of his personal and business affairs before the sale took place, as Winter had lost interest in these matters. Under these circumstances, I hold that Winter was unable to understand the nature and consequences of the transaction, and, therefore, the contract for the sale of land is voidable.

Exercise 2–B

Using Winter as the only precedent, identify the issue and make a list of the relevant facts in the following problem case:

Richard Bower wants to void the contract his uncle Joseph Black made for the purchase of a car shortly before Mr. Black's death on the ground that Black was mentally incompetent at the time he made the contract. Excerpts from the following depositions taken in the case will provide the factual background.

DEPOSITION: DR. MARTIN DREW

(By Ms. Jones, attorney for plaintiff, Richard Bower)

Q: Was Joseph Black a patient of yours?

A: Yes, he was my patient for six years until he died on April 10, 1986, of cerebral apoplexy, what you would call a stroke.

Q: What had you been treating Mr. Black for?

A: Mr. Black had cerebral arteriosclerosis. He suffered from a hardening and shrinkage of the arteries, which reduced the amount of blood that gets to the brain.

Q: What are the symptoms of cerebral arteriosclerosis?

A: Well, since this disease develops gradually, the symptoms develop gradually as well, becoming more and more intense. The most common early signs are memory loss, irritability, anger, confusion, and forgetfulness. In Mr. Black's case, the symptoms were becoming more and more severe. You see, as the amount of blood that got to his brain diminished because the arteries continued to shrink, the amount of his confusion and forgetfulness increased. He also became more stubborn as his memory became more uncertain.

Q: When did you last see Mr. Black?

A: I last saw him on January 31, 1986.

Q: How would you describe his condition?

A: I would say that his arteriosclerosis had become quite severe—not enough that he needed to be hospitalized, but enough so that he needed home nursing care. He would talk to me and then he would forget what he said and tell me the same things again and again. And he thought I was my father, who had been his physician 30 years ago. I asked him to tell me his name and where he lived. He remembered his name, but couldn't tell me where he lived.

Q: Doctor, in your opinion, was Mr. Black able to understand ordinary business transactions?

A: At this point in his life, I would say he would not.

DEPOSITION: RICHARD BOWER

(By Ms. Jones)

Q: Mr. Bower, what is your relationship to Joseph Black?

A: He was my uncle, my mother's brother.

Q: Did you accompany your uncle to Miller Motors on February 12, 1986?

A: Yes I did. He came next door, where I live, and asked me to go with him to Miller Motors, which is around the corner. I couldn't understand why, but I humored him and went with him. When we got there, a salesman came out and said, "Your car is ready, Mr. Black." My uncle had bought a Buick the day before and he wanted me to drive him home in it. I couldn't believe it because he hasn't driven in three years. I don't think he even has a valid license anymore. I asked him how he could do such a thing, because he only had $15,000 left to live on, except for Social Security, and the car cost around $14,000. He wouldn't even be able to make his mortgage payments and eat on what he had left. When I reminded him of that he said it was not a problem because he had only borrowed the car and it only cost a few hundred dollars. Then he said that he could give the car back in a few days. When I told him again that he had spent $14,000 on a car, he started yelling at me and making a terrible scene so I drove him home and put it in the garage beside his house. He never went near it. I started it once a week so that the engine wouldn't rot.

Q: What did you do after your uncle died?

A: I called Miller Motors and said I was my uncle's executor and that I wanted to give the car back. I said I would be willing to pay them for the two months' use of the car, even though we never even drove it. But they refused.

DEPOSITION: ROSE BROWN

(By Ms. Jones)

Q: Ms. Brown, were you employed by Joseph Black?

A: I took care of Mr. Black, though Mr. Bower actually paid me out of a joint checking account he had with Mr. Black.

Q: How long did you take care of Mr. Black?

A: I took care of him from February 3, 1986, until he died on April 10.

Q: What did your work consist of?

A: I did the shopping, cooked, cleaned, helped Mr. Black get dressed if he needed help.

Q: How did Mr. Black occupy his time?

A: He sat around, sometimes watched TV. He didn't read the paper anymore. I had to watch him very carefully because he would wander off, like he did the day he bought the car. But you had to be very careful how you talked to him, because he would get angry and use terrible language. He hated to hear that he had forgotten something and would just get more stubborn.

———

Exercise 2–C

Compare the facts in the Winter case and in the problem case to determine whether the cases are analogous or distinguishable. Under what general classifications would you compare the facts?

---

2. *Issues and Subissues*

In determining whether a case is controlling as precedent, the issue in the precedent should be essentially the same as the one in the new problem. However, sometimes you can define the issue in the precedent more broadly in order to reveal its significance for your problem case. Reread the Jones case. In Jones the issue was a prisoner's intent to change his domicile for diversity purposes. If you wanted to use the case as precedent for other classifications of persons in similar situations, you could frame the issue more broadly, i.e., whether a person can become a citizen of a state to which he has been involuntarily transferred. For example, a serviceman who was involuntarily assigned to another state could try to use the Jones case as precedent and argue that he should be allowed to present facts which would show his intent to change his domicile to the new state.

3. *Holding*

When you are considering the relationship between a precedent and your problem case, you might formulate a court's holding differently from the way you would if you were simply briefing the case. How you formulate the holding depends on how many facts you include as essential and how you characterize those facts. If you describe the facts exactly as they were in the case, then the holding you state will be very narrow. This is sometimes called limiting a case to its facts. If, however, you describe the facts more broadly, then the holding will apply to a larger number of future cases whose facts come within that broader description. The holding in the Jones case, for example, could be stated in terms of the particular facts in Jones's case, in terms of prisoners in general, or, most broadly, in terms of classes of persons who were considered to be legally or psychologically incapable of freely choosing their domicile.

The way you formulate the holding may depend on the result you want to reach in applying that case, the purpose of the document you are writing, and its intended audience. For example, if you are writing to a court and the decision in the precedent case is one that is favorable to your client, then you will try to formulate the holding broadly enough to encompass the facts of your client's case. Or, if the decision in the precedent is unfavorable, you will try to state the holding more narrowly so that it will not include the facts of your client's case. Of course, there are limits to formulating the holding broadly or narrowly. If you manipulate the facts to violate the sense of the case, you will be engaging in unethical behavior and faulty analysis.

Exercise 2–D

Reread Beta v. Adam in Chapter One. Suppose you represented the plaintiff in each of the following three cases. How would you formulate the holding of Beta v. Adam to be most advantageous to your client?

Case 1:

Same facts as in the Beta case in Chapter One, but your client's pocketbook contains only a handkerchief, a comb, and makeup. Your client stays five minutes and leaves.

Which of these two statements would you use as the holding in Beta v. Adam?

a. In Beta v. Adam, the owner of a restaurant confined the plaintiff when he took her pocketbook and told her she could not leave the restaurant until he determined that she had paid her bill.

OR

b. In Beta v. Adam, the owner of a restaurant confined the plaintiff when he took property of value from her in order to detain the plaintiff and detained her for twenty minutes.

Case 2:

Same facts as above but the restaurant owner tells your client that he does not believe that she left the money to pay her bill and asks your client to wait while he gets someone to see if she left the money on her table. The owner does not take anything from her. Your client waits for twenty minutes.

Which of these two statements would you use as the holding in Beta v. Adam?

a. In Beta v. Adam, the defendant confined the plaintiff by duress even though he did not engage in threatening behavior.

OR

b. In Beta v. Adam, the defendant confined the plaintiff by duress by implied threats that if she left the premises she would lose her property.

Case 3:

Your client drove her car into a gas station for gas. An employee of the station who thought she was wanted for bank robbery drained the water from her car's radiator and called the police. Your client had to wait fifteen minutes for a police officer to come and identify her as not being the felon.

Which of these two statements would you use as the holding in Beta v. Adam?

a. In Beta v. Adam, the owner of a restaurant confined the plaintiff when he took her pocketbook, told her not to leave the restaurant, and took twenty minutes to determine whether she paid her bill.

OR

b. In Beta v. Adam, the defendant confined the plaintiff by duress when, although he did not threaten the plaintiff to remain, the plaintiff would have had to leave behind valuable property if she left the defendant's premises.

---

4. Reasoning

The court's reasoning in the precedent case must apply equally well to the facts in your problem case. This would certainly happen when the facts are quite similar, as they would be if you were applying Jones to another case dealing with the domicile of prisoners. However, the court's reasoning may also apply in a different context. For example, mental incompetents traditionally were thought to be incapable of forming the necessary intent to change their domicile. A court might reason that, like prisoners, mental incompetents should not be barred by an irrebuttable presumption that they could not demonstrate the necessary intent to change their domicile, and might adopt the reasoning of the prisoner case.

5. Policy

The court in the precedent may be basing its decision on an articulated (or unarticulated) policy. If the same policy would apply in your problem case, the result should be the same. A court, for example, might decide that just as fairness and flexibility would be promoted by allowing prisoners an opportunity to demonstrate a change of domicile, the same policy would be promoted by allowing mental incompetents to show a change in domicile. Another court, however, might decide it would be inappropriate to make a change in the law on this subject and would leave it to the legislature to make that change, or decide that the irrebuttable presumption rule promotes efficient use of court time.

In general, then, under the principles of precedent and stare decisis, if your problem case is similar to the precedent, the result should be the same. When your problem case is different from the precedent in a significant way, the precedent should not be controlling. In making these comparisons, you will find that a number of possibilities exist.

You could have:

—Your problem case and a case dealing with the same issue and with similar facts—the result should be the same (the case is analogous);

—Your problem case and a case with the same issue but materially different facts—the result should be different (the case is distinguishable);

—Your problem case and a case dealing with a completely different issue—there should be no impact;

—Your problem case and a case with the same issue but based on a policy which is no longer persuasive or has not been accepted by another court—the result should be different (the case is distinguishable).

Consider the following case. If <u>Jones</u> is the precedent, how would this case be decided?

Mr. Wheeler is presently serving a sentence of 5–7 years in the federal prison in Danbury, Connecticut. He wishes to sue his former attorney who lives in Arkansas, where Wheeler lived before his incarceration. Wheeler has written the following letter to his legal aid attorney, who wants to sue in the United States District Court for the Eastern District of Arkansas. Arkansas is within the Eighth Circuit.

"Dear Attorney,

As you can see I'm in the federal pen doing 5–7 for bank robbery, thanks to that rotten lawyer Donald Lindhorst. First he cons me into hiring him and paying him 1500 bucks, my whole life savings, to defend me. Then he didn't do anything for me and just pocketed the cash. He talked to me exactly once before my trial. I should never have listened to this guy I knew but I was in a bad spot. I was living in Little Rock where Lindhorst lives, too. So when I was arrested and charged with bank robbery (something I never did) a guy I know said Lindhorst was OK so I hired him. I'm sick up to here with Little Rock and all the people there. I don't know how the jury could find me guilty, because I told the honest truth under oath. I hate this place. I'm always telling my wife Mary when she comes to visit that I'd be a "free man" if it wasn't for Lindhorst. The food stinks here. I got no recreation and Lindhorst is sitting in his fancy office with the air conditioning on. Mary and our kid moved to Connecticut to be near me. She put all our stuff in our rattle-trap car. Mary got a job near the pen and my kid goes to the public school here. Anything Mary saves we put in the bank here. Mary kind of likes it better because her sister lives in Connecticut and that's all the family she's got. I got one brother but he's moved to Canada. Mary and me are going to "start fresh" in Connecticut when I get out of here. Her sister's husband has a hardware store in Bethel, Conn. and he says he

has a place for me when I get out which is more than anyone
ever said to me in Little Rock. I want to show up that crook
Lindhorst for what he is and get a million bucks for what he did
to me. You can write me here."

To determine how this case would be decided, ask yourself:

a. Is the issue the same as in Jones?

The issue will be the same as the issue in Jones—under what
circumstances can a prisoner change his domicile to the state of
incarceration so that he can sue in federal court based on diversity
jurisdiction.

b. Are the relevant facts analogous or distinguishable?

First, you must identify the facts in Jones which the court
considered to indicate a clear intent to change domicile. Then
classify these facts under general headings which relate to a
prisoner's intent to change his domicile. Consider:

     i.—the family situation

     ii.—the business and financial connections with the for-
mer state of residence

     iii.—the business and financial connections with the state
of incarceration

     iv.—the prisoner's stated intent regarding his domicile

     v.—the length of the prisoner's sentence

Second, analyze the facts in Wheeler's case according to these
classifications. Begin by determining which facts are relevant
and which are irrelevant. Some of the facts in Wheeler's letter
are obviously irrelevant to the question of Wheeler's intent to
change domicile:

     —Lindhorst's lawyering ability

     —the amount Wheeler paid Lindhorst

     —Wheeler's actual guilt

     —the type of food and recreation available in the prison

     —the condition of Wheeler's car

     —the air-conditioning in Lindhorst's office

Most of the other facts in the letter, however, come within the
identified classifications, are relevant to the question of Wheeler's
intent to change his domicile, and should be considered.

Third, determine if the facts are analogous or distinguishable.

An examination of the facts in Wheeler's case shows them to
be distinguishable from the facts in Jones.

     i.—Mr. Jones claimed that his marriage had irrevocably
deteriorated, suggesting that he had no family ties to his former

state of residence. No other facts were provided. Mr. Wheeler's family situation supports his claim that he wishes to change his domicile to Connecticut. His wife and child have moved to Connecticut. His wife has a job in Connecticut and their child goes to school in Connecticut. Mrs. Wheeler's only living relative lives in nearby Bethel, Connecticut. Mr. Wheeler's only relative lives in Canada. There are, therefore, no family connections to Arkansas.

ii.—Mr. Jones continued to have business and financial connections with Missouri. He continued to own real estate in Missouri, and his real estate business in that state had not been terminated. Mr. Wheeler does not appear to have any business or financial connections with Arkansas.

iii.—Mr. Jones appears to have had no business or financial connections with the state of incarceration. Mr. Wheeler has a bank account in Connecticut. He says he is going to work in his brother-in-law's hardware store in Connecticut when he completes his prison sentence.

iv.—Mr. Jones claimed that his legal residence was Kansas. Mr. Wheeler says he is fed up with the people in Little Rock and intends to make Connecticut his home.

v.—Mr. Jones was serving a long prison sentence. Mr. Wheeler was serving a 5–7 year sentence. On this fact, Mr. Jones may show a stronger intent to change his domicile since he will be in the state of incarceration for a longer period of time. This demonstrates that you will not always be able to draw a neat distinction or analogy and will sometimes have to balance one fact which cuts differently against the others.

c. Would the court's reasoning in Jones lead to the same or a different result?

The court's reasoning in Jones would lead to a different result in Wheeler's case. The court in Jones adopted a new rule which, in that circuit, would permit a prisoner to show facts that raised a substantial question of his intention to change his domicile to the place of incarceration. Jones did not demonstrate such facts. However, Wheeler has shown a bona fide intention to change his domicile. Therefore, under the reasoning of the Jones case, a court would likely reach a different result in Wheeler's case and conclude there was diversity of citizenship.

d. What impact, if any, would the policy behind the decision in Jones have on this case?

The policy behind the decision in Jones is consistent with a decision that Wheeler did show a bona fide intention to change his domicile and that diversity of citizenship therefore exists. The policy would change the traditional rule with regard to the domicile of prisoners to a rule which is more flexible and fair.

e. In light of the answers to these questions, is it likely that the holding in Jones would be followed in Wheeler's case?

A court would probably decide that Wheeler's case was distinguishable from Jones, since Wheeler had shown a bona fide intention to change his domicile and should therefore be permitted to sue in federal court basing jurisdiction on diversity of citizenship.

———

Exercise 2–E

Consider whether a court would decide that the plaintiff in these cases could establish federal diversity jurisdiction. Use these five questions as a guide.

a. Is the issue the same or analogous to the issue in Jones?

b. Are the relevant facts analogous or distinguishable?

c. Would the court's reasoning in Jones lead to the same or a different result?

d. What impact, if any, would the policy behind the decision in Jones have on this case?

e. In light of the answers to these questions, is it likely that the holding in Jones will be followed?

1. Mr. Smith is serving a long sentence in the federal penitentiary in Lewisburg, Pennsylvania. He wishes to sue his former attorney for malpractice in federal district court in Pennsylvania. His attorney is domiciled in Ohio, Smith's domicile before he was incarcerated. Smith is 25 years old, unmarried and childless. He has been incarcerated in Pennsylvania since his conviction and will remain in prison for a long time. All of his personal belongings and assets are in Pennsylvania and all of his business transactions are conducted in Pennsylvania. Because of the crime with which he has been charged, he has become an outcast in his community in Ohio and says he does not intend to ever return there if paroled. [The United States Court of Appeals for the Third Circuit includes Pennsylvania within its jurisdiction. Like the court in Jones, the Third Circuit has adopted a rule permitting prisoners to rebut the presumption against their change of domicile.]

2. John Brown, a medical doctor, was drafted into the Army when he was living in Pennsylvania and since then has been stationed in South Carolina. His family remains in Pennsylvania. He and his wife are registered to vote in Pennsylvania and Brown says he plans to vote there in November. He has continued membership in local medical societies in Pennsylvania. He maintains bank accounts in Pennsylvania and filed his latest tax returns there. Dr. Brown's

family will remain in Pennsylvania while he is transferred to Germany. Dr. Brown wishes to sue a building contractor in Pennsylvania in federal district court, claiming that he is a citizen of South Carolina and, therefore, diversity of citizenship exists.

3. Corporation A was incorporated in the State of New Mexico and had its principal place of business in Arizona. The Directors of Corporation A wished to sue Corporation B, which is also incorporated in New Mexico. However, the Directors wanted to sue in federal court. They, therefore, moved Corporation A's place of incorporation to California and sued Corporation B in federal district court in California basing jurisdiction on diversity of citizenship. Corporation B has argued that the district court had no jurisdiction because the diversity of citizenship created by the new incorporation was a sham conducted solely for the purposes of this litigation.

Exercise 2–F

Read the following statement by the court in <u>Jones</u> and the accompanying hypothetical. Then answer the questions that follow these materials.

In <u>Jones</u>, the court noted that one indication of pre-incarceration domicile was that Jones continued to own real estate in Missouri, the state in which he lived before he was sent to prison. Suppose, instead, that the court had spoken more generally, and said that Jones "still owned property in Missouri," and noted that he owned land there (land is classified as real property).

In a case currently at trial, a prisoner, Smith, also owned property in Missouri, but the property was personal property rather than real property. Smith had left household possessions in storage there and money in a safety deposit box in a Missouri bank.

a. What is the impact of this change in facts? How might the differences in the type of property be relevant to the issue of the plaintiff's intent as to domicile? Under these facts can you still use the fact that the plaintiff "still owned property in Missouri" as a factor to show that Smith did not intend to change his domicile to the state of his incarceration?

b. Does the fact that Jones, the prisoner, continued to own land in Missouri necessarily indicate his intention to remain domiciled in Missouri? Can you explain this fact in a way that indicates that even though Jones continued to own land in Missouri, he did not necessarily intend to remain domiciled there? Remember that land is not moveable and for Jones to no longer own the land he must sell it or give it away. Facts can have two faces. They may be interpreted to support different conclusions or at least may raise some questions that can lead to a different conclusion.

Exercise 2–G

1. Read <u>Smith v. Allen</u>. Then write an answer applying <u>Smith</u> to the problem in the <u>Peterson</u> case which follows <u>Smith</u>. How would a court decide the issue of David Peterson, Sr.'s liability?

Smith v. Allen (1980)

Judith Smith alleges that James Allen owned a golf club which he left lying on the ground in the backyard of his home. On April 12, 1979, his son the co-defendant Jimmy Allen, age eleven years, was playing in the yard with the plaintiff, Judith Smith, age nine years. Jimmy picked up the golf club and proceeded to swing at a stone lying on the ground. When Jimmy swung the golf club, he hit the plaintiff on the jaw and chin.

Smith alleges that Jimmy Allen was negligent since he failed to warn her of his intention to swing the club and he swung the club when he knew she was in a position of danger.

Smith also alleges that James Allen was negligent, and was liable for his son's actions. She alleges that although Allen knew the golf club was on the ground in his backyard and that his child would play with it, and that although he knew or "should have known" that the negligent use of the golf club by children would cause injury to a child, he neglected to remove the golf club from the backyard or to caution Jimmy against the use of the golf club.

James Allen demurred, challenging the sufficiency of the complaint to state a cause of action or to support a judgment against him.

The demurrer is sustained. A person has a duty to protect others against unreasonable risks. A person who breaches this duty is negligent and liable for injuries resulting from his negligence. No person, however, can be expected to guard against harm from events which are not reasonably to be anticipated at all, or are so unlikely to occur that the risk, although recognizable, would commonly be disregarded. An unreasonable risk in a case such as this is determined by examining the tool for its obvious and intrinsic danger. A golf club is not so obviously and intrinsically dangerous that it is negligence to leave it lying on the ground in the yard. Unlike a knife, for example, it is not commonly used as a weapon. Thus, the father cannot be held liable on the allegations of this complaint.[2]

Aarons v. Peterson

David Peterson stored a tool chest on the floor in the basement of his suburban home. In it he kept three screwdrivers, two wrenches, a hammer and several boxes of nails. Last Tuesday afternoon, his 11–year-old son, David, Jr., and a nine-year-old neighbor, Phil Aarons, were playing knock hockey in the basement. Their exertions were so strenuous they knocked the side rail loose from the baseboard. Phil, who was losing, was glad. He was tired of playing knock hockey and wanted to

---

2. This example is based on and uses language from <u>Lubitz v. Wells</u>, 19 Conn. Super. Ct. 322, 113 A.2d 147 (1955).

play with David's trains. David, however, wanted to continue the match. Spotting his father's tool chest lying on the floor in the corner, he decided to fix the board. He took a hammer and a large nail out of the chest and, while Phil was playing with the train set, quietly set about repairing the damage. At first the work went well. He placed the nail at the joint and hit it firmly on the head. It pierced the wood and held firm. Then disaster struck. On the next hammer blow, the nail flew out from the wood and struck Phil in the face, chipping his two front teeth, bloodying his nose, and gashing his cheek.

In an action for negligence, is David's <u>father</u> liable for the injuries to Phil?

2. Read the following case summary of <u>Green v. Kermit</u>. This case was decided by a court in the same jurisdiction as <u>Smith v. Allen</u>. Does this decision change your analysis of <u>Smith v. Allen</u>?

<u>Green v. Kermit</u> (1985)

The plaintiff Lucy Green is suing for injuries she received on the Muni Golf Course when she was struck in the knee by a golf ball hit by the defendant, John Kermit, who is eleven years old. Green was walking over a foot bridge about 150 yards from the 8th tee, when Kermit, who was playing in a foursome with his parents and sister, teed off the 8th tee without yelling fore. The plaintiff was in clear view of the tee at the time Kermit teed off and hit her with the golf ball. The issue is the standard of care that the eleven year-old defendant should be held to when he played golf.

A golfer should be required to use reasonable care. But whether John should be held to use the reasonable care of a reasonably prudent child or of a reasonably prudent adult depends on whether he used a dangerous instrument. Minors will be held to an adult standard of care if they used a dangerous instrument. A golf ball is a dangerous missile that can cause injury if it hits someone during its flight. Indeed in some ways hitting a golf ball is more dangerous than firing a gun or throwing a stone, because a person can have more control over the direction of a gunshot or a stone than over a golf ball.

Golf has become a very popular sport and as golf courses have become more crowded, more accidents have occurred, especially accidents involving golf balls. Yet golf is an adult activity involving dangerous instruments. Since a child is, for practical purposes, on the course as an adult, he should be held to an adult standard. John could see the plaintiff, he did not yell fore, and he teed off with the plaintiff in sight. The judgment for the plaintiff is affirmed.

———

What difference does this case make to your analysis of # 1?

———

IV. Synthesizing Cases

You will rarely work on a problem for which there is only one case precedent. More likely, your research for a problem will turn up many cases relevant to the problem. In order to use the principles that those cases offer to resolve your problem, you must relate the cases to each other, that is, synthesize them. In that way, you can understand the applicable area of law and then use the synthesis to analyze your problem.

The courts will frequently have done some synthesis for you. Often, in reading cases, you will see definitions of a claim for relief, like the definition of battery by a court or the Restatement, or statements followed by string citations. Usually these definitions or statements have evolved as courts have put together the decisions of many related cases. The judges who have formulated those definitions or statements have worked inductively. They have analyzed the outcome of each case and then combined those separate analyses into a coherent whole to form general principles about the area of the law. These general principles are then expressed at a level of abstraction that encompasses the particular holdings of all of the individual cases.

When you analyze a legal problem, such as one of your class assignments, you will do further synthesis of your own. Synthesizing is the step between your research and your writing. You do research by reading one case at a time. If in your writing you merely report each case, one at a time, then you have compiled a list of case briefs, but you have not analyzed a topic.

To analyze and write about a topic, you will need to engage in one of three types of case synthesis, or in a combination of these three types:

1)   Grouping cases according to the rule they follow

2)   Creating analytical categories

3)   Defining the factors of an evolving claim or defense

The first type, which is perhaps the least difficult, essentially requires you to group cases. For example, if you read several cases from federal courts on the issue of whether the court will apply an irrebuttable presumption that a prisoner does not intend to change domicile to the state of incarceration, you will find that several federal courts of appeals apply the traditional presumption, and a few courts have adopted the rule in Jones v. Hadican.

To write an analysis of your research, you would group the cases applying each rule, rather than list the cases one by one. You might write as your introduction to this analysis:

The majority of the federal courts of appeals apply the traditional rule that a prisoner is irrebuttably presumed to retain the domicile he had prior to incarceration. See [cases applying this rule]. The reason for this presumption [explanation of reasons.]

A growing number of courts, however, have rejected the irrebuttable presumption and instead permit a prisoner to show that he intends to change domicile to the state of incarceration. See, e.g., Jones v. Hadican, 552 F.2d 249 (8th Cir. 1977); Stifel v. Hopkins, 477 F.2d 1116 (6th Cir. 1973). [Explanation of these cases].

This writer had identified two lines of decisions and described the basic characteristic of each in clear topic sentences. The two categories in this example were based on a legal rule that was explicit in the cases themselves.

A second more difficult type of synthesis is required when courts do not clearly articulate the general principle that explains why various applications of a legal rule to individual cases have led to different outcomes. In this situation you must develop a general descriptive category that makes analytic sense out of decisions involving diverse factual patterns.

This type of synthesis identifies and explains a variety of facts by putting them under the rubric of one general principle that encompasses them. For example, if you were analyzing when the police need a search warrant in order not to violate the fourth amendment, you would find that police need a warrant if their activity invades a criminal suspect's reasonable expectation of privacy. You may have found cases in which the courts isolated the following facts. (In these examples, the police acted without a warrant.)

1. Police broke down the door of the suspect's apartment and ransacked the suspect's bedroom. Police violated the fourth amendment.

2. Police knocked on the suspect's door, were admitted to his home, and strip-searched the suspect. Police violated the fourth amendment.

3. Police used binoculars to look through the windows of the suspect's home. No violation.

4. Police used dogs to sniff the suspect in an airport. No violation.

5. Police put a radar device into a package so it could be traced to the suspect's home. Police violated the fourth amendment.

To synthesize these cases, you need to create an analytic category that makes sense of these diverse facts. Here, for example, you may explain the decisions in these cases on the basis of the degree of intrusiveness into the suspect's home or person. You would then analyze the facts of your own problem by referring to this description, and comparing your facts to the relevant facts in the precedents as to intrusiveness.

A third type of synthesis involves putting together a general principle of law and the relevant factors that have evolved in the case law. The definition of negligent infliction of emotional distress discussed in Chapter 5 is an example of a principle that has evolved in a series of cases.

Read these four case summaries. All the cases involve the question of whether parents are immune from tort suits brought by their children. All suits are in the jurisdiction of Kent where the age of majority is 18. (Full citations are omitted.)

Case 1:

    Jack Abbott sued his father Joseph for negligently pouring hot liquids in the Abbott kitchen so that he burned Jack in the process. Jack is twelve years old. Held: Mr. Abbott is immune from suit. Abbott v. Abbott (1965).

Case 2:

    James White sued his father Walter for battery, an intentional tort. Walter knocked James's baseball cap off his head because James struck out in the last inning of a Little League game. James is ten years old. Held: Mr. White is not immune from suit. White v. White (1968).

Case 3:

    Joan Brown sued her father Matt for assault, an intentional tort, for brandishing a tennis racket at her after she lost her serve in the final set of the women's 25 and under local tennis tournament. Joan is twenty-four years old and lives at home. Held: Mr. Brown is not immune from suit. Brown v. Brown (1969).

Case 4:

    George Black sued his father Paul for negligently burning him in Mr. Black's kitchen by handing him a large hot pot. George is a twenty-four-year-old business man and is married. Held: Mr. Black is not immune from suit. Black v. Black (1982).

These cases involve two factors that determine whether the parent is immune from suit. To analyze the topic, you should identify these factors and consider how they determine immunity. Look at the facts that evidently have led the courts to decide that the parent is immune and at the facts that evidently have led the courts to decide that the parent is not immune. When you can characterize these facts in a way that explains the results, you are ready to begin writing. You would then start your written discussion of these cases with a topic sentence that sets out your identification of the factors.

Notice the difference between the following two discussions of the immunity topic.   Which is more effective and why?

    1. Two factors determine parental immunity from a tort suit in Kent: the type of tort involved and the age of the child.   First, immunity extends to suits for negligence only.   Parents are not immune from suits for intentional torts.   The Kent Supreme Court has held that parents are not immune from their child's suit for assault, Brown v. Brown, and for battery, White v. White.   But the court has held that parents are immune from a negligence suit brought by their child.   Abbott v. Abbott.   Second, parental immunity extends only to a suit brought by a minor child.   Id. (immunity against twelve-year-old child's suit for negligence); Black v. Black (no immunity against twenty-four-year-old son's suit for negligence).

    2. The Kent Supreme Court has decided four cases on parental immunity from tort suits by their children.   In the first case in 1965, the court decided that a parent was immune from suit for negligence brought by his twelve-year-old son.   Abbott v. Abbott (1965).   However, in the next suit, in 1968, the court held that a parent was not immune from a suit for battery brought by a ten-year-old son.   White v. White (1968).   Only a year later in Brown v. Brown (1969), the court affirmed that a parent is not immune from suit for assault brought by a twenty-four-year-old daughter.   The most recent case on this topic is Black v. Black, decided in 1982.   In Black, the court decided another suit by a twenty-four-year-old against his parent, this time for negligence.   The court still decided that the parent is not immune.

In the first discussion, the writer synthesizes the four cases and extracts two factors that explain the cases.   In thinking through the problem, the writer proceeded inductively by analyzing individual cases and then generalizing about these cases, i.e., by identifying two factors that appear crucial on the issue of parental immunity.   For the written product, however, the writer followed a deductive pattern.   The writer put together a general principle to explain Kent law and started the discussion with that principle.   Then she developed that principle, using the cases as authorities for her conclusion.   However, the writer of the second discussion has not analyzed the problem.   She has written no more than a historical narrative of the four cases.   The paragraph's only organizing principle is one of chronological order. The writer has recreated her research process, but has left the job of making sense of the cases to the reader.

Exercise 2–H

    Consider these cases along with the preceding cases about parental immunity.

Case 5:

Bob Peepe sued his father Larry for negligence for driving his car into Bob while Bob was riding his bicycle. Bob is nineteen and a senior in high school. He lives at home. Held: Mr. Peepe is immune from suit. Peepe v. Peepe (1979).

Case 6:

Marilyn Smith sued her father Richard for negligence for riding his bicycle into Marilyn while she was gardening. Marilyn is nineteen years old, unmarried, and a part-time college student who lives at home. She is not self-supporting. Held: Mr. Smith is immune from suit. Smith v. Smith (1984).

Case 7:

Steve Andersen sued his mother Gretel Andersen for negligence for stumbling against Steve and pushing him against the hot pottery she had just removed from her kiln. Steve is twenty, married and lives in another city. Held: Mrs. Andersen is not immune from suit. Andersen v. Andersen (1985).

How might you synthesize these three cases and add them to the preceding four? What additional factor is raised by these cases?

Exercise 2–I

Read these three excerpts from cases from the same federal court. The issue before the court is whether a prisoner has shown an intent to change domicile to the state of incarceration. Write a topic sentence to a paragraph that synthesizes these cases.

1. There are no facts in the plaintiff's complaint that indicate a bona fide intention to change his domicile. For example, plaintiff's complaint indicates that he continues to own certain "choice" real estate in Missouri and that his business there has not been terminated.

2. The plaintiff owned no real or personal property in the state of her original domicile. She never owned her own home, and before she was incarcerated she sent all her personal possessions to her parents' home which is in the state of her incarceration. This fact could manifest an intent to change domicile to the state of incarceration.

3. The plaintiff continued to own a small house in the city in which she lived before she was incarcerated in another state. Although the market for real estate in that part of the city was good and she could have received a favorable price, she has retained the property. This indicates that she plans to return after she has served her term.

Chapter Three
Analyzing Legal Authority:
Statutes

I. Reading the Text

Just as you should know how to read and analyze a judicial opinion, you should also know how to read and analyze a statute. And just as there are layers of analysis involved in analyzing case law, from briefing a single opinion to synthesizing a group of related cases, there are layers of understanding involved in statutory analysis.

The first step in statutory analysis, as with analysis of any written material, is to read the text carefully. Your analysis of a statute begins with its exact text; you must know what the statute says. Among other things, you must read the statute to know to whom it is addressed, the exact conduct it prohibits, requires, or permits, and how the parts of the statute relate to each other. Your next step is to isolate the issue in your problem by determining what question is raised by the statutory language in terms of the facts of your case.

Often, your assignment involves only one section of a larger statute. Even so, you should look at that section within the context of the statute as a whole. Federal statutes, for example, often include explanatory preliminary sections, some of which can be helpful to you in interpreting the section at issue. Start by reading the title of the statute, which can help you understand its area of application. For this same reason, read any preamble or statement of policy or purpose which appears at the beginning of many statutes. This statement may tell you, for example, that the statute was written to codify the existing common law. If so, then the case law decided prior to the enactment of the statute may still be authoritative. If the statute was written to change the common law, then that case law should no longer be controlling. Frequently overlooked, but important to know, is the date that the statute took effect. This information will be in the statute and it may be crucial; for example, the statute may not have been in effect at the time of the conduct at issue in your problem. Also, read through the other sections of the statute to see if any of them affect your problem. Look especially for a definition section, and determine whether any of the terms in the sections that apply to your case are defined there.

For example, a state statute, § 10 of the Probate Code, permits a person to revoke a will "by a subsequent will which revokes the prior will." Your client's mother left a will and a separate signed paper dated after the date of the will that said only, "I revoke my will." Your client wants to know if the revocation is valid. If you had read only § 10, you would have told your client that the revocation was not valid because the statute requires a person to revoke by means of a later will and the second paper is not a will. In order to advise your client correctly, however, you should also have read the Definitions section of the entire Probate Code. There you would have seen that the word "will" in § 10 is defined to include "any instrument that revokes another will." The second instrument is, thus, a valid revocation.

When you read the text of the sections with which you are concerned, look at the overall structure to see how one part of the text relates to the rest. If, for example, some language of the statute is in the alternative, that is, connected by the disjunctive "or," then only one of those parts needs to be satisfied. If, on the other hand, parts of a statute are connected by the conjunctive "and," then both parts must be fulfilled. Consider this statute:

Burglary in the Third Degree

1. A person is guilty of burglary in the third degree if he knowingly enters or remains unlawfully in a building, and

2. does so with the intent to commit a crime.

Under this language, the person charged needs either to have entered a building unlawfully or to have remained there unlawfully. He need not have both entered and remained unlawfully in order to be guilty. For example, a person may have entered a building while it was open to the public, but remained unlawfully after the building had closed.

In contrast, both part 1 and part 2 of the statute must be satisfied because they are connected by the conjunctive "and." The prosecutor must prove that the person charged with burglary in the third degree either entered or remained in a building unlawfully and also that he did either of those with the intent to commit a crime.

Analyze also how the modifiers are used. Usually a modifier is placed before or after the verb or noun it modifies. In this statute, interpretation is complicated by the presence of two adverbs, "knowingly" and "unlawfully," and two verbs, "enters" and "remains." Although a reader could legitimately infer that "knowingly" modifies only the adjacent word "enters" and that "unlawfully" modifies only the adjacent word "remains," common sense dictates a different interpretation. It is not a crime to enter a building merely because one knowingly enters it, even if one intends to do a criminal act. And it is probably a crime of a lesser degree if one remained in a building unlawfully but was unaware that remaining was unlawful. Because an interpretation based on normal adverb placement renders the statute nonsensical, the more likely interpretation is that a person must either knowingly enter a building unlawfully or knowingly remain in a building unlawfully in order to violate this statute.[1] The statute would probably be clearer if its drafters had written "if he knowingly and unlawfully either enters or remains in a building."

Exercise 3–A

A Kent statute permits a person to execute a will without witnesses to the execution if the will is "entirely written, dated, and signed" in the handwriting of the testator. John Bloom hand wrote and signed his will. He dated the will May, 1980. Is the will valid? What does that depend on?

II. Finding the Statutory Issues

When you read the statute in light of the facts of your problem case, you should identify the issues concerning how the statute applies to those facts. The first dispute may be whether the statute applies at all to your case. For example, one of the parties to litigation may rely on Article 2 of the state's Commercial Code, which applies to sales of goods. If the case concerns the leasing rather than the sale of goods, then one issue is whether the requirements of Article 2 apply to a contract for the lease of goods.

---

1. You will also interpret the statute's meaning according to the techniques described in Part III.

Exercise 3–B

Does the following statute apply to either of these sets of facts?

Statute: Deceptive Collection Practices Act

A collection agency or any employee of a collection agency commits a deceptive collection practice when, while attempting to collect an alleged debt, he or she adds to the debt any service charge, interest, or penalty, which he or she is not entitled to by law.

Facts 1:

John Brown, an interior decorator, loaned $3000 to his employee. When the employee had made no efforts to return the loan, Brown began harassing him for repayment and also claimed a usurious interest rate. The employee threatens to sue Brown under the Deceptive Collection Practices Act.

Facts 2:

Oscar Green, a secretary for Acme Collection Agency, plays poker with five friends every Tuesday evening after work. One night his friend Felix ran up a $500 debt that he couldn't pay, and Oscar loaned him the $500. Two weeks later, when he asked Felix to repay him, Oscar added a $25 charge.

What information about the statute's coverage might you want to know besides the section above?

————

Once you have determined that a statute applies to your case, then identify the issues in terms of whether the statute was violated. What conduct does the statute permit or not permit? Does your client's or the other party's conduct come within the statutory description?

Exercise 3–C

Identify the statutory issues in these problems.

1. Statute: Wills

In order for a will to be valid, the will must be signed by the testator in the presence of two witnesses.

Facts:

Mr. Beal signed his will while one witness, Ms. Smith, stood next to him, and the other witness, Ms. Byrd, was in the adjoining room getting her pen. Ms. Byrd was facing Mr. Beal and saw him bend over the paper at the time he signed.

2. Statute: Solid Wastes

No garbage dump shall hereafter be established within the corporate limits of any city or town, nor shall any garbage dump be established within 250 yards of any residence without the consent of the owner of the residence.

Facts:

The People's Garbage Dump was opened by the city in 1950. Three years later, Tom Smith built a house on a lot near the dump. The city acquired a tract adjoining the dump and within 200 yards of Smith's residence. The city plans to enlarge the dump with the new tract of land. Smith opposes the enlargement.

3. Statute: Distribution of Damages in Wrongful Death Action: [2]

The jury in any wrongful death action may award such damages as may seem fair and may direct how the damages shall be distributed among the surviving spouse, the children, and grandchildren of the decedent.

Facts:

Martha Smith, for whose death a wrongful death action was brought, was survived by her husband, a natural born child, an adopted child, and her illegitimate child.

4. Statute: Worker's Compensation

If an employee suffers personal injury by an accident arising out of and in the course of the employment, the worker is entitled to recover under this Act.

Facts:

Nathan Hail was employed by a university's tennis facility as a teacher at its tennis camp for children. The facility sold summer passes and also solicited people to contribute as subscribers. The director of the facility made clear that the teachers should be friendly to the subscribers. Sam Hardy, a subscriber, asked Nathan to play one afternoon after Nathan got off work teaching tennis classes. During the match, Nathan twisted his ankle and had to stop working for the rest of the season.

———

When you brief a case in which there is a statutory issue, your brief should reflect the statutory nature of the case. You should state the issue to reflect the exact question that the statute raised and you usually should include verbatim the operative language of the statute. Your statement of the holding of the case should answer that question, also in terms of the statute and its exact language.

2. A wrongful death statute provides a civil recovery against a person who caused the death of another.

The following are examples of issues written for a case brief.

1.   Is a handwritten will that is dated with the month and year, but not the day, a will "entirely written, dated and signed by the testator" as required by the Kent Probate Code?

2.   Does a person who without authority goes into a tent pitched in a park enter a "building" within the meaning of the Oz burglary statute?

3.   Is a signed writing that says only "I revoke my will," a "subsequent will which revokes the prior will" as required by the Kent Probate Code?

Exercise 3–D

Write the issues for the four exercises beginning on page 54 as you would write them for a case brief.

Exercise 3–E

For the following exercise, read the statute and the facts to which you will apply the statute.

Statute: Theft of Lost or Mislaid Property

A person who obtains control over lost or mislaid property commits theft when that person:

(1) Knows or learns the identity of the owner or knows of a reasonable method of identifying the owner, and

(2) Fails to take reasonable measures to restore the property to the owner, and

(3) Intends to deprive the owner permanently of the use of the property.

10 Oz Rev. Stat. § 20 (1985).

Facts:

Bill Smith saw a 14k gold locket on the ground of the park softball diamond at 1:30 p.m., just after a team from the YWCA had been practicing there. The diamond is located just west of a residential area of Oz and is in a large park that also contains children's playground facilities and tennis courts. The locket was engraved with three initials. Although he did not know the people on the team, Smith knew the name of the team because of the YWCA uniforms they wore. Smith was making deliveries for a nearby supermarket, where he worked a 10 a.m. to 4 p.m. shift. He also worked evenings for a newspaper.

Smith picked up the locket, looked it over, saw it was stamped 14k gold and saw that the initials were the same as those of his sister, who was in school 300 miles away. The locket needed polishing and had two pictures inside it. One was of a movie star. Smith pocketed the locket. He walked toward the street for his next delivery, in the opposite direction from the YWCA. About a block from the place where he picked up the locket, Bill Lyons robbed Smith of the groceries, Smith's own money, and the locket.

Someone who knows Smith saw him pick up the locket and gave his name to the police, who claim he violated the statute.

––––––––––

a. What does the prosecutor have to prove in order to convict Smith of Theft of Lost or Mislaid Property?

b. What are the statutory issues?

c. What are the legally relevant facts?

III. *Techniques of Statutory Interpretation*

Once you identify the exact dispute about the application of the statute, you then analyze what the statute means in order to resolve how the statutory language applies to the facts of the case. Because a legislature enacts a statute to apply to future conduct, some of which is unforeseen at the time of enactment, rather than to a particular situation that has already occurred, legislative language is often more general than is the language in a judicial opinion. In written opinions, judges can tailor their language specifically to apply to the events that gave rise to the litigation. Statutory language may not be as specific to the events, however, and judges cannot rewrite the text of the statute, although they can direct its application.

In statutory litigation, then, the judge must often decide how the relatively general language of legislation, such as language that refers to a class of things, applies to a particular case. For example, a statute may require registration of motor vehicles. A court may have to determine which specific types of vehicles are included in that category, such as whether the requirement applies to a person's private airplane. Besides being general, statutory language may also be vague, sometimes purposely so. The statute may use terms like "fair use" or "reasonable efforts." The court must then determine the content of those vague terms within the framework of specific litigation. Statutory language, like all language, may also be ambiguous; it may have more than one meaning and the court may have to decide which meaning to apply. For example, a municipal ordinance revokes the license of a cab driver if he is convicted for a "second time of any offense under the Motor Vehicle Act." This statute may mean that the driver must be convicted twice of the same offense, but may also mean that the license will be revoked upon a conviction for a second but different offense. In all of these situations, a judge may be called upon to interpret what the text means.[3]

3. See R. Dickerson, The Fundamentals of Legal Drafting, 31–43 (1986).

A. *Legislative Intent*

The court determines what statutory language means by asking what the legislature intended it to mean. Often the court determines a legislature's intended meaning from the language of the statute itself or from other evidence about the statutory language. Moreover, a court may seek to determine what policy the legislature intended to pursue through the statute by determining the purpose of the statute. Then the court interprets the statute in a way that furthers that policy.

Courts employ a variety of approaches to determine what the legislature intended the statute to mean. The first step for most courts is to determine whether the statute has a single plain meaning. This process also can determine whether the parties may submit evidence besides the statute itself to support their interpretations of the language. If the court can interpret the statutory language according to a plain meaning, then it often will decide not to permit the parties to submit other evidence to explain the statute's meaning; it will use only the statute itself to indicate what the legislature meant.

For example, the Freedom of Information Act requires government agencies to disclose documents to any person who requests disclosure, subject to several statutory exemptions. One of those exemptions, Section 7, excludes from disclosure federal records that are compiled for law enforcement purposes if the production of those records would "disclose the identity of a confidential source." The plaintiff sought the production of documents from the government which the government argued were exempt from production because they would disclose confidential governmental agency sources. The plaintiff argued that the exemption referred only to human sources and not to foreign, state or local law enforcement agencies. The court decided, however, that the plain and ordinary meaning of the language "confidential source" is any confidential source without distinction among types.

"Plain meaning" is often, but not always, the ordinary meaning, sometimes the dictionary meaning, rather than a technical meaning of the statutory words. However, words in some statutes, such as statutes that regulate a particular industry, may more appropriately be interpreted according to their technical meanings in that industry.

If the court cannot determine a plain meaning from the statutory language itself, but decides that the language is "ambiguous" (used in this sense to mean doubt exists about the meaning of the language), then it will permit the parties to introduce other evidence to show what the legislature intended the statute to mean. There is also considerable case law to the effect that these may not be exclusive steps. For instance, a court can use other evidence as aids in construing the statutory language even if it can ascribe a plain meaning to the words. Often, even if a plain meaning is discernible, a court will permit the parties to submit evidence explaining what the legislature intended in order to show that an ambiguity exists, or to show that enforcing the first meaning would lead to absurd or to unintended results.

For example, a federal statute prohibits importing aliens "under contract to perform labor or service of any kind in the United States." Has a church violated this statute by contracting and bringing from England an English minister to perform services as minister for the church? If it seems absurd to construe this statute to impose a monetary penalty on a church because it employed a minister from England, then the court will admit evidence to show that Congress did not intend the statute to prohibit that type of employment.

The most favored evidence that parties employ to determine the legislature's intended meaning is the legislative history of the statute. A legislative history consists of different elements. One part of a legislative history is the predecessor statutes to the one at issue. Legislative history also consists of the documents that were produced during the statute's legislative journey from its beginning as a bill introduced in the legislature, through proceedings in the committee or committees to which it was assigned, and to its passage into law. You use this type of legislative history to find legislators' statements about what they meant by the disputed language. In the case of the statute that prohibits importing aliens, for example, the transcripts of committee hearings, the committee report, and the Congressional Record account of the debate on the floor of Congress all show that Congress intended to prohibit importation of contract labor crews to perform unskilled labor, not to prohibit hiring an individual from abroad to perform professional services.

If, however, the documents do not reveal the legislators' intended meaning or if they show that the legislators never thought about the application of the statute to the particular problem posed by the case, then you read the documents to try to find the more general purpose of the statute and you interpret the language in a way that promotes that purpose.

For federal statutes, the legislative history can be considerable, the most favored source being committee reports. For example, committee reports played a considerable role in one court's interpretation of Exemption 6 to the Freedom of Information Act. This section exempts from mandatory disclosure "personnel and medical files and similar files the disclosure of which would constitute a clearly unwarranted invasion of personal privacy." The section required judicial interpretation because of an ambiguous modifier. It is unclear which terms are modified by the phrase: "the disclosure of which would constitute a clearly unwarranted invasion of personal privacy." The restriction could apply only to similar files or it could modify personnel files, medical files, and similar files.

If the restriction applies only to "similar files," then personnel and medical files are under a blanket exemption from disclosure regardless of whether their disclosure would constitute an invasion of privacy. A person requesting disclosure of personnel files would interpret the restriction to apply to all three descriptions of files. The government agency would interpret the restriction to apply only to "similar files."

Because of the ambiguous syntax of Exemption 6, the statute's plain language is unhelpful. Thus, the court facing this issue of statutory interpretation used the following information and reasoning to decide that the "invasion of privacy" restriction applied to all three types of files.

1. That court had already interpreted the policy behind the entire FOIA statute as one of disclosure, not secrecy.

2. The Congressional committee reports included language that applied to all of Exemption 6. That language requires a court to engage in a balance of the two policies of protecting an individual's private affairs from unnecessary public scrutiny and of preserving the public's right to governmental information. A court would not engage in that balance for medical and personnel files if those files were under a blanket exemption from disclosure.

3. The committee reports had no language about blanket exemptions in Exemption 6.

The court used these sources to decide that the limiting language modified the three types of files listed so that none was under a blanket exemption from the Act.[4] By doing so, the court interpreted the statutory language to promote the statute's policy of disclosure.

Unlike the materials available for federal statutes, the legislative materials available for state statutes may be meager. Even if a considerable amount of state or federal materials exist, however, they may be inconclusive as to what the legislature intended the litigated language to mean or how the purposes of the statute bear on the application of the particular language to the facts of the case.

---

4. Based on Department of Air Force v. Rose, 425 U.S. 352 (1976).

Exercise 3–F

Some of the relevant legislative history of the Freedom of Information Act § 7 exemption described previously is set out below. Based on this legislative history, did the court interpret the § 7 exemption correctly? Was the statute intended to mean only human sources?

    1. Original version of statute:

The original version of § 7 exempted records that would "disclose the identity of an informer." The term "informer" was changed by the committee to which the bill was referred to "confidential source."

    2. Committee Report:

The Committee Report contains the following statements:

    a. "The substitution of the term 'confidential source' in § 7 is to make clear that the identity of a person other than a paid informer may be protected if the person provided information under an express assurance of confidentiality."

    b. "The bill in the form now presented to the Senate . . . has been changed from protecting the identity of an 'informer' to protecting the identity of a person other than a paid informer. . . . Not only is the identity of a confidential source protected but also protected from disclosure is all the information furnished by that source to a law enforcement agency. . . ."

    3. Congressional debate:

The debate on the floor of the Senate recorded in the Congressional Record contains the statement by a senator on the committee, "we also provided that there be no requirement to reveal not only the identity of a confidential source, but also any information obtained from him in a criminal investigation."

———

How do you evaluate the following arguments in support of the court's plain meaning interpretation that § 7 applies to all sources including other law enforcement agencies?

    a. The use of the word "person" in the Committee Report is similar to the use of any collective noun and refers to a variety of entities in addition to human beings.

    b. The singular masculine pronoun, such as the "him" used by the senator, is often used where the sex of the referent is unknown or where it refers to a collective noun consisting of entities of more than one sex. A person using a pronoun during debates is not grammatically precise.

    c. Congress was concerned that it not impair the ability of federal law enforcement agencies to collect information. The plaintiff's interpretation of § 7 would make other law enforcement agencies or other entities reluctant to share information with federal agencies.

    d. The legislative history materials are themselves ambiguous and should not control the customary meaning of words in the statute.

Exercise 3–G

For the following exercise, read the facts of the problem. The case following the facts will provide some arguments relevant to the issue in the problem.

Facts:

The Oz Licensed Nursing Home Act § 15 provides a hearing for any licensee that has been charged with abusing a patient. The section provides "The Department shall commence a hearing within thirty days of the receipt of a nursing home's request for a hearing."

On April 10, 1986, the Department determined that TranQuil Nursing Home had abused a patient. TranQuil then requested a hearing on May 1, 1986. The Department, however, overlooked the request and did not schedule a hearing until December 1, 1986. At the hearing, the Department again determined that TranQuil was guilty of abuse. The home now seeks judicial review of that determination and has moved to dismiss the Department's proceedings for lack of timeliness because it was held after the thirty day period.

Adam v. Personnel Board

The Personnel Code of Oz § 20 requires that the Personnel Board provide a review for all state personnel protesting their discharge. Section 20 provides that the review "shall be held within 60 days of a discharged employee's request for review." Donald Adam requested review on September 1, 1980. The Personnel Board hearing, which confirmed his discharge, was held January 15, 1981. Adam has asked this court to void the Board's decision on the grounds that it was not timely.

The plain meaning of the word "shall" is that of a mandatory verb. The dictionary so defines it. The word has sometimes been construed as directory, however. If the statute states the time for performance but does not deny performance after a specified time, then "shall" is usually considered directory. If the time period safeguards someone's rights, it is mandatory.

Section 20 is designed to protect the rights of government employees who protest their discharge. A delay in their hearing could prejudice their rights. We therefore interpret the section as mandatory.

a. Which statutory argument will the plaintiff TranQuil Nursing Home make?

b. Which arguments will the state make?

c. Which arguments are better?

B. *The Canons of Construction*

Another long-standing—and frequently criticized—method of determining statutory meaning is to apply what are called "canons of construction." These canons are maxims or guides that suggest possible interpretations of certain verbal patterns in statutes and certain types of statutes. The canons, however, often yield inconclusive results.

A well-known canon used to interpret verbal patterns is the canon known as *ejusdem generis*. *Ejusdem generis* is applied to mean that whenever a statute contains specific enumeration followed by a general catchall phrase, the general words should be construed to mean only things of the same kind or same characteristics as the specific words (*ejusdem generis* means "of the same genus or class"). For example, in the language "no one may transport vegetables, dairy, fruit, or other products without a certificate of conveyance," the catchall words "or other products" could be interpreted to mean food products but not manufactured goods. However, the term may also be interpreted to include non-manufactured goods that are not foods, such as fresh flowers or lumber. To determine the scope of this phrase, it may be more important to know that the legislature's purpose in requiring a certificate of conveyance was to ensure sanitary conditions during transport.

Another example is a criminal code that makes illegal the shipment of obscene "books, pamphlets, pictures, motion picture films, papers, letters, writings, prints or other matter of indecent character." In a prosecution under the statute for mailing obscene phonograph records, application of the rule of *ejusdem generis* would require that the statute be interpreted to not include obscene phonograph records because the enumerated list includes matter taken in by sight, not by hearing.

The Supreme Court, however, did not use the canon to construe this statute because to have done so would have defeated the obvious purpose of the statute, which was to make illegal the use of the mails to disseminate obscene matter. The Court read the entire statute, beyond the portion under which the defendant was charged, to construe the statute as a "comprehensive" one that should not be limited by a mechanical construction.

Another well-known canon, which is again always referred to in Latin, is *expressio unius, exclusio alterius* (expression of one thing excludes another), usually shortened to *expressio unius*. *Expressio unius* is applied to mean that if a statute expressly mentions what is intended to be within its coverage, then the statute excludes that which is not mentioned.

For example, the statute that prohibits importing aliens contains a section that excludes actors, artists, lecturers, professional musicians, and domestic servants, but does not exclude ministers. A court applying *expressio unius* would interpret the list of exemptions as an exclusive one, yet the legislature may not have intended the enumerated exclusions to be exclusive or may not have thought about other categories of people who should also have been excluded from the statute's broad coverage.

A third well-known canon is "statutes in *pari materia* (on the same subject matter) should be read together," that is, they should be interpreted consistently with each other. For example, a section of the Family Law Code on the topic of adopted children provides, "the adopted child shall be treated for all purposes as the natural child of the adopting parents." A section of the Probate Code provides that the property of a person who dies without a will shall be distributed "one-third to the surviving spouse and two-thirds to the surviving children." If this statute and the section of the Family Law Code are to be read in *pari materia* so as to be consistent with each other, then the word "children" in the Probate Code should be interpreted to include adopted children of the decedent.

Of course, the statutory language of one or both statutes may show that the statutes should not be interpreted together. For example, the Family Law Code may provide that the adopted child be "treated for all purposes, including relations with the kin of the adopting parents, as the natural child of the adopting parents." The Probate Code, however, may provide only that "the adopted child shall inherit from the adopting parents as would a natural child." If the issue is whether the adopted child inherits from an adopting parent's mother (where the adopting parent has died), the differences in language between the statutes now make a difference. The Probate Code does not employ the specific language about "kin of the adopting parents," nor does it define the child as a natural child "for all purposes." Because the drafters of the Probate Code did not use that language, they may not have intended that the statute apply to all the situations to which the Family Law Code applies. Of course, the drafters also may not have read the Family Law Code, and had not thought about problems arising from interpreting the two statutes consistently. The court will have to decide if it should do so, or whether the more narrow language of the Probate Code should control because it is the statute that more specifically applies to this problem.

Some canons are used to help interpret types of statutes by the presumed policy behind those statutes. An example is "a penal statute should be strictly construed." This means that if it is not clear whether the language of a criminal statute (or a civil statute that imposes a penalty) applies to a particular defendant's conduct, the statute will be interpreted narrowly in favor of the defendant. This type of construction is based on a policy that people should have fair warning of conduct that is punishable. Other canons of this type are the somewhat outdated "statutes in derogation of the common law should be strictly construed," and "remedial statutes should be liberally construed." If the remedial statute is one that changes (is in derogation of) the common law, however, such as a worker's compensation act, then the two canons' presumptions conflict.

Canons do not explain what the legislature meant in enacting the particular statute being analyzed. Rather, they suggest what people usually mean by common language patterns. A canon such as "a penal statute should be strictly construed" supplies a presumption about how any legislature enacting that type of statute would intend the statute to be interpreted. Thus, because the canons do not analyze the reasons for the particular statutory language being applied, a canon should not by itself compel a particular interpretation.[5] Indeed, in the case involving the criminality of sending obscene phonograph records through the mail, the Court did not interpret the statute according to this canon either. Instead, it read the statute as a whole to determine the enacting legislature's purpose. You should become familiar with the canons because many courts employ them as aids in construing language, especially if there is no legislative history available, but they are not conclusive about meaning.

Statutory interpretation often can be a difficult process of analyzing the language of text, the pre-enactment legislative history materials related to that text, other materials related to the statute, such as proposed amendments, and the canons of construction. But just as you apply case law to further the policies behind legal precedents, you use the techniques of statutory analysis to determine the legislative policy in enacting the statute and to interpret the text to further that policy.

C. Stare Decisis and Statutes

Once a court interprets a statute, the principle of stare decisis applies and the court will then follow the interpretation it has previously adopted unless it overrules it. For each new case with the same statutory issue, the court then reasons by analogy to the facts of the prior cases in order to apply the statute to the new case.

When you write about a problem that involves statutory analysis and arguments, you should include these analytic steps in your written analysis. Discuss the statutory language and its possible interpretations. Summarize the relevant legislative history and its interpretations, and, if the canons are relevant, explain how they apply to the language. If the statute has been inter-

5. As has been pointed out, some canons point to opposite conclusions. See Llewellyn, Remarks on the Theory of Appellate Decision and the Rules or Canons About How Statutes Are To Be Construed, 3 Vand. L. Rev. 395 (1950).

preted by the courts, discuss the case law. If there is binding precedent interpreting the statute, explain how that interpretation applies to the facts of your problem. You will find that after a statute has been interpreted by the courts, its history becomes less important to its interpretation.

Exercise 3–H

The following two exercises are examples of constitutional issues for which a court has already applied the disputed constitutional provision in a precedent. For the purposes of these exercises, consider that the same principles of stare decisis apply to prior interpretations of constitutional language as to statutory language. Use Case 1 in each exercise as the controlling precedent for Case 2.

1. Does a city's display of a creche at Christmas time violate the establishment clause of the first amendment to the United States Constitution that says "Congress shall make no law respecting an establishment of religion"?

Case 1

A city owned and displayed a Christmas scene in a privately owned park located near a shopping area. The display consisted of many figurines and decorations, including a Santa Claus and sleigh, a decorated tree, several carolers, animals, clowns and a creche scene. The court decided that the display of the creche did not violate the establishment clause of the first amendment, which prohibits government activity that establishes religion. One part of the test of whether the establishment clause has been violated is whether the activity has the effect of advancing religion. The court decided that although the creche by itself is a religious symbol, within the overall context the display was a seasonal rather than religious display, and the creche demonstrated the historical origins of the holiday. Thus, the city did not act unconstitutionally by including the creche scene because the scene did not have the effect of advancing religion.

Case 2

Another city, one of the ten largest in the country, displayed a city-owned creche in the lobby of the City Hall. The city also decorated the lobby with Christmas wreaths above the elevators, a large Christmas tree just inside the entrance, and a Santa Claus and sleigh in the lobby, which it designated as the collection spot for food donations. These decorations are from ten to ninety feet away from the creche. Is this city's creche an unconstitutional endorsement of religion?

Compare Case 2 with Case 1. You must determine if Case 2 should be decided differently from Case 1 for purposes of whether the city endorses religion by displaying a creche. You do that by examining whether the facts are essentially analogous or distinguishable.

In Case 1 the creche is one part of a large diverse display. In Case 2 the creche is not side by side with other figures. Is it a self-contained religious exhibit because it is ten to ninety feet from other holiday decorations? Or is it just one element of an ensemble of seasonal holiday decorations? Are the two cases analogous or distinguishable on this point?

In Case 1, the holiday display was owned by the city but set up in a privately owned park. In Case 2, the city-owned display is in the lobby of City Hall. Does this difference in location and the ownership of the display make the cases distinguishable in terms of whether the two cities endorsed religion by setting up a creche at Christmas time?

2. Does the fourth amendment require that police acquire a search warrant in order to accomplish aerial observation of a person's premises within the fenced area around the person's home?

Case 1

Municipal police, acting without a search warrant, used a small airplane to fly 1000 feet over the house and backyard of the defendant. The yard was completely enclosed by a ten-foot fence. From the airplane, the officers saw marijuana plants growing in the defendant's yard. The court held that the police, although acting without a search warrant, did not violate the fourth amendment by their observation of the defendant's backyard. The fourth amendment is interpreted to mean that a person is entitled to its search warrant protections if he has a reasonable expectation of privacy in the object of the challenged search. This defendant's expectation of privacy from observation was unreasonable because the police were in an airspace open to public navigation, viewing what was visible to the naked eye.

Case 2

Municipal police acting without a search warrant flew in a helicopter at 400 feet over the defendant's premises. Police observed the defendant's greenhouse adjoining his house. The officers were able to look through openings in the greenhouse roof and sides to see marijuana growing inside the greenhouse. Did the officers violate the defendant's reasonable expectation of privacy and thus conduct an illegal search under the fourth amendment by observing the premises from a helicopter without getting a search warrant?

Does Case 1 require a decision that the police did not need a search warrant in Case 2? What are the analogies between these two cases? What are the differences that are relevant to the question of whether the defendant had a reasonable expectation of privacy that was violated?

Exercise 3–I

John Hume is charged with violating 18 U.S.C. § 2114 (1988), which provides:

> whoever assaults any person having lawful charge . . . or custody of any mail matter or of any money or other property of the United States with intent to rob or robs any such person of mail matter or of any money or other property of the United States shall be imprisoned . . . .

Hume assaulted an undercover Secret Service agent while attempting to rob him of $2000 of United States money entrusted to the agent to "purchase" counterfeit money from Hume.

Hume's defense is that the language in § 2114 "any money or other property" applies only to crimes involving robbery of postal money or postal property. The predecessor statutes to § 2114 all applied only to mail robbery and appeared in the section of the Criminal Code about offenses against the Post Office. The Postmaster General requested Congress to amend the statute to include robberies of money and other valuables as well as mail from a Post Office.

How would you evaluate the following arguments about the question of what the statutory language means? Which arguments would be used by the prosecutor and which by the defendant?

1. The statutory language is plain and unambiguous: the statute applies to any lawful custodian of three distinct classes of property. Nothing on the face of the statute limits its reach to offenses against custodians of postal money or postal property.

2. The principle of *ejusdem generis* demonstrates that the general terms "money" and "other property" should be limited by the specific term "mail matter" to postal money or postal property.

3. The bills introduced to amend the predecessor statute, which broadened its language, were referred to the Post Office Committees of both the Senate and the House of Representatives. A member of the House Post Office Committee said on the floor of the House that "the only purpose of the pending bill is to extend protection of the present law to property of the United States in the custody of its postal officials, the same as it now extends the protection to mail matter in the custody of its postal officials."

4. The Committee Reports of both the House and Senate Committees say that "the purpose of the bill is to bring within the provisions of the Penal Code the crime of robbing or attempting to rob custodians of government moneys."

5. The federal Criminal Code § 2112 contains a general statute penalizing thefts of government property with a much lesser sentence than the one imposed by § 2114.

6. In an earlier case, the Solicitor General of the United States conceded that § 2114 covered only postal crimes.

Chapter Four
Writing a Legal Document:
The Legal Memorandum

I. Introduction

In the previous chapters we have discussed how to analyze
and apply legal authority. We have also discussed how to write a
case brief, which law students usually write for their own use.
Most legal writing, however, is done to communicate with others.
As a first-year law student, you will receive legal problems and
will be asked to analyze the problem and write up the results of
that analysis. The typical vehicle that lawyers use to do this is
the legal memorandum. When you write a memorandum, you
will make use of the several analytical skills you have been
developing. This chapter explains the form and content of a legal
memorandum. The next chapters go into more detail about how
to write a legal analysis within a memorandum.

A. Purpose of a Memorandum

A legal memorandum is a document written to convey information within a law firm or other organization. It is a written
analysis of a legal problem. The memorandum is usually prepared by a junior attorney or by a law clerk for a more senior
attorney early in the firm's handling of a legal dispute. The
writer analyzes the legal principles that govern the issues raised
by that problem and applies those principles to the facts of the
case. The attorneys will then use the memo to understand the

issues that the case raises, to advise the client, and to prepare later documents for the case.

The memorandum should be an objective, exploratory document. It is a discussion in which you explore the problem, evaluate the strengths and weaknesses of each party's arguments, and reach a conclusion based on that analysis. It is not an advocacy paper in which you argue only for your client's side of the case. The memorandum should be persuasive only in the sense that you convince your reader that your analysis of the problem is correct.

B. Audience

When you write a memorandum, you should be aware of your reading audience and its needs and expectations. The hypothetical audience for a student memorandum assignment is usually an attorney who is not a specialist in the field. Most attorneys for whom you write will be very busy and will have certain expectations that you must fulfill. For example, they will expect to receive a core of information about the controlling law and its application to the facts of the problem, but will not expect to be given a lesson in fundamental legal procedure. Because the reader is an attorney, you will not have to explain the legal process steps of the sort that you have been learning the first weeks of law school. You need not explain, for example, "This case is from the highest court of this state and so is binding in this dispute." You may wish to give this information to a lay reader, but a lawyer knows that a case decided by the jurisdiction's highest court is binding. On the other hand, the lawyer probably does not know the facts, holding, and reasoning of that case and does expect that you will supply that information.

C. Writing Techniques

Your reader will also have expectations about how the memorandum should be written. The legal profession is dependent on language. However unfamiliar you are with legal analysis and its presentation in a professional document, you are still writing English and you should continue to follow the principles of good written English. The general characteristics of good writing need to be cultivated because legal analysis can be complicated and involve difficult ideas. In order to communicate these ideas clearly to your reader, you must have a firm control over language. Chapters Eight and Nine and Appendix A explain the principles for clear writing.

The memorandum is a formal document in that it is a professional piece of writing. Thus, you should use standard written

English and avoid slang, other kinds of informal speech, and overuse of contractions. For example, you should not write, "for starters, we have to decide if John Doe's parents are immune from suit." Say instead, "the first issue is whether John Doe's parents are immune from suit." On the other hand, you should not be pompous and stuffy. Use simple, direct words and sentence structures. You do not have to say, "one can conjure multiple scenarios for fulfillment of these objectives." Say instead, "the agency can fulfill its goals in several ways." In addition, you should not write a verbose sentence like, "in applying the above precedent, it is clear that the lack of action by the school implies that the incident was not considered to be unlawful." Just say, "the school's inaction implies that school officials did not consider the incident unlawful." Since the revised sentence is of reasonable length and contains no empty phrases, it is easier to understand. Moreover, since the sentence is written in the active voice, there is no ambiguity about who considered the incident lawful.

Another aspect of presenting yourself as a legal professional is that you are writing as the client's attorney. Many students forget that role, and, for example, may write, "John Doe's attorney moved for a continuance." Remember that you are John Doe's attorney, or part of a team of attorneys, and instead should write, "we filed for a continuance." You should not, however, inject yourself into your legal analysis. The purpose of the memorandum, and of many other legal documents, is to analyze the law and facts. You want to communicate that analysis persuasively and convincingly, not present it as your opinion only. For example, you should say "in Doe v. Doe the court held . . .," not "I believe [or I think] that in Doe v. Doe the court held. . . ."

One problem of legal writing that deserves particular attention is the problem of legalese. Lawyers frequently are criticized for using archaic terms and incomprehensible sentence constructions in legal documents. This criticism is especially aimed at the form documents that many attorneys use. An example is a form that begins "whereas the party of the first part," and uses expressions like "herein" and "hereinbefore." This type of legalese usually does not afflict law students, and we hope it will not afflict you. In the end, you will sound more professional and more in control if you use a vocabulary and syntax with which you feel comfortable.

Some legal terms are substantive, however, and you should use them. For example, you should use the operative language of a statute or of a judge's formulation of a rule when that language controls the analysis of a problem on which you are working. Although that language may not strike you as admirable, it supplies the general principle of law to which you must give meaning. Your reader should be told what that language is and will expect you to repeat those operative terms.

Your language should also be responsive to your audience. You will be writing for several different audiences during your legal career and you will have to adjust your prose accordingly. Not all of your readers will be lawyers. For example, often you will write to your clients, to administrative personnel, and to other government officeholders. Although you should write accurately about the law, you should also explain your message in good written English, using terms that a non-lawyer can understand. When you write to lawyers, you should also use good written English, although you may use legal terms without as much explanation. Keep in mind that each audience has a different need, but that all audiences need and appreciate good writing.

Nonetheless, if as a law student you face the particular challenge of navigating between legalese and terms of art, in most respects, legal writing requires only what any thoughtfully written paper requires. As long as your prose adheres to the rules of standard written English and composition and respects legal terms, you will fulfill your reader's expectations for memorandum style.

II. *Format*

Most office memoranda are divided into sections that are assembled in a logical order. You do not need to write the memorandum in the order you assemble it, however. Instead, you may first want to write tentative formulations of certain sections (such as the Question Presented) and then rewrite those sections when you have a final draft of the part of the memo that is pivotal to your writing process, usually the Discussion. After that pivotal section is written, you should rewrite the sections you wrote earlier to ensure they are in accordance with the finished section. This type of writing process requires drafts and revisions before you reach your final copy.

There is no required format that all lawyers use or that all law schools use for a legal memorandum. Most memoranda, however, are divided into from three to six sections, each of which performs a particular function within the memo and conveys a necessary core of information: the Statement of Facts, the Question Presented, the Short Answer or Conclusion, the Applicable Statutes, the Discussion, and perhaps a final Conclusion. Under some formats, the Question Presented may come before the Statement of Facts, as it does in the sample memo, Appendix C.

The memorandum usually begins with a heading with the following information:

> To: Name of the person for whom the memo is written
> From: Name of the writer
> Re: Short identification of the matter for which the memo was prepared
> Date:

Then the body of the memo may be divided into the sections described below.

A. *Statement of Facts*

Because the heart of legal analysis is in applying the law to the facts, the facts of the problem can be the most important determinant of the outcome of a case. Each case begins because something happened to someone or to some thing. The Statement of Facts introduces the legal problem by telling what happened.

The purpose of this section is to state the facts and narrate what happened. Therefore, use only facts in this section; do not give conclusions, legal principles, or citations to authorities. This section should include all legally relevant facts, all facts that you mention in the other sections of the memo, and any other facts that give necessary background information. If the problem for your memo is already in litigation, you should include its procedural history.

Facts are relevant or irrelevant in relation to the legal principles at issue. In order to know which facts are relevant, you will need to know what the issue in the problem is. If the issue is whether the client committed a crime, then you must know the elements of that crime. The relevant facts are those that are used to prove or disprove those elements.

Do not omit facts that are unfavorable to your client. The attorney for whom you are writing the memo may rely on the Statement of Facts for negotiations with other attorneys and to prepare other documents for the case. Without the complete facts, the attorney for whom you are writing will be surprised and unprepared while handling the case.

Be careful to use objective language. The facts should not be slanted, subtly or not so subtly, toward either party. Sentence one of each of the following sets describes facts using partisan language inappropriate for a memorandum. Sentence two of each set uses language more appropriate for a memorandum.

1. John Smith endured three hours of his family's presence.
2. John Smith remained with his family for three hours.

1. Because Ms. Jones deserted her husband, he was left the unenviable task of raising three children.

2. After Ms. Jones left her husband, he raised his three children by himself.

Whether you are given the facts with your assignment or you gather them yourself, you should sort them out and organize them rather than repeat them as the information came to you. Put the crucial information first. Generally, in the first paragraph, you should tell who your client is and what your client wants. By doing so, you provide a framework for the problem. The reader then can more easily evaluate the rest of the facts within that framework. For example, compare these two paragraphs, each of which was written as the first paragraph of a Statement of Facts for the same problem.

> 1. John Davis is a high school graduate who has been unable to keep a job. He first worked as a machinist's apprentice, but after two years he was asked to leave. Since then he has worked at various trades, including carpentry and plumbing, in retail stores, and at McDonald's. None of these jobs lasted more than a year.

> 2. Our client, William Mathews, has been sued by John Davis for fraud. The charge stems from statements that Mathews made to Davis in the course of a stock investment proposal.

Example 2 is better because it tells the reader the context of the problem. The reader of the first paragraph does not know what the problem is about. Is it an employment contract case? An unemployment compensation application problem? The reader of the second example knows that she should read the rest of the facts with an eye toward a fraud suit.

Use the rest of this section to develop the facts. Explain who the parties are and give any other descriptions that are necessary. Always group like facts together. For example, if your memo topic is a false imprisonment topic about a person confined in a room, you may want to present in one paragraph or series of paragraphs all the facts that describe the physical appearance of the room.

For many of the assignments you receive, the best and easiest way to develop the events is chronologically, that is, in the order in which the events occurred. For some problems, however, a topical organization in which you structure the facts in terms of the elements you need to establish or by the parties involved, if there are many parties, may work better.

You also may want to include what relief your client wants, or what you have been asked to analyze in the memo. This information often provides a natural ending to the section.

Exercise 4–A

Which Statement of Facts about the Wheeler case described in Chapter Two is best? Why?

1. Mr. Fred Wheeler is a prisoner in the federal prison in Danbury, Connecticut. Wheeler was convicted of bank robbery in Arkansas, which was his domicile at the time of the robbery. He has asked us to sue his attorney in that case for malpractice. The attorney, Donald Lindhorst, is a domiciliary of Arkansas. We would like to sue in the United States District Court if we can establish diversity jurisdiction.

Wheeler is in the second year of a five-to-seven year prison term. His wife and son moved to Danbury four months ago, and his wife is now working here. His son is enrolled in the Danbury public school. Mrs. Wheeler has registered to vote in Danbury and has opened an account at a bank there. The Wheelers have no financial interests in Arkansas. His wife's sister, who is her only family member still alive, lives in nearby Bethel, Connecticut. Wheeler's brother-in-law has offered Wheeler a job there after Wheeler's release from prison. Wheeler has said he will not return to Arkansas, and that he wants to "start fresh in Connecticut."

This memo analyzes whether Wheeler is a citizen of Connecticut for purposes of federal diversity jurisdiction.

2. Donald Lindhorst is a lawyer in Little Rock who unsuccessfully defended Fred Wheeler against a bank robbery charge in Arkansas. Wheeler is now in federal prison here in Danbury and wants to sue Lindhorst for malpractice. Wheeler has called Lindhorst a "rotten lawyer" and "a crook," who was only interested in getting his legal fee from him.

Wheeler is serving his second year of a five-to-seven year prison term. He hates the prison because of the food and lack of recreational facilities. His wife has moved to Danbury with their son and visits him often. Wheeler wants to remain in Connecticut when he gets out of prison and take a job offered him by his brother-in-law in nearby Bethel. His wife is working in Danbury and his child is in school here.

Lindhorst had been recommended to Wheeler by a mutual friend in Arkansas, and now Wheeler is sorry he hired him. He says that Lindhorst spoke to him only once, and did not interview any witnesses before the trial. He has asked us to handle his malpractice case. We would like to sue in the United States District Court in Hartford if we can establish diversity jurisdiction.

3. On March 4, 1986, Fred Wheeler was convicted of bank robbery in the federal district court in Arkansas. At his sentencing hearing in May 1986, he was sentenced to a five-to-seven year term in federal prison in Danbury, Connecticut. Wheeler was represented by a Mr. Donald Lindhorst, an Arkansas attorney, in the bank robbery case.

Wheeler now wants to sue Lindhorst for malpractice, and wrote us on March 10, 1988, asking us to represent him in this suit. We want to sue in the federal district court in Hartford. When I interviewed him last month, Wheeler told me that he does not intend to return to Arkansas and wants "to start fresh in Connecticut."

Mrs. Wheeler moved to Danbury in January, 1987. That month she enrolled their son in the public school and opened a bank account. In February, she started work in Danbury, and has remained with that job. Mrs. Wheeler visits her husband frequently. Her brother-in-law has offered Wheeler a job in Connecticut when he gets out of prison.

B. Question Presented

The most important inquiry for the memo writer, as it is in other legal inquiries, is "what is the legal issue in this problem?" The Question Presented is a sentence that poses the precise legal issue in dispute that the problem turns on. There are two ways to formulate the questions for a memorandum. The first, and easier way, is to be very specific to the problem and identify people by name and identify events by reference to them. This type of question works if the reader already knows the facts of the problem. For example, suppose you have a contract problem and the fact statement includes the facts that Mr. Smith is mentally incompetent and Mr. Jones is Smith's guardian. If the issue is written as "is the contract between Mr. Smith and Mr. Jones valid?" the reader who has read the facts will probably understand that the problem in the case is whether a contract between a mentally incompetent person and his guardian is valid. Many law firms require only this type of specific identification in the Question Presented of a memorandum. If you write a very specific question, the important things are to be sure that the reader knows the facts already and that you identify the issue correctly.

The other way of formulating issues is to write them so that they can be understood by a reader who does not know the facts of the problem. It is usually necessary to write the Question this way if the Question Presented precedes the Statement of Facts. Then the Question Presented should be written to include not only the legal principle that controls the claim, but the key facts that raise the issue. A Question written this way does not describe people or events specifically by name, however, because the reader does not know who or what they are. Instead, the issue must be written more generally by describing the relevant characteristics or relationships of people and events. This type of question is written to apply to anyone in the position of the person described in the question. For example, the contract question would be written, "Is a contract between a mentally incompetent adult and his guardian valid?" This question does not name the parties to the contract but describes their relationship and the relevant characteristics that raise the contract issue. It is a good idea to identify people by relationships appropriate to the cause of action. For an adverse possession problem, for example, you could identify the parties as a "possessor of land" and a "title holder."

You can write the Question Presented either in the form of a question as in sentence one below, or as a statement beginning with the word "whether," as in sentence two. Issues written as questions usually begin with a word such as "does" or "is."

  1. Does a prisoner's domicile change to that of the state in which he is incarcerated for purposes of satisfying federal diversity jurisdiction?

  2. Whether a prisoner's domicile changes to that of the state in which he is incarcerated for purposes of satisfying federal diversity jurisdiction.

You may find it helpful at first when you begin research for the problem to isolate the issue in specific terms (Is the Smith–Jones contract valid?), but then after you begin writing the memorandum, you should rewrite that specific question into more general terms.

Typically, the question should identify the cause of action, either a common law cause of action or the statutory or constitutional provision that the plaintiff is suing under, the key relevant facts, and the people involved described in general terms.

An exception to this pattern exists, however, if the problem involves a question of law only rather than a question of law applied to facts. For example, the issue may be whether a jurisdiction will adopt a new cause of action, or an element of an established cause of action. Then, the question may not require specific facts of the problem. In the following set of questions for a memo, the first issue is a question of law. The second issue asks how the law (assuming the law is adopted) applies to the facts. The second question thus includes specific facts of the problem.

  1. In Illinois, must a plaintiff in a false imprisonment claim be aware of the confinement?

  2. If so, is a plaintiff who believes a door will not open because it is stuck, when it has been locked by the defendant, aware of his confinement?

If the problem contains more than one issue, such as an assault and a battery, then set each out as a separately numbered question. If the problem has one issue, but two or more sub-issues, you may consider using an inclusive introduction and then sub-parts. For example, a wills issue could be written:

Is a handwritten will valid under the Oz Wills Act if

  a. the will is dated with the month and year but not the day, and

  b. the will is written on stationery that contains a printed letterhead?

One important decision you must make is the level of generality to use for your description of facts. To identify parties, we have suggested that you not name the parties specifically, but, instead describe them more generally in relation to the claim at issue. "Mr. Smith" then becomes "a mentally incompetent person" and Mr. Jones is "his guardian." But do not generalize the category so much that you obscure the issue in the problem. For example, if the case involves the duties of a school district to provide services, then "an arm of the county government" is not specific enough. The proper level of generality here is probably just "a local school district".

The facts other than the identities of the parties should be described specifically, however. The issue in a problem involves how the law applies to those particular facts. If a contract is at issue between Smith and Jones, call it a contract, not a business relationship. If the school district is being sued for not providing a sign language interpreter to a deaf student, do not write "appropriate instructional aids" instead. If the defendant is sued for building a one-car garage over a property line, do not write "a small structure." One benefit of using specific facts is that you will avoid inappropriately inserting judgments into the Questions. For example, if you called a garage a "small structure," you have made a judgment about the size of the structure that intrudes over the property line. If you said a "one-car garage," you avoided that judgment.

Consider these other suggestions for a good Question Presented.

1. Isolate the specific issue. The issue should not be so broadly stated as to encompass many possible issues under the cause of action. For example, "Was Carey denied due process?" is a poorly conceived question because due process refers to many different legal issues and the question does not specify the relevant one. A question that adequately isolates the issue is, "Is a juvenile denied due process because he is not represented by counsel at a delinquency hearing?"

2. Do not make conclusions. The Question should pose the inquiry of the memorandum, not answer it. You will avoid making conclusions if you use facts and legal principles. For example, if the case law in a jurisdiction establishes that a person can be guilty of criminal contempt if he disobeys a court order intentionally or recklessly, the following question contains a conclusion: "Is a person guilty of criminal contempt if he recklessly does not read a court order and disobeys it?" By concluding that the defendant acted recklessly, the writer has concluded that the defendant is guilty. The writer should have asked whether the

defendant is guilty under these facts, as in the question, "Is a person guilty of criminal contempt if he disobeys a court order because he did not listen to or read the order?"

3. Keep the question to a readable length. You should not include all the relevant facts in the question, just the key ones that raise the issue. The following question includes too many facts: "Is a person guilty of criminal contempt if he disobeys a court order that he never read because he left the country for several weeks, his attorney's letter was lost while he was gone, his seven-year-old daughter forgot to write down the telephone messages she took, and his cat shredded the messages from his wife?"

4. If the question does become complicated, keep it readable by moving from the general to the specific. One way of doing that is to first identify the claim and then move toward the specific facts, as in these examples.

> Did a person commit theft of lost or mislaid property when he pocketed a locket that he had found on a baseball field just after the conclusion of a YWCA team practice, and that locket was stolen from him as he walked away from the field?

> Whether a prisoner's domicile changes for purposes of federal diversity jurisdiction when he is incarcerated in another state, the prisoner's family moves to the state of incarceration, and the prisoner has secured employment there upon his release from the penitentiary.

5. Questions are less ambiguous and are easier to understand on a first reading if they begin with a short concrete subject that is quickly followed by an active verb, rather than if they begin with a long abstract subject. For example, for these questions, the writers have used abstract nouns (the failure, the refusal) as the subjects of their sentences:

> Whether the failure to appear in court for a scheduled trial by an attorney is contempt of court if he was notified of the date of the trial but never wrote it in his calendar.

> Was the refusal to give a requested entrapment instruction by the trial court because the defendant pleaded not guilty to the crime reversible error?

The subjects of these questions are nominalizations, that is, they are nouns or noun phrases that have been constructed from verbs. Sentences that begin with nominalizations are often difficult to understand because the reader has to unpack the event described in the nominalization (the failure to appear in court . . . by an attorney) and then fit that event into the question.

Another type of abstract subject that can be difficult to understand on first reading is a subject that is a gerund. A gerund is a present participle of a verb that is used as a noun. Because a gerund is a form of a verb, it may be ambiguous whether the word is the subject or the verb of the sentence. In the following question, "refusing" is a gerund.

> Did refusing to give an entrapment instruction by the trial court because the defendant pleaded not guilty constitute error?

In this question, "refusing" is the subject. But the sentence is about the trial judge. "Refusing" is what the trial judge did.

These questions should be rewritten so that they use short concrete subjects.

> Did an attorney commit contempt of court when he failed to appear for a scheduled trial if he was notified of the trial date but never wrote it in his calendar?

> Did the trial court commit reversible error when it refused to give the defendant's requested entrapment instruction because the defendant had pleaded not guilty to the crime?

See Chapter Nine for more information about nominalizations and concrete subjects.

C. The Short Answer or Conclusion

The function of this section is to answer the Question Presented and to summarize the reasons for that answer. This section can be written in either of two ways. One way is to write a short answer of one or two sentences, such as "Yes, a juvenile is denied due process if he is not represented at a delinquency hearing. Due process does not require that the juvenile be represented by an attorney, however." To write this form of Answer, you answer the Question Presented and add a sentence that summarizes the reason for your conclusion or adds a necessary qualification to the answer. Some lawyers write only one or two sentence answers to the Question. For your assignments, the Short Answer may be more appropriate for a short memorandum, such as one of three or four pages.

The alternative form is a section, here called a Conclusion rather than a Short Answer, that answers the Question and then summarizes the reasons for that answer from the Discussion section of the memo. A Conclusion should be longer than the Short Answer, but it still should be a summary only, and it should answer the Question. Depending upon the complexity of the problem and the length of the memorandum, the Conclusion may be one or two paragraphs or, for a long memorandum, it may require a few paragraphs. You should have a Short Answer or

Conclusion for each Question Presented and number each to correspond to the number of the Question it answers.

Sometimes you cannot confidently reach a conclusion because the law is too uncertain, or you need more facts. In that situation, explain briefly why your conclusions are tentative, or what the alternatives are, or which additional facts you need.

The following are suggestions for writing this section.

1. Be conclusory. A Short Answer or Conclusion should be an assertion of your answer to the issue you have posed. But it is not a discussion of how you evaluated strengths and weaknesses of alternate arguments in order to reach that conclusion. That evaluation and a full discussion of your reasons for the conclusion belong in the Discussion. Which of these examples is conclusory?

1. Jones was falsely imprisoned because he reasonably believed that he was confined by Smith's dog. Jones's belief was reasonable because the dog growled at him and Jones knew that the dog had bitten other people in the past.

2. Jones may have been falsely imprisoned depending upon whether he reasonably believed that Smith's dog would bite him if he moved. Several facts show that Jones could have reasonably believed he was in danger because the dog had bitten other people before. But some facts do not. For instance, the dog had been sent to obedience school after those incidents. The issue depends on the importance of these latter facts.

Example one is conclusory. The writer has reached an answer to the Question Presented. The writer of example two is discussing and weighing alternate arguments.

2. Do not include discussions of authority. Although your answer to the question will necessarily come from your analysis of the relevant primary and secondary authorities, your discussion of those authorities belongs in the Discussion section. In the Conclusion or Short Answer, you need not discuss or name particular cases or other authorities you rely on.

Which of the following examples is better?

1. The Popes adversely possessed the strip of land between their lot and Smith's. Although they occupied the land mistakenly believing it was theirs, their mistaken possession should be considered hostile as to Smith's ownership.

2. Whether the Popes adversely possessed the strip of land between their lot and Smith's if they mistakenly believed that the strip is theirs depends upon whether the Oz court relies upon old decisions that a claimant's mistaken possession cannot be hostile to the title holder. Several courts in other jurisdictions recently have decided that a person who possesses land mistakenly thinking it is his own can still possess the land hostilely to the

true owner. The Oz court has strongly indicated that it may adopt those rulings.

Example two is a discussion of authority but not a conclusion about the adverse possession problem. Example one is an answer to the problem.

One exception to this rule arises when the problem is a statutory issue, in which case you should refer to the statute and include the essential information about the statutory requirements.

> Smith did not violate the Theft of Lost or Mislaid Property Act, 12 Oz Rev. Stat. § 2 (1960). The statute applies only if a person "obtains control over lost or mislaid property." Because Lyons robbed Smith of the locket almost immediately after Smith found it, Smith never obtained control over the property.

Another exception occurs if one case is so crucial to deciding the issue that it controls the analysis and cannot be omitted. In this situation, you should also include the citation.

> The defendant attorney should be liable for malpractice even if the plaintiff is not in privity of contract with him. The Oz Supreme Court has held that a notary public who practiced law without a license by writing a decedent's will was liable to the decedent's beneficiary for his negligence. Copper v. Brass, 10 Oz 200 (1965). This decision should apply to attorneys as well as to notary publics. If so, the defendant will be liable to Jones for negligently drafting the Jones will.

Exercise 4–B

Evaluate the following pairs of Question Presented and Conclusion. Which pair is best? Why? What is wrong with the others?

1. QP: Whether an attorney should have been convicted of criminal contempt of court for negligently failing to appear at a scheduled trial and not representing his client if he was told the date, had cases in other courts that same day, and had already failed to appear in court once before.

Conclusion: The attorney should not have been convicted. Applying the precedents to this case, his failure to record the trial date and his failure to appear will not be criminal contempt.

2. QP: What shall determine if an attorney's failure to appear in court for his client's trial constitutes criminal contempt?

Conclusion: In Oz, whether an attorney is in criminal contempt for failure to appear at trial depends on the attorney's intent. If the attorney shows that the failure to appear was not willful disregard of duty, then there is no contempt. Mr. Toto should be able to show that.

3. QP: Is an attorney who does not appear in court for his client's trial guilty of criminal contempt if he was notified of the trial date but did not record it, and on the day of the trial, had the case file in his briefcase along with files of cases for which he did appear?

Conclusion: The attorney should not be held guilty of criminal contempt. In Oz, the attorney's failure to appear must have been willful, deliberate, or reckless. Mr. Toto did not act with the intent required. Instead, he inadvertently did not appear in court because he forgot to write down the court date and never took the case file from his briefcase in the rush of his other court appearances.

4. QP: Does an attorney who fails to appear at his client's trial commit criminal contempt of court under Oz law?

Conclusion: In Oz, an attorney is in criminal contempt of court if he acts willfully, deliberately, or recklessly in disregarding a court order. The court will have to decide. If the court can be persuaded that Mr. Toto did not so act when he did not appear for his client's trial, then Toto will not be in contempt.

D. Applicable Statutes

If your problem involves the application of a statute, a section of a constitution, or an administrative regulation, set out the exact language of the pertinent parts in block quote form. Include the citation.

A block quote is indented, single spaced, and does not include quotation marks.

E. Discussion

Up to this point, the memorandum contains the facts of your problem, poses the specific legal question that those facts raise, briefly answers that question, and sets out the relevant enacted law. In the Discussion, you will analyze the question by applying the relevant legal principles and their policies to the facts of the case. The process of analyzing is a process of breaking down a subject into its component parts. To analyze a legal subject, you break it down into its issues and then break each issue down into subissues. You give content to the abstract legal principles you have found by examining the facts of the cases from which the principles came and in which the statutes were applied. You also examine the reasons for the principles. Only then can you determine what those principles mean. The purpose of this inquiry is to reach a conclusion and predict the outcome of the problem, that is, to determine whether the requirements for that claim are satisfied by the facts of your problem. This analysis provides the reasons for your conclusion about the outcome.

Because a memorandum is used to advise a client or prepare for further steps in litigation, the reader is looking in this section for a thorough analysis of the present state of the law. Thus, the Discussion should not be a historical narrative of the relevant case law and statutes or a general discussion of that area of the law.

Instead, you should discuss the law specifically as it controls your problem.

The Discussion provides an objective evaluation of the issues. Thus, you should evaluate all the interpretations possible from applying the law to the facts, not just the interpretations that favor your client. Analyze as many arguments for your client that you can think of, but also analyze those arguments against your client. In addition, evaluate which ones are most persuasive. Do not predict an unrealistic outcome only because that outcome favors your client. If you will need more facts than you have been given in order to reach a conclusion, then explain which facts you need and why they are relevant.

A legal discussion is written according to certain patterns of analysis. The next two chapters explain in detail how to identify the issues in a claim and how to write a legal discussion.

F. *Conclusion*

In some formats, where the memorandum includes a Short Answer of one or two sentences after the Question Presented, the memorandum ends with a Conclusion section that summarizes the Discussion. We have explained this type of Conclusion in Part C above.

Editing Checklist: Memoranda

A. Statement of Facts

    1. Have you included all the facts that bear upon the analysis of the problem and are necessary to understand the problem?

    2. Have you omitted distracting and irrelevant facts?

    3. Did you provide an introduction that sets out the context of the problem?

    4. Did you then arrange the facts in an organization that is easy to understand, such as chronologically, topically, or chronologically within a topical organization?

    5. Does this section include only facts and not analysis or argument?

B. Question Presented

    1. Have you identified the correct and the specific issue?

    2. Unless the issue is solely a question of law, have you incorporated the facts that raise the issue?

    3. Have you identified the facts as specifically as appropriate, rather than use an overly generalized description?

4. If there is more than one issue, have you organized the issues in a logical order, which you will adhere to through the memo?

C. Conclusion or Short Answer

1. If you use a Short Answer, have you accurately and clearly answered the Question Presented?

2. If you use a Conclusion

    a) have you accurately and clearly answered the Question Presented? and

    b) have you summarized the analysis in the Discussion and briefly applied the controlling law to the facts of your problem?

D. Discussion (See Chapters 5–7)

1. Did you begin with a thesis paragraph, the length of which is appropriate to the length and complexity of the discussion?

2. Have you organized your discussion logically?

    a) Is the discussion organized into separate claims that are presented in a logical order?

    b) Is each claim broken down into the issues and sub issues by which the claim is analyzed?

3. For each issue and sub-issue do you

    a) analyze the controlling statutes and case law and the persuasive authorities?

    b) apply the legal principles in those statutes and cases to the facts of your problem?

    c) draw analogies and distinctions to the precedents?

    d) objectively evaluate and explore all credible interpretations?

4. Does your analysis reflect an accurate synthesis of the authorities so that you explore all the ramifications of a topic as a related analysis?

5. Have you kept firmly to what is relevant for the claim or defense you are analyzing?

6. Have you explained and supported your conclusions with adequate reasons? Do you analyze all interpretations before coming to an unqualified conclusion?

7. Are you creative in using facts and analogizing to similar issues?

8. Have you supplied citations to authority and are they accurate?

E. Writing Style (See Chapters 8–9)

    1. Are your paragraphs unified around a topic and is that topic clear?

    2. Do you use transitions to show the logical relationships between sentences and between paragraphs?

    3. Do your sentences carry the reader forward rather than bog the reader down?

        a) Are your sentences a readable length without too many interrupting phrases and clauses?

        b) Do the verbs of your sentences carry the action or have you nominalized the verbs?

        c) Do you use concrete nouns as subjects rather than abstract ones?

        d) Are most of your sentences in the active voice?

        e) Did you edit out unnecessary throat clearing words and phrases?

    4. Have you checked for correct grammar and punctuation?

    5. Do you use past tense for events that already occurred?

    6. Do you use quotations only when necessary and do you fit them into your text?

Chapter Five
Organization of a Legal Discussion: Large–Scale Organization

I. Introduction

In this chapter, you will learn how to identify the legal issues that are relevant to analyzing a problem and to use these issues to organize the Discussion section of your memorandum. In Chapter Two, in the context of briefing a case, we used the word "issue" to describe the basic question that the court has to answer to resolve the dispute between the parties. Here we use the word "issue" to describe the points that must be discussed in the analysis of a claim.

As we pointed out in previous chapters, the process of analyzing is a process of breaking down a subject into its component parts. To analyze a legal subject, you first identify the claims or defenses (which we will call the claims) in your problem. Then you break each claim down into its parts. Then where needed, you break each part down into its sub-parts. Once you have identified the parts and sub-parts, you must arrange them in a logical order. This logical order forms the organizational structure of your Discussion.

II. Organizing a Discussion

A. Overall Organization

The first organization, that of the entire Discussion section, is dictated by the topic of your memo. If your problem contains only one claim, then your entire Discussion will be an analysis of that claim. If your memo contains more than one claim, then you discuss each separately. For example, if your client has two claims, one for assault and one for battery, you should divide the Discussion into two main sections, one for assault, and one for battery. You will have identified these claims in your Questions Presented, and you should discuss them in the same order as they appear there.

The order in which you discuss the claims depends upon the particular problem. If the problem requires resolution of a threshold question or a question that logically must precede the others, then you should analyze it first. A threshold question is one that the court will answer first because its decision on that question will determine whether the litigation will continue or whether the court must decide the other issues.

An example of a threshold question is whether the plaintiff waited too long to file a complaint and whether the period for filing that type of complaint (governed by legislation known as a statute of limitations) has expired. A court will resolve this first, because if the plaintiff has waited too long to file, the court will dismiss the complaint. Therefore, you should discuss it first in your memorandum. Your resolution of the threshold question, however, should not end the discussion. Analyze the rest of the claims also. The judge may disagree with your conclusion on the threshold question and go on to consider the other claims or your reader may want an analysis of the entire subject.

If there are no threshold questions, you may want to organize the claims by degree of difficulty. You may decide to analyze the simpler claim first to dispose of it quickly and then work toward the more difficult one. Or you may decide to attack the more complex claim first while you have the reader's attention, and then follow with the claim that you think is easier to establish.

B. Organization Within One Claim—Identifying the Issues

After identifying the claims in your assignment and deciding the order in which you will discuss them, you must break down each claim into its constituent parts, that is, into the legal issues raised by that claim. These issues may come from an established definition, such as the elements of a tort or crime. Or they may be factors that the courts have previously considered in determining how to decide particular cases. In any event, you need to identify these issues and analyze each separately. They will form the organizational framework for your analysis. The fundamental principle to remember is that when you analyze a claim, you must organize your analysis around the issues that the claim raises. You cannot merely describe the relevant cases and statutes.

There are several different ways of finding these issues.

1. A court's opinion may explicitly identify the issues.

2. The issues may be raised by the terms of a statute.

3. You may have to extract the issues from one court's opinion.

4. You may have to extract and synthesize the issues from a series of opinions.

1. The Court's Opinion Explicitly Identifies the Issues

Sometimes, a court opinion will tell you what issues must be discussed in a claim by setting out a definition which identifies those issues, for example, the elements of a tort. Read the following opinion to find out what the elements are of the tort of intentional infliction of emotional distress. These elements will provide the organizational framework for the analysis of this claim.

Davis v. Finance Co.

Luella Davis (Davis) sued Finance Company (Finance) seeking to recover on the theory of intentional infliction of emotional distress.

In this jurisdiction, the courts have adopted the definition of intentional infliction of emotional distress provided in the Restatement (Second) of Torts. First, the defendant's conduct must be extreme and outrageous. Liability will be found only where the conduct has been so outrageous in character, and so extreme in degree, as to go beyond all possible bounds of decency.

Second, the plaintiff's emotional distress must be severe. Mental conditions such as fright, horror, grief, shame, humiliation, or worry are not actionable. The distress inflicted must be so severe that no reasonable person could be expected to endure it.

Third, the conduct must be intentional, or at least reckless. If reckless, the conduct must be such that there is a high degree of probability that severe emotional distress will follow and the actor goes ahead in disregard of it.

In this case Finance's conduct was not so extreme and outrageous as to constitute a basis for recovery under this tort. Davis claims that agents of Finance called her several times weekly, that they went to her home one or more times a week, and that they twice called her at a hospital where she was visiting her sick daughter. She alleges that Finance continued its practices even after she told them she was on welfare and was unable to make any additional payments. Davis, however, was legally obligated to Finance and had defaulted in her payments. A creditor must have latitude to pursue reasonable methods of collecting debts. Finance was attempting to collect a legal obligation from Davis in a permissible though persistent and possibly annoying manner. Such conduct is not outrageous, and therefore, Davis does not state a cause of action for intentional infliction of emotional distress.[1]

———

In the <u>Davis</u> case, the court identifies three elements to the tort. First, the defendant's conduct must be outrageous. Second, the plaintiff's distress must be severe. Third, the defendant's conduct must have been intentional or, at least, reckless. The plaintiff must prove each of these in order to succeed. Therefore, you would organize an analysis of a problem dealing with intentional infliction of emotional distress around the three elements of the tort. They become the issues you would discuss. Using the simplest of all organizational structures, you could discuss each issue in a separate paragraph.

You may find, however, that some issues will require extensive analysis, and others need be discussed only briefly. For example, in <u>Davis</u>, the most difficult issue to resolve was whether the company's conduct was extreme and outrageous. Finding that it was not, the court did not need to discuss the other two issues, since all of the elements of the tort must be met for the claim to succeed. If your facts paralleled those in <u>Davis</u>, you would discuss all of the elements in writing a memorandum on this subject. But you would devote more space to your analysis of whether the defendant acted outrageously than to the other issues, because it was the most complex. Moreover, you might want to discuss that issue first because of its importance in the analysis.

Sometimes, however, you may want to organize a discussion by mentioning the less controversial issues first in order to dismiss them quickly. Then you would go into detail on the most problematic issue. For example, in another case dealing with intentional infliction of emotional distress, the real controversy might be over whether the plaintiff's distress was severe. You might decide that the analysis of whether the defendant acted outrageously and intentionally was so clear-cut that it could be disposed of quickly. You would then discuss extensively the more complex issue of whether the plaintiff's distress was severe. The discussion might run several paragraphs and be organized this way:

Paragraph 1— The defendant's conduct was unquestionably both outrageous and intentional.

Paragraph 2— The plaintiff's distress was not severe because X.

---

1. This example is based on and uses language from the case of <u>Public</u> Finance Corp. v. Davis, 66 Ill. 2d 85, 360 N.E.2d 765 (1976).

Paragraph 3— The plaintiff's distress was not severe because Y.

Paragraph 4— The plaintiff's distress was not severe because Z.

Exercise 5–A

Read the following case and identify the three elements of the tort of
false imprisonment. Each element will be an issue in the analysis of a
false imprisonment claim. Does the court break down any of these issues
into subissues?

East v. West

Carol West appeals from a judgment that she falsely imprisoned
the three plaintiffs.

The plaintiffs were comparing voter registration lists with names
on mailboxes in multi-unit dwellings. They intended to challenge the
registration of people whose names were not on the mailboxes.
Plaintiffs testified that they entered West's house through the outer
door into a vestibule area which lies between the inner and outer
doors to West's building. They were checking the names on the
mailboxes when West entered and asked what they were doing. They
replied that they were checking the voter lists. She first told them to
leave and then changed her mind and asked if they would be willing
to identify themselves to the police. Plaintiffs said they would. West
then asked her husband to call the police. While they waited, she
stood by the door, but neither threatened nor intimidated the plaintiffs. In addition, the plaintiffs did not try to get her to move out of
the way. When the police came, they said the plaintiffs were not
doing anything wrong and could continue to check the lists. Plaintiffs later sued West for false imprisonment.

An actor is liable for false imprisonment if he acts intending to
confine the other or a third person within boundaries fixed by the
actor; if his act directly or indirectly results in such a confinement of
the other; and if the other is conscious of the confinement or is
harmed by it.

The evidence here is not sufficient to support the conclusion that
West's acts directly or indirectly resulted in the plaintiffs' confinement. Confinement may be brought about by actual physical barriers, by submission to physical force, and by threat of physical force.
The question in this case is whether confinement was brought about
by threat of physical force. We think it was not. Plaintiffs acknowledge that West did not verbally threaten them. Since none of the
plaintiffs asked her to step aside, they could no more than speculate
whether she would have refused their request, much less physically

resisted. Moreover, the three of them are claiming confinement by a single person. Accordingly, the judgment below is reversed.[2]

According to the East case, what are the three elements of the tort of false imprisonment? These are the three basic issues and provide the organizational structure for your discussion. Of the three elements, on which does the court focus its discussion? As to this element, what are the different ways in which it can be met? These different ways suggest subissues that you must also consider in organizing your analysis of a false imprisonment problem.

Make an outline of how you would organize a false imprisonment problem. First, list the three elements of the tort—the basic issues that you must consider. Then look at the opinion and see how each of these elements is met. If any element can be met in different ways, list those ways beside the element. These are the subissues in the problem. This list provides the basic organizational structure for your analysis. Remember that subissues may also merit different degrees of analysis, depending on their applicability to the facts of your case, their intrinsic complexity, and the other subissues involved.

2. *The Terms of a Statute Identify the Issues*

If you are analyzing a problem which is governed by a statute, the terms of the statute itself may identify the major issues you must analyze. These are the requirements for the statutory claim. The language will tell you to whom the statute applies and the kind of conduct it governs.

Consider the following statute, also discussed in Chapter Three:

§ 140.20 Burglary in the Third Degree

1. A person is guilty of burglary in the third degree if he knowingly enters or remains unlawfully in a building, and

2. does so with the intent to commit a crime.

Most criminal statutes are composed of elements of a crime, each of which must be proved at trial. As with the elements of a common law claim like a tort, the elements of a statute become the issues that you will discuss. The elements in this statute provide the organizational structure for an analysis of the crime of burglary.

---

2. This example is based on and uses language from the case of Herbst v. Wuennenberg, 83 Wis. 2d 768, 266 N.W.2d 391 (1978).

To determine those elements, first consider the overall structure of the statute. If any parts of the statute are given in the alternative, only one element need be satisfied but you may have to analyze each. If parts of a statute are connected by the word "and," both parts must be considered.

Once you have a sense of the overall structure of a statute, you can go on to identify its elements. You identify the elements of the crime by looking at the terms of the statute. Each term may be significant and require some discussion. However, as with a common law claim, some elements will require detailed analysis, while others need be analyzed only briefly.

The statute defining burglary in the third degree is short and fairly simple. However, even this short statute includes a number of terms which identify the elements of the crime that must be analyzed.

According to the statute, guilt of burglary in the third degree is established if:

    (1) [a] person

    (2) (a) knowingly enters unlawfully [in a]

             or

       (b) knowingly remains unlawfully [in a]

    (3) building

    (4) [with] intent

    (5) [to commit a] crime

You might organize your analysis by disposing of some elements, such as whether the defendant entered a "building", in a sentence or two and by analyzing others in a paragraph or series of paragraphs. Some elements may be so obvious, i.e., that the defendant is a person, that they need not be mentioned at all. As with the elements of a common law claim, your treatment of each statutory element depends on its complexity in relation to the facts of your case.

Exercise 5–B

Consider what issues are raised by the following statute, a section of the Uniform Commercial Code.

§ 2–315. Implied Warranty: Fitness for Particular Purpose

Where the seller at the time of contracting has reason to know any particular purpose for which the goods are required and that the buyer is relying on the seller's skill or judgment to select or furnish suitable goods, there is, unless excluded or modified under the next section, an implied warranty that the goods shall be fit for such purpose.

According to the statute, to whom does the statute apply? What time period is relevant? What type of warranty is created? What must the seller know for the warranty to arise? How may the warranty be excluded or modified?

Make an outline showing the organizational structure of an analysis of implied warranty of fitness for a particular purpose.

Exercise 5–C

According to the following statute, what are the elements of burglary in the second degree? Notice that the structure of this statute is more complex than burglary in the third degree.

§ 140.25 Burglary in the Second Degree

A person is guilty of burglary in the second degree when he knowingly enters or remains unlawfully in a building with intent to commit a crime therein, and when:

1. In effecting entry or while in the building or in immediate flight therefrom, he or another participant in the crime:

   (a) is armed with explosives or a deadly weapon; or

   (b) causes physical injury to any person who is not a participant in the crime; or

   (c) uses or threatens the immediate use of a dangerous instrument; or

   (d) displays what appears to be a pistol, revolver, rifle, shotgun, machine gun or other firearm; or

2. The building is a dwelling.

To identify the elements of this crime, you must first examine the overall structure of the statute. Look for the relationships among the words connected by "and" and "or." Notice that the statute contains two sections that follow the introductory section. You must determine how sections 1 and 2 relate to each other and to the introductory section. By considering questions like these, you will be able to identify the essential elements of the crime.

In a memorandum analyzing whether someone had committed burglary in the second degree, you would have to decide which, if any, of the subsections of section 1 you could prove. You might decide that of the subsections of the statute, subsection (b), was totally irrelevant to your case, and that three subsections (a), (c), and (d) might be relevant. You might decide to briefly dispose of the irrelevant section, and then fully discuss those subsections that seem to be relevant to your case.

Make an outline showing the organizational structure of an analysis of burglary in the second degree, assuming that subsection (b) is not relevant to your problem.

3. *You Must Extract the Issues From the Court's Opinion*

When a court explicitly identifies the elements of a common law claim for you, or when the language of a statute supplies the elements, you will not find it too difficult to know which issues to analyze. Often, however, a particular common law or statutory claim is defined generally rather than by explicit elements. Here the courts will frequently flesh out the requirements by identifying certain factors that are particularly relevant to deciding whether the plaintiff has a remedy. For example, in the <u>Jones</u> diversity jurisdiction case in Chapter Two, we identified several factors, not contained in the language of the federal diversity jurisdiction statute, which were important to whether the plaintiff intended to change his domicile to the state of incarceration. These factors included the location of the plaintiff's family and the location of his business and other economic interests. In a written discussion, these factors would form the organizational structure of your analysis.

Suppose your client, Mr. Smith, wishes to hire a new employee. He wants the employee to sign a covenant not to compete with him if the employee decides to leave Smith's employment in the future. Read the following case. What factors does the court in this case consider relevant in determining whether a covenant not to compete will be enforced? These factors will constitute the issues you will focus on when analyzing Mr. Smith's problem.

Columbia Ribbon v. Trecker

We are required to determine whether a covenant made by a salesman not to compete with his employer after the termination of employment is enforceable in whole or in part.

Defendant Trecker was employed by Columbia Ribbon as a salesman for several years. He signed an employment contract with the following restrictive covenant:

  1. The employee will not disclose to any person or firm the names or addresses of any customers or prospective customers of the company.

  2. The employee will not, for a period of twenty-four months after the termination of his employment, sell or deliver any goods of the kind sold by the company within any territory to which he was assigned during the last twenty-four months prior to termination.

After Trecker was demoted, he terminated his employment with Columbia Ribbon and took a job with a competitor, A–1–A Corporation. Columbia then sued to enforce the terms of the covenant.

There are powerful considerations of public policy against depriving a person of his livelihood. Restrictive covenants are, therefore, disfavored in the law. They will be enforced only if they are limited in time and geography, and then only to the extent necessary to protect the employer from unfair competition which stems from the employee's use or disclosure of trade secrets or confidential customer lists. If, however, the employee's services are truly unique or extraordinary, and not merely valuable to the employer, a court will enforce a covenant even if trade secrets are not involved.

The broad sweeping language of the covenant in this case has no limitations keyed to uniqueness, trade secrets, confidentiality, or even competitive unfairness. The affidavits make no showing that any secret information was disclosed, that Trecker performed any but commonplace services, or that any business was lost. Moreover, nothing in the purely conclusory affidavits by Columbia contravenes the points in Trecker's own affidavit that no trade secrets had been involved in his employment, that he had taken possession of no customer lists, and that all customers were publicly known.

Accordingly, Columbia's showing was insufficient to defeat summary judgment. Therefore, the order below denying enforcement is affirmed.[3]

In the Columbia Ribbon case, the court tells you two basic things. First, it identifies the broad public policies which govern cases dealing with restrictive covenants. Courts look upon these covenants with disfavor because they do not want people to be deprived of their livelihoods. Therefore, courts will enforce them to protect the employer only under specific circumstances. Second, the court identifies these circumstances by stating the factors it will consider in deciding whether a particular covenant should be enforced. The court points out that only if the employer can show that trade secrets or confidential customer lists have been disclosed, or that the employee's services were unique, will a court enforce a covenant. Even then, the time and place limitations must be reasonable. These factors are like the elements of a tort or a crime. They, too, provide the organizational structure for the analysis of the problem.

An analysis of the enforceability of a covenant not to compete could use this organizational structure:

A. Public policy considerations:

    1. employee's livelihood

    2. protection of the employer from unfair competition

B. Factors affecting enforceability:

    1. existence of trade secrets

or

    2. existence of confidential customer lists

---

3. This example is based on and uses language from the case of Columbia Ribbon & Carbon Manufacturing Co. v. A-1-A Corp., 42 N.Y.2d 496, 369 N.E.2d 4, 398 N.Y.S.2d 1004 (1977).

or

3. uniqueness of the employee's services (even if no trade secrets)

C. Further considerations if a factor in section B is present:

1. reasonable time restriction

2. reasonable place restriction

Notice the order of issues in this problem. The time and place restrictions are relevant only if a factor in section B is present. Since their relevance depends on the presence of section B factors, section B factors are threshold factors and must be discussed before section C factors.

Exercise 5–D

In the following case, the defendant has moved to quash service of process. He argued that he was immune from service of process because he came into the state to be a party in a judicial proceeding. Read the case and determine which factors a court will consider in analyzing whether to grant a motion to quash service.

<u>Finch v. Crusco</u>

The question before this court is whether a Delaware resident who brought a contract claim in Pennsylvania is immune from service of process in an unrelated action, if he was served in Pennsylvania while attending court proceedings in his contract claim. Philip Crusco was in Pennsylvania to testify in his breach of contract claim. When he came out of the courthouse, he was served in an unrelated tort action.

The courts in this state have long provided that non-resident parties and witnesses in civil actions are immune from service of process. The purpose of this grant of immunity is not to protect the individual, but to assure that the courts' business is expedited and that justice is duly administered. The rule provides an incentive to those who might not otherwise appear whose attendance is necessary to a full and fair trial.

However, courts should deny immunity where it is not necessary to provide this incentive. Where both cases arise out of the same transaction, the courts should not grant immunity. Under this circumstance, the reason for granting immunity would be outweighed by the importance of fairly resolving the full dispute between the parties. Nor should the courts grant immunity to someone who is in the jurisdiction as a defendant in a criminal action. That person needs no incentive to appear, since a criminal defendant has no choice but to appear. Finally, the courts need not grant immunity to a party or witness who is in the jurisdiction to serve his own interest, since he, like the criminal defendant, does not need an incentive to appear.

Mr. Crusco falls into the last category. He did not require an incentive to appear in the state court since he had brought the suit himself and was personally benefiting from the court hearing. Therefore, his motion to quash service of process is denied.

———

This opinion identifies a number of factors that are relevant to a court's determination of whether to grant a motion to quash service of process.

What is the general rule regarding immunity from service of process? What is the purpose for the general rule? Under what three circumstances will the courts deny immunity and what are the reasons for the denial in these circumstances?

Make an outline of an analysis of immunity from service of process.

4. You Must Extract and Synthesize the Issues From a Series of Opinions

Organizing an analysis is most difficult when the relevant issues are not found in a single case, but must be synthesized from a series of cases. One case may provide the basic standard without identifying all of the factors or issues that are relevant. Then you must read other cases on the general topic to identify which other factors the courts have considered and how the courts have treated them.

Read the following summaries of cases about the tort of negligent infliction of emotional distress. All of them are from the same jurisdiction and all are relevant to this topic.[4]

Sinn v. Burd

The plaintiff, Robert Sinn, sued to recover damages for the emotional injuries he suffered when he saw his minor daughter struck and killed by a car. Mr. Sinn became hysterical and then lapsed into a depression, sustaining severe emotional distress and repeated nightmares. He has had to spend considerable amounts of money for medical care. Mr. Sinn was not in any personal danger of physical impact when he saw the accident from the front door of his home.

Under the traditional rule, bystanders could not recover for mental injury unless they also suffered physical injury or were within the zone of danger, that is, they were in personal danger of physical impact. This rule, however, is unreasonably restrictive in cases where a parent views the death of a child, a situation which would cause at least as much emotional distress as being within the zone of danger. Here the injury was foreseeable since the plaintiff was the child's father, the plaintiff was near the scene of the accident, and the shock resulted from his sensory

4. Case summaries in this example are based on Sinn v. Burd, 486 Pa. 146, 404 A.2d 672 (1979); Kratzer v. Unger, 17 Pa. D. & C.3d 771 (Bucks Co. 1981); and Cathcart v. Keene Industrial Insulation, 324 Pa. Super. 123, 471 A.2d 493 (1984).

and contemporaneous observance of the accident. Therefore, the court below incorrectly dismissed the claim.

Kratzer v. Unger

The plaintiff sued the driver of a car, which struck and seriously injured her foster child, for negligent infliction of emotional distress. The child had lived with the plaintiff for over eight years. The plaintiff may bring a claim for negligent infliction of emotional distress.

Cathcart v. Keene

Mrs. Cathcart sued her husband's employer for negligent infliction of emotional distress. She alleged that he had contracted asbestosis on the job and that she suffered emotional distress in witnessing his continual deterioration and death. Although the plaintiff did have a close relationship with the victim, this court must dismiss her claim since her injuries did not arise from the shock of viewing a single, identifiable traumatic event.

Long v. Tobin

Mrs. Long sued the driver of a car for negligent infliction of emotional distress caused by her viewing her neighbor's child being struck by a negligently driven automobile. She alleged that she became nervous and upset as a result of seeing the accident, since she has a child of the same age.

This court will grant the defendant's motion to dismiss the claim. Mrs. Long does not have the requisite close personal relationship with the victim. Moreover, the mental distress she alleges is not sufficiently severe to warrant recovery. The type of stress required is that which no normally constituted reasonable person could endure.

————

In reading through the case summaries, you will have noticed that the most extensive discussion of this tort is given in Sinn v. Burd. Sinn is the leading case in the jurisdiction on the claim of negligent infliction of emotional distress. It sets out the basic standard for recovery: a person may recover for negligent infliction of emotional distress if the emotional distress is foreseeable. Distress is foreseeable when the plaintiff was the parent of the victim, when the plaintiff was near the scene of the accident, and when the distress resulted from a sensory and contemporaneous observance of the accident. The case also describes the nature of the distress Mr. Sinn suffered.

The other cases either elaborate on the factors raised in Sinn or introduce other factors. For example, the decision in Kratzer indicates that relationships other than parent to child can qualify. Mrs. Kratzer was not a parent, but a foster-parent. The Cathcart decision elaborates on the relationship between plaintiff and victim by extending the coverage of the tort to spouses. In addition, the court in <u>Cathcart</u> raises a different point. To be actionable, the distress must arise from a single, identifiable traumatic event. Finally, the court in <u>Long</u> defines the nature of the emotional distress that is required.

If you had identified the factors the courts address in determining whether a plaintiff states a claim for negligent infliction of emotional distress and made a list, the list would look something like this:

1. whether the plaintiff was closely related to the victim

2. whether the plaintiff was near to the scene of the accident and whether the plaintiff's shock resulted from a sensory and contemporaneous observance of the accident

3. whether the shock resulted from a single, identifiable traumatic event

4. whether the plaintiff's distress was severe

Each of these factors becomes an issue that you would discuss in analyzing the tort.

Exercise 5–E

Read the following cases, all of which deal with the question of a hospital's liability for the suicide of one of its patients. Ask yourself what the basic rule is regarding the standard of care and what factors the courts will consider in determining a hospital's liability.

Ross v. Brown Hospital

The plaintiff's wife committed suicide four days after she was admitted to the defendant mental hospital. The patient had twice tried to commit suicide before her admission to the hospital. The last time was the day before she was admitted.

The court denied the defendant's motion to dismiss and stated that the hospital owed the plaintiff a duty of exercising reasonable care to protect her from injuring herself. That duty was proportionate to her needs and constituted such reasonable care as her known mental condition required.

Smith v. Stevens Hospital

An acutely depressed patient was left unobserved in his hospital room by his nurses for successive periods of two hours each during the night and early morning. During the last of these periods, he hung himself with a bed sheet. The court held that the hospital did not exercise reasonable care in supervising the patient and was liable.

Moore v. United States

The patient voluntarily admitted himself to a hospital. His preadmittance diagnosis was arteriosclerosis. His examination revealed no signs of suicidal tendencies or any psychiatric disorder. He had no history of mental illness. The doctors accordingly placed him in an open ward.

Four days later, the patient's behavior changed. He became paranoid and in fear for his life. The doctors then transferred him to a closed ward. The doors were kept locked and heavy screens were placed over the windows. The attendants routinely counted the silverware on his meal tray. There was a high number of personnel per patient in this ward. Nurses observed the patient several times and saw no unusual behavior. One night the patient pried open the screen in front of a window and jumped out. The court held that the hospital had used reasonable care in diagnosing the patient in light of his history and in treating him.

Brown v. General Hospital

The plaintiff's wife had attempted suicide and had voluntarily admitted herself to the psychiatric department at General Hospital. For five months she was in a closed ward and received electroshock treatment. When her condition improved, her doctor transferred her to an open ward.

Under modern psychiatric theory, allowing patients as much freedom as possible is consistent with reasonable care. Doctors believe that an open ward is more conducive to the establishment of a therapeutic atmosphere in which the patient comes to trust the doctor than is a closed ward. Ms. Brown's doctor recommended a program of drug treatment and occupational therapy. For six months, Ms. Brown remained in the open ward, her condition continuing to improve. She then took her life. The court held that the hospital had used reasonable care in supervising her and was not liable for negligence.[5]

What is the basic standard that the courts use in determining whether a hospital is liable for the suicide of one of its patients? Make a list of the factors the courts consider in analyzing this standard. These factors are the issues that you would discuss in analyzing the hospital's liability. They form the organizational structure of your analysis.

5. Case summaries in the example are based on Stallman v. Robinson, 364 Mo. 275, 260 S.W.2d 743 (1953); Smith v. Simpson, 221 Mo. App. 550, 288 S.W. 69 (1926); Moore v. United States, 222 F. Supp. 87 (E.D. Mo. 1963); Gregory v. Robinson, 338 S.W.2d 88 (Mo. 1960).

Chapter Six
Organization of a Legal Discussion: Small–Scale Organization

I. Introduction

In Chapter Five, we discussed the need to organize the discussion section of an office memorandum around the legal issues of each claim for relief. In this chapter, we focus on the organization of a discussion of a single legal issue and suggest an organizational pattern that will enable you to write a clear analysis of that issue. The pattern presented here is a fairly standard format for fact-based legal problems because it logically orders the steps necessary in this type of legal reasoning. We focus here on fact-based problems because these are common assignments in both legal practice and first-year legal writing courses. Be aware, however, that a different kind of legal problem—one involving the meaning or the validity of a law, for example—will require you to adapt this pattern so that your focus is on statutory construction, weight of authority, judicial reasoning, or underlying policies rather than on factual comparison (see Chapter Ten).

With this caveat in mind, a useful pattern for analyzing a single legal issue often has the following structure.

1. Explanation of the applicable rule of law

2. Examination of the relevant case law

3. Application of the law to the facts of the case and case comparison

4.　Presentation and evaluation of opposing arguments

5.　Conclusion

In other words, begin by explaining the controlling legal principle in the jurisdiction in which your problem is located, or if there is no controlling rule in that jurisdiction, then in other jurisdictions. The general rule comes from the elements of a statute or statutes and from the holding of a previous case or from a synthesis of holdings from more than one case on a topic. Go on to explain and discuss those authorities that have established and applied that principle. Then, apply that principle to the facts of your case, and compare and contrast the facts of those precedents to the facts of your problem. Follow this application with a discussion of the counterarguments and exceptions that may apply. Finally, evaluate the arguments and counterarguments to reach a conclusion as to the outcome or probable outcome of your problem.

Adherence to this pattern ensures that the reader gets necessary information in an order which is readily understandable. You should not begin the discussion with a summary of the facts of your case, for example, because the reader cannot assess the legal significance of those facts without your having first examined the relevant case law and the kinds of facts courts have previously decided were legally significant. Therefore, you usually examine relevant case law before you discuss how the law applies to the facts of your own case. Similarly, you should raise and answer opposing arguments before you reach a conclusion because the success with which you handle an opposing argument should be reflected in your final conclusion.

Sometimes the analysis of an issue is so clear cut that you can include all five analytic steps in a single paragraph. For example, if the case law in your jurisdiction on false imprisonment requires that a plaintiff be aware that he was confined and the plaintiff in your problem was clearly aware of his confinement, you can treat that requirement quickly. For most issues, however, you will need to break your analysis into parts. You can subdivide your discussion without sacrificing its logical structure if your paragraphs reflect those steps. You should also use topic and transition sentences to remind the reader what you have covered and to indicate where the discussion is going.

A.　*Steps and Organization of a Legal Analysis on a Single Legal Issue Using a Single Case*

The following pages attempt to illustrate the development of a discussion of one element in an action for intentional infliction of emotional distress. The client, plaintiff Livia Augusta, wants to sue Olympia Department Store for emotional distress suffered while the store attempted to collect payment for a debt she never incurred. The discussion is based on one primary authority, a case from the same jurisdiction as the problem, and on one secondary source (full citations are omitted).

1. *Paragraph or Paragraphs on the Rule of Law*

The discussion of a particular legal issue should begin with a sentence or one or more paragraphs that set forth and explain the governing rule of law. When the rule of law appears to be both straightforward and clearly articulated, a complete paragraph explaining it may be unnecessary. In these instances, you would still need to begin with a topic sentence informing the reader of the governing rule, but you could follow this sentence with a discussion of its application in decided cases. When the intent and the scope of the law is more complicated, however, you may need to write an entire paragraph or more amplifying and clarifying its meaning or components. These explanations may require you either to analyze the language of a constitution or a statute, to set out the tests governing a law's application, or to summarize a court's discussion of that rule or a pertinent discussion in a secondary authority, which has, perhaps, been adopted in that jurisdiction.

A paragraph that explains the applicable law governing a defendant's outrageous conduct might look as follows (the marginal comments refer to the paragraph's mode of construction).

Topic Sentence
Announcing
Element

Explication of
Rule

> The first element for intentional infliction of emotional distress is whether the defendant's conduct was extreme and outrageous. Davis. Outrageous conduct is distinguishable from minor insults, threats, or annoyances. Id. A defendant has engaged in outrageous conduct only if he has engaged in a "prolonged course of hounding by a variety of extreme methods." W. Prosser, Law of Torts 57 (4th ed. 1971). Such methods include abusive language, shouting, repeated threats of arrest, withdrawal of credit, and appeals to the debtor's employer. Davis.

2. *Paragraph or Paragraphs on Case Law*

After analyzing the governing rule of law, your next step is to examine the relevant case law from which that rule came or in which it has been applied. In a fact-based problem, you should recount the relevant facts of the precedents because it is by identifying how the rules of law were applied to the facts of those cases that you give the rules meaning. Then by identifying similarities and differences between the facts of the precedents and those of your client's case, you predict the outcome of an action. It is also necessary to give the court's holding since, under stare decisis, it is the holding for each important case which establishes how the facts are to be interpreted. Finally, you should summarize for the reader the reasons and policies behind a court's determination of an issue. This type of analysis provides a basis for generating arguments about whether the legal requirements of that claim will be satisfied in your case. We illustrate this step with one paragraph because this discussion is based on only one precedent. A more complex discussion will require more than one paragraph.

It is important to remember that you are examining these cases to shed light on the legal principle you introduced in the opening paragraph. You must, therefore, connect the case discussion to that principle. If you fail to show how the precedent illustrates, limits, expands or explains the law, the discussion falters. One general rule of thumb here is to avoid beginning this paragraph with a sentence giving the facts of a case, as "In East v. West, where a defendant stood in front of a door to prevent three men from exiting, the court found no basis for recovery." Rather, start either with a topic sentence setting forth the legal principle that case shows or with a transition sentence that makes it clear you are continuing the same topic.

Topic Sentence on Legal Principle

Holding

Reasoning

Pertinent Facts

> When the defendant is a creditor, it may use reasonable if somewhat embarrassing and annoying methods to collect legitimate debts. Davis. In Davis, the court held that Finance Corp.'s conduct was not outrageous when it made numerous phone calls and visits to Mrs. Davis at her home and at the hospital where she visited her ailing daughter. Id. Finance Corp. made these phone calls for seven months. The Davis court reasoned that a creditor must be given some latitude in collecting a past due obligation and that Finance Corp.'s conduct fell within reasonable limits. Indeed, Mrs. Davis herself did not allege that Finance Corp.'s agents used abusive, threatening, or profane language. Id. Although the court said that Finance Corp. acted wrongly when it induced Davis to write a bad check, it found that one isolated act was inadequate to show the prolonged course of harassment that is required for a showing of outrageous conduct. The court permitted the creditor reasonable latitude to collect its debt, which it had a legal right to do. Id.

3. Paragraph or Paragraphs on Application of Precedents

The next step in a legal analysis involves applying the facts, policies, and reasons of decided cases to your case. In a memorandum, you should set out and evaluate the similarities and differences between the precedent and your case and determine their importance. The central job in this stage of analysis is to compare each relevant fact in the decided cases to those in your own case and to evaluate the strength of the claim you wish to make in light of these comparisons. You also apply the reasoning or policies of a decided case to your own case.

It is helpful to begin this step with a transition sentence which weighs the merits of the client's case in light of established precedent.

Transition
Sentence
Distinguishing
Cases

Augusta's situation is distinguishable from that of Mrs. Davis in two ways. First, Augusta does not owe a debt to Olympia. Thus the reasoning in <u>Davis</u>—namely, giving a creditor latitude to collect debts—does not apply to Olympia. Olympia was not doing what it had a legal right to do. Second, Olympia's conduct was more extreme than that of Finance Corp. For example, the language of Finance Corp.'s personnel was neither abusive nor vituperative. Olympia's language, however, became increasingly abusive and vituperative—an employee called her "a welsher and a four flushing bastard." Thus, Augusta can establish a type of conduct that the court said was not present in <u>Davis</u>. In addition, Olympia's wrongful conduct was not an isolated act, like inducing a plaintiff to write a bad check, but occurred over a period of many months. The billing department sent daily letters that demanded payment and that threatened to cancel her charge account and to report her delinquent account to the Credit Rating Bureau.

Distinguishing
Facts

When you believe your adversary has no authentic opposing argument on this issue, do not feel compelled to create one. Instead, end your discussion with a conclusory sentence, for example, "Since these letters continued arriving for three months, Olympia engaged in a prolonged course of harassment." Normally, however, your adversary will have a valid opposing argument which you must assess before coming to a conclusion. See steps 4 and 5 below.

4 & 5. Paragraph or Paragraphs on Presentation and Evaluation of Opposing Arguments and Legal Conclusion

A thorough discussion requires you to present and evaluate opposing arguments. Discuss those precedents and those facts from your problem that your opponent is going to rely on. Opposing counsel will highlight facts which are clearly unfavorable to your client or which can be interpreted differently by the parties.

Evaluation of an opposing argument is usually the last step before the conclusion in a legal analysis. When the refutation is complex, it may require an extended analysis of one or more paragraphs. Some ways you can diminish the importance of opposing arguments are by showing: 1) that your opponent's arguments are based on legally insignificant or incomplete facts or on a misapplication of the law to the facts; or 2) that your opponent relies on inapplicable reasons or policy arguments in coming to a legal conclusion; or 3) that your opponent's reasoning is illogical. On the other hand, your analysis of the opposing argument might convince you that your client cannot prevail on this issue. If this is the case, you should say so. Remember an office memorandum is an objective exploration of your client's legal situation and the basis for legal advice. You do not want to be misleading in a document of this nature.

The final sentence should be the legal conclusion, a conclusion grounded in the prior analysis of the law, precedent, and facts. This conclusion differs from the one given in the thesis paragraph that begins the Discussion section of the memorandum. (See Chapter Seven.) That conclusion offers an assessment of a client's overall chance of winning a suit or defending himself against a charge. Here, the conclusion refers only to the issue that has been under discussion.

Topic Sentence: Opposing Argument

Opponent's Facts & Reasoning

Opponent's Conclusion

Arguably, Olympia has not done anything as extreme as Finance Corp. Whereas Finance Corp. induced Davis to write a bad check and then phoned an acquaintance of Davis to inform her that Davis wrote bad checks, Olympia did nothing so publicly humiliating. Whereas Finance Corp. called Davis several times a week, frequently more than once a day, for a period of seven months, Olympia sent out daily letters and made daily phone calls only over a three month period. The court in Davis found that Finance Corp.'s numerous phone calls did not establish a prolonged course of hounding because there was no indication that the agents of Finance conducted themselves other than in a permissible manner during those calls. Thus, even if less extreme conduct is actionable when the plaintiff is not a debtor, Augusta may not be able to establish a prolonged course of harassment involving more than minor insults and threats.

Transition Sentence: Rebuttal

Facts & Reasoning Supporting Rebuttal

Legal Conclusion

This argument should not prevail, however. Even if Olympia did not commit such an extreme action as inducing Augusta to write a bad check, and even if its course of harassment was four months shy of Finance's, Olympia's abusive language and threats of ruination of credit are not permissible conduct under Davis. Had Augusta actually been a debtor, Olympia's conduct in comparison to that of Finance Corp. might nonetheless have stated a claim. Given that Augusta was not a debtor, and that the reasoning of Davis is therefore inapplicable, Augusta will satisfy the element of outrageous conduct in an action for intentional infliction of emotional distress.

Although you usually handle counterarguments in separate paragraphs, it is possible, if also more difficult, to weave rebuttal into your analysis and application of the case law. (In the fact application paragraph of step three, for example, the writer begins to rebut potential opposing arguments by distinguishing the facts of the cases.) When the opposing argument or the rebuttal is complex, however, or when the opposing argument is based on policy or reasoning rather than precedent, it is preferable to handle the rebuttal separately, as in the paragraphs above.

Exercise 6–A

In order to win a suit against Olympia Department Store on the grounds of intentional infliction of emotional distress, Livia Augusta must show that the conduct of the store was intentional or reckless. Read the following summary of Davis v. Finance Corp. on the requirement of reckless conduct. Then read Augusta's account of Olympia's reckless conduct. After this, write a discussion on whether Augusta can show Olympia acted recklessly.

Davis v. Finance Corp.

Defendant's conduct must be intentional or at least reckless to be actionable. If reckless, the conduct must be such that there is a high degree of probability that the plaintiff will suffer severe emotional distress and the actor goes ahead in conscious disregard of it.

Mrs. Davis told Finance Corp. that its visits to her at the hospital where she visited her ailing daughter were upsetting her daughter so much that her recovery was being impeded. Davis added that she herself was becoming extremely anxious, worried, and angry that Finance was dragging a patient into a dispute that "was none of the patient's doing." Upon hearing this, Finance Corp. suspended its visits to the hospital. At a later date, Davis informed Finance that "its harassment was driving her nuts."

The court held that the conduct of Finance Corp. was not reckless because it suspended its visits to the hospital when it became apparent that there was a high degree of probability that severe emotional distress would follow from those visits. It also stated that Davis's warning that Finance was "driving her nuts" did not sufficiently establish reckless conduct leading to severe distress since the phrase is routinely used to describe such trivial reactions as a parent's irritation at a child's misbehavior.

Livia Augusta told her attorney that she began informing Olympia personnel that its harassment was causing her insomnia, nightmares and weight loss after three weeks of abusive phone calls. After four weeks, Livia wrote the following letter to the president of Olympia.

> The conduct of your personnel in pursuing payment for a purchase I never made is having a horrendous impact on my health and emotional stability. My physician is giving me tranquilizers around the clock to control the acute anxiety I have been experiencing. This situation is intolerable, and I expect you, as president of the store, to clear this matter up before I become a complete wreck.

Augusta never heard from the president, nor did the store change its behavior. In fact, Olympia wrote a letter threatening to report her delinquent account to the Credit Rating Bureau a week and a half after Augusta had mailed her letter to the president.

B. *Case Synthesis in a Legal Analysis of a Single Legal Issue*

Occasionally, one case like <u>Davis</u> will provide all of the authority you need to resolve a legal question. More frequently, however, you will need to use more than one case to analyze that question. The following example is an analysis of one part of a false imprisonment case brought by Alma Kingsford against her former employers. The requirements of this tort are that the defendant must actually have confined the plaintiff, that the defendant intended to confine the plaintiff, and that the plaintiff was aware of or harmed by the confinement. This part of the memorandum is an analysis of the first element: actual confinement. In researching this problem, you will have found a number of cases dealing with the elements of a false imprisonment action. For the moment, set aside all of the cases that decided elements other than actual confinement. You will address those cases later.

In examining your cases on the element of confinement, you will discover that confinement can be brought about in several different ways. Kingsford's argument is that the defendant confined her in a room to question her by threatening to use physical force if she left the room. Your focus should therefore be on those cases that show confinement by threat of physical force.

Your discussion of confinement by threat of physical force must make sense of all the different factual situations which courts have held establish that requirement. In other words, you must synthesize the cases your research has turned up by articulating general principles that make analytic sense of decisions involving diverse fact patterns. In this false imprisonment problem, your case synthesis will reveal that a threat of physical force can be established by a defendant's actions, tone of voice, or size advantage. The cases also reveal two other factors necessary to a finding of confinement by threat of physical force, namely, that the defendant had the ability to carry out the threat and that the confinement was against the plaintiff's will. You should discuss each of these factors separately, and you should begin each discussion with a topic sentence that states how those factors can be established.

When you synthesize cases in your discussion, do not feel compelled to give all cases equal treatment. First, always give more weight to and begin with precedents from the jurisdiction of your problem than to precedents from other jurisdictions. Second, let your treatment of a case depend on its relevance to your client's situation. Some cases, for example, may not provide useful facts for comparison but may provide a rule of law or relevant policy. In this situation, a one sentence summary of the rule or policy may be all you need to use. Where, however, a case is especially relevant to your problem—either for the facts or for its discussion of the rule—your discussion of the precedent should be more extensive. In reading through the sample discussion that follows, notice when a one sentence summary is used to state a rule or to characterize a set of facts and when a case is more thoroughly treated.

Notice also that the sample discussion begins with an introductory paragraph, the first sentence of which introduces the element of whether the plaintiff had been confined. The paragraph then defines confinement and concludes with a statement about whether the element can be satisfied in the problem case.

The rest of the discussion demonstrates how the basic technique for organizing a discussion of an issue when working with a group of cases is similar to that used when working with one case—the rule is presented, the precedent or precedents are discussed, the facts of your case are compared, opposing arguments are raised and evaluated, and finally, a conclusion regarding that issue is stated. Notice in the sample discussion that when a requirement can be easily established, all the analytic steps described above are covered in a single paragraph. When the discussion is complex or case law abundant, however, the discussion is subdivided into paragraphs indicative of the steps in a legal analysis. Also notice that opposing arguments are not always raised. When opposing arguments seem insubstantial, this step can be omitted or incorporated into the fact application paragraph. Note, full citations have been omitted.

Pattern of an Analysis Involving Case Synthesis

Topic Sentence: Confinement

Case Used for General Rule (Not Used Again)

Cases Provide Rule For 1st Subissue: Threat

Kingsford must show that her supervisors, Peterson and Smith, did, in fact, confine her. In Kent, a defendant can confine a plaintiff by physical barriers, overpowering physical force, threats to apply physical force if the victim goes outside the boundary fixed by the defendants, submission to other types of duress, and submission to an asserted legal authority. Johnson v. White (adopting Restatement (Second) of Torts). Kingsford's chances of establishing confinement depend on her showing that the defendants threatened physical force. A plaintiff may be confined through threat of physical force by a defendant's action, see Atkins v. Barton, or by a defendant's tone, see Smith v. Jones.

For 2nd Subissue:
Ability

For 3rd Subissue:
Involuntariness

Legal Conclusion

Topic Sentence:
1st Subissue

Case on 2 Ways
Threat Can Be
Made

Comparison with
Problem Case

Transition
Sentence on
Opposing
Argument

Pertinent Facts

Cases Support
Rebuttal

Legal Conclusion

Topic Sentence
On 3rd Way to
Show Threat

Case Provides
Example

Comparison with
Problem Case

Under any of these circumstances, the defendant must also have the ability to apply force. East v. West. Finally, the restraint must be against the plaintiff's will. Id. If the plaintiff voluntarily agrees to stay, he or she has not been falsely imprisoned. Lopez v. Winchell. Kingsford was confined because Peterson and Smith were able to carry out the threat they made and she submitted to them against her will.

An action so intimidating that its effect is to confine the plaintiff by threat of physical force may result from the defendant's movement and gestures and from the plaintiff's perception of the defendant's size advantage. Atkins v. Barton. In Atkins, the plaintiff successfully sued a deprogrammer, Barton, for false imprisonment. Barton was 6'2" and 225 pounds. When he stepped in front of the door to the plaintiff's bedroom, blocking her exit, she reasonably believed that she was confined by threat of physical force even though he did not say a word. Id. Similarly, Ms. Kingsford may have been confined by the threatening gestures of her supervisors. Smith moved to the door and leaned against it when Kingsford rose from her chair as if to leave. In addition, Smith has a size advantage. At 5'6" Smith is five inches taller than Ms. Kingsford. She is also athletic and works out at a health club several times a week.

Nonetheless, because Smith is significantly smaller and lighter than the defendant in Atkins, defendants will doubtlessly argue that Kingsford's reliance on Atkins is misplaced. In addition, whereas the female plaintiff in Atkins perceived the male defendant as having an unfair physical advantage because of his gender, there is no gender disparity between Kingsford and Smith. Yet these differences are probably not significant. Courts have consistently regarded the comparative sizes of the parties as more important for establishing initimidation than size or gender alone. See Cane v. Downs (defendant was six inches taller and fifty pounds heavier than plaintiff); Carey v. Robier (although defendant was only 5'5", plaintiff was four inches smaller). See also Mussel v. Wimple (defendant was a 5'11" male, plaintiff a 5'6" male). Thus, based on their gestures and size advantage, the defendants threatened physical force.

If the defendant does speak, his tone may be sufficient to establish a threat of physical force, even if he made no explicit threat. In Smith v. Jones, the defendant accused the plaintiff of stealing money from his car. The defendant demanded that plaintiff be searched in front of his fellow workers. The defendant's confrontational manner and his belligerent tone of voice made it clear that there would be serious trouble if the plaintiff did not allow himself to be searched. Id. In calling his friends over to witness the "frisk," the defendant created a threatening atmosphere. Id. In Ms. Kingsford's case, threats of physical force, if not actually articulated, were at least implicit in Peterson's tone of voice, which Kingsford described as "loud" and

S., W. & F.–Writing and Analysis 2nd Ed. FP—5

"harsh." She also referred to a lot of "screaming and shouting." Thus, the defendants' actions and tone established a threat of physical force.

The ability to carry out a threat is established when defendants outnumber the plaintiff. See Appley v. Owens (two defendants confined plaintiff); Atkins (parents and deprogrammer confined a single woman). Like the defendants in these cases, Peterson and Smith outnumbered the plaintiff. As Kingsford said, "there were two against one."

Finally, there is no confinement unless the plaintiff remains involuntarily. East v. West. In Lopez v. Winchell, the plaintiff, who was accused of stealing money from her employer, remained voluntarily. She decided to remain in the store with her employers so that she could clear her name. Similarly, the plaintiffs in East remained voluntarily. When told the police had been called, they agreed to wait. Id.

Kingsford may also have remained voluntarily. Peterson and Smith had initially summoned Kingsford to their office to fire her. They also wanted her to agree to leave their firm without receiving severance pay. When Kingsford said that she would never agree to such a condition and that she would not hang around to be bullied into submission, Peterson told her that if she left, he would not only give her a bad reference but would spread the word that she was a sullen, incompetent, and lazy employee. Threatened by the prospect of both present and future unemployment if Peterson did as he said, Kingsford agreed to remain in the office to discuss the matter further, as Lopez did to clear her good name.

Yet this similarity between Lopez's situation and Kingsford's is probably not dispositive. A submission which is procured by an act or threat to take something of value from the plaintiff is not voluntary. Goodhart v. Butcher Restaurant. In Goodhart, a restaurant owner took and held onto a patron's wallet until he could determine if the patron had paid his bill. During this time, the patron remained because he did not want to lose the wallet's valuable contents. The court held that the plaintiff had not remained voluntarily when the defendant took something of value from the plaintiff in order to ensure the plaintiff remained. Id. Although Peterson did not take a tangible object like a wallet, he did have control over Kingsford's professional reputation, which is a thing of value. In contrast, although the plaintiff in Lopez was worried about her "good name," her employer did not threaten to give Lopez a bad reference if she left. Thus, Goodhart is the controlling case here, and Kingsford should be able to show that she was confined against her will. All three requirements for confinement by threat of physical force can, therefore, be established.

Marginal annotations (left column):

Conclusion

Topic Sentence On 2nd Subissue: Ability

Parentheticals Give Relevant Facts

Comparison

Topic Sentence on 3rd Subissue: Involuntariness

Case Analysis

Transition Sentence Suggests Opposing Argument

Pertinent Facts

Transition Sentence: Rebuttal

Case Supports Rebuttal

Distinguishing Adverse Decision

Restatement of Legal Conclusion

Two important writing techniques for handling case synthesis have been used in this discussion. First, the paragraphs often begin with topic sentences that state in general terms the principles that have been extracted from the precedents. Thus, the fact that the plaintiffs in Appley v. Owens and Atkins v. Barton were outnumbered is the basis of the author's general claim, made in the topic sentence of paragraph four, that "the ability to carry out a threat is established when defendants outnumber the plaintiff." Similarly, the defendants' overbearing size and movements in Atkins v. Barton, Cane v. Downs, and Carey v. Robier give rise to the topic sentence in paragraph two that "an action so intimidating that its effect is to confine by threat of physical force may result from the defendant's movements and gestures and from the plaintiff's perception of the defendant's size advantage." Constructing such general statements is one important way of bringing to your reader the results of your analysis. The topic sentences also promote clear organization by orienting the reader to the paragraph's place in the analysis.

The second important writing technique used in this discussion is the writer's considered use of parenthetical discussion. Because the deprogrammer Barton is such a clear and dramatic example of size advantage, the author discusses Atkins thoroughly in order to establish the main point. The references to Cane v. Downs and Carey v. Robier are necessary because they refine the point that size advantage can be relative, but the facts can be parenthetical because these cases are used to supply details and general support of Atkins. By using these parentheticals, the author keeps the text free from the specific factual details of these cases.

Exercise 6–B

To win a suit against Olympia Department Store, Livia Augusta needs to establish not only that Olympia used outrageous collection tactics, but that her distress was severe. Read Augusta's account of her emotional state and the following summaries of controlling precedents. Then write a discussion on the issue of whether Augusta can show her emotional distress was severe.

Augusta reports a variety of reactions to Olympia's tactics, including insomnia, nightmares, and weight loss (15 lbs.). When she began hyperventilating after each phone call from Olympia, Augusta became worried about her health. She went to see her doctor, who diagnosed her as suffering from acute anxiety. He gave her a prescription for 10 mg. valium and told her to take one tablet four times a day. Although Augusta has been following this regimen, she complains the medication has been interfering with her job performance and social life. She has trouble concentrating, dozed off during an important meeting, and feels too lethargic to go out in the evenings. Her employer has told her to "shape up." The tranquilizers have helped to control her anxiety and sleeplessness, but Livia is worried about their long term effect on her physical health.

Davis v. Finance Corp.

The tort of intentional infliction of emotional distress requires a showing that the distress is severe. Mental conditions such as fright, horror, grief, shame, humiliation, or worry may fall within the ambit of the term emotional distress. However, these mental conditions alone are not actionable. The distress inflicted must be so severe that no reasonable person could be expected to endure it. The court decided that Davis's distress was severe because she suffered shame and anxiety and required medical attention, but it dismissed the case because Davis was unable to establish the separate element of outrageous and reckless conduct.

Marlboro v. First Bank of Gilford

June Marlboro, a fifty-five-year-old widowed schoolteacher, was diagnosed as suffering major depression in June 1987. Four months prior to this diagnosis, Marlboro had defaulted on a home improvement loan from the First Bank of Gilford because she had lent her retired brother money to purchase a new car. In the month following the default, Marlboro received daily threatening letters. Later, the bank's collection agent began making nightly, obscene phone calls. June found herself going on eating binges after these calls. After the bank called the principal of her school to inform him of her default, June's symptoms of depression became more pronounced. She was often fatigued and began taking naps during the day and oversleeping in the mornings. She experienced a loss of self-esteem. She was unable to make decisions. She gained twenty pounds. She went to her physician, who found that her weight increase had raised her blood pressure. He put her on a salt-free diet and told her that she had to lose weight. He also referred her to a psychiatrist. The psychiatrist testified that June's mental health has been seriously threatened. The court found Marlboro's distress so severe no reasonable person could be expected to endure it.

Dale v. New City Hospital

Jim Dale lost his job when his employer went bankrupt. In the months that followed, money became increasingly tight. Then, Mrs. Dale was hospitalized with leukemia. Dale, who had never bought medical insurance to replace his old employee coverage, was unable to pay the hospital bills. The hospital turned his account over to a collection agency, which began hounding him for payment. Shortly thereafter, Dale sank into a serious depression. He suffered from an emotional paralysis so severe that he was unable to leave his apartment. He refused to visit his wife in the hospital and missed several job interviews. His physician placed him on anti-depressants. Although the court found Dale's distress so severe as to interfere with normal functioning, it concluded that his distress was not the result of the defendant's actions, but of his wife's diagnosis and his unemployment.

Histrionic v. Credit Inc.

Histrionic, a seasoned actor in rehearsal for an off-broadway musical, defaulted on his payments to Credit Inc. When Credit Inc. attempted to collect the debt, Histrionic reacted emotionally. He broke down several times during rehearsal, ranting about Credit Inc.'s persecution of him and weeping that he was misunderstood. On more than one occasion, he threw himself down on the stage, pounding the floor and moaning that he was ruined. His doctor testified that Histrionic's response to Credit's collection methods was extreme and that he had prescribed a mild sedative for Histrionic. Although Histrionic tended to forget his lines while on this medication, the musical, when it opened, was a smashing success. Histrionic was singled out for his excellent performance. The court found Histrionic's emotional distress not actionable. It said that Histrionic's feelings of hysteria and anxiety had not grossly impeded his functioning and that his behavior was in some measure consistent with his prior character and professional training.

Chapter Seven
The Thesis Paragraph

The discussion section of an office memorandum should begin with a paragraph that introduces the reader to your client's claim for relief, to the legal issues it involves, and to your reasoned conclusions about their probable resolution in your client's situation. This paragraph is frequently called a thesis paragraph because it states your thesis, that is, your position on the outcome of a client's prospective case. One benefit of providing this kind of introduction early in the discussion is that it makes it easier for your reader to evaluate the analysis as it is being built. Another benefit is that it sets out the organization of the discussion.

One logical way of arranging relevant introductory material in a thesis paragraph is to

1. Identify the claim or defense in your problem;

2. Set out the rules that govern that claim in the order you intend to discuss them and explain how those rules relate to each other;

3. If length permits, or complexity requires, briefly apply those rules to your facts;

4. State the thesis (your legal conclusion).

If your memo is fairly simple, however, or if your professor or firm requires a Conclusion section rather than a Short Answer section, you may want to shorten your thesis paragraph by eliminating or abbreviating some of the steps outlined above. One thing you can do is to eliminate step 3, the application of the law to the facts. You can also combine steps 1 and 4 and begin with a thesis sentence that introduces the topic of the discussion and gives your conclusion as to the claim or defense in your problem. After this, you could still indicate the organization of your discussion by introducing the rules that govern that claim in the relevant jurisdiction or, in a case of first impression, in other jurisdictions.

———

Assume you are writing a memorandum about a due process problem based on the following facts:

Alice Doone, mother of three minor children, receives payments under the Aid to Families with Dependent Children program (AFDC), a federal program administered by the state. Her payments were reduced when she enrolled in a work-training program which paid her a stipend. Having unsuccessfully challenged the reductions at an administrative hearing of the state Social Services Department, Doone sought to appeal to the State of Kent Court of Appeals. Such appeals are authorized by state law. However, under state law, the filing of a civil appeal requires a $40 filing fee. Ms. Doone claimed she was unable to pay the fee and sought leave to proceed in forma pauperis (permission to proceed without liability for court fees); leave was denied without an opinion. Alice Doone would now like to file suit in the United States District Court for the Western District of Kent, claiming that application of a fee to indigent appellants violates the due process clause of the fourteenth amendment.

You might begin your Discussion section with a thesis paragraph like the one below.

Topic Sentence on Claim

Applicable Rules

Application

Legal Conclusion

> To proceed with her claim against AFDC, Ms. Doone needs to show that the statutory $40 filing fee, as applied to her, violates the due process clause of the fourteenth amendment to the United States Constitution. Due process demands that an indigent person not be denied access to the courts for failure to pay a fee when (1) the court is the only forum for resolving the dispute, (2) the underlying subject matter is itself of constitutional significance, and (3) the constitutional interest overrides a countervailing state interest. Boddie v. Connecticut, 401 U.S. 370 (1971). In this case, the court is the only forum in which Ms. Doone can challenge the Department's reduction of her benefits. However, the underlying subject matter, an increase in welfare payments for family support, is not constitutionally significant. Thus, the state's interest in defraying the costs of the judicial system will override Ms. Doone's interest. The filing fee will, therefore, probably be found constitutionally permissible under the due process clause.

This paragraph is an effective introduction in that it clearly states the legal question, the relevant legal tests and their applicability to the client, and the author's conclusion. A lot of this information is in the next sample thesis paragraph but in a less explicit manner.

> In Boddie v. Connecticut, 401 U.S. 371 (1971), the Court held that requiring a filing fee from an indigent seeking access to a state court for dissolution of a marriage was unconstitutional. Ms. Doone's situation is similar to that of the Boddie plaintiffs. Therefore, a court will probably find the fee must yield to Ms. Doone's right to have an opportunity to be heard in court regarding her challenge to the reduction of her AFDC payments. The court is the only forum for resolution of a dispute involving Ms. Doone's ability to provide basic necessities.

There are a number of problems with this thesis paragraph, foremost of which is the absence of a topic sentence which clearly sets forth the legal claim. By introducing the topic in terms of the Boddie holding, the sentence incorrectly identifies the paragraph as being only about Boddie. The first sentence also introduces the discussion too narrowly. It is unclear if the Boddie ruling on the constitutionality of filing fees extends to an indigent's appeal on grounds other than divorce. In order to avoid this kind of confusion, it is a good idea to begin a thesis paragraph with a topic sentence that sets out the legal claim in general terms, or in terms of your client, instead of tying it to the facts of a particular case.

Another shortcoming of this paragraph is that it does not make it clear that Boddie created standards for determining the constitutionality of filing fees. In the last sentence, two of the three Boddie standards are referred to in passing, but we are not specifically told that they are the tests announced in Boddie—nor is it clear that the statement about Ms. Doone's ability to provide basic necessities is the writer's attempt to establish the required presence of a fundamental, constitutionally protected interest. Thus, as readers, we are uncertain of the legal issues and legal principles involved and unclear about where the discussion is heading.

Because a memo is supposed to include a fully developed discussion of the thesis, it is important to delineate the legal issues and conclusions carefully. A weak discussion is frequently one which begins with a vague introductory paragraph that leaves the reader unclear about which issues need to be discussed, how they relate, and how they will be resolved.

Although you want to provide an introduction that orients your reader to the analysis that follows it, be careful that the length of your thesis paragraph is proportionate to the length of your discussion. Although you must introduce the reader to a synthesized statement of what you will analyze, the thesis paragraph is not the place to offer an elaborate explanation or application of a rule. If your problem involves many rules of law and intricate facts, shorten or eliminate your application of the rules to the facts of your case.   After listing the prongs of the controlling test, for example, you could conclude by saying, "Because Ms. Doone cannot satisfy all three prongs, it is unlikely the court will allow her to proceed in forma pauperis."   Another way to keep your thesis paragraph to a manageable length is to begin with a thesis sentence that presents both the claim and your conclusion about that claim, as in, "Jane Simon will not be convicted of assault in the second degree for failing to act to prevent the injury of a minor whom she had taken care of for five years."

————

The Doone memorandum involved only one claim and thus it was possible to announce and apply all three legal requirements. When several claims are involved, however, each of which has several elements requiring discussion, you may need to rethink your strategy in order to prevent your thesis paragraph from becoming too long.   One helpful tactic is to write a thesis paragraph that sets out all the claims and that explains how they relate and how they will be resolved.   Then write separate introductory paragraphs which set out the elements of each claim, placing each introductory paragraph at the beginning of your discussion of that claim.

Assume, for example, that your client is embroiled in a dispute arising out of a contract within which there is a mandatory forum selection clause.   Your client wants to know if that clause is enforceable.   You might begin your Discussion with the following thesis paragraph (citations are omitted).

Topic Sentence on Claim

In deciding whether paragraph thirteen of the contract between Alta and MMI ousts it of jurisdiction over a dispute arising from the contract, the Southern District of New York must first

First Issue

decide whether the paragraph should be interpreted as a mandatory forum selection clause conferring exclusive jurisdiction on the courts of Milan, Italy for any dispute arising out of the contract, or simply as consent to Milan jurisdiction should a related action be brought there.   Even if it finds that the Milan court has exclusive jurisdiction, however, the court may in its

Second Issue

discretion decline to enforce the provision if it finds that to do so would be unjust and unfair under the circumstances. On the first issue, the court is likely to find that the language of paragraph

Conclusions

thirteen unambiguously provides Milan with exclusive jurisdiction.   In addition, it will probably find that it is reasonable to enforce the forum selection clause in this case.

This thesis paragraph, which bridges the issues and synthesizes the analysis, might then be followed by a more detailed introduction to the rules governing the first issue.

Topic Sentence on Rule Governing First Issue

To determine whether the language of a forum selection clause is mandatory or permissive, New York courts generally examine whether the language is clearly mandatory and all-encompassing,

Factors

or whether there are two opposing, yet reasonable, interpretations of the clause. In particular, courts look for words like "shall" or "must" since these words commonly signify a command. If they fail to find that language, they will usually apply the traditional contract rule of interpreting ambiguous language against the drafter.

After this introduction to the factors involved in construing the language of a forum selection clause, the writer would analyze this issue in depth. Upon finishing that analysis, the writer would then write an introduction to the second issue, listing the five factors courts use to determine the reasonableness of enforcing a forum selection clause.

Of course, not all problems involving multiple issues or claims are necessarily complex. When you have a problem involving a couple of relatively uncomplicated issues or claims, you may still use one thesis paragraph to introduce all the issues, their relation to each other, their governing rules and their disposition. This is the situation in the following problem where Paul Hart is contesting his late father's will.

Topic Sentence on Claim

First Issue

Application & Conclusion

Second Issue

Application & Conclusion

Paul Hart has two different grounds upon which to challenge his father's will disinheriting him. The first ground is that the will is invalid because his father, who had been adjudicated insane, lacked the capacity to execute a will. An insane person can execute a valid will, however, if he is lucid at the time he executes it. Arnold v. Brown, 200 Kent 50 (1962). Because the evidence shows Mr. Hart was lucid when he executed the will, Paul's first challenge should fail. The second ground is that even if the will is valid, his father's will did not effectively disinherit him under Kent Rev. Code § 100 (1975), which requires a parent's will to show an intent to disinherit a child. Mr. Hart's will does not do so. Thus, Paul Hart's second challenge should be successful. Under Kent Rev. Code § 150 (1975), he will be entitled to a one-third share of his deceased father's estate.

If you wanted to shorten this thesis paragraph, you could rewrite as follows:

Topic Sentence on Claim
First Issue

Second Issue

Conclusion

Paul Hart has two different grounds upon which to challenge his father's will disinheriting him. The first ground is that the will is invalid because his father, who had been adjudicated insane, lacked the capacity to execute a will. The second ground is that even if the will is valid because his father was lucid when he executed it, his father's will did not effectively disinherit him under Kent Rev. Code § 100 (1975). This section requires a parent's will to show an intent to disinherit a child. This second challenge should be successful, and under Kent Rev. Code § 150, Paul Hart will be entitled to a one-third share of his deceased father's estate.

After either of these two introductions, you would discuss each ground separately.

Exercise 7–A

1. Your client, John Wheeler, wants to sue Donald Lindhorst in a federal district court in Connecticut for negligence. There is a threshold question, however, as to whether the district court would have the power to hear this case. Lindhorst is a citizen of Arkansas. Wheeler lived in Arkansas until he was sent to serve a prison sentence in Connecticut, where he is still an inmate. If Wheeler is still a citizen of Arkansas, the federal court will lack diversity jurisdiction. Which thesis paragraph for this problem is better and why?

Thesis A

Wheeler is a citizen of Connecticut based on the decision in Ferrara v. Ibach. In Ferrara, the court ruled that serviceman Ibach was a citizen of South Carolina because of his physical presence there and his intention not to return to his former domicile in Pennsylvania. He established domicile by moving his family to South Carolina, renting a house there, enrolling his children in public school there, and maintaining a bank account there.

Thesis B

John Wheeler, a domiciliary of Arkansas before his incarceration in a Connecticut prison, would like to bring suit for negligence against Donald Lindhorst, an Arkansas domiciliary. In order to sue in federal court, however, Wheeler must be a domiciliary of Connecticut for the purposes of establishing diversity jurisdiction under 28 U.S.C. § 1332 (1982). In cases involving a person's involuntary relocation, there is a presumption in favor of an original domicile over an acquired one. Nonetheless, this presumption can be overcome by showing that the person clearly and unequivocally intended to make the new domicile home. Jones v. Hadican. The Wheeler family's actions and Wheeler's statements demonstrate such clear intent to make Connecticut the Wheelers' new home that diversity jurisdiction can be satisfied.

2. Livia Augusta wants to sue Olympia Department Store for emotional distress suffered while the store attempted to collect payment for a debt she never incurred. Which thesis paragraph is a clearer introduction to the problem?

Thesis A

Ms. Augusta's claim for damages rests on Olympia Department Store's negligence in billing procedures. The claim for damages from severe emotional distress depends on the store's intentional employment of outrageous collection methods which Ms. Augusta asserts precipitated her severe emotional distress. Also Olympia's collection department was harassing Ms. Augusta without right since she was not indebted to them.

Thesis B

Olympia's liability to Livia depends on her satisfying the three standards that establish intentional infliction of emotional distress in the state of Kent. First, the defendant's conduct, which gives rise to the distress, must be extreme and outrageous. Second, the plaintiff's distress must be severe. Third, the defendant's conduct must have been intentional or reckless. Davis v. Finance Corp. The Kent courts have extended considerable latitude in interpreting these standards in favor of creditors pursuing legal debts. In this case, there was no legal debt, so Olympia's actions will not be granted that latitude. Livia Augusta will be able to satisfy the tests for this tort because Olympia threatened Livia for over six months, her distress required medical attention, and Olympia knew that its harassment would cause such distress.

3. Read the following facts and rules of law and then write a thesis paragraph on whether John Star and Alice Doe can recover for negligent infliction of emotional distress as a result of Pennsylvania Deluxe Hotel's negligence in hiring and supervising the security guard who fired at Jane Star (you can assume the negligence for the purpose of this exercise).

———

On Election Day, John Star, the husband of candidate Jane Star, and Alice Doe, Jane's great aunt and former guardian, decided to watch the television election coverage at campaign headquarters at Pennsylvania Deluxe Hotel. They were waiting for Jane to return to the hotel after visiting her supporters at local campaign offices. The campaign had been marred by numerous threats of violence against the candidate and her family.

At 9:30 p.m., Jane and several staff members arrived at the hotel, and Jane began walking to the hotel's entrance. Halfway there, a psychotic hotel security guard pulled out a pistol and shot at Jane. The television cameras picked up the guard pointing and shooting his pistol in Jane's direction. The shot was heard on the T.V. The cameras did not actually show Jane being hit and falling, but they did immediately show her lying on the sidewalk, unconscious, in a pool of blood.

John and Alice were watching the T.V. as the entire scene unfolded. They say they realized immediately after the shot was fired that Jane was seriously hurt. John immediately collapsed, and Alice became hysterical.

Although Jane's injuries were not fatal, both John and Alice were extremely depressed in the months following the incident. Alice was put into a sanitarium to recover from a breakdown. John was too shaken to work for three months. John and Jane's marriage suffered as John insisted that Jane resign the post she had just recently won. Neither John nor Alice has any physical ailments associated with their emotional problems.

———

As you may recall from Chapter Five, case law establishes the legal requirements of this tort as follows:

1. The plaintiff must be closely related to the victim, as opposed to being distantly related or unrelated;

2. The plaintiff must have been near enough to the scene of the accident that the ensuing shock was the direct result of the impact of a sensory and contemporaneous observance of the accident, as opposed to shock which results from learning about the accident from others after its occurrence;

3. The shock must have resulted from a single, identifiable traumatic event; it cannot be the result of a condition that occurs over time;

4. The plaintiff's distress must be severe, although there need not be a physical manifestation of a psychic injury.

Chapter Eight
Effective Paragraphs

I. Introduction

A paragraph is often described as a group of sentences developing a dominant idea that is usually expressed in a topic sentence. A paragraph should have both unity and coherence. It has unity when every sentence relates to the topic. It has coherence when there is a smooth and logical flow between sentences and a clear and explicit connection between any one sentence and the topic of the paragraph.

While unity and coherence are essential for any effective paragraph, well written paragraphs in a lengthy discussion have an additional function. They must not only be understandable internally, but they must also indicate their place in the overall argument. Clear writing depends on providing the reader with signals so that the direction and point of an analysis are always apparent. The most common way of achieving continuity and logical progression is to begin paragraphs with topic and transition sentences. Topic sentences introduce new issues and sub-issues and show their connection with the thesis presented in the thesis paragraph. Transitional sentences bridge subjects or connect the steps within an analysis.

II. Topic Sentences and Paragraph Unity

A paragraph is a subdivision of a text indicating that the sentences within the subdivision develop one idea. That idea is usually expressed in a topic sentence which pulls the lines of a paragraph together by summarizing the basic idea developed in

124

that paragraph. Without this summarizing sentence, the reader may have difficulty understanding the paragraph and its place in the analysis. Thus, the topic sentence expresses the writer's intention for the paragraph the way a thesis paragraph expresses the writer's intention for a paper. And just as a thesis paragraph ought to be the first paragraph in your discussion, so a topic sentence should generally be the first sentence of a paragraph.

Topic sentences can unify ideas which might appear unrelated by establishing a context which makes their relation and the point of a paragraph clear. Consider this paragraph.

> In Red v. Black, five-year-old Johnny Black broke a windshield while throwing rocks. The court held him to the standard of conduct of a reasonable person of like age, intelligence, and experience under like circumstances. Id. Similarly, a twelve-year-old was held to a child's standard of care for his negligence in swinging a badminton racquet and hitting a teammate. Nickelby v. Pauling. However, the same court held an eight-year-old to an adult standard of care when the infant defendant injured a spectator while driving a go cart on a golf course. Delican v. Cane. That decision was affirmed two years later when an adult standard was applied to an eleven-year-old girl who shot another child with an arrow during archery practice. Marion v. Hood.

Although each sentence seems vaguely connected to the others, the reader does not understand their precise relation. The discussion suffers from the vagueness that often occurs when a paragraph begins with the facts of a case rather than with a topic sentence. A topic sentence eliminates this vagueness or confusion by establishing a context for understanding the cases. For example,

> Infants are held to a child's standard of care for damages occasioned by their tortious acts, except when those infants engage in adult activities involving dangerous instruments for which adult skills are required. Delican v. Cane.

Thus, topic sentences play a key role in ensuring paragraph unity by forcing the writer to articulate the point and the function of the paragraph. If the topic sentence given above was added to the sample paragraph, the author would have at least presented the principle explaining how these cases fit together instead of having offered a mere summary of her research. In fact, if the author had written that topic sentence, the substance of the rest of the paragraph might have improved. The writer would probably have realized the relevance of the courts' explanations of why archery and go cart driving are adult activities, and would have included those discussions in her paragraph.

Not only do you need topic sentences to present your analysis of a case or group of cases, but you need topic sentences to introduce legal issues and subissues. In a problem involving the admissibility of expert testimony on the Battered Wife Syndrome, for example, you would need a topic sentence to introduce each prong of the test that is used to determine admissibility. For example,

> To determine the admissibility of expert testimony, courts first decide if the subject matter is so distinctly related to some science, profession, or occupation that it is beyond the ken of the average juror.

Because the first sentence in a paragraph plays a crucial role in informing the reader of the point of the paragraph, it should not be wasted on a citation. Citations often distract the reader from the point you mean to stress. The following sentence should have introduced the claim, not the facts behind a precedent which recognized that claim.

> In Apple v. Baker, 100 Mass. 406, 688 N.E.2d 600 (1988), the plaintiff brought an action for breach of warranty based on the blighted quality of 20% of the wheat delivered to him.

It would have been preferable to use the first sentence to introduce the basic idea of the paragraph. Then, if appropriate, follow with a citation that shows your authority. After this, you can use the case as an illustration of the basic idea.

> An implied warranty of merchantability is breached when the goods are not fit for their ordinary purposes. See Apple v. Baker, 100 Mass. 406, 688 N.E.2d 600 (1988). In Apple, the plaintiff brought an action for breach of warranty based on the blighted quality of 20% of the wheat delivered to him.

In addition, you do not want to waste your opening statement on a sentence that merely "treads water," that is, one that does not go anywhere and that immediately needs to be explained.

> The court has had to deal with the issue of a child's suit for loss of parental consortium. In a recent case, the court has held that the child has no cause of action.

The paragraph should immediately say that the court has held against the claim, not that the court "dealt" with it.

Although topic sentences play a major role in orienting your reader to your organization, not every paragraph requires a topic sentence. A complicated topic will require several paragraphs to explain, and thus a new paragraph may just be continuing the topic of the preceding paragraph. For this series of paragraphs, you would use a topic sentence in the first paragraph, and then use transitional words or sentences to begin the next paragraphs. Transitions are discussed in section III of this chapter.

After you have written a first draft, you can focus on your topic sentences as a method of editing your work. Topic sentences, or the lack of them, can help you to assess paragraph unity. You can check the body of a paragraph against the topic sentence to see if the paragraph contains more than one topic, wanders into an irrelevant digression, or lacks development. If so, you should divide, edit, or develop the paragraph to achieve unity. If you find yourself unable to state the topic in a sentence, your paragraph needs to be sharpened, focused, or omitted.

Evaluate the following two paragraphs for unity.

Example 1: In determining whether an infant will be held to an adult standard of care, courts first examine the infant's activity to see if that activity involves a dangerous instrument which requires adult skills. In Marion v. Hood, archery was considered an adult activity because of the intrinsic danger of arrows and the skill required in operating a bow and arrow. See also Delican v. Cane (go carts are intrinsically dangerous and require skill in handling). In contrast, in Nickelby v. Pauling, a badminton racquet was found so lightweight as not to constitute an intrinsic danger.

Example 2: An infant will be held to an adult standard of care if the infant was engaged in an activity involving a dangerous instrument for which adult skills are required. Marion v. Hood. Because of the intrinsic danger of arrows and the skill required in using a bow and arrow, archery was found to be an adult activity in Marion v. Hood. In Delican v. Cane, an infant driving a go cart was held to an adult standard of care because of the intrinsic danger of go carts and the skill required in their handling. Although the court in Ashley v. Connor did not scrutinize a squash racquet for its intrinsic danger, it found squash to be an adult activity because knowledge of the game's traditions and customs is required to mitigate the potential risks of the game. In squash, it is customary for a player to yell "clear" before taking a shot directed at the partner in order to avoid striking that player.

Example one has a clear topic sentence supported by the succeeding sentences. The paragraph exhibits direction and unity. Each sentence develops the general principle articulated in the topic sentence by setting forth authority for that principle.

Example two lacks unity because it introduces a factor not announced in the topic sentence. The paragraph begins well. It initially focuses on one factor the courts examine to determine whether a game is an adult activity: whether the instrument used in the activity is so inherently dangerous as to require adult skill. Yet the writer gets sidetracked in the last two sentences. The Ashley court's silence on the first factor leads the author to a second: whether traditions and customs have evolved to mitigate the risks of the game. This is an important factor and deserves discussion. But the discussion should begin in the next paragraph and should be announced in a separate topic sentence. Having written a topic sentence that refers to the first factor only, the author should be guided by it.

Attention to paragraph unity and topic sentences may help with paragraph length also. Long paragraphs—paragraphs the length of a page or more than 250 words—should send you looking for logical subdivisions which are often natural places for paragraph division. In contrast, a very short paragraph, when used other than for emphasis, is often part of a larger discussion and should, therefore, be combined with another paragraph. A one sentence paragraph, for example, is frequently the conclusion of a prior paragraph or an introduction to the next. If it is not, a short paragraph should be examined for lack of development.

Examine the following paragraph for a logical subdivision.

A landlord's duty to maintain the premises in safe and sanitary condition does not require the landlord to provide protection from criminal activities directed against persons lawfully on the premises. Pippin v. Chicago Housing Authority. Pippin was a wrongful death action against the landlord concerning not so much the conditions, but the policing, of the premises. Pippin had been an acquaintance of one of the tenants in the building. During an argument with the tenant, Pippin was fatally stabbed. The Pippin decision was a simple restatement of the common law in Illinois: a landlord does not have the duty to protect a tenant from criminal acts nor does it have a duty to protect a third party lawfully on the premises from criminal activities. Nonetheless, a landlord who has provided part-time guard service may have a duty to make security provisions for the hours when the guards are not on duty. In Cross v. Wells Fargo Alarm Services, the court held the landlord responsible for the safety of the building during those hours for which it had not provided guard service. The court relied on the theory that the provision of part-time guard service had the effect of increasing the incidence of crime when the guards were not there. The plaintiff had been injured by several unknown men at a time when the guards were not on duty.

The paragraph breaks naturally after the fifth sentence when the writer begins explaining an exception to the common law rule that a landlord has no duty to provide protection from criminal activity. The writer should indent and begin a new paragraph there.

Decide which of the following paragraphs can be logically combined with another.

In Holley, the plaintiff paid $5.00 a month as a security fee, aside from the regular rent. The court stated that this fee created a contractual duty on the landlord to provide protection to the tenants. Ms. Parsons was charged a $10.00 a year security fee. This fee, like the one in Holley, was for the purpose of maintaining a security system. Although Ms. Parsons paid $50 a year less than the plaintiff in Holley, the $10 fee could establish a contractual duty for Fly-by-

Night to provide the plaintiff with protection against third party crimes occurring on the defendant's premises.

If the duty is not contractually established, Fly–by–Night may still be under a duty to protect the tenant from the results of reasonably foreseeable criminal conduct. <u>See Ten Associates v. Mc-Cutchen</u>.

For example, in <u>Stribling v. Chicago Housing Authority</u>, the plaintiff was a tenant whose apartment was burglarized on three separate occasions. On each occasion, the thief entered the plaintiff's apartment through a wall shared with a vacant adjacent apartment. The landlord negligently failed to secure the apartment after the first burglary, despite many demands by the plaintiff. The court held that the landlord was liable because the second and third burglaries were reasonably foreseeable.

The second paragraph should be combined with the third. That sentence provides a transition from the first paragraph and introduces the issue illustrated by the third.

III. *Paragraph Transitions*

Transitional phrases or sentences are often used to show the relationships between an individual paragraph and the preceding and succeeding ones. They tend to appear either at the end or at the beginning of paragraphs and are used to summarize what has been covered and introduce what is to come. They are particularly important in long or complex discussions to prevent a reader from feeling lost. Although you can expect your reader to read carefully, you should not expect that reader to do your work, to provide the clarity, structure and development which are not in the paper itself. You can avoid overreliance on your reader if you use transitional phrases or words to show how a paragraph advances your discussion.

Sometimes transitions announce a change in subject. Thus they can underscore a shift in topic which might otherwise be announced in a heading or topic sentence. Sometimes transitions track the steps in an argument, informing the reader, for example, that a case just described is now going to be distinguished or that a rule just discussed will now be applied. There are numerous ways to effect these transitions.

1. You may want to raise a new point with a sentence that summarizes a completed discussion while relating it to the upcoming issue.

> Although the prosecution will have little difficulty showing assault, it may have trouble proving battery.

2. You may want to keep track of the issues with enumeration.

> The second exception to the employee-at-will rule arises when there are implied contractual provisions such as terms in an employee handbook.

3. You may want to show the relation between paragraphs by showing a substantive connection.

> A. There is no causal connection offered to link Joan's prior passivity with her present aggressive activity.
>
> > A similar causal element was missing in the expert testimony on the battered wife syndrome offered in Buhrle v. Wyoming.

OR

> B. The Tarasoff holding has been applied in this jurisdiction.

4. You may want to link paragraphs with a simple transitional word or phrase showing the logical connection one paragraph has with another.

> Therefore, although a court will not enforce that part of the contract which is unconscionable, it will generally refuse to award punitive damages.
>
> > In Frostifresh, however, the court awarded the seller not only the net cost but also a reasonable profit.

Since transitions play so central a role in showing the reader how you are building the argument, it is especially important that your transitions be thoughtful. You should not mechanically insert transitional words or phrases between your paragraphs without thinking about the relationship you wish to establish. Imprecise, erroneous, or ambiguous transitions can be misleading because they point the reader in the wrong rather than the right direction. The list of transitional expressions provided below, therefore, should be used cautiously. Although it supplies some of the phrases that establish particular kinds of logical relationships, you must still check that the transition you have selected is the one most appropriate for the connection you wish to establish. You should also be sure that you are entitled to use the transition. For example, the word "therefore" signifies a conclusion. Yet, before you can persuasively signal your conclusion with "therefore," you must be sure that you have provided supporting reasons.

Transitional Expressions

1. To signal an amplification or addition:

> and, also, moreover, in other words, furthermore, in addition, equally important, next, finally, besides, similarly, another reason, likewise.

2. To signal an analogy:

    similarly, analogously, likewise, again, also.

3. To signal an alternative:

    in contrast, but, still, however, contrary to, though, although, yet, nevertheless, conversely, alternatively, on the other hand.

4. To signal a conclusion:

    therefore, thus, hence, as a result, accordingly, in short, consequently, finally, to summarize.

5. To establish a causal consequence or result:

    because, since, therefore, thus, consequently, then, as a result, it follows, so.

6. To introduce an example:

    for example, for instance, specifically, as an illustration, namely, that is, particularly, in particular.

7. To establish temporal relationships:

    next, then, as soon as, until, last, later, earlier, before, afterward, after, when, recently, eventually, subsequently, simultaneously, at the same time, thereafter, since.

8. To signal a concession:

    granted that, no doubt, to be sure, it is true, although.

Exercise 8–A

1. Reread Exercise 6–B. Write a topic sentence synthesizing the holdings in Dale v. New City Hospital and Histrionic v. Credit Inc.

2. Reread Exercise 2–H. Write a topic sentence synthesizing the holdings in cases 5, 6 and 7.

3. Read the following discussion. Then provide topic and transition sentences where appropriate.

    Ellen Warren must show that Diethylstilbestrol (DES) was more than a merely possible cause of her various injuries in order to present her negligence claim against the manufacturers to the jury. Since statistics show that DES is a probable cause of adenosis, distortion of the uterus, and cervical cancer, the question of the defendant's liability for Ellen Warren's injuries should be presented to the jury. However, Ellen Warren will have a harder time showing that DES is more than a merely possible cause of her infertility, although she can probably establish this also.

    In Wilkins v. Kramer Service Inc., the defendant negligently cut the plaintiff's skin. Two years later a skin cancer developed at the spot. Two medical experts testified. One said the cancer was not caused by the cut; the other said it was possible that the cut caused the cancer, but the chances were only one out of one hundred. The court ruled that this evidence was not sufficient to permit the jury to find the defendant liable for the cancer. The court held that a plaintiff must show more than a merely possible connection between the defendant's negligence and the plaintiff's injury to permit a jury to consider whether the negligence caused the injury.

Ellen Warren's evidence includes the FDA decision to ban DES for use during pregnancy; the statistics that a substantial percentage of women exposed to DES develop cancer; and her doctors' diagnoses that adenosis, distortion of the uterus, and cervical cancer are characteristic of DES exposure. These facts demonstrate that DES is more than merely a possible cause of those injuries.

Ellen Warren's family has a hereditary history of cancer. Because heredity does not seem a more likely cause than DES, particularly in light of Warren's combination of DES-related disorders, this argument does not negate the evidence that DES is a probable cause of her cancer.

While DES causes or contributes to infertility in a substantial percentage of exposyed women, many women are infertile without exposure. Moreover, Warren has suffered some other reproductive disorders that may be to blame. Nevertheless, given her combination of DES-related symptoms and the statistical evidence the DES contributes to infertility, Warren still has more evidence of causation than Wilkins did and should be able to present the issue to the jury.

IV. *Paragraph Coherence*

A paragraph has coherence if it promotes continuity of thought. Even a unified paragraph—that is, a paragraph with a single topic—can seem choppy and disconnected if the sentences are not in a logical order or are not clearly related to each other.

Paragraph coherence depends in part on clear paragraph organization; you must arrange your sentences in a logical order. If the final sentence of a paragraph contains information that the reader needs in order to understand the first sentence, then the paragraph will be hard to understand, regardless of the clarity of these sentences.

Although logical sequence promotes easy comprehension, it alone does not ensure paragraph coherence. Smooth progression from one sentence to the next often requires you to use connectors or transitions, just as you use transition sentences to get from one paragraph to the next. Sometimes, of course, you can juxtapose two ideas and feel confident the reader can infer their logical connection. For example, a reader can probably infer the connection between the following sentences: "You said you put the check in the mail a week ago. I have not received it." The discrepancy between these two events alerts the reader to the writer's skepticism about the first assertion, even without a connector like "but." Sometimes, however, the specific relation of one sentence to the next is not obvious. In this situation, part of your second sentence must be devoted to giving directions which enable your reader to perceive an otherwise buried connection. One way writers do this is by repeating key words or by using transition words and connectors. Another way writers promote continuity of thought is to overlap their sentences so that a new sentence begins with a brief summary of an idea in the prior sentence. By moving from old, known information to new information, the writer links the sentences together and moves the reader forward.

Of course, coherence on the paragraph level cannot be achieved without sentence coherence, that is, there must be clear and logical connections between the parts, even the words, of a single sentence. See Chapter Nine for suggestions on how to achieve sentence coherence.

A. *Paragraph Coherence: Organization*

The sense of a paragraph becomes clearer when ideas are put in a logical order. What is logical depends, of course, on the purpose of a paragraph. If, for example, you are trying to narrate events, such as in a Statement of Facts, you would probably use a chronological order. If you are developing an analysis, however, the order of ideas will probably follow either a deductive or inductive pattern of reasoning. Although thought processes are frequently inductive—that is, an examination of particulars enables you to formulate a generalization—most written arguments benefit from a deductive presentation—that is, the argument opens with a generalization which is then supported by particulars.

When ideas are not in a logical order, as in the following paragraph, the sense of that paragraph is hard to understand.

> A mental hospital has a duty to provide its patients with such care as would be reasonable to prevent self-injury given their individual mental problems. Stallman. Ms. Brown was a nonviolent suicidal patient whose cure had been progressing steadily during her sixteen month hospital stay. The standard of care is based upon the reasonable anticipation of the probability of self-inflicted harm. Gregory. In Stallman, the court found the duty breached when a violently suicidal woman was left unattended for 30 minutes. Based on Ms. Brown's progress, the doctors would not have reasonably anticipated her suicide.

If the writer had discussed the test defining a hospital's duty of care before launching into the facts of Brown, i.e., if the ideas had been organized deductively, this paragraph would have been easier to understand.

> A mental hospital has a duty to provide its patients with such care as would be reasonable to prevent self-injury given their individual mental problems. Stallman. The standard of care is based upon the reasonable anticipation of the probability of self-inflicted harm. Gregory. In Stallman, the court found

the duty breached when a violently suicidal woman was left unattended for thirty minutes. Ms. Brown was a nonviolent suicidal patient whose cure had been progressing steadily during her sixteen month hospital stay. Based on Ms. Brown's progress, the doctors would not have reasonably anticipated her suicide.

B. Paragraph Coherence: Sentence Transitions

1. Transition Words and Coherence

For a reader to follow your thought processes, you must provide transitions that signal where you are taking your analysis next. After finishing a discussion of a general rule, you must clearly indicate to the reader that you now want to explain an exception. If you have just described two requirements for a cause of action, announce that you are now going on to the third. Transitions (perhaps "nevertheless" in the first instance, "in addition" or just "third" in the second) will tell the reader what you are doing.

The following passage is an example of a paragraph which lacks coherence because the sentences are not explicitly connected to each other.

> Express oral contracts between unmarried, cohabiting couples are enforceable. Implied contracts in these situations are unenforceable. Vague terms render a contract unenforceable. Jessica Stone and Michael Asch expressly agreed that Mr. Asch would repay his share of their living expenses once he began practicing law in exchange for Ms. Stone's support for three years. They entered into an enforceable contract. Ms. Stone may bring an action for its breach. Ms. Stone's understanding that Mr. Asch would support her during graduate school is unenforceable since it is an implied agreement. Mr. Asch's boast to "take care of" Ms. Stone forever is too vague to be enforced.

The sense of this passage would be clearer if more transitional expressions were used to establish the logical relationship one sentence has with another.

> Although express oral contracts between unmarried, cohabiting couples are enforceable, implied contracts in these situations are unenforceable. Vague terms also render a contract unenforceable. Because Jessica Stone and Michael Asch expressly agreed that Mr. Asch would repay his share of their living expenses once he began practicing law in exchange for Ms. Stone's support for three years, they entered into an enforceable contract. Ms. Stone may, therefore, bring an action for its breach. Ms. Stone's understanding that Mr. Asch would support her during graduate school is unenforceable, however, since it is an implied agreement. Similarly, Mr. Asch's boast to "take care of" Ms. Stone forever is too vague to be enforced.

2. *Other Connectors*

Transition words are used to show the reader the logical connection between sentences. Other kinds of connectors orient your reader in time or place or inform your reader that you are looking at the material from a particular point of view or perspective. The underlined phrases in the following passages illustrate the use of these kinds of connectors.

> During Mardi Gras week 1989, Jeffrey Bond boarded a trolley in New Orleans and sat down in the rear of the car. At a later stop, three teenage boys, Joseph Claiborne, Robert Landry, and Thomas Vallee, boarded the trolley. The four boys wore stockings over their heads and streamers around their necks. They were obnoxiously loud and drunk. At one point, Claiborne, who was 6'7" tall, turned to Bond and demanded, "What are you looking at?" The two other boys gathered in behind Claiborne, blocking Bond's exit through the aisle. Given these circumstances, Bond thought it best not to antagonize this group of teenagers; thus he averted his eyes and kept quiet. From a tactical point of view, however, this proved to be a mistake. Claiborne started screaming, "Answer me when I speak to you!" Then he stood up, drew a gun, and shot Bond in the leg.

3. *Overlapping Sentences*

Cohesion is often achieved when a new sentence opens with a brief reference to all or part of the prior sentence. In other words, you begin a sentence with old information and then move on to new information. This overlapping of sentences leads your reader gently into the new idea. The underlined phrases in the following passage illustrate overlapping.

> Ms. Moultry has been addicted to crack for the past two years. During this time, she gave birth to a son, a baby born with a positive toxicology. After his birth, Ms. Moultry placed her child into temporary foster care so that she could enter an in-patient drug rehabilitation program. While there, she repeatedly said that her resolve to come "clean" would weaken if she was denied visitation with her infant. To prevent such a relapse, Ms. Moultry's foster care worker sanctioned visitation. The initial visits went smoothly; the foster parents were supportive of Ms. Moultry and Ms. Moultry felt good about the care her baby was receiving. Then Ms. Moultry learned she tested positive for the AIDS virus. When the foster parents learned she was HIV positive, they refused to admit her into their home. Ms. Moultry disappeared three days later.

4. *Coherence and Complex Sentences*

Complex sentences—sentences with a dependent and independent clause—often establish relationships more economically than do compound sentences—sentences consisting of two independent clauses joined by a coordinating conjunction. Dependent clauses begin with subordinating conjunctions which establish that clause's temporal or logical connection with the main sentence. Therefore, complex sentences clarify relationships between ideas within a sentence. There are many subordinating conjunctions, but some key ones are because, since, if, when, while, although.

In contrast, independent clauses joined by the coordinating conjunction "and" are clauses which are juxtaposed but not related. "And" is a vague connector; it joins sentences without establishing a logical connection between them.

Example: Richard began suffering from arthritis in 1981, and he stopped working.

Rewrite: Because Richard began suffering from arthritis in 1981, he stopped working.

5. Coherence and the Repetition of Key Words

Continuity is better served by the repetition of key words than by elegant variation. For example, transitions and key words effectively bridge these paragraphs.

Thus the only factual distinction between Hughes and this case seems to be the emotional nature of Mr. Jackson's response.

Emotions, however, are at the core of many family matters, especially those involving finances.

It is also important to use consistent terminology when referring to the parties to a suit. In the following sentence, it is unclear whether the court is referring to one person or two persons. It is also unclear whether the court is referring to the particular defendant before it or is stating a principle of law:

In Windley, the court stated that if a person has any personal or financial interest in bringing trade to the seller, then the defendant was not acting solely as an agent for the buyer.

Some of the ambiguity in this sentence also comes from the change in verb tense. Propositions of law should be stated in the present tense while the facts of a case should be described in the past tense. Thus, the sentence should be rewritten in one of the following two ways.

In Windley, the court stated that if a person has any personal or financial interest in bringing trade to the seller, then that person is not acting solely as an agent for the buyer.

or

In Windley, the court stated that if the defendant had any personal or financial interest in bringing trade to the seller, then the defendant was not acting solely as an agent for the buyer.

Exercise 8–B

1. Reorder the sentences in the following paragraph to improve organization.

In <u>Kelly</u>, the court found that the defendant, who had demonstrated a long and broad experience with the legal process, had knowingly and intelligently waived counsel, although the trial judge made no detailed inquiry. <u>Kelly v. State</u>, 663 P.2d 967, 969 (Alaska App. 1983). In some cases a defendant may be permitted to waive his right without detailed inquiry. <u>Id</u>. Furthermore, unlike Miller, Kelly availed himself of some of the services of court appointed counsel while defending himself. <u>Id</u>. Here, although Miller stated that his mother had married an attorney after his father's death, this cannot be construed as meaningful legal experience. Because a waiver of the right to counsel may not be lightly inferred, <u>Ledbetter v. State</u>, 581 P.2d 1129, 1131 (Alaska 1978), the degree of the court's inquiry must be tailored to the particular characteristics of the accused. <u>O'Dell v. Anchorage</u>, 576 P.2d 104, 108 (Alaska 1978).

2. Add transition words to improve the coherence of the following passage.

The degree of judicial inquiry will also depend on the complexities and gravity of the legal issues raised by the charge against the defendant. <u>O'Dell v. Anchorage</u>, 576 P.2d 104, 108 (Alaska 1978). Traffic misdemeanor cases are easily understood by lay persons and the consequences are usually not severe. <u>Id</u>. The inquiry in such cases need not be extensive. <u>Id</u>. Miller, if convicted, faces a mandatory jail term and not a simple parking fine. The severity of the charges mandated a more extensive inquiry by the judge.

3. Rewrite to improve the coherence of this paragraph. Use transition words, connectors, subordinate clauses, and sentence overlapping.

The state's suppression of evidence in a criminal prosecution may constitute a violation of the defendant's due process rights. Whether the defendant's rights were in fact violated depends on four conditions. The state must be responsible for the loss of the evidence. The evidence must have had exculpatory value that was apparent before it was lost. Then the defendant must show that he would be unable to obtain comparable evidence by any other reasonable means. If the evidence was only potentially exculpatory, the defendant must demonstrate that it was lost due to bad faith on the part of the state. Rich Kant can show that the state was responsible for the loss of the alleged murder weapon, the car. The car disappeared before it was examined. Its exculpatory value was never demonstrated. It would be difficult to determine what comparable evidence might consist of. The record offers little to prove that the loss of the potentially exculpatory car was due to bad faith on the part of the police. Kant cannot meet the conditions for determining violation of his due process rights because of state suppression. The court will most likely deny the motion for dismissal.

4. Rewrite the following paragraph to improve its organization and coherence.

The parties agree that First Sergeant Valiant of C. Company first picked up the phone to learn who was being called. During the first few seconds after picking up the phone, Valiant overheard a conversation between members of His Company that began "Do you have any of the good stuff?" He recognized the speakers, who were later court martialed on drug charges. Valiant had not "intercepted" the conversation. The sergeant's act in picking up the phone must be considered in the ordinary course of business. When the use of an extension comes within the ordinary course of business, no unlawful interception of the defendants' communication occurs. When there are several extension phones, as there are in the orderly room, it is not unusual that when a call comes in, a person will pick up the receiver to see who the call is for.

V. *Paragraph Development*

You cannot write clearly if you assume too much knowledge on your reader's part. Your papers must be self-explanatory; they must follow through on an idea, consider its meaning and significance, and come to a logical conclusion. Do not cut your discussions short; develop them. It is only in the development that the meaning of a paragraph becomes apparent.

The principal methods of development include: A) comparison, B) illustration, C) classification, D) definition, E) cause and effect, and F) description and chronological narration. Frequently, these methods of development occur in tandem. If you are defining prosecutorial misconduct, for example, you might define it by offering illustrations of what constitutes misconduct and what does not.

A. *Comparison*

Paragraphs developed by comparison are common in legal writing since the principle of stare decisis requires factually similar cases to be decided by application of the same rule of law and to result in the same decision. By comparing and contrasting the facts of your problem with those of the precedents, you will be able to show how the rules of those cases fit your case.

For a comparison to be fruitful, you must compare things which are not only alike, but which are relevant and significant. For example, in a claim involving a hospital's negligent failure to prevent a mentally ill patient's suicide, a central issue is whether the patient received reasonable supervision given that patient's medical history. Thus, it might be fruitful to contrast the care of a patient who had attempted suicide twice to the care of a mentally ill patient who had no history of self-inflicted injury, as the difference is germane to the issue of supervision. On the other hand, it would be fruitless to spend time establishing that one patient did watercolors as occupational therapy and the other did weaving because the difference is irrelevant to the issue of reasonable supervision in light of the medical history. A comparison is useful, therefore, only if you are comparing relevant and significant things.

You must also take care to compare like things. It would be meaningless to compare the supervision of an acutely depressed patient with the supervision of a patient with chronic back pain because one condition involves a patient's psychiatric history and the other involves a patient's medical history. You must, therefore, compare similar things for a comparison to be illuminating.

It is generally easier to avoid the impact of a previous decision by distinguishing your facts from the precedent facts than by asking a court to overrule its previous decision. Thus, comparisons are as central a device in writing a persuasive argument as they are in predicting the outcome of a suit in a memorandum. In the following example, the author distinguishes Carol Smith's situation from that of the victim in a decided case in order to overcome that adverse decision.

Example: Comparison

The right of confrontation includes the literal right to confront adverse witnesses face-to-face when they testify. <u>Dowdell v. United States</u>; <u>Mattox v. United States</u>. Thus, lower courts have repeatedly held that procedures which prohibit face-to-face confrontation violate the defendant's constitutional right of confrontation. In <u>Powell v. Texas</u> and <u>Long v. Texas</u>, the defendants' confrontational rights were held to be violated where children who were victims of sexual abuse testified on videotape without having to hear or see the defendants. However, in <u>State v. Sheppard</u>, the court permitted testimony without face-to-face confrontation because the crime involved was incest and the witness was a child testifying against her father.

Carol Smith's situation is distinguishable from that of the victim in <u>Sheppard</u>. Not only had the defendant in <u>Sheppard</u> lost his confrontation rights because he had physically threatened and abused his child, but the crime was more serious than that charged in the present case. Williams is charged with lewd conduct, not incest. In addition, he did not physically threaten or abuse Carol Smith. Thus Carol's situation is more akin to that of the victims of sexual abuse in <u>Powell</u> and <u>Long</u>. Although the trial court permitted Carol to testify without being able to see or hear Williams, the Court of Appeals will probably find the defendant's confrontation right was abridged.

B. *Illustration*

Paragraphs may be developed by illustration. A general principle, the meaning of which is abstract, can be made concrete, and thereby clarified, by examples. In the following passage, two illustrations clarify when a party owes a duty to an incidental beneficiary of a contract.

Example: Illustration

A putative wrongdoer may be liable to one with whom he or she does not have a contractual relation if by acting or failing to act, the wrongdoer works an injury to the non-contracting party. The court in Rensselaer offers two examples of a putative wrongdoer's liability to a third party. An auto manufacturer may be liable to third parties who are injured as the result of its failure to inspect. Similarly, an engineer is liable to a casual bystander who receives burns as a result of that engineer's failure to shut off the steam. See H.R. Moch Co. v. Rensselaer Water Co.

C. Classification

Classification is a process which involves locating the class to which an object belongs in order to gain greater understanding of that object. Classifying requires you to identify the common characteristics of that category or class. After identifying the class by articulating the significant property shared by all the members of that class, you may want to divide that class into subclasses. In subdividing, the relationships between classes become sharper because division clarifies which classes are subordinate to others and which are coordinate with others.

In law, classifying is routinely done. Lawyers classify factual situations as particular causes of action. They also develop legal arguments by classifying their clients' facts as falling or failing to fall under the categories established in a decision or a statute. When courts interpret law, they do it by formulating their holdings in such a way that the classifications involved have either a broad or narrow reach. When courts make law, they erect new categories. Thus, classification is an essential part of legal analysis and legal writing.

Classifying is often crucial in attempting to clarify and establish a legal conclusion, as in the following example.

Example: Classification

The issue is whether Pappagano is violating the state's Wild Animal Act by keeping birds in his aviary. The statute prohibits the capture or restraint of wild animals and applies only to animals known in the common law as *ferae naturae*. This classification consists of animals usually found at liberty. J.W. Blackstone, Commentaries 349 (1845). The statute does not apply to domesticated animals, which are those that are accustomed to living in association with humans and that are not disposed to escape. Id. Pappagano keeps birds such as robins, blue jays, and sparrows in his aviary. Because the birds are usually found at liberty, flying freely, and migrating with the seasons, they are *ferae naturae*, and Pappagano is violating the statute.

D. *Definition*

Definition provides the meaning of a term by establishing its borders, that is, by announcing what it does and does not refer to. In clarifying what is and is not distinctive about a term or concept, definition further refines classification and strengthens it as an analytical tool. A formal definition begins by placing the term within a class and then differentiating it from other members of that class. Sometimes a term requires an entire paragraph before it is adequately defined. Such extended definitions are developed or built by example, comparison, analysis, stipulation, or function (defining what something is by describing what it does).

Example 1: Definition

> A wrongful threat exists when one party to a contract threatens to breach the contract by withholding goods unless the other party agrees to a further demand. The court in Austin found a wrongful threat when a subcontractor would not deliver on a first subcontract unless it got a second contract. It is, however, not wrong to threaten if there is a legitimate contract dispute. In Muller, a delay in construction increased the costs of construction. The builder said the defendant must pay those costs or face a slowdown. Defendant then served notice to terminate the construction contract. The court found there was no wrongful threat since the threat to terminate the contract was related to a relevant dispute about the contract.

Definition can be a method of persuasion in legal writing. Although the meaning of a rule is partially fixed by its wording or its application, there is frequently room for maneuver, room for your own explanation of what is or is not meant by the term. In the following paragraph, the author argues that under even a broad definition of delivery, Davis was improperly served with a summons.

Example 2: Definition

> Generally, service under C.P.L.R. § 308[1] is accomplished by delivering the summons within the state to the person to be served. However, a line of cases has interpreted "delivery" more broadly and upheld service under C.P.L.R. § 308[1] even if the summons was not handed to the person to be served. Thus, in Daniels v. Eastman, the court upheld service although the process server erroneously handed the envelope to Dr. Zippen instead of Dr. Lutker when the two were sitting together. The court ruled that the erroneous delivery and the subsequent redelivery to the intended recipient were "so close in time and space that [they] can be classified as part of the same act." Id. The delivery to Ms. Jones, however, was not so close in time and space to the redelivery to Mr. Davis as to constitute one act. Whereas, in Daniels, Dr. Lutker was sitting with Dr. Zippen at the time of delivery, Davis was not even present when the process server deliv-

ered the summons to Ms. Jones. Moreover, Ms. Jones did not redeliver to him until later in the day.

E. Cause and Effect

A cause and effect analysis requires a writer to explain the reasons for an occurrence. Because one frequently engages in causal analysis of facts, it is important to be alert to the complexity and subtlety of establishing and developing causal connections. Although a cause must precede an event, you cannot assume that whatever precedes an event causes it. Even if event X precedes event Y, X may be entirely unrelated to Y. You should not confuse seriality and causality, i.e., the temporal and the logical orders. To do so is to commit the fallacy of *post hoc ergo propter hoc* (after this therefore because of this). It is also important not to be too superficial or simplistic about identifying causes. A cause can be either necessary, contributory, or sufficient. A necessary cause is one which must be present for an effect to occur but which cannot alone produce that effect. A contributory cause is one that may produce an effect but cannot produce it alone. A sufficient cause is one that alone produces the effect. Do not, therefore, identify one cause but ignore others of equal significance. Many events involve multiple causes.

Example: Cause & Effect

Not only was Bob's failure to repair his refrigerator a breach of his duty to protect a business invitee against dangers he knew or should have known about, but that breach was the proximate cause of Bull's injury. When the refrigerator tray broke, frozen hamburgers spilled onto the counter, knocking the mugs that were there onto the floor. Bull slipped on the spilt liquid and fell onto the shards of the broken mugs. As a result of this fall, he broke his ankle and cut his hands. Therefore, there was a reasonably close causal connection between the duty breached and the resulting injury. Bob's failure to have the refrigerator unit inspected and repaired was the proximate cause of the accident from which Bull suffered injuries.

F. Narration and Chronology

For a paragraph concerned with narration—as in the Statement of Facts—you will probably want to develop events in clear chronological order, that is, the order of their occurrence. You would also follow chronology to describe a process; for example, you would relate the steps necessary for filing a suit in small claims court in the order required by the court. When writing a chronological narrative, be careful not to confuse the reader by changing the sequence of events or by omitting important events.

In a descriptive paragraph, you may need to convey to your reader the setting in which some event occurred by establishing the location of persons or objects in a scene. Although there is no one way to describe a person, a place, or the location of persons or things in a scene, you will need to supply such spatial directions as "to the right," "in the foreground," or "five yards from the fire hydrant."

———

In the heat of creation, you may not be aware of how you developed a paragraph. At the less frenzied stage of rewriting, however, you may become aware that an idea needs explication and that one of these methods of development would clarify and strengthen your argument.

Exercise 8–C

The following exercise is a review exercise of some of the principles covered in earlier chapters and in Appendix A. Reread Exercise 2–G; then read and edit the following sample answer to the Peterson exercise in Chapter Two. Consider the following questions:

1. Does the statement of the issue include enough information about the rule of law and relevant facts?

2. Does the "thesis" or introductory paragraph end with a conclusion that relates the law to the facts of the case? If not, write one.

3. Can you eliminate wordiness and improve sentence coherence?

4. Do the topic sentences effectively introduce the point of each paragraph?

5. Does the writer include the relevant law and facts from the precedent in the second paragraph?

6. What problems with paragraph unity does the third paragraph have?

———

The issue that we must explore in this case is the question whether the father is responsible for the injuries resulting from his son's misuse of a hammer. The applicable rule would be that a person has a duty to protect another against unreasonable risks. A person who breaches this duty is negligent and liable for injuries resulting from his negligence. It must be shown that leaving the tools in the basement was an unreasonable risk.

In the present case, the father left his tools in the basement. Tools are not "obviously and intrinsically dangerous." The case must be discussed in light of relevant precedent. The Smith case clearly applies to the case herein. In Smith, the court sustained defendant's demurrer to the complaint, challenging the sufficiency of the complaint. In Smith, the children were playing with a golf club. Many similarities obviously can be pointed out between <u>Smith</u> and the present case. The children were identical in age. The instruments were left in an area played in by children; the accidents occurred without warning the victims.

Plaintiff herein may claim that the tools should not have been left where children could reach them. Defendant may state that in <u>Smith</u>, the golf club was left in the backyard, also a play area for children. The golf club was not held to be intrinsically dangerous. We must also be concerned with whether tools, although not inherently dangerous, can be considered more dangerous in the hands of a child than a golf club. Tools are like a golf club because they are not weapons; however, they may be misused by a child.

Chapter Nine
Sentence Structure

As discussed in the chapter on paragraphs, the flow of a discussion depends on the effective use of topic and transition sentences, paragraph organization, and transition words. But coherence on the paragraph level cannot be achieved unless there is coherence on the sentence level as well. Poor diction, grammar, and sentence construction break a chain of thought by forcing readers to stop to decipher the meaning of a particular sentence. Thus, even if law students and lawyers do everything else right (display deft organization and incisive analogies), they are not communicating effectively if their sentences need translation.

It is surprising—but true—how many lawyers have sentence level problems, a phenomenon caused in part by the complex ideas that are the core of many legal documents. To write about these complex matters clearly, to communicate effectively with such diverse audiences as law professors, clients, colleagues, judges, witnesses, and juries, law students and lawyers need to pay special attention to syntax: they must make clear and logical connections between the parts, even the words, of a single sentence. The bulk of this chapter is, therefore, devoted to giving you specific suggestions that will help you avoid common sentence level problems. Before enumerating these "do's and don'ts," however, it might be fruitful to reflect a little on what a sentence actually is.

A sentence is traditionally defined as a set of words that expresses a complete thought and that contains, at the very least, a subject (a noun) and a predicate (a verb). Yet this is a somewhat bloodless definition that directs a writer to grammatical requirements of a sentence at the expense of giving a writer a "feel" for readable sentence structures.

It takes only a moment's reflection to realize that many sentences are narratives about real characters who perform real acts. Less apparent is the impact this realization should have on sentence structure. Yet the fact that sentences are often narratives about characters and their actions should lead you to write sentences that follow the action of the narrative rather than sentences that bury the characters and their actions in passive voice constructions or that begin with abstract nouns. Sentences are clearest when the character in the sentence is the subject of the sentence and when the verb in the sentence describes what the character did, does, or should do.[1]

In this regard, you should be aware that many sentences about abstract ideas—principles of law, for example—are nonetheless also sentences with characters who perform actions. Sometimes these characters are mistakenly concealed:

> Contractual choice-of-forum clauses are "prima facie valid" and should be enforced unless it can be shown that enforcement would be unreasonable or that the clause was affected by fraud or overreaching.

The characters in this sentence go unidentified, although a reader could guess at their identities. The character who should enforce a choice of forum clause is the court, and the character who must show unreasonableness or fraud is the resisting party to the suit.

Because your reader probably needs information about each party's responsibilities, the sentence should chart those parties and their obligations, as in the following rewrite:

> Because a contractual choice-of-forum clause is "prima facie valid," a court will enforce it unless the resisting party can show that enforcement would be unreasonable or that the other party to the suit procured the clause through fraud or overreaching.

Of course, not all sentences are about actions. Some describe people, things or conditions. Others are about ideas and concepts. Sentences about ideas often have abstract nouns as their subjects and frequently define or comment on that subject, as in, "Truth is Beauty," or "The necessity of protecting the first amendment rights of the press from the chilling effects of defamation actions makes summary judgment an appropriate procedure." In most analytic writing, some sentences will inevitably begin with abstract subjects. Yet abstract subjects, or long subjects which present a lot of new and complex information, tend to strain the reader's concentration. To alleviate that strain, you should begin

1. See Joseph M. Williams, Style: Ten Lessons in Clarity and Grace, (3rd ed. 1989) for a fuller discussion of some of the ideas in this chapter.

as many of these sentences as possible with easily comprehensible, short, and specific subjects: "Summary judgment is an appropriate procedure for protecting the first amendment rights of the press from the chilling effects of defamation actions."

A first-year law student might worry that short, specific subjects and simple active voice sentences will fail to impress professors, associates, clients, and courts. Yet legal writing is often a lawyer's single opportunity to tell a client's story and to reveal its legal significance to audiences that are pressed for time and unwilling to translate archaic diction and contorted sentence constructions. Thus, simple and direct sentences are more effective than convoluted sentences. In fact, the ability to write about complicated matters in a straightforward manner is the art of lawyering.

The following suggestions will help you write clear and persuasive sentences.

1. *Whenever Possible, Use Short, Concrete Subjects*

A subject is that part of a sentence about which something is being said. It may consist of a single word or of many words (a simple subject and all its attendant modifiers). The easiest sentences to read, however, have short subjects that use concrete rather than abstract nouns. No reader wants to wade through a fifteen word subject, comprised in the following sentence of "use" and its modifiers.

> Defense counsel's use of racially discriminatory preemptory challenges arising out of a state-created statutory privilege deprives excluded jurors of their equal protection rights.

Your reader would much prefer you to start with a short, concrete noun.

> Jurors are deprived of their equal protection rights by defense counsel's use of racially discriminatory preemptory challenges arising out of a state-created statutory privilege.

2. *Use Short, Active Predicates—Not Nominalizations*

The predicate is that part of a sentence that says something about what the subject is or is doing. Sentences are more dynamic and more concise when you use short verbs that express actions rather than states of existence.

> **Not:** The actions of the transit authority in firing appellants for criticizing fare increases were a violation of the appellants' first and fourteenth amendment rights.

> **But:** The transit authority violated the appellants' first and fourteenth amendment rights when it fired them for criticizing fare increases.

Sentences are more forceful if they focus on a verb rather than on a noun. Yet many writers convert verbs into cumbersome nouns called nominalizations. Instead of writing "the judge decided to continue the trial," they write "the judge made a decision to continue the trial." Instead of writing "the defendant knew injury could result from his negligence," they will write "the defendant had knowledge that injury could result from his negligence." The latter sentence, with the nominalization "had knowledge," dissipates the energy of the verb.

3. *Whenever Possible, Use Active Rather Than Passive Voice*

In the introduction to this chapter, we suggested that sentences focus on characters and actions. To achieve such a focus, you should write most of your sentences in the active voice, that is, you should follow a subject-verb-object sequence (actor—action—object of action). Active voice sentences are easier to read because they begin with a short specific subject who then explicitly does something to someone. They have the additional virtue of being somewhat shorter than passive voice sentences.

A passive construction follows an object-verb-subject sequence (object of action-action-actor). It is constructed from forms of the verb "be" and the past participle of the main verb. In passive construction, you do not have to include the actor to have a grammatical sentence, although you risk obscuring the narrative if you end the sentence without identifying the actor.

Passive voice may be appropriate, however, if you do not know or do not want to emphasize the actor or subject, if the object of the sentence is more important than the actor, or if the actor is obvious, as in "a new mayor was elected." Finally, passive voice sentences are appropriate when they promote paragraph coherence. Beginning a new sentence with the object of the prior sentence is one way of overlapping and connecting sentences.

a. Unclear Use of Passive Voice

Example: In balancing the interests, full factual development is needed in order to ensure the fair administration of justice. (Who needs full factual development? Who is balancing?)

Rewrite: To balance the interests, the court needs full factual development in order to ensure the fair administration of justice.

b. Wordy Passive Voice

Example: A duty of care to the plaintiff was breached by the defendant when the slippery floor was left unmopped by the defendant.

Rewrite: When the defendant failed to mop the slippery floor, she breached her duty of care to the plaintiff.

c. Appropriate Use of Passive Voice

Example: Under Rule 11 of the Federal Rules of Procedure, factual errors alone are not enough to justify sanctions. Sanctions would be granted, however, if the attorney knew there was no factual basis for the complaint. (Here, passive voice promotes paragraph coherence in that the second sentence picks up where the first left off and focuses the reader on what is really at issue: grounds for sanctions.)

4. *To Promote the Main Idea of the Sentence, Do Not Separate the Subject From the Verb With Intruding Phrases and Clauses*

A sentence does not begin to become an intelligible thought until the reader knows its subject and verb. When you separate the subject and the verb with a series of interrupting phrases and clauses, you leave the reader in limbo. To be reader-friendly, keep the subject of the sentence near the verb and the verb near the object. You can move interrupting phrases and clauses either to the beginning or the end of a sentence. You can also break the sentence in two.

Example: In 1987, the patients of Kent Family Planning Center, 50,000 in number, 35% of whom were adolescents, 50% of whom were at or below the poverty level, received in the mail a sex education manual published by the Center.

Rewrite: In 1987, Kent Family Planning Center published and mailed a sex education manual to its 50,000 patients, 35% of whom were adolescents, 50% of whom were at or below the poverty level.

Or

In 1987, Kent Family Planning Center published and mailed a sex education manual to its 50,000 patients. Thirty-five percent of these patients were adolescents, and fifty percent were at or below the poverty level.

Example: Officer Miller, who at the preliminary hearing on August 8 had said the car did not look like it had been in an accident, fell ill just before the trial was due to begin and never testified.

Rewrite: Although Officer Miller had said at the preliminary hearing on August 8 that the car did not look like it had been in an accident, he fell ill just before the trial was due to begin and never testified.

5. *Keep Your Sentences Relatively Short (under 25 words)*

Although varying the length of your sentences makes your writing less monotonous and more interesting, it is not a good idea to pack several ideas into one unreadably long sentence. If you have written a long and involved sentence, consider dividing it into shorter ones.

It is easy to split apart a compound sentence (two independent sentences joined by a coordinating conjunction). Instead of joining those sentences with a coordinating conjunction (and, but, or, nor, for, so, yet), put a period between them. You can also divide a long complex sentence (a sentence that has a dependent and independent clause). To do so, you must make the dependent clause independent by deleting the word that makes the clause dependent. These words are called subordinating conjunctions and include, among others, such often used words as *because, since, while, when,* and *although.* You can also shorten a sentence that ends with a long modifier tacked on to the end by converting that modifier into an independent sentence.

When you break long sentences into shorter ones, link your ideas with transition words that carry a preceding idea into the next sentence. Put these transition words early in the sentence so that the specific relation between the sentences is quickly apparent.

> **Example:** Although the Kent statute authorizes a court to sentence a defendant for criminal contempt, the statute does not define contempt, and the Kent courts have been left with the task of defining contempt, which they have interpreted as requiring intent to disobey the orders of a court, a requirement similar to those in other jurisdictions.

> **Rewrite:** Although the Kent statute authorizes a court to sentence a defendant for criminal contempt, the statute does not define contempt. The Kent courts have, <u>therefore</u>, been left with the task of defining contempt, which they have interpreted as requiring an intent to disobey the order of a court. This requirement is similar to those in other jurisdictions.

6. *Maintain Parallel Sentence Structure (Parallelism)*

Repeating a grammatical pattern is a good way of coordinating ideas in a sentence and maintaining control over complicated sentences. By making phrases or clauses syntactically similar, you are emphasizing that each element in a series is expressing a relation similar to that of the other elements in the series. Such coordination promotes clarity and continuity.

To maintain parallelism, nouns should be paired with nouns, infinitives with infinitives, noun clauses with noun clauses, etc. Faulty parallelism results when the second or third element breaks the anticipated pattern. "Hypocritical and a fraud" shows faulty parallelism, for instance, because an adjective is paired with a noun. Parallelism can be restored either by changing "hypocrit-

ical" to the noun "hypocrite" or "fraud" to the adjective "fraudulent."

> **Example:** She also served on the Board of the Fresh Air Fund, as a
> participant in the YMCA programs, and she worked for
> Planned Parenthood.

> **Rewrite:** She also served on the Board of the Fresh Air Fund,
> participated in the YMCA programs, and worked for
> Planned Parenthood.

> **Example:** An agency defense depends upon whether the agent was
> acting as an extension of the buyer and not for himself, if
> the agent was motivated by compensation, and finally,
> was salesman-like behavior exhibited.

> **Rewrite:** An agency defense depends upon whether the agent was
> acting as an extension of the buyer and not for himself,
> whether the agent was motivated by compensation, and
> finally, whether the agent acted like a salesman.

When you are coordinating ideas in a sentence, you normally
begin your coordination after the subject, that is, with the verb (as
in the first example above) or with the complement (as in the
second example). A complement is that part of the sentence
which completes the meaning of the subject and predicate. For
example, if you said only, "They made," your thought is unfin-
ished. You must add a complement to complete the idea: "They
made a last effort to settle out of court." If you have a series of
parallel complements or verbs + complements, you should build
your sentences so that the shortest unit of the series comes first
and the longest comes last, unless logical order dictates otherwise.

> **Example:** Some of the factors a court considers in determining the
> reasonableness of enforcing a forum selection clause are the residence
> and citizenship of the parties, the proximity of the contractual forum
> to probable witnesses, and the comparative convenience for the par-
> ties of litigating in each forum.

Here, the parallelism begins with the complements and the complements are arranged in order of length.

7. *Avoid Misplaced and Dangling Modifiers*

Aside from the primary parts of a sentence (the subject,
predicate, and complement), sentences have secondary parts called
modifiers. Modifiers are words, phrases, or clauses that describe
or define one of the primary parts or that further describe or
qualify one of the modifiers (as in, "a court may impose sanctions
upon an attorney who solicits clients that are still hospitalized").

Modifiers must be placed so that there is no uncertainty about
the word or phrase they modify. A modifier should, in general,
stand as close as possible to the word it modifies.

a. A modifier is misplaced if it modifies or refers to the wrong word or phrase. You can correct this situation by shifting the modifier closer to the word being modified. If this is not possible, rewrite the whole sentence.

Example: The court reached these conclusions by applying the "general acceptance" test for the admission of evidence resulting from the use of novel scientific procedures first articulated over sixty years ago. (The test was first articulated over sixty years ago, not the use of novel scientific procedures.)

Rewrite: The court reached these conclusions by applying the general acceptance test, which was first articulated over sixty years ago, for the admission of evidence resulting from the use of novel scientific procedures.

Or

The court reached these conclusions by applying the general acceptance test for the admission of evidence resulting from the use of novel scientific procedures. The test was first articulated over sixty years ago.

Example: Undercover agent Jones walked up to a group of teenagers standing in front of a store with the intention of buying some cocaine. (Did Jones intend to buy cocaine or did the teenagers?)

Rewrite: Intending to buy cocaine, undercover agent Jones walked up to a group of teenagers standing in front of a store.

b. A dangling modifier points to a word that is not in the sentence. Revise by inserting the word which is being modified.

Example: In Kent, a plaintiff whose spouse has been wrongfully killed has no cause of action for loss of consortium, denying, in effect, recovery for the destruction of the marital relationship.

Rewrite: In Kent, a plaintiff whose spouse has been wrongfully killed has no cause of action for loss of consortium. This ruling denies, in effect, recovery for the destruction of the marital relationship.

Example: After dismissing the claim, the plaintiff filed an appeal.

Rewrite: After the court dismissed the claim, the plaintiff filed an appeal.

8. *Identify and Punctuate Restrictive and Nonrestrictive Modifiers Correctly*

There are two kinds of modifiers, restrictive and nonrestrictive. Restrictive modifiers are those that narrow the denotation of a word, that is, they narrow the class of things or persons covered.

Example: Courts that recognize loss of parental consortium as a cause of action emphasize the child's best interest.

Here, the modifier—"that recognize loss of parental consortium as a cause of action"—is restrictive because it limits the number of courts under discussion.

A nonrestrictive modifier adds information about a primary element in the sentence but does not define that element.

> **Example:** Trial courts, unless faced with a case of first impression, tend not to make policy decisions but rather follow precedent.

In punctuating your modifiers, notice that nonrestrictive modifiers are surrounded by commas while restrictive modifiers are not. It is important to recognize the difference between restrictive and nonrestrictive modifiers, and to punctuate accordingly, because of the impact they have on the meaning of a sentence. If you write, "the court is opposed to loss of consortium damages that are speculative," you have limited the number of consortium damages to which the court is opposed. If you write, "the court is opposed to loss of consortium damages, which are speculative," you imply the court opposes all consortium damages because they are speculative in nature. Far too often litigation arises because of disputes over whether a modifier is restrictive or nonrestrictive, as in "the employee will not disclose to a competitor the names on the customer list which are not publicly known." Is the employee prohibited from revealing all names or only those names not publicly known?

Besides using commas to indicate restrictive and nonrestrictive meaning, you should be aware that the relative pronoun "that" is properly used when it introduces restrictive modifiers. "Who" and "which," however, are used to introduce both restrictive or nonrestrictive modifiers. Conventional usage also requires you to use "who" or "that" when referring to specific individuals, "that" when referring to a class composed of persons, and "which" or "that" when referring to things or ideas.

9. *Eliminate Unnecessary Words*

Aim for economy and simplicity of phrasing.

a. Substitute Simple Words for Cumbersome Words.

> **Example:** By reason of the fact that the witness was out of the country, the trial was postponed.
>
> **Rewrite:** The trial was postponed because the witness was out of the country.

b. Avoid "Throat–Clearing" Introductions to Sentences

Start right away with an argument. If you make the argument well, you do not have to tell the reader that you are about to do so. Most "throat-clearing" introductions are padding. They can usually be replaced with a word or omitted entirely.

>   **Example:** After discussing this question, it is important to consider the possibility that Michael's "acceptance" may have been a counter-offer.

>   **Rewrite:** A second question is whether Michael accepted the offer or, instead, counter-offered.

10. Use Quotations Sparingly

In using quotations, be selective, grammatical, and accurate. Quotations should be used selectively for two main reasons. First, a heavy reliance on quotations is frequently a signal of adequate research but inadequate analysis. Second, a paper littered with quotations is often disjointed; differences in style may jar your reader. Before you use a quotation then, think about whether the quote is necessary or whether it can be eliminated from your paper. You may be able to put the idea into your own words more efficiently and effectively. Whether you quote or you paraphrase, make sure that you then cite to the source of the idea.

It is sometimes appropriate to quote the holding of a case, and you should quote language that supplies the controlling standard for a particular area of the law. When you quote the controlling language of a statute, it is important to repeat the exact wording of the statute as you apply it to your problem. Besides using necessary quotes from the language of precedents, you might want to quote some judges for their particularly eloquent or apt language.

Generally, you should not quote a court's description of the facts. However, you should quote, rather than paraphrase, the words of a party or a witness if they are important to your case.

>   **Example:** The witness said, "I killed him and I'm glad."

Not

The witness dramatically confessed.

A quotation that is embedded in a longer sentence must fit into that sentence grammatically and logically. This sometimes takes some juggling. It is frequently easier to recast that part of the sentence which is not a quotation than to alter the quotation. The following sentence needs to be revised because the possessive pronoun "its" in the quotation wrongly refers to the parent company. "Its" is meant to refer to subsidiaries.

>   **Example:** The court found it decisive that the parent company, through its American subsidiaries, had "continued to engage in the market penetration and expansion that are its raison d'etre. . . ."

Rewrite: The court found it decisive that the American subsidiaries of the parent company had "continued to engage in the market penetration and expansion that are its raison d'etre. . . ."

Keep quotes short. But if you do use a long passage of fifty words or more, you must set out the quote in block form, that is, indented and single spaced. You do not use quotation marks when you set out a quote in block form. Put the citation as the first nonindented text after the quotation.

11. Use the Appropriate Tense

English is a language that has many tenses; this characteristic is a sign of the importance we place on accurately reporting the sequence of events and conveying the relation of one event to another. In legal writing, it is particularly important to pay attention to tenses when narrating facts and discussing case law. You should use the past tense to state all facts that have already occurred. Thus, you should use the past tense to discuss precedents. However, use the present tense to state a proposition of law.

Example: The court held [past tense] that due process requires [present tense] court-appointed counsel.

12. Make Your Comparisons Complete and Logical

A comparative sentence must have two terms. Do not say "Jones has a stronger case." Finish the comparison by adding the second term: "Jones has a stronger case than you." In addition, make sure you are comparing like or comparable things. Do not compare, for example, your facts to a case. Compare your facts to the facts in a case. Do not say "Smith's fraudulent statements are like John v. Doe." The proper comparison is "Smith's fraudulent statements are similar to those of the defendant in John v. Doe."

13. Check That the Words in Your Sentence Have a Rational Relationship

The subject of your sentence should be able to perform the action expressed by the verb; if the subject cannot, your sentence lacks coherence. A court, for example, does not *contend* or *argue* that a defendant is negligent. It "holds" the defendant negligent. A court is not an advocate in the litigation; the attorneys are the advocates. Nor do courts *feel* or *believe;* their decisions are presumably based on reasons, not emotions or beliefs. What then might a court do? The court may have said something, or decided, stated, concluded, held (for propositions of law), found [that] (for facts), weighed, reasoned, indicated, implied, considered, stressed, noted, compared, added, analyzed.

A court, for example, might "apply" a balancing test or might "balance" the state's interest against a private interest. It would be incorrect, however, to write that a "test" balances those interests. A "requirement" does not "show" a "foreseeable injury," although a test might "require" a plaintiff to "show" the defendant could have foreseen injury. In other words, make sure the subject, predicate, and object of a sentence rationally relate to each other.

14. Select Concrete, Familiar, and Specific Words: Avoid Vagueness and Imprecision

We have already recommended that you use concrete words as subjects instead of abstract nouns. You should also use concrete facts in your descriptions rather than words that characterize. Instead of saying, "The defendant drove several miles over the speed limit," report that the defendant drove sixty miles per hour in a fifty mile zone. If you say, "After a period of time, Roche purchased the drugs," we do not know whether minutes elapsed or years.

Do not be afraid to use a familiar vocabulary, one you feel comfortable with. To sound professional, you do not need to inflate or strain your diction. You need not say, "The car accident victim expired." Simply tell us that he died. You run far more risk using a word the meaning of which you are uncertain than you do using a familiar vocabulary.

15. Avoid Jargon, Informal, and Esoteric Language

a. You need not be a slave to jargon or legalese. Delete expressions like "hereinafter" and "cease and desist" (unless the phrase describes the remedy that is being asked for). You should, however, use the wording of a court when applying a particular test that a court uses to evaluate claims and use the exact statutory language that you are applying.

b. As an attorney, you will be writing mostly formal documents. Informal expressions in these documents jar the reader because of their inappropriate tone. Do not say, "the car's rear end abutted the public road." Say, "the rear of the car abutted the public road."

c. Although courts sometimes employ an esoteric vocabulary, you need not parrot that language. If a court says, "the statute does not pass constitutional muster," you can paraphrase that statement in a more contemporary idiom. For example, you could simply say that "the statute is unconstitutional."

16. *Avoid Qualifiers and Intensifiers; Do Not Overuse Adjectives and Adverbs*

It is better to demonstrate the clarity of an idea by supplying supporting arguments than to insist on it with adverbs like "clearly" or "certainly." Do not overuse adjectives and adverbs. One apt adverb is more effective than many. (For a fuller discussion on adjectives and adverbs see Chapter 13, G, 1.)

17. *Avoid Sexist Language* [2]

The legal profession has become increasingly sensitive to the use of sexist language. To avoid antagonizing colleagues and clients, it is important to use gender neutral language when you write.

a. The generic use of the pronoun "he" should be avoided.

— Use plural nouns and plural pronouns.

Example: The attorney must represent his client to the best of his ability.

Rewrite: Attorneys must use their best abilities in representing their clients.

— Substitute articles for pronouns or use "who" instead of he.

Example: The judge handed down his opinion on June 1st.

Rewrite: The judge handed down the opinion on June 1st.

Example: If an attorney solicits a client, he may be disciplined.

Rewrite: An attorney who solicits a client may be disciplined.

— Substitute one, you or we for "he" or delete pronouns altogether.

Example: The litigator must exercise his judgment in selecting issues.

Rewrite: The litigator must exercise judgment in selecting issues.

— When all else fails, try the passive voice.

Example: The judge handed down his opinion on June 1st.

Rewrite: The opinion was handed down on June 1st.

2. The recommendations made in this section are adapted from the "Guidelines for the Nonsexist Use of Language" written for the American Philosophical Association by Virginia L. Warren. They were published in PROCEEDINGS AND ADDRESSES OF AMERICAN PHILOSOPHICAL ASSOCIATION, vol. 59, no. 3 (Feb.1988), at 471–84. Copyright © 1988 by the American Philosophical Association; reprinted by permission.

b. The generic use of "man" and other gender specific nouns should be avoided.

— Use person, individual, human, people.

— Use spouse instead of wife or husband, sibling instead of sister or brother

c. Address people by their titles whenever possible.

— Use Dr., Prof., Ms., Editor, Colleague, Chair or Chairperson.

Exercise 9–A: Sentence Structure

Diagnose error and correct.

1. On arriving at the age of majority, a parent no longer has to support a child.

2. In calculating the cost of replacing Mrs. Markham's services, the salary of the full-time housekeeper was considered to be the greatest expense.

3. Since an express agreement between unmarried cohabitants is a valid contract, Asch can be directed to keep his promise.

4. The guidelines should be applied with flexibility and not as rigid standards.

5. The movement toward the present circuit court publication plans began in 1964, when the Judicial Conference of the United States recommended that the federal courts authorize "the publication of only those opinions which are of general precedential value."

6. Canon 9, which prohibits both impropriety and the mere appearance of impropriety, and which alone is a basis for a disqualification motion, reflects the Bar's concern with protecting the integrity of the legal system.

7. The decision established that fraudulent conduct barred setting up the privilege of infancy.

8. A trial by jury was requested by defendant.

9. Keith Johnson's case is more factually similar to <u>Ziady v. Curley</u>.

10. Contractual modifications and limitations of remedies are allowed in the UCC in order to allow parties to allocate risk in accordance with sound business practice.

11. The court admitted into evidence the decedent's will charging her husband with cruelty, indifference, and failure to support, emphasizing that admitting the will did not violate the statute.

12. A determination of the awarding of consequential damages is done largely on a case-by-case basis.

13. The state interest in setting a filing fee relates to revenue raising and arguably to act as a deterrent to unmeritorious use of judicial time.

14. Unlike <u>Elliot</u>, Keith's mother had never relinquished her custody.

15. A finding of specific jurisdiction can be held.

16. In order for a plaintiff to state a claim, it must be shown that he suffered severe emotional distress.

17. When utilizing the statute, it is critical to establish whether the doctor administers first aid.

18. Smith is distinguishable from our case because in Smith the court is interpreting § 5–305, and the court says that it is limiting its decision to the peculiar facts of the case.

19. Any instrument, article, or substance which, under the circumstances in which it was used, is capable of causing death or serious injury is a dangerous instrument.

20. The jury, knowing the prosecutor has the authority of the government behind her, and aware of her access to the files, gave her words great weight.

21. The proscription against a prosecutor expressing his personal opinion goes to the heart of a fair trial.

22. The McCaren–Ferguson Act makes an exemption for the business of insurance.

23. Breach of the implied warranty of habitability can occur even without a violation of city building and housing codes.

24. The familial relationship between the deceased and the devisees and the sentimental value attached to the gifts is influential to the distribution of the gift in dispute.

25. The court ruled for the landlord because the noise was not characterized as repetitious and affected the tenants in a detrimental manner on one occasion only.

26. Turn the material below into a sentence with parallel structure.

    Jones made these suggestions for financial planning:

    - Analyze insurance coverage.
    - New investment strategies.
    - Organize budget.
    - Retirement planning.
    - Move their savings to money market fund.

27. Turn the material below into a sentence with parallel structure.

    The landlord agrees to:

    - Provide heat.
    - All utilities will be paid for.
    - Premises to be in good order.
    - He will keep the air-conditioning system maintained.

Chapter Ten
The Complex Memorandum

I. Introduction

The examples of legal analysis we have used so far have mostly involved fairly straightforward applications of established statutory language and precedents to new facts. Legal analysis, however, often requires you to apply a more complex combination of statutory and case law authority and to reach conclusions that are less certain than many we have illustrated. Some assignments may require you to balance competing elements or legal policies to determine which one a court would implement, or may require you to weigh facts when a decision depends on a totality of circumstances. Other assignments will involve you in questions of law rather than questions of fact. Problems like these require you to consider and choose from a variety of analytic strategies and organizational patterns.

II. Balancing of Interests

One type of more complex analysis requires you to analyze and balance competing interests in order to assess a legal claim. In this process, you must determine the weight and importance of each interest involved as compared to the others. Several different situations require this type of analysis.

A. Defining the Claim Itself

A balancing approach is sometimes demanded by the definition of the claim itself. For example, the Supreme Court of the United States has interpreted the due process clause of the four-

160

teenth amendment to require that an indigent who cannot pay a court's filing fee must satisfy three conditions in order to have access to the court: 1) the court must be the only forum to resolve the dispute; 2) the subject matter of the dispute (the indigent's "interest") must be constitutionally significant; and 3) the constitutional interest must override a countervailing state interest. Thus, the court's three-part test explicitly requires you first to identify and then to balance the individual's interest in access to the court and the state's interest in requiring a filing fee.

To analyze a due process issue under this test, you must discuss each part of the legal standard separately, according to the pattern demonstrated in Chapter Six for each element of a claim. Then, you must balance (that is, weigh the importance of) the interests inherent in the last two parts of the test against each other. For example, a plaintiff may argue that she has a protected interest in restoring cuts to her Aid to Families with Dependent Children payments, which she needs for family support. Neither welfare payments nor other economic relationships have ever been classified as fundamental interests protected by the Constitution. However, family relationships are constitutionally protected, and the plaintiff's interest could be characterized as protecting her family relationships. If so, you would then balance this interest—admittedly one of attenuated constitutional significance—against the state's interests in requiring filing fees, which are to raise revenue for the state and, arguably, to deter frivolous litigation. We set out a thesis paragraph for this type of discussion in Chapter Seven, Thesis Paragraphs, in the Alice Doone example.

B. *Balancing Competing Policies*

This due process hypothetical provides an example of the sort of balancing you must do in applying an established rule to new facts. A second situation which involves balancing arises when a new rule must be fashioned to resolve a dispute because the existing law is silent or ambiguous. In such a case, you may engage in weighing competing policies in order to implement the more important policy.

We can illustrate this type of balancing with a statute of limitations problem in which you must analyze when the statute's time period begins to run. For personal injury claims, many statutes dictate that the plaintiff file an action within a specified time (often two years) after the claim "arises." Assume that a plaintiff who filed suit for personal injury in 1980 was a builder who worked with a manufacturer's asbestos materials from 1970–74. Assume also that the plaintiff was diagnosed in 1979 as suffering from a form of cancer frequently caused by exposure to asbestos. Given a two-year statute of limitations, the plaintiff's suit would be barred if the claim "arose" at the time of the exposure, but not barred if it "arose" when he discovered he had cancer. Indeed, if the court chooses the former time, the plaintiff's suit would be barred before he ever knew about the cancer and had any reason to file a claim.

To assess when the claim arose, you must balance two competing policies that your research will reveal. The first is a policy that underlies statutes of limitations: fairness to a defendant who, if the claim "arose" at the time of discovery, would have to defend against old claims for which evidence may be unavailable, or may be stale and unreliable if the plaintiff discovered the injury many years after the event occurred. The opposing policy recognizes the unfairness to a plaintiff who would be denied any opportunity to litigate if the claim arose at the time of the injury.

You would analyze and organize this type of balancing according to the same processes already demonstrated: break the policies being balanced into their constituent parts and arrange them in logical order. You might find that the policy behind the statute of limitations can be organized by two factors: requiring a plaintiff to prosecute claims promptly, and avoiding difficulties of proof associated with old claims. One ordering principle would be to evaluate each factor and to analyze it from the perspective of the two opposing policies. After evaluating each of the factors, determine which policy should prevail.

You could also handle your analysis and counteranalysis by a different organization: discuss all the reasons behind one policy, then all the reasons behind the opposing policy, and then compare the strength of each. Finally, you would conclude as to which policy should prevail.

C. *Weighing the Totality of Circumstances*

A third situation in which you engage in balancing occurs when you apply a set of criteria to a particular claim in order to determine whether the facts of that claim satisfy the established criteria. In this situation, while the criteria do not explicitly require balancing, you may have to balance because it may not be clear whether each criterion must be fulfilled, or to what degree each must be fulfilled. If the claim only minimally fulfills one or two factors, but clearly fulfills the others, then you may have to weigh all the factors to determine which ones are more important than the others. This procedure is often called a totality of circumstances approach.

For example, in Chapter Two, in analogizing Jones v. Hadican with the Wheeler case, we pointed out that one of the factors in Wheeler's situation (the short length of his prison sentence) cut against his intent to change domicile to the state of incarceration, and that that factor would have to be weighed against others indicating that he intended to change domicile.

You may organize a totality of circumstances discussion by analyzing each factor separately. Your discussion then should include an explicit evaluation of the strength of each factor. Then you should analyze whether all the criteria must be satisfied, and, if not, how important the criteria are, relative to each other.

At other times, however, it may make more sense to organize a totality of circumstances problem around the principles the court has articulated for weighing the factors, if a court has done so. For example, in determining whether to deny or grant a defendant's motion for a court to decline jurisdiction on the grounds of forum non conveniens (inconvenient forum), a court must consider such factors as the ease of access to sources of proof; the availability of compulsory process for attendance of unwilling witnesses; the cost of obtaining attendance of willing witnesses; the state law that will govern the case; the local interest in the controversy; and the plaintiff's ability to enforce a judgment in another forum.

Instead of taking each of these factors separately, you may want to use the court's guidelines for assessing these factors and to organize accordingly. For example, if the court previously has said that, if a transfer of forum would result in substantial hardship to a plaintiff, a plaintiff's choice of forum should rarely be disturbed, then you could assess these factors by grouping those that would cause hardship to the plaintiff and weighing that hardship against the factors that cause inconvenience to the defendant and injury to aspects of the public interest.

III. Questions of Law

A. Introduction

The analysis of a question of law is often complex because it requires you to examine a variety of sources, to be sensitive to the weight of these sources and their interrelationships, and to develop analytic strategies that will enable you to resolve the question in a logical and persuasive manner. These analytic strategies and skills involve determining the weight of the relevant authorities, framing broad and narrow holdings, employing alternative analyses, evaluating underlying policies, and considering the relevance of related legislative activity.

In this section, we will analyze a complex problem and use it as the vehicle for explaining these more sophisticated patterns and strategies that a lawyer would use. For the purpose of this exercise we rely on primary authorities only, although for a more thorough analysis, we also would have relied on interpretations found in secondary research materials. To demonstrate this type of analysis we will take you through a series of steps for one particular case, but these strategies are appropriate for many other difficult issues and combinations of authority.

B. Factual Background: People v. Trent

We will use as a primary example a hypothetical Illinois criminal prosecution that involves an entrapment defense. The defendant John Trent, who is your client, was charged with knowing possession of a controlled substance. He was arrested when he lit a pipe that contained crack cocaine. Trent was with an old friend who had given him the pipe, but who was acting as a police informer. At his trial, Trent denied knowing that the pipe contained cocaine and pleaded not guilty. His attorney requested that the court instruct the jury on entrapment. The trial judge refused the request on the ground that Illinois law does not permit a defendant who denies the crime by pleading not guilty to also raise an entrapment defense.[1] The court reasoned that because entrapment presupposes commission of a crime, the defenses of not guilty and entrapment are inconsistent. Trent was convicted and you appealed on the ground that the court should have instructed the jury on entrapment.

For this problem, the relevant authorities are:

— an Illinois statute, § 7–12,[2] which provides for the entrapment defense in state criminal prosecutions but says nothing about how the defense applies to a defendant who enters a not guilty plea

1. Entrapment is a defense based on the claim that the government "set up" the defendant. In the Supreme Court case cited most often as authority for this defense, the Court explained that entrapment occurs "when the criminal design originates with the officials of the Government, and they implant in the mind of an innocent person the disposition to commit the alleged offense." Sorrells v. United States, 287 U.S. 435, 442 (1932). Entrapment thus is interpreted as a two-part test: The criminal design must originate with the government and the defendant must not be predisposed to commit the crime.

2. "A person is not guilty of an offense if his conduct is incited or induced by a public officer or employee, or agent of either, for the purpose of obtaining evidence for the prosecution of such person. However, this Section is inapplicable if a public officer or employee, or agent of either, merely affords to such person the opportunity or facility for committing an offense in furtherance of a criminal purpose which such person has originated."

— two cases from the Illinois Supreme Court on the particular issue in this case, People v. Realmo,[3] and People v. Fleming,[4] and

— a case also directly on point from the Supreme Court of the United States, Mathews v. United States.[5]

We will incorporate analysis of each of these sources of law at relevant points in the discussion below.

C. *Legal Background: The Weight of Authorities*

Analysis of any legal issue requires you to consult a variety of legal sources. For this problem, we have gathered important primary authorities, and we begin by considering the weight of these authorities. Our purpose is to identify the controlling precedent that a court will apply.

As a threshold matter, because a United States Supreme Court case is involved, you must first ascertain the basis of that decision to determine whether it is binding on a state court. In Mathews v. United States, the Court held that the defendant could deny any element of the crime and still receive an entrapment instruction if there was enough evidence of entrapment to go to the jury.

If Mathews was based on the United States Constitution or on a federal statute in an area of law for which federal law takes precedence over conflicting state law, then that decision would be the authority with the greatest weight. The proper analysis then would be to apply the rule in Mathews to the facts of the Trent case, which is a fairly straightforward task. You would conclude that an appellate court would reverse the trial court's decision.

If it is not clear whether Mathews was decided as a constitutional matter or on the basis of a controlling federal statute, then you would first need to analyze the basis for the Mathews decision and determine whether the case controls a state criminal prosecution. Because in fact Mathews was not decided on either of those grounds, but was decided as a matter of federal criminal law, it is not binding on this problem.

With no controlling federal or constitutional precedents, this issue is a matter of state law. Thus, the Illinois entrapment statute is the authority with the greatest weight. However, it is silent as to whether a defendant can deny the elements of the crime and also enter an entrapment defense. As is true for many state statutes, there is no legislative history for this particular

---

3. 28 Ill. 2d 510, 192 N.E.2d 918 (1963).

4. 50 Ill. 2d 141, 277 N.E.2d 872 (1971).

5. 485 U.S. 58 (1988).

section of the state's criminal code. And although the section was published with the Committee Comments, those Comments do not mention the issue of inconsistent defenses. The Comments do say that the statute codifies the general definition of entrapment that already had been adopted by the Illinois courts.

Thus the available legislative materials lead you to common law definitions of entrapment, and your most important authorities then become the Illinois Supreme Court cases that implement the statute, People v. Realmo and People v. Fleming, summarized here.

1. People v. Realmo.

Defendant was convicted of the unlawful sale of narcotics. He denied selling or possessing narcotics on the date charged. The court held that a defendant may not raise an entrapment defense where he denies "the commission of the acts constituting the offense." The court said that since the defendant denied committing the acts, it was inconsistent also to claim that he had committed the acts but was induced to perform them.

2. People v. Fleming.

The defendant, a Chicago police officer, was convicted of soliciting and receiving a bribe from a physician in exchange for not filing a complaint charging the physician with unlawfully prescribing a dangerous drug. The physician, at the instruction of the police, paid part of the bribe to the defendant, but then turned away to open the office door to a policeman. The defendant did not have the money on him when he was searched. The defendant entered a not guilty plea and denied requesting or receiving any bribe from the doctor. The trial court refused to instruct the jury on entrapment.

The court affirmed the conviction, invoking what it considered the Illinois rule, "one may not at once deny the commission of the offense and claim entrapment."

In addition to Realmo and Fleming, you may find cases on point from lower Illinois courts. These would be used for their interpretations of Realmo and Fleming. Nonbinding precedent from the Supreme Court of the United States, such as Mathews, and cases on point from other states have less weight than the Illinois cases, but still will be useful for their reasoning or for determining how recent cases are being decided. Decisions from the lower federal courts that pre-date Mathews are valid only for their reasoning, provided those decisions permitted the inconsistent defense.

In summary, for this discussion we evaluated the relevant materials in this order:

— constitutional or federal law that controls state law

— state statutory materials

— precedents from the state supreme court and from the state appellate courts

— nonbinding precedent from the Supreme Court of the United States

— precedents from other jurisdictions.

D. *Analytic Strategies*

The methods that you use to analyze and organize this problem include many that we already have suggested for legal analysis and discussion, such as analogizing and distinguishing cases. Unlike many of our earlier examples, however, this entrapment problem poses a legal question rather than a factual one. Therefore, the problem is to decide which legal standard the court will apply, and how to interpret that standard.

Here, the legal issue is whether a defendant who pleads not guilty to a criminal charge may also use an entrapment defense. In analyzing the issue, your task is to consider the sources—statutes, cases, and policies—on which a court in the jurisdiction would base its ruling, and then to engage in these different types of legal reasoning:

— Statutory interpretation: first analyze the controlling statutory language and its legislative history;

— Case law analysis: then analyze how the cases interpret the statute, and analogize or distinguish this case with reference to the Illinois Supreme Court precedents;

— Policy analysis: if you cannot distinguish this case from the Illinois precedents, then analyze policy reasons which explain why the precedents should or should not be overruled. For the Trent problem, you find these reasons in

• Persuasive precedents of the Supreme Court of the United States and of other jurisdictions

• Analogies to similar areas of law

• Consequences of applying the existing law or a competing rule

— Legislative analysis, including an examination of legislative activity or inactivity as it affects this area of law.

E. Analysis of The Trent Problem

1. Statutory Interpretation and Case Law Analysis

Because the entrapment statute, § 7–12, is silent with respect to the question of whether a defendant can receive an entrapment instruction if he pleads not guilty, your analysis of the problem will focus on the case law. Two strategies are most important. First, analogize and distinguish relevant cases with respect to your case, that is, analyze whether the precedents are binding as to their outcome.   Second, analyze whether your court would be willing to overrule the precedents. Keep in mind that courts prefer to distinguish cases rather than to overrule a precedent. When you analyze whether a court may overrule a decision, however, it is important to consider if the case is going to be heard by a court that is lower than the court that established the rule, because a lower court cannot overrule a higher court's decision; it can only distinguish it. Therefore, exhaust every possible analysis in favor of distinguishing a precedent before recommending an argument for a court to overrule.

In this example, we will analyze how the state and the defendant would analyze Realmo and Fleming, the Illinois Supreme Court cases. The problem for the defendant is whether the cases are distinguishable. Through a very narrow interpretation, the defendant can limit those decisions to their facts. With a broader interpretation, the state can show that the cases can apply beyond their own facts. The discussion below illustrates the difference between a narrow and broad reading of the Illinois cases, and the importance of a careful reading of the judicial language.

Both Realmo and Fleming involved defendants who denied engaging in the criminal acts with which they were charged, yet who also wished to enter the defense that the acts were committed at the instigation of a government officer. The prosecution's argument is that these precedents clearly control the Trent case and that their holdings dictate that Trent cannot plead not guilty and also receive an entrapment instruction.

In Realmo, the court held that a defendant may not raise the defense where he denies "the commission of the act constituting the offense." Mr. Trent, however, does not deny the act itself. He denies only the intent element of the crime. Trent admits holding the pipe, but he denies knowing that the pipe contained cocaine. Therefore, the question here is whether the defendant can distinguish the cases by interpreting the Realmo court's statements about Illinois law in light of the difference in the facts of Trent's case.

Read narrowly, the Illinois rule against inconsistent defenses would apply when the defendant denies committing the acts charged, but might not apply when the defendant admits the act charged but denies the intent element. The defendant's analysis would thus categorize the facts of Realmo as "denial of the acts," a more narrow category than "denial of the crime." If Trent admits the act of possession but denies knowing that the pipe contained cocaine, then the Realmo court's statement does not apply, and Trent may receive an entrapment instruction.

An argument against this narrow interpretation is that the more recent case, Fleming, used slightly different language than Realmo did. In Fleming, the court spoke more broadly and said the defendant could not "deny the commission of the offense and claim entrapment." However, in Fleming, as in Realmo, the defendant also had denied committing the acts charged. Thus, in both cases, the court applied broad language to the same type of more narrow facts, and Trent would construe these cases to restrict them to their facts: a defendant who denied committing the criminal act. By identifying the facts upon which the courts based their rule, Trent would argue that the rule applies only to the particular facts common to both cases, which are different from the facts that prompted his not guilty plea.

2. Policy Reasons

The second type of argument, employing the policy bases of persuasive precedents, is an alternative to the first, in which the writer focuses on binding precedents. Here again, the analysis requires you to marshal reasons for and against the Illinois rule. For the defendant, the first strategy would be to interpret Illinois precedents as not foreclosing Trent from receiving an entrapment instruction because those precedents apply only to defendants who deny committing the act charged, not the intent element. If, however, the Illinois rule is interpreted to apply to a defendant who denies the criminal intent, then the next logical step, and an alternative argument for Trent, is to contend that the court should overrule those cases for the reasons that led the United States Supreme Court to decide Mathews v. United States as it did.

Although Mathews is not binding on the Illinois courts (because it is not based on the Constitution), a case from the Supreme Court directly on point carries great weight and requires careful treatment. In Mathews, the Court held that a criminal defendant who denies any element of the crime is entitled to an entrapment instruction, so long as sufficient evidence supports the defense. Since the defendant in Mathews denied the intent element of the crime, that case is more factually analogous to the problem than are the Illinois cases. More importantly, the defendant will want to use the Court's reasons for its decision in <u>Mathews</u> to persuade the Illinois court to adopt its rule.

In <u>Mathews,</u> the Court used two types of reasoning often used in complex analysis. First, it employed analogies to other areas of law. The Court noted that alternative pleadings and defenses are permitted in civil litigation under the Rules of Civil Procedure and in other criminal defenses such as self defense.

Second, the Court examined the behaviorial consequences of its rule. One reason that courts had decided against allowing defendants inconsistent defenses was their view that to allow such defenses would encourage perjury. The Court answered that line of argument, however, by pointing out that the risk was minimal that a defendant would commit perjury by first denying the crime, and then saying he did it because he was entrapped. By offering such conflicting testimony, the Court opined, a defendant's credibility would be so greatly reduced as to discourage perjury.

The state, of course, would seek to minimize the importance of the Supreme Court's reasoning. For example, the state might take the approach of explaining why rules for criminal trials may logically differ from the Rules of Civil Procedure that control civil trials.

In addition, if there is relevant case law in other jurisdictions, those decisions can be used to strengthen the reasons to overrule or not overrule. Besides the Supreme Court's decision in <u>Mathews,</u> there may exist precedents in other jurisdictions that dealt with the issues more recently than the Illinois court's decision in <u>Fleming.</u> If so, the next step is to analyze the state court decisions on this issue, giving careful attention to the level of the courts and the reasons for their decisions. These authorities may also be persuasive to an Illinois court, especially if a strong majority of the highest courts of those states adopted the same rule.

It is important to realize, however, that decisions from other states do not bind an Illinois court. Therefore, you must analyze these decisions to show how the other jurisdictions have decided this issue, and to show why the reasons for their decisions may be ones the Illinois court would wish to adopt or reject. Treat these decisions as part of a complex pattern of reasons; they cannot themselves compel the Illinois court's decision.

3. *Legislative Activity*

A final strategy suggested here is one that takes into account legislative activity or the lack of it on the particular issue before the court. On some issues, a court may defer to the legislature as being the proper body to implement a new rule. In this case, however, because the "no inconsistent defenses" rule was originally a judge-made rule, the court would not be likely to defer to the legislature to change it. On the other hand, a court could interpret the legislature's failure to change the <u>Realmo</u> and <u>Fleming</u> decisions as approval of its rule. It may reason that if the legislature had disagreed with those decisions it could have overruled the court's decisions by amending § 7–12.

4. *Summary*

We have taken you through the analytic steps of the Trent entrapment problem. For a written discussion of the Trent problem, our organization would look like this:

— identification of the controlling precedents

— analysis of those precedents and determination of how their holdings bind this case

— analysis of alternative arguments to overrule or not overrule the state cases, including reasoning from

  • persuasive cases

  • legislative activity

The exercises below suggest other analysis to employ in this and a related issue.

Exercise 10–A

1. What additional interpretations could you have used if the Illinois legislature had amended § 7–12 to add that for all criminal acts occurring after January 1991, a defendant who denies any element of the crime may not raise an entrapment instruction?

2. What if, instead, this amendment was voted on but defeated in the Illinois legislature?

3. What if the legislature amended § 7–12 in other ways, but never referred to this issue?

4. What if, in a very recent case, the Illinois Supreme Court decided that a homicide defendant may be entitled to a self-defense jury instruction even where he testifies that he accidentally killed the victim?

Exercise 10–B

Write a thesis paragraph for an analysis of the Trent problem.

Exercise 10–C

When John Trent was arrested for possession of a controlled substance, he was with his friend Timothy Lot who had given him the cocaine-filled pipe. Suppose that Lot was not a police informer, and indeed did not know that it was an undercover police officer who supplied him with cocaine. Suppose also that the undercover officer urged him to provide the drugs to his "special friends in government positions," and Trent was a local government official.

The Illinois statute cited in footnote 2 of this chapter provides the entrapment defense for a person whose conduct "is incited or induced by a public officer or employee, or agent of either." The statute does not define "agent."

The trial court denied Trent's request for an entrapment instruction on the ground that Lot was not an agent of a public officer because he did not knowingly act on the officer's behalf.

1.   List the types of materials you would research to analyze whether an agent must be a knowing agent under the Illinois statute.

2.   Which types of analytic strategies would you want to use? How would you organize your analysis?

3.   Read the arguments set out below. What kinds of strategies are each of these writers using? Evaluate the strength of each. Which ones would you prefer to use? And which ones would you avoid? Organize the strategies you would use in a memorandum analysis as they pertain to 1) statutory arguments, 2) case analysis, and 3) policy analysis, including consequential arguments.

Arguments:

a.   Section 7–12 does not define the term "agent." However, the Committee Comment suggests that the legislature did not intend to require a knowing agent. The Comment provides:

> The defense has been recognized as proper not only when the person alleged to have incited the offense was a government officer or agent, but also when he was an investigator privately hired and acting without contact with law enforcement authorities. One case sometimes cited as an entrapment case involved a burglary of a private office, planned and executed by a detective with the knowledge of the owner of the office, to cause the arrest and prosecution of several men who were suspected of having perpetrated a series of burglaries. Although the Illinois Supreme Court referred to the entrapment situation, the basis for the reversal of the judgment was that the "victim" consented to the conduct, and since lack of consent is an element of the offense, no burglary was committed.

b.   If the legislature intended to require a knowing agent, it would have said so. For example, § 4–3 of the Criminal Code generally defines the mental state element for the entire Criminal Code and says that "knowledge is not an element of an offense unless the statute clearly defines it as such."

c.   Two Illinois appellate courts have reached opposite conclusions as to whether a defendant is entitled to an entrapment instruction where a private person unknowingly worked with an undercover policeman to buy drugs from the defendant.

In one case, in which the appellate court held that the trial court correctly rejected the instruction, the private party had initiated the contact with the police officer. He also had initiated the contacts with the defendant, and urged the defendant to sell the drugs. In the other case, the private party's only role was to directly communicate the government's inducements to the defendant. The appellate court held that the trial court should have instructed the jury on entrapment.

    d. The lower federal courts are split as to whether the middleman must know he is acting for the government.

    e. Recognition of entrapment where the police use an unknowing middleman is necessary to prevent the police from engaging in unchecked abuses. Otherwise, police will avail themselves of this technique and unfairly induce people to commit crimes.

    f. When the police instruct a middleman to target a particular person, all courts permit that person to raise the entrapment defense. In this case, the police did not name Trent as the target but described the target in a way that logically led Lot to Trent.

    g. If the legislature were opposed to police using middlemen, it would have legislated against it.

    h. Law enforcement agencies can best control abuses administratively by issuing clear guidelines to their personnel.

    i. Section 7–12 defines the terms "public officer" and "public employee" as well as several other terms. In light of this specificity, the fact that the section does not define "agent" implies that the legislature intended not to restrict its meaning.

    j. Black's Law Dictionary defines agent as "one who represents and acts for another under the contract or relation of agency."

    k. If a police officer is not present during the transaction between a defendant and a middleman, an entrapment defense would present the danger of collusion between the defendant and middleman and would encourage false statements at trial.

Chapter Eleven
Research Strategies

I. Introduction

When you work on a problem, your research goal is to find the relevant mandatory and persuasive primary authorities of law. However, a law library also contains many materials that will help you find those primary authorities, and will help you analyze the issues you are researching. This chapter will not explain the basic bibliographic information about those resources. Instead, it gives advice for using them for different types of research projects that you may encounter as a law student.

A client will come to you with a story, not an identified claim or defense. To determine how to proceed, you should gather all the facts that you can. You need a complete account of what happened, of the problems your client currently faces, and of the result the client seeks.[1] As a lawyer, your goal is to convert the facts from your client's narrative into a legal claim that states a cause of action, or into a viable defense to plausible legal claims. If you are an experienced attorney, the client's information may suggest to you a claim or a line of defense, and the issues that are involved, without your having to do research to identify them. If you are an inexperienced attorney or a law student, however, you may have to do research first to identify the relevant claims and then to diagnose the problem and find an appropriate solution.

---

1. See D. Binder and S. Price, Legal Interviewing and Counseling 2 (1977).

The facts of your client's problem are important at all stages of your work. Initially, you want to identify the important facts and use them both to determine which legal claims will be involved and to provide search terms with which to begin your research. After you have begun your research and have read some of the primary and secondary authorities, you will be able to make a more sophisticated identification of the legally relevant facts. Then you can use those facts not only as search terms for your research, but also analytically to help you prove or disprove the elements of the cause of action and to provide analogies to the important precedents.

In your legal writing assignments, you may be told the nature of the claims and the particular issues to research and write about. If not, then first you should determine the general body of law that is involved. For example, the facts and the relief your client wants may bring your client's problem within the body of contract law because the problem involves a written or oral exchange of promises.

After making this general classification, try to identify the more specific problem within that body of law. If you identify the cause of action as a tort, for example, determine which particular tort or torts are involved. If you face a property law problem because your client is a tenant who has a disagreement with his landlord about terms in a lease, then you probably are concerned only with landlord-tenant law. Or the problem may be a statutory one in which a governmental agency is requiring your client to comply with a statute or with the agency's regulations.

Your research methodology depends on the nature of the problem and the knowledge you have to begin with. If you are not familiar with the cause of action and do not know, for example, which particular torts the client's facts suggest, then you need to begin differently from the way you would if you had previously done research in that area of law and knew relevant cases and statutes. The scope of your research will also depend on other factors, most importantly, the jurisdiction of the problem. Because the law of that jurisdiction governs, you should examine the law of that jurisdiction first. Other factors that affect your research are whether you need state or federal materials or both, whether the problem involves statutes or common law, and whether it involves a new cause of action or statute or a well-settled body of law.

II. *Types of Research Materials*

The traditional classification of legal research materials includes three types: primary materials, secondary materials, and search materials. Some materials, such as the annotated A.L.R. series, combine features of primary and secondary sources.

Primary materials are published in forms that are difficult to gain access to for your research. Case reporters report cases by jurisdiction and in a roughly chronological order, rather than by topic. But when you do legal research, you will need to find case law about a particular topic. In order to do so, you will need to use the secondary and search materials published for this purpose which classify materials by topic.

Enacted laws are published in a variety of sources. A jurisdiction's statutes are first compiled and published as session laws, which are the statutes passed during each session of the legislature. Because the session laws are published in chronological order and not by subject matter, they too are difficult to use for research. Instead of using session laws to find statutory materials, a researcher uses the statutory publication called a code in which the jurisdiction's statutes are arranged by subject matter. In a code, all statutes pertaining to a topic are grouped together (for example, the criminal laws) in numbered chapters or titles.

The commercial publishers' unofficial editions of each jurisdiction's code are especially valuable for research because they are annotated and provide you with citations to the cases that have applied each statute, or part of it. The codes also contain other information about the statutes, such as historical information that can help you begin a legislative history.

A jurisdiction's constitution and court rules of procedure are published in separate volumes along with the publication of its code. Administrative regulations usually are published separately in official publications and in publications by commercial publishers.

Case reporters, session laws, and codes are examples of published forms of primary authorities. Most of the other research materials that you will use, such as legal encyclopedias, treatises, and legal periodicals, fall into the next category of materials— secondary sources. They provide text that explains and analyzes legal topics. If you use quotations from or paraphrase the texts of these sources, or if you use ideas from them, you must cite them in your written work. Secondary sources also provide citations to primary sources of law and to other secondary materials. Unlike primary authority, however, the secondary sources do not supply binding law. They are persuasive authority only.

Search materials, the third category, are tools that help you find the other materials. A familiar example is an index. The more specialized legal search tools are the digests and the Shepard's citators. Search materials contain no original text of their own, and you never cite them in your written work. Computerized legal research, that is, LEXIS and WESTLAW, are both search tools and sources of primary materials. You may cite to a computerized source for primary authority if the primary authority has not yet been published, but is available on a computer.

As you do your research and writing, you should become aware of the differences among these materials, not only as to the information they provide, but also as to their value as authorities. Primary sources are always the most important legal authorities. Primary sources do not all have the same weight, however; among primary authorities, always look first for the binding authority in the jurisdiction of your problem, and then look for sources from other jurisdictions and from analogous areas of the law.

Secondary materials are generally of less weight than persuasive primary authorities. However, not all secondary materials have the same weight. For example, a well-written treatise by a named author who specializes in that field is more authoritative than an encyclopedia article about that topic. Certain treatises and law review articles may even be more authoritative to some judges than some case law. Many non-legal research materials, such as statistical or sociological studies, are also secondary materials and can prove very useful to your research.

For each source that you use, become familiar with the means of access to its text, that is, its indexes and tables. Learn the type and scope of the information it contains, its method of updating, and the ways it is the same or different from other sources.

Whichever sources you use to find primary authority, be sure that you yourself read the relevant primary sources. It is not acceptable research to rely on the descriptions of those sources in the secondary materials.

III. *Beginning Your Research*

A. *Statutory Research*

When you begin your research for a problem, you should determine if there is a statute that governs. Even if no state statute applies, a federal statute may, or both federal and state statutes may apply.

1. *Starting With Known Relevant Citations*

If you know statutes relevant to the subject matter of your problem, you can begin your research differently from the way you begin if you do not know of relevant materials. When you know citations to statutes that are relevant to your problem, read the statutes immediately, and then expand your search as described in Part 2. If your client is being sued for violation of a statute, for example, then the litigation has already identified the statute, and you should find the statute in that jurisdiction's code. Although proper citation form is to the official code, for research purposes you probably will want to read the statute in the unofficial code because of its annotations. Then, proceed with your research as explained below.

2. *Starting With No Research Information*

If, as you begin your research, you do not have citations to relevant statutes, then you have to search for them yourself. Unless you are very familiar with the structure of the jurisdiction's code and can go directly to the title that includes the subject matter of your problem, start by using the index volume of the code to find whether there are statutes related to your topic. Indexing techniques and problems associated with indexing are discussed below in Part B(2). You can also find statutes of some jurisdictions by using one of the computer services.[1] If there are statutes that appear relevant, read them to determine whether they apply to your case. Then use the statutory annotations or the computer services to find the cases applying that statute.

You must update the statute in the code by using the pocket parts to the statutory index and to the code volume, and also by using the interim annotation services that accompany codes. Besides providing citations to more recently decided cases applying the statute, these sources also tell you whether the statute has been amended or repealed, or whether a new statute has been passed. The statute on a computer's data base will already be updated.

Other reference sources besides the code volumes and computer services supply information about statutes. For example, you can use a Shepard's statutory citator for information about the legislative changes in the statute, such as amendments, and for cases that cite the statute. Also use the indexes to legal periodicals, which include tables of statutes with citations to articles about them. Loose-leaf services, either of national or state-wide scope, are especially helpful for specialized statutory subject matter. But you usually would not use an encyclopedia or other general secondary source for research on statutory issues.

1. As yet, not all state statutes are in the computer data bases.

B. Case Law Research

1. Starting With Known Relevant Citations

If you already know an important case and know its citation, either from an annotated code or another source, and you want to limit your research to finding other relevant cases, one way to proceed is to begin with that case.

For example, you may read the case and use the headnotes in the West reporter to work from the case to the most relevant topics and key numbers. Then use the key number to look through the relevant digests or do a key number search on WESTLAW to find more cases on the point of that key number. Another method of finding the key number, if you know the case name but not its citation, is to look up the case in the Table of Cases of the appropriate West digests. The Table of Cases provides citations and key numbers for the case.

The case itself will give you citations to earlier cases that the court regarded as relevant. The context of the opinion should help you to determine which cases you should track down and read. Even more important, you can find more cases using the case citation by Shepardizing the case. By using Shepard's volumes or the Shepard's function on the computers, you can find more recent cases citing your original case that are likely to be relevant to your topic. If you have the time, Shepardize the cases that the court relied on in your original case.

To find out more about the case and its subject matter, use the Table of Cases in a relevant treatise to find whether the case is discussed there. Indexes to legal periodicals also contain Tables of Cases that will direct you to articles and comments about that case.

2. Starting With No Research Information

If your problem is a common law problem, and you start with no citations to cases, then you must find relevant cases by using the secondary sources or the digests, which are search tools that are, in effect, an indexing system for published case law. You can gain access to these materials by using the facts of your problem to provide words for your search.

a. Using Secondary Sources

If you know little or nothing about the area of law involved, then you may want to begin with a secondary source. These materials provide background information and citations to relevant cases. If you have identified the large area of law in which the problem belongs, such as tort or contract, then a good place to start your research may be a treatise in that field. You might also begin with an A.L.R. annotation or a legal encyclopedia article. Then seek out articles in law reviews and other periodicals. For many conventional legal problems, however, articles in periodicals may be too specialized to use at the beginning of your research. But if your problem involves a fairly new claim, then a periodical article may be a useful place to begin. You probably would not use computerized research at this point because you would not be able to formulate accurate search terms. However, some people use a computer to begin if the problem involves very distinctive terms that provide accurate search terms.

For most of these sources, you will need to use the index to find the relevant text, although a treatise table of contents will frequently be sufficient. Use the indexes by identifying and searching under key words or ideas you have developed from the facts of the problem. Concentrate on the relationships among the parties, the underlying events, and their chronology. These concepts will describe people, relationships, places, things, and events that supply search terms. Remember also the legal theory that appears to be involved and the relief your client is asking for. If your client wants someone to stop doing something, for example, then your research should concentrate on the requirements for injunctive relief, not for civil damages. Some publishers advise you to begin a search with terms that describe the remedy or the legal theory. If you do search an index under a general remedy such as "damages," or if you look up a broadly defined cause of action such as "torts," you probably will encounter a longer search for relevant information than is necessary because of the breadth of these topics.

If you have used the book before or otherwise already know the publisher's or author's categories, for example, the classifications in the encyclopedias, you may work more efficiently by turning immediately to that particular book chapter or article in the encyclopedia. Encyclopedia articles and chapters in many treatises begin with a table of contents, which some publishers call an index. Look over this index to see how the article or chapter is organized; the index or table often is more efficient to use than the general index. However, unlike the general indexes, these indexes and tables may not provide cross-references to other chapters or articles that treat the subject matter.

Many of the secondary sources provide cross-references to other materials published by that same publisher. These cross-references save search time in the other volumes. The Am. Jur. 2d encyclopedia articles, for example, cross-reference to relevant annotations in the A.L.R. series because both are published by the Lawyers Co-operative Publishing Company. Many West publications cross-reference to other West materials and provide the key number designations for the West digests.

b. Using Digests

If you do not need explanatory or analytical text from a secondary source but immediately want to find relevant cases, then you may want to start your research with a digest. Although other publishers publish digests, the most extensive digest system is that of West Publishing Company, which digests every case it publishes in its case reporters. To use the digest system, you must identify the topic and the key number for the point you are researching. To do so, use the Descriptive Word Index.

Using a general index such as a Descriptive Word Index to a West digest sometimes is a simple task, but also can be a frustrating one, and one that requires creativity. For certain problems, it is easy to formulate index search terms, but finding the proper entries in a general index may still be a circuitous process. For example, if you represent an attorney who has been charged with criminal contempt for not appearing at his client's trial, you probably would select the terms "attorney" and "contempt" as the key words in this problem. The person's status as an attorney is a key fact to the concept of contempt. And contempt is a key word because it is the legal action involved. In this example, you might also decide that "trial," "appearance," and "failure to appear" describe important facts in the problem.

If you looked up "Attorney" in the general index of the recent decennial (the ten-year compilation of the American Digest), however, you will find no relevant entries and no cross-references. You will, however, find "Attorney and Client" if you look down the page. This topic has a long entry, including the sub-entry "Contempt"; however, there are no references relevant to your problem. If you also had looked up "Lawyer" or "Counsel," you would have found no entry for the former and a very short entry for the latter, irrelevant to your problem. Thus, although the publisher suggests that you look under words describing the people involved, that suggestion is not useful in this topic.

You might then turn to "Contempt," and its sub-entry "attorneys." There you will find an entry for "trial, willful absence from" designated key number 20. If you had looked in the topic index at the beginning of the Contempt topic in the digest volume, however, you would have seen a list of all the key numbers along with their descriptions, and you would have noted that the more specific and better key number for your problem is key number 10, "Misconduct as Officer of the Court." Key number 20 is designated "In General." Yet no Descriptive Word Index entry under

"Contempt," sub-entry "Attorneys," refers you to key number 10. To find key number 10 in this index, you would have had to find sub-entry "Appearance" under the "Contempt" entry. If you knew the correct topic, then the topic index would have been more efficient.

Thus, even a relatively straightforward topic requires perseverance and willingness to search under a variety of words that describe the problem when the first attempts fail. Be prepared to use synonyms for your original search terms. For example, try the word "counsel" as well as "attorney." If your problem involved a doctor, you could look under "physician" or "surgeon" as well as doctor; if your problem involved a car, you could look up "automobile."

You should also be ready to formulate broader categories, using more general terms, such as "motor vehicle" instead of automobile. Remember, however, that the more specific the term is to your problem, the more relevant the materials your research turns up should be. Also remember that at a certain point, categories can become too broad to be accurate. Although "litigation" instead of "trial" may not go far afield from your needs, the term "professional" instead of "attorney" would. You also must be prepared to use terms describing other aspects of the problem, such as "contempt" in addition to "attorney." Finally, you need the patience to look line-by-line through an index entry that is long and contains many sub-divisions, such as "Contempt."

Once you have found the most relevant topic and key number, you can use them to look through the entire West digest system to find cases for your problem. You also can employ the key number to update your research in the digest supplements, the General Digest volumes of the American Digest System, and the West case reporters published since the most recent digest supplement. Each case reporter includes a key number digest of the cases in that volume.

The key number also can be an entry for a WESTLAW search. Once you know the key number, you can search on WESTLAW instead of using the digest or you can update the digest by using the computer.

Remember that the digest entry for each case is not necessarily the holding of the case. Rather, the abstracts are statements about a point of law mentioned in the case. Sometimes those statements will be unimportant to the main issues in the case and you will find that the digested case is irrelevant to your problem. You must read the case yourself before you cite it for the point of law at issue. Moreover, even if a case is in the digest, the case may have been reversed or overruled. To find that information, you must use the Shepard's citators, either the Shepard's volumes or the computer services.

You may be using indexes compiled by different publishers for different types of research materials. The search term that proved successful for one resource may not be correct for another. For example, if you look for A.L.R. annotations about the contempt problem in the Index to Annotations under "Contempt," you will find that the most relevant sub-entry in the index is not "Attorney," but "Delay," and "Absence and Presence."

You can avoid the limitations imposed by the publishers' indexing systems by using computerized research, although this form of search has some limitations of its own. To use the computer for your research, you formulate your own search terms. The computer will search through the texts of cases and will retrieve every case in which those words or groups of words appear. Before you can use these systems effectively, however, it is usually advisable to read enough cases and other materials to find the words that describe your problem, and use those exact words in your search.

Computerized research permits you to create your own search terms by identifying the key words in the cases and combining these words to show their relationships. The computer does not free you from thinking about alternative formulations, however. Indeed, it is quite literal and you must use the exact words used in the decisions. For example, if you search under "attorney" and "contempt," you will not retrieve cases in which the court has used "lawyer" or "counsel" instead of "attorney."

IV. *Tailoring Your Research*

A. *Researching Federal Law*

The nature of your research depends not only on how much information you already know about the problem, but on the scope of your problem. When you are doing research on a problem governed by a federal statute, your approach will frequently be different from the approach you would use in doing common law research or even researching a state statute. The digest approach will not give you an overview of the problem. Moreover, reading the annotations to the statute may not be an effective way to begin if the statute is complex and has hundreds of annotations.

You may find it more helpful to begin this type of research by reading law review articles. They can give you an overview of the problem, identify the major issues, and provide references to other materials analyzing the problem. In addition, since even the best law reviews cannot tell you about cases decided after their publication, you will find looseleaf services particularly helpful. You could use either a general looseleaf service, like United States Law Week, which can identify recent cases on a variety of topics, or a specialized looseleaf service that deals with a particular subject area, like labor law or securities law. Specialized looseleaf services are widely used in legal practice and it is wise for you to become familiar with them.

If you are doing research on a federal constitutional issue, you might begin with a treatise, and then go on to law reviews for a more detailed analysis. Some looseleaf services are also very important when researching constitutional issues. The Supreme Court edition of Law Week will tell you whether and how the Supreme Court has dealt with an issue; the general edition of Law Week will provide the lower courts' treatments of important issues. A looseleaf service for a specific subject area, like criminal law or first amendment law, should also be consulted.

If your case involves issues of federal law only, then you will use some different sources from the ones you would use for issues of state law.[2] If your research concerned only a federal statute imposing penalties for criminal contempt, you would find that legislation in the United States Code, the United States Code Annotated, the United States Code Service, and in the session laws published as Statutes at Large. Federal administrative cases and regulations are published separately. In addition, some research tools publish separate volumes for federal law. Thus, you could use the various series of West federal law digests and the Lawyers Co-operative Supreme Court digest to find cases from the federal courts only. You could also look for annotations in the A.L.R. Federal and in Supreme Court Reports, Lawyer's Edition. Moreover, various treatises discuss federal law topics, such as civil procedure or securities law.

B. Researching the Law of One State

You can also narrow your research if your case involves the law of only one state. If, from your own experience, or from the instructions with your assignment, you limit your research to one state's law, then you can use sources limited to that state's law. Start with the state code to find relevant statutes. Use the state's annotated code not only for citations to cases applying the statute, but also for its cross references and for citations to such sources as law review articles about state law. See if there is an encyclopedia of that state's law. Use the digest or digests that are limited

2. Of course, some problems involve research into both federal and state law.

to that state. For each state, West publishes either a state law digest or a regional digest including that state; other companies publish digests of individual state laws. An assignment limited to one state's law permits you to limit your Shepardizing to the Shepard's state citator, where you will also find references to state law materials such as the attorney general's opinions. You may also find that the state's Continuing Legal Education publications are helpful.

You can limit your search in LEXIS and WESTLAW by selecting a data base limited to the local scope of your problem. For example, in LEXIS, choose the proper library and file to restrict the search to cases from a particular state.

V. *Doing Your Research*

Before you begin your research, make sure that you understand your problem and its issues. If the problem is from a class assignment, read it carefully to determine exactly what you have been asked to do. Try not to waste your time by going off on tangents. Make preliminary identifications of the jurisdiction of the problem, the claim involved, the issues within that claim, and the most relevant facts. Identify statutes that may be applicable and other relevant reference materials. Reserve computer time if your library provides sign-up reservations.

When you begin your research, take steps that will save you time later. If you read the cases to determine their relevance before you photocopy, you may save time and money. Even if you photocopy and highlight information on your copies, you should read the cases as you go along and take notes about what you are reading. Your notes should identify your emerging analysis of the issues and facts and which cases are relevant to them. In that way you are not faced with a mass of undifferentiated highlighted copies when it is time to analyze the problem and write. You may want to start an outline right away. The outline should identify the issues and break them down into their component parts. Then preliminarily fill in the cases and statutes you need for each part.

Copy important information so you will not have to retrieve it later on. Be careful to put quotation marks around all exact quotes so that if you use a quotation in your written work, you will identify it as such. Write down the page numbers of the text you are quoting or paraphrasing to use in the citation. Remember that you must attribute paraphrases and ideas from the texts with citations to their sources, including the pages on which they are found.

Take down full citation information of all authorities when you read them, including parallel citations, the courts and dates of the cases, and the edition numbers of books such as treatises. If you read a case in which more than one issue was decided, write down the headnote numbers for those issues relevant to your research. You will shorten your search in Shepard's and eliminate the reading of cases cited for statements about issues different from yours if you search with the relevant headnote numbers.

One of your most difficult judgments will be to decide when to stop your research. On the one hand, a little more digging may turn up the perfect case. On the other hand, that time, for which you will be charging your client, may yield nothing that you have not seen, perhaps many times. When you already have found and read the cases and secondary sources that are cited in the new materials you are turning up, then you probably have done enough research.

Often, you will find deficiencies in your research when you outline or begin to write. At those stages of your work you may find that you have not done enough research in certain areas of the problem. You may not have thought through every relevant line of analysis, or you may not have enough support for a particular conclusion. Once you start writing and thus must commit your reasoning to paper, you should confront these flaws in research or analysis. If you begin writing early enough, you leave time to evaluate your progress and your understanding of the problem. Then you can continue research in those areas in which you are not satisfied with your work.

As you do your research you should be continually refining your understanding of the problem. You started your work by identifying important facts. As you then read through the sources, you identified the general rules those facts bring into play, and the particular issues that are raised in your problem. The cases and statutes you found should have suggested how to organize an analysis of those issues. You would then have determined those types of facts that courts have considered especially relevant to these issues. Your focus on relevant facts should enable you to refine your understanding of the problem, and to narrow your research to cases most similar to your problem.

For all research, remember: (1) learn which sources are most useful for particular research; (2) be resourceful when you use indexes; (3) update all sources by using pocket parts and supplements; (4) eliminate sources that merely duplicate what you already have done; (5) Shepardize all primary authorities you rely on; (6) evaluate the authoritative value of the sources and the quality of their analyses.

Chapter 12
Writing to the Court

I. Introduction to Persuasive Writing

A. Purpose, Tone, Audience

In Chapter Four we discussed how to write a legal memorandum that would be used within a law office to analyze a legal problem. The purpose of such a memorandum was to analyze the problem in an objective exploratory way and reach a conclusion based on that analysis. When you are writing to a court, however, your purpose is very different. You are then writing as an advocate representing one side in a dispute and your purpose is not to explore, but to persuade. Everything you write should be designed to persuade the court to rule in your client's favor.

Although the purpose of an advocate's writing is to persuade, you do not achieve this purpose by adopting a strident, wildly argumentative tone. Persuasion is not achieved by belligerence. Your tone will certainly be more assertive than it is in a memorandum. However, your ability to be convincing will ultimately depend on the underlying strength of your arguments, the language you choose to make those arguments, and the credibility you achieve with the court.

The documents that you submit to the court will be the first source of this information. (Oral argument is the second source.) It is appropriate to assume that judges have a general understanding of the law. However, they may not be familiar with the particular legal principles that govern your case and will have no knowledge of the facts of the case. Accordingly, you should include all relevant material, both factual and legal, that the court will need to render a decision.

B. Documents Written to Trial and Appellate Courts

A document written for a trial court may be called a memorandum of law, an advocacy memorandum of law, or a trial brief. A memorandum of law seeks to persuade the court of the validity of one point of view. It is frequently submitted in support of or in opposition to a motion. Attorneys may also submit a memorandum of law to present their side of any disputed issue, to summarize the evidence, to support or oppose post-trial motions, and to request particular instructions to the jury. Finally, attorneys may file extensive post-trial briefs at the end of the litigation to present the court with their final arguments based on the facts adduced at trial. A memorandum of law tends to be shorter than an appellate brief and less rigid in format.

An appellate brief is a formal document submitted to an appellate court by which an advocate presents a case to a court for review. An appellate brief differs from a memorandum of law in that it is written from a record on appeal and is written to affirm or reverse a lower court's decision. An appellate court does not hear evidence in the case as does a trial court. Rather, the appellate court reviews the trial court's decision to determine whether, based on the record below, the trial court committed error in hearing or deciding the case. An appellate court's review is limited by the power of the court to review particular questions, by the standard of review that is appropriate to the court and to the case, and by the record in the court below.

II. Court Rules

Whether you are filing a motion before a trial court or filing an appeal before an appellate court, you must familiarize yourself with the applicable court rules. Some rules apply to all courts of a certain type, such as the Federal Rules of Civil Procedure (governing civil cases filed in all federal trial courts) or the Federal Rules of Appellate Procedure (governing cases filed in all federal appellate courts). Other rules apply to particular local courts. Often, more than one set of rules will be relevant. For example, an attorney suing in federal district court in the Eastern District of New York will have to be aware of both the Federal Rules of Civil Procedure and the applicable local court rules of the Eastern District. An attorney filing an appeal in the Court of

Appeals for the Second Circuit would be bound by both the Federal Rules of Appellate Procedure and the rules of the Second Circuit.

Rules cover a variety of points, some substantive and some technical. For example, Rule 23 of the Federal Rules of Civil Procedure establishes the prerequisites for a class action, but Rule 6 is only technical, describing the method for computing periods of time under the Federal Rules. Local rules governing motion practice may prescribe the content of a memorandum in support of or in opposition to a motion, set out time and page limitations, or require attorneys to confer with opposing attorneys before bringing any motion to compel discovery.

You must familiarize yourself with the applicable court rules at the start of your case. Failure to do so could be disastrous.[1] You do not want to discover the night before you submit a 75 page brief that the page limit for your type of brief is 65 pages, and that an application to file a longer brief had to be submitted 15 days ago. Nor do you want to miss a deadline for filing a brief because you thought you had 20 days to file a reply brief and the correct period of time is 14 days.

III. The Memorandum in Support of or in Opposition to a Motion

A. Introduction

When you have a case before a trial court, it may be necessary or advisable for you to file one or more motions with the court.[2] A motion is a request to the court for a ruling on a legal question.

---

1. For example, see this excerpt from Swicker v. Ryan, 346 N.W.2d 367, 369 (Minn. App. 1984):

While we are mindful of . . . the court's discretionary authority to consider the matter on the merits irrespective of legal procedural defects, the case load before Minnesota appellate courts in 1984 requires a firm application of the new rules of appellate procedure. The bench and bar had sufficient time since August 1, 1983, the effective date of the new rules, and November 1, 1983, the effective date of the implementation for the Court of Appeals to become aware of the necessity for firm judicial and calendaring administration. Failure of counsel to follow the rules, or to timely make appropriate motions cannot be countenanced. Unfamiliarity with the rules, a heavy work load, or overwork is not good cause. The rules must be viewed as the guideposts for efficient court administration. We intend to apply them firmly and reasonably.

Failure of appellant to process an appeal, appealing from a non-appealable order and failure to timely order a transcript, are sufficient grounds to grant the motion of dismissal. This matter is dismissed.

2. See generally R. Haydock, D. Herr, J. Stempel, Fundamentals of Pretrial Litigation (1985)

The court will respond to a motion with a ruling called an order. You may make the motion on your own initiative or the court may request that all parties file memoranda on a legal question that has arisen in the course of litigation. Motions are usually accompanied by: 1) a "notice of motion" which will notify the other side that a motion has been filed, 2) a memorandum of law which supports the motion, and 3) a proposed order (a ruling in your favor which the judge could sign). Supporting documents, like affidavits (a person's written statements either sworn to or affirmed), may also be appropriate.

Attorneys make motions at many different stages of litigation. You will probably discuss these motions in your Civil Procedure class. The plaintiff's attorney may file a motion for a preliminary injunction at the same time that the complaint is filed. The defendant's attorney may respond to the complaint with a motion to dismiss the complaint for failure to state a claim. If the case proceeds, the plaintiff's attorney may make a motion for certification of a class. The defendant's attorney may move for summary judgment. Either attorney may make a motion to compel discovery, or make a motion for a directed verdict at the close of the evidence offered by an opponent at trial. Finally, a party who has lost after a trial may make a motion for a new trial or to alter or amend the judgment.

Behind every motion that you file will be your theory of the case. The theory of the case combines two elements: the legal framework from which you present your client's position and the facts in your client's "story" which would justify relief under that legal framework.[3] It summarizes the reasons why your client deserves to win. For example, the plaintiff's theory in a negligence case may be that Dr. X was negligent in failing to provide due care to patient Y by leaving a surgical sponge in the patient's abdomen. Dr. X's theory of the case, his defense, may be that he used due care and that another doctor's actions caused whatever harm may have occurred. Or the plaintiff's theory of the case in an employment discrimination suit may be that affirmative action for blacks and hispanics is necessary to achieve real racial equality while the defendant company would characterize such relief as reverse discrimination.

Your theory of the case will provide an analytical foundation for any motion that you file. However, you also need to be aware

---

3. M. Berger, J. Mitchell, R. Clark,
Pretrial Advocacy: Planning, Analysis,
& Strategy 18 (1988).

of the technical standards that govern the particular motion that you are filing. For example, a motion to dismiss the complaint under Rule 12(b)(6) of the Federal Rules of Civil Procedure for "failure to state a claim upon which relief can be granted" is based entirely on the allegations of the complaint. All of the facts in the plaintiff's complaint will be taken as true, and the question is whether, under those facts, the plaintiff is entitled to any legal relief. In support of the motion to dismiss, you would try to convince the court that even accepting the facts as the plaintiff states them, the plaintiff cannot recover under any legal theory and the complaint must be dismissed. A motion for summary judgment under Rule 56 of the Federal Rules of Civil Procedure is based on a different standard. Under the standard for that motion, the moving party would argue that the pleadings, discovery materials, and affidavits filed show that "there is no genuine issue as to any material fact," and that the moving party is entitled to judgment as a matter of law. Accordingly, the attorney's focus should be on whether there are any material facts in dispute, and why, based on the indisputable material facts, the attorney's client is entitled to judgment as a matter of law.

B. *Format of a Memorandum in Support of or in Opposition to a Motion*

There is no required format for the memorandum in support of a motion. Courts generally require that the moving party set forth both the grounds for the motion with citation to supporting authorities and the specific relief sought. Memoranda may be divided into the following sections: the Caption and Title, the Introduction, the Statement of Facts, the Question(s) Presented, the Argument, the Conclusion, and any supporting affidavits or appendices.

1. *Caption and Title*

The first page of a memorandum contains at a glance the basic information about the case: the caption includes the name of the court, the names of the parties, the docket number, and the initials of the judge to whom the case has been assigned. It also includes the title of the memorandum in support of or in opposition to the motion. The cover page of the memorandum will usually contain the same information along with the name, address, and phone number of the attorney. A sample caption and title follows:

IN THE UNITED STATES DISTRICT COURT FOR THE
SOUTHERN DISTRICT OF NEW YORK

JANE SMITH, JOAN JONES, and MARY DOE, individually and on behalf of all others similarly situated, Plaintiffs, -against- CONSOLIDATED ELECTRIC CORP., Defendant.	89 Civ. 284 (M.R.W.)

MEMORANDUM OF LAW IN SUPPORT OF
PLAINTIFFS' MOTION FOR DETERMINATION OF THE CLASS

2. Introduction

The Memorandum of Law may contain an Introduction designed to provide a context for the motion and to provide the court with basic information about the case. The Introduction should at least identify the parties, the nature of the motion, and the relief sought. For example,

Introduction

Plaintiffs Jane Smith, Joan Jones, and Mary Doe sued defendant Consolidated Electric Corporation alleging discrimination in employment on the grounds of sex in violation of Title VII of the Civil Rights Act of 1964, as amended, 42 U.S.C. § 2000e et seq. (1988). This memorandum of law is submitted in support of plaintiffs' motion pursuant to Rule 23(c)(1) of the Federal Rules of Civil Procedure for an order:

(a) allowing this action to be maintained as a class action pursuant to Rules 23(a) and 23(b)(2) of the Federal Rules of Civil Procedure, and

(b) defining the class represented by plaintiffs as all female employees of Consolidated Electric Corporation who have unsuccessfully sought or who, but for the discriminatory acts and practices of the defendant, would have sought management positions with Consolidated Electric Corporation.

If the memorandum deals with a legal question that is not complex, some attorneys dispense with the Introduction entirely.

3. Statement of Facts

The Statement of Facts usually includes the procedural history of the case as it relates to the motion and the relevant facts. Keep two main points in mind as you write it. First, because the court is dealing with many different matters and cannot be expected to be familiar with the facts of your case or even the basic legal arguments that are relevant to the motion, you must provide this information. Second, because you are looking for a favorable ruling, you must present the facts of your case in such a way that the court will be inclined to decide the motion in your favor.

If your Memorandum contains an Introduction, you will need to decide which information should be stated in the Introduction and which in the procedural history of the case. The procedural history in the example above could be written:

Statement of Facts

On February 21, 1989, plaintiffs Jane Smith, Joan Jones, and Mary Doe filed a complaint individually and on behalf of others similarly situated challenging a course of conduct by defendant Consolidated Electric Corporation. Plaintiffs alleged that the defendant discriminated on the basis of sex in the terms and conditions of employment relating to hiring and promotion for management positions.

After the procedural history, you would present the facts of the case that support your motion. To do this effectively, you must be familiar with the legal standards that govern the motion that you are bringing. A class action motion in federal court, for example, is governed by Rule 23. This Rule outlines certain prerequisites for class certification, including the requirements in Rule 23(a) that

"(1) the class is so numerous that joinder of all members is impracticable, (2) there are questions of law and fact common to the class; (3) the claims or defenses of the representative party are typical of the claims or defenses of the class, and (4) the representative parties will fairly and adequately represent the interests of the class."

Therefore, you would include facts that support the requirements of numerosity, commonality, typicality, and representativeness. These facts would likely come from pleadings, discovery documents (interrogatories and depositions), and affidavits. You should cite to these documents in the Statement of Facts. In the sex discrimination case, for example, you could include facts showing that the class is so numerous that joinder of all members of the class would be impracticable because Consolidated Electric has offices in five different states and because more than 80 women are potential members of the class.

In addition to the legal standard, you should think of how you can present the facts in a way that would be most convincing. Although it is inappropriate in the Statement of Facts to adopt an argumentative tone, it is still possible to arrange facts in such a way that they incline the court to see the case and the motion from your perspective. More detailed suggestions on writing a Statement of Facts are contained in section III of Chapter Thirteen.

4. *Question Presented (Statement of Issues)*

Some memoranda of law include a section in which the attorney states the legal questions that the motion raises. A memorandum could have one or more Questions Presented. This section could either precede or follow the Statement of Facts or be omitted altogether.

The Question should both focus the court's attention on the basic issues in your motion and suggest an answer that would support a decision by the court in your favor. Each Question combines the relevant facts of a case and a legal rule. For example, a person seeking to intervene in an action in federal court pursuant to Fed. R. Civ. P. 24 must make a "timely application". Therefore, one ground on which to oppose a motion to intervene is that the motion was not timely. A question presented raising this issue could be stated:

> Is the agency's motion to intervene timely when it was made more than three years after the action was commenced and almost ten months after the judgment was entered?

To intervene as of right pursuant to Fed. R. Civ. P. 24(a)(2), an applicant must also show a legally protectable interest. A party opposing the motion could state:

> Did a preliminary injunction remedying racial discrimination against non-whites create a legally protectable interest, within the meaning of Fed. R. Civ. P. 24(a)(2), for white persons who seek to intervene as plaintiffs to obtain union membership for themselves?

The question in both of these examples focuses on a legal issue that the court must consider in deciding whether to grant or deny the motion (timeliness, legally protectable interest) and is framed in such a way that the attorney's argument is clear. More detailed suggestions on writing a Question Presented can be found in section II of Chapter Thirteen.

5. *Argument*

The Argument is the heart of your memorandum. In it you provide the facts, citations to authority, and reasoning to convince the court to rule in your favor on the motion. The Argument is often divided into sections representing the main legal arguments in the memorandum, although a short memorandum may only have one basic argument.

You may begin each section with a point heading that states the conclusion that you want the court to reach on that legal point. The point heading is a conclusory sentence which combines the facts of the case with the legal principles analyzed in that section. For example,

> The Requirement that Public Health Sanitarians be Citizens of the United States Violates the Equal Protection Clause of the Fourteenth Amendment to the United States Constitution.

If your motion is based on a rule which sets out certain requirements, then you may have a separate section in your memorandum for each of these requirements. As noted in the section on the Statement of Facts, a plaintiff who wishes to bring a class action must satisfy all four requirements of Rule 23(a). It may be appropriate, then, to discuss each requirement in a separate section.

As to the order of arguments, you should begin with any threshold arguments which are present, or if there are none, then with the strongest argument supporting your position on the motion. Remember to interweave the facts of the case with the legal points. An Argument which is only an abstract discussion of the law will not be effective. Extensive suggestions on writing an Argument are contained in Chapter Thirteen.

6. Conclusion

The Conclusion is a brief statement, often one sentence, reminding the court of the relief you are seeking. It is often followed by a phrase like "Respectfully submitted", and then by the signature and name, address, and telephone number of the attorney of record. For example,

> For the foregoing reasons, plaintiff's motion for a preliminary injunction should be granted.

Respectfully submitted,

ATTORNEY'S NAME
Attorney's address
Attorney's phone number

Attorney for Plaintiff Jane Doe

IV. The Appellate Brief

A. Introduction

An appeal is not a re-trying of a case. Appellate courts do not hear evidence in the case as do trial courts. Rather, an appellate court's review is typically limited to a review of the trial court's decision to determine whether, based on the record of the evidence, the trial court committed error in hearing or deciding the case. The function of the appellant's attorney is, therefore, not to fashion a new theory of the case on appeal, but to search the record to determine what errors the trial court may have committed, to select the issues that have the best chance of convincing an appellate court to reverse the decision below, and to shape the arguments as convincingly as possible. The primary function of the appellee's attorney is to argue in favor of affirming the judgment below.

B. Standard of Review

An attorney must also consider the standard of review that is appropriate to each case. The standard of review that an appellate court uses will depend on a number of factors, including the court itself (federal, state, intermediate appellate, highest appellate), the nature of the case (civil, criminal), and the type of error alleged. It is important, though not always easy, for the attorney to determine the appropriate standard of review. The standards of review cover a wide range: [4]

- review of questions of law—

    An appellate court does not have to defer to the trial court's opinion on a question of law and can decide the issue de novo (without regard to the lower court's determination).

    E.g., Can an unmarried cohabitant sue for loss of consortium?

    Did a School Board violate its students' first amendment rights by denying them access to their high school for meetings after school?

- review of questions of fact—

    a) jury trials—

    An appellate court will give great deference to a jury verdict and will generally not reverse that verdict. In civil cases, a jury verdict will be reversed only if it

---

4. The categories were taken from the discussion of the Standard of Review in <u>Appellate Advocacy Principles</u> and Practice: Cases and Materials 67–104 (1990) by U. Bentele and E. Cary.

is unsupported by any evidence. If the verdict is supported by some evidence, however, to get appellate review of the weight or the sufficiency of the evidence, the attorney must have made a timely motion below. In criminal cases, the verdict will be set aside if the appellate court determines that no rational jury could have found the elements of the crime beyond a reasonable doubt.

b) trials by the court—

Findings of fact made by a trial court are also given significant deference, though not as great as that given jury verdicts. Under the Federal Rules of Civil Procedure Rule 52(a), for example, a federal trial court's findings of fact will not be set aside unless they are "clearly erroneous".

E.g., Was the trial court's finding that the promotions were not the result of discriminatory intent clearly erroneous?

• review of mixed questions of law and fact—

The standard of review is difficult to characterize because the courts have not adopted a single approach as to whether these questions should be treated more like questions of law or questions of fact.

E.g., Was the plaintiff constructively discharged from his job?

• discretion of the trial court—

Trial courts have discretion to determine certain issues. For example, many statutes give the trial judge discretion to award attorneys' fees. A discretionary decision by the trial court may be reversed for abuse of the discretion, for improvident exercise of the discretion, or for a failure to exercise discretion. The extent of the trial court's discretion will depend on the matter at issue.

E.g., Did the trial court abuse its discretion in denying the plaintiff back pay in an employment discrimination suit?

In analyzing your case and in writing your brief, you should include a reference to the appropriate standard of review, and, if necessary, an argument as to the correct standard. The standard of review that the appellate court uses can determine the outcome of the case. Therefore, in writing an appellate brief, the attorney should be aware of the strength of the issues not simply in terms of the merits but also in terms of how likely the appellate court is to reverse the trial court's decision.

C. *Format of an Appellate Brief*

In the rest of this chapter, we describe the parts of a brief that most appellate courts require. In the next chapter, we discuss some of these parts in detail and offer more specific suggestions on writing and strategy.

1. *Title Page*

The Title Page is the outside front cover of your brief. At the top of the page you identify the court to which the case is being appealed and provide the index number to your case. The Title Page also includes the name of the Appellant and Appellee and may identify the Plaintiff and Defendant below. Under this information, you name the court from which the case is being appealed, the party whose brief this is, and the name and address of the attorney representing that party.

2. *Table of Contents*

The Table of Contents should contain page references for each section of your brief, including the other introductory tables. These sections usually are the:

Table of Authorities

Question Presented

Statement of the Case

Summary of Argument

Argument

Conclusion

Appendix (if any)

In addition, the Table of Contents includes the point headings (and subheadings, if any) for the sections in the Argument. The outline of the point headings gives the court a quick summary of the content of the Argument and permits the reader to find the page at which any particular point begins. Type the headings in the Argument in upper case; type the subheadings in upper and lower case, indented and underlined.

3. *Table of Authorities*

In the Table of Authorities you provide page references in your brief for the authorities you relied on in the Argument. Ordinarily, you divide the authorities into categories. Cases, put in alphabetical order, with citations, are given first. (If a case is repeatedly cited, use <u>passim</u> instead of a page reference.) Then list the Constitutional and Statutory Provisions, and the Administrative Regulations. Other authorities may be put under the heading of Miscellaneous, or you may set out other categories.

Some schools will require that their students' briefs conform to the format required by the Rules of the Supreme Court of the United States. Under these Rules, the brief should also include sections entitled Opinion Below, Jurisdictional Statement, and Constitutional and Statutory Provisions Involved. See Sample Appellate Brief, Appendix D.

4.   *Question(s) Presented*

The Question Presented sets out the legal issues that the parties will argue, incorporating the key facts of the case, in order to tell the court what the appeal is about. Like all other parts of the brief, the Question Presented is also intended to persuade the court of the correctness of your client's position. You can use the Question Presented as a way of getting the court to see the issues in the case from your client's point of view by framing the question so that it suggests a response in your favor.

The number of Questions generally corresponds to the number of issues in the case.

5.   *Statement of the Case*

In the Statement of the Case, you have an opportunity to tell the court what happened in the case from your client's point of view. The Statement of the Case frequently includes two components: an opening paragraph and a Statement of Facts. The opening paragraph, often called the Preliminary Statement, includes procedural information about how the case got to that court. It describes the nature of the action, the parties involved, the wrongs alleged, the losses sustained, and the relief requested. It also tells the court the type of order from which the appeal is taken.

In the Statement of Facts, you should present the material facts of the case, but in a way that inclines the court to your client's perspective. By selecting and arranging the facts, and by artful writing, you may accurately portray the events giving rise to the litigation, yet still present those events from your client's point of view. All material facts, however, even those unfavorable to your client, must be included. Your tone in the Statement of Facts to some extent should be objective even though the purpose of this section is not only to tell the court about the case but also to incline the court to view your client's position favorably. Strident declamations, exaggerated characterizations, exclamation points, and argumentative statements only detract from an effective presentation of the facts.

6. *Summary of the Argument*

The Summary of the Argument is a clear condensation of the arguments made in the body of the brief. Write the Summary in ordinary prose; do not merely string the headings together. Discuss each major section of the brief in a separate paragraph.

The length of the Summary will vary according to the complexity of the case. However, it should be in proportion to the length of the Argument itself. A fifteen page Argument should have neither a five line nor a five page Summary. A more appropriate Summary would be between one and two pages.

Generally, you should not include citations in the Summary, unless a case is so central to an argument that it is impossible to summarize the Argument without referring to it.

7. *Argument*

The Argument is the heart of the brief. It is the place where you present the arguments that you hope will persuade the court that your client's position is correct.

The Argument is usually divided into sections representing the main legal arguments in the brief, although occasionally a brief will have only one basic argument. Begin each section with a point heading that states the conclusion that you want the court to reach on that legal point. The point heading is a conclusory sentence which combines the facts of the case with the legal principles analyzed in that section. Where warranted, a section may be divided into subsections, each beginning with a separate subheading. It is unwise, however, to divide the argument into too many small subsections. An overly divided argument may be choppy and flow poorly.

Remember that an Argument which is only an abstract discussion of the law will not be effective. Therefore, you should always relate the legal points to your argument back to the facts of your case. Otherwise, the Argument will become a law review article on a general topic, not a persuasive piece of writing focused on your particular case.

8. *Conclusion*

The conclusion is very brief. It is not another summary of the arguments. Instead it specifies the relief which the party is seeking. It is followed by a closing, like "Respectfully Submitted," and then your name and address as attorney of record.

Chapter Thirteen
Writing the Appellate Brief

I. Introduction

The purpose of an appellate brief is to convince a court to grant relief to your client for the issues on appeal. Thus, your task as a brief writer is to present persuasively those arguments and that evidence which would convince a court that your client's position is the only one that comports with law and justice. In a brief, you should not present an objective analysis of the law and facts, as you do in a memorandum. Nor should you plead patently frivolous claims in highly emotional and bombastic language. Because persuasiveness in a brief is closely tied to credibility, you should present your arguments reasonably, but with conviction and thoroughness.

A. Selecting Issues for Appeal

Normally, the first step in preparing an appeal is to review the record closely and research the law carefully in order to narrow the issues to those that are truly arguable. Because you want your brief to be credible, you need to avoid making both frivolous claims and too many claims. As the Supreme Court recently observed, "a brief which treats more than three or four matters runs serious risks of becoming too diffuse and giving the overall impression that no one claim of error can be serious." Jones v. Barnes, 463 U.S. 745, 752 n.5 (1983).[1] In the Court's estimation, if you cannot win on the merits of your stronger

---

1. Quoting the Committee on Federal Courts of the Association of the Bar of New York, Appeals to the Second Circuit 38 (1980).

points, you will not win on your weaker points; an attorney should, therefore, winnow out the weaker arguments. Id. at 751–52.[2] In first-year legal writing courses, the issues may have been selected for you by your instructors. You should be aware nonetheless of some of the considerations that go into selecting issues for appeal.

For a real appeal, you would begin by reading the record to get a feel for the case.[3] Since the facts surrounding each legal issue give rise to initial impressions about your client's claims, appraise the record first from this viewpoint. Also examine as possible grounds for appeal each motion or objection made by trial counsel and decided adversely to your client. Then try to grasp the trial counsel's and the opposing counsel's theories of the case. After this, research the legal issues thoroughly.

On the basis of this initial research, begin to plot out your strategy. Ascertain which facts are material, which arguments are consequential (that is, which arguments would give your client the greatest relief, like a dismissal of charges), and which arguments are persuasive (that is, which are likely to convince a court to rule in your favor but which will not necessarily give your client the same degree of relief, like a new trial or a modified sentence). After you identify those arguments for which there is a basis of appeal, decide which combination of persuasive and consequential arguments would most help your client. You have now, at least tentatively, selected your issues.

B. Choosing Arguments in Support of an Issue

Once you have decided which issues to appeal, you must decide which arguments to raise in support of your claims. Usually your research will suggest the legal arguments and the policy arguments you ought to put forward. When considering these options, however, be careful not to raise contradictory, inconsistent claims. You can argue, for example, that a court improperly denied a request for an adjournment because, although trial counsel exercised due diligence, he was unable to interview a key witness who was in the hospital. If you make this point, however, you cannot also argue that a court improperly denied a request for

---

2. Note also that the Code of Professional Responsibility, DR7–102A(1), says, "A lawyer shall not bring or defend a proceeding, or assert or controvert an issue therein, unless there is a basis for doing so that is not frivolous, which includes a good faith argument for an extension, modification or reversal of existing law." See also Model Rules of Professional Conduct, Rule 3.1.

3. The suggestions offered here are paraphrased from W. Hellerstein, "Appeal to Intermediate Appellate Courts," in Basic Criminal Law Practice (1985).

an adjournment because a key witness was never interviewed due to ineffective counsel who failed to exercise due diligence.

Also, consider whether raising an argument in the alternative is strategically appropriate. It is appropriate when your client could materially benefit even under the alternative argument. Assume, for example, that a child defendant in a negligence suit was held to an adult standard of reasonable care because the child was engaged in an adult activity. On appeal, you might argue first that the lower court applied the wrong standard because an exception to the rule applied. Under that exception, very young children can be held to a child's standard regardless of their participation in an adult activity. You would go on to show that your client is not liable under the child's standard of reasonable care. Then, if you think the facts would warrant a reversal even under the adult standard, it would be appropriate to raise this as an alternative argument. If you think that this argument has no merit whatsoever, however, you would not include this alternative argument in your brief.

C. Ordering Issues

After selecting your issues, you must decide how to order them. Generally, a brief follows the order of importance, that is, you begin with the most persuasive and consequential argument and move in a descending order down to the least important argument. There are two primary reasons for organizing your brief this way. First, the realities are such that a judge might not read your entire brief; in order to ensure that your most important argument will at least be read, you will want to put it in a prominent place in the brief. Second, by beginning with your most important argument, you set a positive tone for your brief as well as establishing yourself as a serious, credible, and thoughtful advocate. Of course, to organize a brief in order of importance, you must determine which of your arguments is the most important. Logic and strategy must be considered.

Strategy involves weighing the merits of your most persuasive argument (that which is most likely to succeed) against the merits of arguments affording your client greater relief. You must come to a realistic decision about whether your client is best served by beginning with the most persuasive argument or with the most consequential. When your arguments are of unequal strength, most attorneys advise beginning with your most persuasive argument, i.e., that argument which has the greatest chance of success based on the law and the facts. When your arguments are of comparable weight, however, most attorneys advise that you begin with your most consequential argument, i.e., the one which will most benefit your client. Common sense dictates that if you can argue a point that will give your client substantial relief as convincingly as a point that gives less relief, you begin with the argument which has greater consequences.

There may be times, of course, when you wish to depart from these established conventions. If, for example, your most persuasive argument really will not materially assist your client, you might decide to begin with the argument which would most benefit your client. You might also consider whether your client has expressed a strong preference for one argument or whether the court to which you are appealing is more receptive to one kind of a legal argument than another. An intermediate court of appeals, for example, would probably be more receptive to a fact-centered or doctrinal argument. A state supreme court, however, might be more open to a policy-centered argument (one which focuses on the purpose of the rule and the desirability of the end) or to an institutionally-directed argument (one which focuses on whether a legislative body or a court should create a rule).

Strategy is not the only factor in ordering your issues. You must also consider logic. Discuss threshold issues before other issues. Threshold questions—involving, for example, jurisdiction or a statute of limitations—take logical priority over other issues because the court's decision with respect to the former may obviate and preclude the court from considering the latter. If you have interdependent issues such that one question must be resolved before another question can be meaningfully addressed, logic dictates that you treat the threshold question before the dependent question. For example, a decision must be rendered on whether a party consented to a search before an argument can be made about whether that party revoked consent.

Other problems will present you with different types of legal questions, for example, a constitutional and a statutory question. Barring special considerations, you would deal with the statutory question first and the constitutional question second. For example, a state sodomy statute would be scrutinized first for whether the defendant violated the statute. If the defendant did not violate the statute, then the court need not decide whether it is unconstitutional.

The interrelation of some issues might also be a factor in ordering issues. You might decide to shift a persuasive argument into a less prominent position in order to follow one point with discussion of another, related point. Assume, for instance, that you have a persuasive argument that the trial judge unduly interfered with the cross-examination, a moderately strong argument that someone was improperly excused for cause during jury selection, and a weak argument that the prosecutor made an inflammatory summation. You might decide to follow the argument on the prejudicial conduct of the judge with the argument on the prejudicial conduct of the prosecutor simply because the two issues may involve similar facts and legal questions.

These, then, are some of the factors you consider in ordering your issues. To check on the order and organization of issues and subissues, many people prepare an outline which helps to clarify the logical relationships among ideas (rules of outlining are discussed in the section on Point Headings). Once you have decided upon an order, make sure your Questions Presented, Point Headings, and Arguments adhere to that order.

II. *Questions Presented*

Under most court rules, the Questions Presented must appear at the beginning of the brief. Thus, the Questions Presented are in effect the introduction to your brief and will be the first part that the judges read. The Question or Questions must introduce the case to the court by setting out the legal issues that the parties will argue and by providing a factual context that explains how those issues arose. Rule 15.1(a) of the Supreme Court of the United States requires that the questions be "short and concise." They should also be understandable, preferably on first reading.

If your topic contains more than one issue, then you must pose more than one Question. Put your Questions in the order in which they will be argued. Each Question should be written in the same form, either as a statement beginning with "whether" or in question form, beginning, for example, with "may" or "does."

Some suggestions for writing the Questions follow.

A. The Questions should include a reference to the constitutional provision, statute, or common law cause of action under which the case arises. For example:

> Is the decision by a private nursing home to transfer a patient from a skilled nursing care facility to a health-related facility subject to the procedural requirements of the due process clause of the fourteenth amendment?

This Question identifies the due process clause as the constitutional provision at issue in this case. For a lesser known cause of action, for example, one that arises under a statute, you may want to include the operative statutory language in the Question.

> Did a person violate 18 U.S.C. § 1071, which prohibits harboring or concealing a person for whom a federal warrant has been issued, when he gave a fugitive money and lied about the fugitive's whereabouts?

B. The Question should also provide the facts of the case as they relate to the issue. Because a judge must decide each case

according to its facts and must apply the established principles of
law to those facts, the Question should include some of the factual
aspects of the case which gave rise to the legal question. Try,
therefore, to avoid "label" or abstract questions that identify the
type of action that is before the court but tell nothing about the
particular facts of the case. An example of a label question is:

> Did the police seize the evidence in a search of petitioner's
> residence that violated his fourth amendment rights?

This Question labels the case as a search and seizure problem but
does not indicate the particular nature of the fourth amendment
problem. The sentence could be the issue in almost every fourth
amendment case. The writer of this Question should have identified why the police seizure of evidence may have violated the
fourth amendment.

> Was the evidence seized in a search of petitioner's residence inadmis-
> sible on fourth amendment grounds when petitioner gave his consent
> to search only after the police officer implied he had legal authority
> for the search regardless of consent?

Similarly, the nursing home question provides the facts of the
case as they relate to the requirements of the fourteenth amendment. When you provide a factual context, you help the court by
defining the particular issue your case poses.

Note, however, that appeals based on questions of law (rather
than on questions of fact or mixed questions of law and fact) need
not include the particular facts that gave rise to the dispute.
Instead they should include details about the rule under judicial
scrutiny.

> Does a statute that bans the advertisement of tobacco products in
> places offering "family" oriented entertainment violate an adver-
> tiser's first amendment right to free speech?

Or again, in the question below, it is unnecessary to relate specific
facts establishing the child witness's likely trauma if forced to
testify in front of the accused because the question is about the
constitutionality of the statute, not its applicability to the particular child witness in this trial.

> Is a statute valid under the sixth amendment right of confrontation if
> it allows a child witness in a sex-offense prosecution to testify outside
> of defendant's presence by one-way closed-circuit television when the
> statute can be applied only upon a showing of individualized, clear,
> and convincing trauma to the witness?

C. State the Question as a general principle that would apply
to anyone in the particular situation of these parties. One consequence of placing the Questions Presented first is that the reader
knows nothing about the parties. Therefore, you should identify
the parties by general description rather than by name. In the

following example, the appellant is identified as a member of the bar, not as "appellant" or by name.

> Do the first and fourteenth amendments protect a member of the bar from disciplinary action when she advises members of an organization of their rights and discloses the price and availability of legal services?

Another consequence of placing the questions first is that you must avoid general and vague references to facts that the reader has not yet been given. For example, do not say:

> Under the circumstances of this case, were the petitioner's fourth amendment rights violated by the manner in which police secured consent?

Instead, flesh out the "circumstances":

> Is an individual's consent to a search of his premises coerced and involuntary under the fourth amendment when that consent follows a statement by a law enforcement officer implying legal authority for the search regardless of consent?

D. Let the Question suggest an answer favorable to your client, but do not overstate your client's case. Most court rules require that the Question not be argumentative. The Question should, therefore, appear neutral. Probably the best way to write a persuasive Question that is not unduly slanted is to incorporate facts and to use word choice and placement advantageously. For example, a Question that is posed favorably but which is not unduly slanted might be:

> Was the evidence that defendant provided a fugitive with some worn clothing and an occasional dinner insufficient to prove a violation of 18 U.S.C. § 1071, which prohibits committing acts of support sufficient to constitute harboring a fugitive so as to prevent the fugitive's discovery?

Incorporating the facts into the Question ensures a measure of objectivity by telling the court what the parties actually did. In the Question above, the writer suggests the evidence is insufficient to establish a violation of the statute, but the court is given room to come to its own decision.

Some writers disagree with the advice that the Question Presented should be framed to suggest the answer favorable to the client, but instead advise that you formulate the issue so neutrally that the opposing counsel will accept it.[4] The nursing home question would meet this criterion.

E. Do not usurp the function of the court by coming to conclusions that assume a favorable resolution of legal and factual

---

4. See, e.g., R. Martineau, Fundamentals of Modern Appellate Advocacy 145 (1985).

issues which the court must decide. The underlined phrases in the examples below are improper because they are conclusions of law.

> Did the respondent Disciplinary Commission's reprimand of the petitioner <u>for actions not likely to cause substantial harm</u> violate the petitioner's rights to freedom of expression and association under the first amendment?

> Is the evidence obtained from a warrantless search conducted pursuant to consent inadmissible on fourth amendment grounds where <u>the consent is not voluntarily given</u> and where the <u>search conducted exceeds the scope authorized by that consent</u>?

In these Questions, the author assumes the very point that is at issue: whether the actions were likely to cause substantial harm; whether the consent was voluntary; and whether the search exceeded the scope authorized by that consent.

Be equally careful not to give away your case in the Question by conceding arguments to the opposing party and then trying to recapture them. The following Question does this:

> Whether a search, conducted pursuant to consent by the defendant, is unreasonable merely because it exceeds the bounds of the consent given.

By concluding that the search exceeded the defendant's consent, the writer has conceded that the search was not valid. The word "merely" will not retrieve the lost case.

F. Although you should not concede an argument, your Questions may pose alternative arguments. You may appear to concede a contested point in order to argue the next issue that follows logically from the first point. When you use this sort of alternative argument, you are implicitly saying, "but even if I am wrong on the first point, then the other party still should not prevail because of my arguments on point two." Utilizing this technique, the writer concedes the first point only for the purpose of meeting opposing counsel's next argument.

In the fourth amendment search and seizure problem, for example, the appellant can make an alternative argument: even if he did consent to the search initially, he then withdrew that consent. Appellant admits to the consent only for the limited purpose of making his second argument. Such a Question might look as follows:

> Even if the petitioner initially consented to a search, is the evidence obtained from that warrantless search nonetheless inadmissible on fourth amendment grounds because the petitioner withdrew his initial consent to that search? .

G. Finally, to make questions readable, keep related ideas together. For example, use the first half of the sentence to pose the legal question. Then use the second half to raise the legally relevant facts. Take particular pains to keep the subject of the sentence near the verb since this type of construction is the easiest to understand. Do not separate the subject of the sentence from the verb with a series of interrupting clauses or modifiers. The following question is hard to comprehend because eighteen words (those modifying the main noun) intervene between the main noun (statute) and the verb.

> Whether a statute allowing a child witness in a sex-offense prosecution to testify outside of defendant's presence by one-way closed-circuit television is valid under the sixth amendment right of confrontation when the statute can only be applied upon a showing of individualized, clear, and convincing trauma to the witness.

The question is more readable if the main noun of the sentence is near the verb, as in our earlier version of this question.

> Is a statute valid under the sixth amendment right of confrontation if it allows a child witness in a sex-offense prosecution to testify outside of defendant's presence by one-way closed-circuit television when the statute can be applied only upon a showing of individualized, clear, and convincing trauma to the witness?

Exercise 13–A

1. The following Questions Presented have been prepared for appellant, Alice Bell. Ms. Bell is suing her husband Alan Bell for civil damages under a federal statute popularly known as the federal wiretapping act or Title III of the Omnibus Crime Control and Safe Streets Act of 1968. Alice Bell claims her husband wiretapped her business telephone. Which is the best Question and why? What is wrong with the other Questions?

    A. Did the trial court err in dismissing Ms. Bell's claim against her husband for damages for using an extension telephone to intercept her private communications without her consent?

    B. Does Title III of the Omnibus Crime Control and Safe Streets Act prohibit the appellee's interception of the appellant's telephone conversations?

    C. Did the trial court err in dismissing the appellant's claim since her husband's unauthorized actions of intercepting her oral telephone communications are clearly prohibited by Title III of the Omnibus Crime Control and Safe Streets Act and do not come within the exceptions to the Act?

    D. Does Title III of the Omnibus Crime Control and Safe Streets Act, which prohibits an individual from intercepting any wire or oral communication, provide a cause of action for a wife against her husband who eavesdropped on an extension telephone and secretly recorded her private telephone conversations?

2. The following Questions Presented have been prepared for Juliet Stone's appeal of the trial court's dismissal of her wrongful life claim

against Dr. James Eagle. The issue is whether there is a legal remedy for the injuries she has sustained. (For more information, see section VI, F.) Which is the best Question and why? What is wrong with the other Questions?

A. Whether infant Juliet Stone may sustain a claim for wrongful life against an obstetrician who negligently failed to inform the infant's parents of the advisability of having an amniocentesis test, thereby depriving them of the choice to abort, when the infant has suffered legally cognizable injuries.

B. Whether an infant born with severe congenital birth defects has a legally cognizable claim against her mother's physician.

C. Can an infant born with severe birth defects sustain a claim for wrongful life when the obstetrician failed to inform the parents of the risk of Down's Syndrome and the availability of amniocentesis, and thereby deprived them of making an informed choice about terminating the pregnancy?

3. Assume you are a prosecutor appealing a pre-trial order suppressing evidence of the photographic identification of a robber by the only eyewitness to a bank robbery. The judge had found the photographic identification procedure conducted by the police was (1) "unduly and unnecessarily suggestive" and (2) the identification itself was not "independently reliable." Your student intern has written two versions of the question presented. You find one of them conclusory and both of them unpersuasive and unreadable. Using the information they provide, write a persuasive and readable question.

A. Whether the court properly suppressed the eyewitness's photographic identification testimony, where photographs, each one basically resembling the others, were shown to the witness from which she identified the accused as the perpetrator of the crime without any influence from the police officer, and where during the course of the crime, the witness, who had an excellent opportunity to view the criminal, attentively observed the criminal for about a minute in strong light, thus enabling her to give a detailed description of the criminal that closely resembles the accused, on the ground that the procedure was unduly and unnecessarily suggestive and the identification itself was unreliable.

B. Whether the pretrial photographic identification was unnecessarily and impermissibly suggestive when, weighing the various factors which affected the reliability of the witness's description of the perpetrator against the level of suggestiveness of the photographic procedure, there does not exist, in light of the totality of the circumstances, a substantial likelihood of irreparable misidentification, given the facts that the witness, although terrified, had seen the robber at close quarters and the agent's only comment after she tentatively identified the defendant's photo was that she was "doing just fine, a good job."

III. The Statement of the Case

Few attorneys dispute the importance of the Statement of the Case. The Statement is your opportunity to focus only on the facts and to present your client's version of those facts so convincingly that a court is ready to rule in your client's favor even before reading the Argument.

The contrast between the appellant's and appellee's Statements of the Case in most appeals illustrates that the same transcript can be used to convey very different impressions of the facts. These different impressions result from the attorney's judicious selection and arrangement of facts and are legitimate advocacy as long as you also honor your obligation to state your facts accurately and fairly. A lawyer who knowingly misstates the facts violates the Code of Professional Responsibility.[5] You must not only be accurate about the facts which you include, but you must include all the known facts that are material to the case so as to avoid giving a distorted impression of the events. If you misrepresent the facts or allow a misleading inference to be drawn, you not only lose credibility, but will be quickly corrected by opposing counsel—to your client's disadvantage.

Some students become so preoccupied with writing the facts to persuade that they confuse the reader as to what the case is actually about or what actually happened. Be careful, therefore, that you include and logically order all the material facts, favorable as well as unfavorable, so that the court need not rely on the opposing brief to understand the dispute.

Nonetheless, the significance of a fact or event may well become apparent only after you have put it in a meaningful context; facts do not speak for themselves. Thus, although your portrait should ultimately be fair and understandable, you should arrange the facts in a context which is as advantageous to your client as possible.

Your initial selection of facts and interpretation of their significance should, therefore, be provisional. The interpretation, the selection, and the ordering of facts may need to be changed to reflect your growing understanding of how they can be used in your legal arguments. If you write your facts with this purpose in mind, the court, after reading the Statement of the Case, ought to be aware not only of the boundaries within which it must work, but of the legal arguments to come.

---

5. Canon 7, DR7–102A(5) says in pertinent part, "In his representation of a client, a lawyer shall not knowingly make a false statement of law or fact." See also Model Rules of Professional Conduct, Rule 3.3(a)(1) (which have been adopted in some jurisdictions and prohibit a lawyer from making false statements of material fact or law).

A. The Opening Paragraph or Paragraphs

Many brief writers begin the Statement of the Case with a brief synopsis of the case from a procedural point of view. The overview should be given in the opening paragraph of the Statement and include procedural information about how the case reached that court as well as information about the nature of the action, the parties involved, and the relief requested. Make sure you explain the background of procedural issues if your appeal involves any. For example, if you are appealing a judge's refusal to give an instruction to the jury, include in the procedural facts the party's request for the instruction and the judge's denial of the request. Some lawyers also summarize the lower court decision in the opening paragraph(s). Others, however, conclude the Statement of the Case with this information (see section III, C).

Some attorneys separate the procedural history from the summary of relevant evidence by having separate headings for each. The procedural history may go under the heading "Preliminary Statement." The summary presenting the facts goes under the heading "Statement of Facts."

Example of a Preliminary Statement

This is an appeal from a judgment of the Supreme Court, New York County, rendered October 9, 1986. A jury convicted the appellant, Sam Mann, of burglary in the third degree, N.Y. Penal Law § 140.20 (McKinney 1975), and the court sentenced him to a prison term with a maximum of seven and a minimum of three-and-a-half years.

The appellant filed a timely notice of appeal, and on November 19, 1986, this Court granted appellant leave to appeal as a poor person on the original record and typewritten briefs. On July 14, 1987, Una Bent, Esq., was assigned as counsel on the appeal.

B. Developing the Facts

1. Organization

To sustain your reader's interest, you want to develop the facts in a coherent and sympathetic narrative. Usually, a chronological order works best. Before you begin this chronological narrative, however, it is sometimes appropriate to have a paragraph recounting significant emotional facts which might elicit the reader's sympathy or antipathy. If you are a prosecutor, for example, you might want to begin with the details of the murder. If there are many issues and the Statements of Facts is somewhat lengthy, you may want to use a topical organization instead of a simple chronological organization. If you divide the facts into topics, you may use short topical headings before each new section if your fact statement is lengthy. You might organize the facts into topics like the evidence at trial, the conduct of the trial court, and the charge to the jury. The subsections summarize and organize the facts pertinent to a legal issue you intend to address in the Argument section of the brief. You would still organize the facts relevant to each topic chronologically.

Before you actually write the Statement of the Case, you may want to identify the events to be covered and the facts material to them. Work out a structure that frames and maximizes the facts most favorable to your client and that limits the impact of facts damaging to your client. Bury damaging facts in the middle of the narrative and in the middle of paragraphs and sentences; juxtapose unfavorable facts with favorable facts; place favorable facts in positions of emphasis (at the beginning and end of sentences, paragraphs, and the narrative). Finally, allocate space according to importance. For example, as attorney for appellant in a criminal case, you would emphasize, even repeat, facts establishing your client's innocence or the closeness of the case, but condense and bury unfavorable material.

2. *The Narrative Approach*

Although the Statement of the Case is not an occasion for displaying talent in creative writing, it is a prose narrative and should unfold logically. To promote the narrative flow, you should usually refrain from parroting the record in a witness-by-witness procession and instead concentrate on integrating the testimony of the witnesses and using that testimony to describe events. It is perfectly legitimate to mix direct and cross examination if doing so strengthens and clarifies the narrative flow.

To avoid monotony, you may also want to include quotations from the record. Although direct quotation should be used sparingly because it threatens to interrupt the continuity of the narrative, testimony that seems to capture the true significance of an event can have a dramatic impact on the narrative. It may, for example, be worth quoting the following statement in a prosecutor's brief, "When the officer said he was going to write out a speeding ticket, the appellant said, 'maybe there is something I could do to make you change your mind, maybe you're short of cash or something'."

Direct quotation should be buttressed by summaries of the record. Indeed, summaries are preferable to frequent quotation because they promote continuity. Make sure, however, that your summaries are borne out by the record.[6] Remember, although you are trying to create a narrative, you are not creating fiction. You must be accurate: you cannot add to or change the record; your direct quotations must be meticulously correct; you must support your assertions in the Statement of the Case with reference to the page or pages in the record (R.) where the supporting facts can be found, or to the page or pages in the opinion below from which the facts came.

One last technique for promoting narrative continuity and coherence is to supply visual details. Visual details help the reader to conceptualize the events. If you are trying to discredit an eyewitness's identification of a suspect, for example, you should describe how far away the witness was, the dim lighting conditions, the shadows cast by an adjacent scaffold, etc.

3. Persuasive Writing Techniques

Several writing techniques will help you to shape this section of the brief persuasively.

a. If the record allows, include emotionally significant facts and significant background facts—even if they do not have any strict legal significance—since such information might influence a court to look favorably on your case by establishing a context for understanding the events, by personalizing your client, or both. (Defendant's Statement of the Case on page 217 makes use of significant background facts.)

b. Personalize your client. Even if the record for your class assignments does not reveal any personal information about your client, you can help the court view him or her as a person deserving of fair treatment by referring to the client in a dignified way, as, for example, "Mr. Gonzales" rather than "Gonzales" or "Petitioner." This sort of personalization was achieved in the following paragraphs:

> Ms. Maria Fox, the petitioner in this case, was charged by the Attorney Registration and Disciplinary Commission of the State of New Java for "soliciting employment" in violation of Disciplinary Rule 2–103(A). (R.1).

> Ms. Fox has practiced law for ten years and has successfully resolved legal problems for the Northwest Community Women's

---

6. The New York Bar Association, Practitioners Handbook for Appeals to the Court of Appeals gives the following good advice on page 60:

> If inference is relied on, a summary should make that clear and not simply cite a record page in the expectation that the reader will draw the

same inference. Moreover, all of the record references supporting the inference should be cited so that a reader disagreeing with the inference from the first reference may nevertheless accept it because the other references bear it out.

Organization (NCWO) of which she is a member. (R.2). Ms. Fox followed up a request for business cards with personal letters to NCWO members who attended a counseling session at which Ms. Fox was asked to speak. (R.3).

c. Characterize facts favorably. In the following example, the writer suggests the possibility of police coercion by first characterizing the officer's words as a threat and then restating the exact words of the officer:

> Officer Brown wanted permission to enter and to search the apartment. When Mr. Gonzales refused, Officer Brown threatened to seek a warrant and to leave an officer outside the door until his return. He said, "I can always go ask for a warrant. I'll leave the other officer outside till I get back." (R.1.) Mr. Gonzales then acquiesced to the search.

d. De-emphasize unfavorable facts.

i. You may de-emphasize unfavorable facts about your client's activities by using the passive voice. Passive voice will create a distance between your client and the activity described in the sentence. For example, instead of saying, "Ms. Fox mailed her letters to all the people who had signed the sheet," you would say, "The letters were mailed to the women whose names were on the sign-in sheet." By using passive voice, the writer avoids naming Ms. Fox as the person who mailed the letters.

ii. Another way to de-emphasize your client's conduct is to use the other parties involved as the subjects of the sentences. For example, instead of saying that Gonzales had the stolen bank money in his apartment where it was found, you can focus on the police activity and say, "The police seized crucial evidence, money stolen from a bank, without a warrant."

iii. You can also emphasize or de-emphasize a fact by using independent and subordinate clauses carefully. An independent clause is a sentence containing a complete thought, such as "Sam Paley is an excellent lawyer." That clause can be joined in a sentence with a subordinate or dependent clause which has a subject and verb but is an incomplete thought, such as "Although Paley's memory is poor." Because a subordinate clause depends on the independent clause for meaning, a reader's attention focuses on the independent clause. Therefore, it is helpful to put unfavorable facts into a dependent clause which is joined to a more favorable independent clause, such as "Although Paley's memory is poor, he is an excellent lawyer." This sentence leaves the impression of Paley's excellence as a lawyer. If you reverse the information in the clauses, "Although Paley is an excellent lawyer, his memory is poor," or "Even if Paley is an excellent lawyer, his memory is poor," you emphasize the negative information about Paley's memory.

e. Vary sentence length. After several long sentences, a short sentence can have a dramatic impact.

f. Choose your words to take advantage of their descriptive power. In a brief, you may describe events using loaded words that would not have been appropriate in a memorandum. It is legitimate, for example, to describe a boy as having applied "emotional blackmail" when he threatened to find a new girlfriend if his present one continued to resist his sexual advances, although such a description would be inappropriate in a memo.

You should also use vigorous verbs (smash rather than hit) and pointed adjectives and adverbs for facts you want to emphasize. On the other hand, use colorless verbs and few adjectives or adverbs for facts you wish to de-emphasize.

Do not interpret this advice to mean, however, that you should write in an openly partisan manner. The Statement of the Case should be written to appear neutral—even if it is not. Partisan characterizations and partisan choice of language must be subtle, or not attempted at all.

Other persuasive writing techniques are described in section VI, G of this chapter.

The following paragraphs show how the appellee and appellant might each have presented the facts of the case on appeal. In the initial suit, plaintiff had sued Gothic Memorial Chapel for the negligent infliction of emotional anguish and distress, claiming that the defendant's conduct was negligent, that the negligence was the cause-in-fact of her emotional anguish and distress, and that her anguish was severe and disabling. At trial, the court held that although the defendant had been negligent and Miss Morte had suffered severe emotional distress, her distress was not the result of defendant's actions but of her grief at the loss of her father. Defendant was held not liable. The issue on appeal is whether defendant's negligence was the cause-in-fact of plaintiff's distress.

The plaintiff's lawyer might present the facts as follows. (Procedural paragraphs and citations to the record are omitted.)

> On the day of George Morte's funeral, in full view of the decedent's daughter, Maria Morte, the hired bearers of defendant undertaker dropped the coffin in which the body lay, causing the lid to spring open and the corpse to crash to the ground. With greater alacrity than diplomacy or agility, the employees heaved the dead man's body up and swung it back into the coffin. In the process, they banged George Morte's head against the side of the coffin, smashing his nose and ripping open his right cheek as it caught on the lock mechanism.

This grotesque disruption took place as the funeral party was watching the pall bearers load the coffin onto the hearse for the motorcar procession to the graveyard. At that time, Maria Morte was standing less than four feet from the coffin and the hearse. Her horror at witnessing the defendant's employees manhandle her dead father's body was quickly apparent. She fell into hysterics and began to vomit convulsively. Among the assembled friends and mourners who immediately attempted to assist and soothe Miss Morte was a medical doctor. He insisted on administering a strong tranquilizer to Miss Morte in order to calm her sufficiently to accompany her beloved father's body to his grave.

For several months after this incident, Miss Morte suffered from a dramatic loss of appetite and weight. She had trouble concentrating, wept easily, and seemed alternately depressed, panicky, and stunned. She was frequently awakened by recurring nightmares about graveyards, mangled corpses, and open coffins.

The defendant's lawyer might present the facts as follows.

Plaintiff in this action is an unmarried woman of 58 who for the last several years of her 85-year-old and ailing father's life served as his constant companion and nurse. Her mother had died when she was a child and she had no other surviving relation. Miss Morte had never married and had always lived in her father's house. The relationship between this elderly, dying father and his aging, spinster daughter has been described as exceptionally close.

The accident which is the basis for this action took place as the funeral party for George Morte was preparing to leave for the cemetery. The employees of Gothic Memorial Chapel inadvertently dropped the casket in which the deceased lay as they were sliding it into the hearse, requiring them to recover his fallen body from the ground. In the process of lifting the body back into the casket, the decedent's face was disfigured.

After the accident occurred, plaintiff, who had been standing with the other mourners nearby, seemed to become somewhat shaken. Friends came to her assistance and one of them, a medical doctor, gave her a tranquilizer. In a little while, she was able to accompany the deceased to his final resting place.

For several months after the accident, Miss Morte suffered from the symptoms of grief and mourning which are the natural aftermath of losing a beloved parent. She cried easily, felt depressed, and experienced nightmares and loss of appetite.

Although most cases will not offer you such dramatic and gruesome possibilities, these two versions of the facts illustrate the very different impressions you can convey even when working from the same transcript. Miss Morte's account portrays the employees of Gothic Memorial Chapel as crassly negligent and unfeeling. The narrative begins with a detailed description of the pall bearers' actions and the resulting disfigurement to her father. The verbs are evocative, the nouns blunt, the tone intentionally macabre. The last paragraph, which describes the rather ghoulish content of Miss Morte's nightmares, suggests that her distress is directly tied to the pall bearers' activities. In the middle is buried the somewhat unfavorable fact that Miss Morte was not so distraught as to be unable to proceed to the cemetery. By suggesting that it was only the doctor's administration of the tranquilizer which made it possible for Miss Morte to carry on, this fact is minimized.

Miss Morte's attorney does not dwell in the statement on the close relation of this father and daughter or on her subsequent solitariness because to do so would portray Miss Morte's distress as the natural mourning of an unmarried, middle-aged daughter. On the other hand, appellee's attorney begins with these emotionally significant background facts as a way of minimizing the impact the incident in question had on her mental state. The last paragraph reiterates the idea that Miss Morte experienced nothing more or less than the natural grief of a daughter upon the death of her sole parent. Buried in the middle is the incident itself, which is rather quickly summarized and neutrally reported. The nouns are euphemistic, the verbs colorless, the tone factual. Miss Morte's rather immediate reaction to the manhandling is minimized by the suggestion she recovered rather quickly.

C. Closing Paragraph

You may end the Statement of the Case by relating the facts back to the legal issue before the court and by giving a short summary of the decision of the court below. The appellee will ordinarily want to place greater emphasis on the decision of the court below than the appellant would, since that decision was favorable to the appellee.

Contrast these examples from appellant's and appellee's briefs. Notice that the appellant summarizes the arguments made before the trial court while the appellee summarizes the trial court's reasons for its decision.

Appellant

> The defendant appealed his conviction on two grounds. The first was that his consent to the search was not voluntarily given in that he "was coerced into agreement by the threat inherent in Brown's language that a future search was inevitable." (R.2.) The second was that the evidence was seized after he had clearly indicated a desire to terminate the search. Id. A divided court

of appeals affirmed the conviction. Id. This Court granted certiorari on the question of whether the police officer's search violated the fourth amendment.

Appellee

The United States Court of Appeals for the Twelfth Circuit affirmed the defendant's conviction and rejected the defendant's claims that his consent was coerced. Instead, the court held that defendant's consent was freely and voluntarily given in an attempt to allay suspicion and on the assumption that nothing would be found. (R.2) The court also found that the defendant's attempt to stop the search was an attempt to "obstruct the search" in the face of discovery of the evidence. Id.

Exercise 13–B

1. In the following examples, the defendant is appealing the trial court's decision granting closure of the courtroom during the testimony of a thirteen-year-old victim of a brutal assault on the ground that his sixth amendment right to a public trial had been violated. Which Statement for the defendant is more persuasive and why? Citations to the record are omitted.

Example A

Daniel McGee was indicted for Attempted Murder in the Second Degree and for Assault in the First Degree on June 15, 1986. Five days prior to the indictment, Mr. McGee allegedly assaulted thirteen-year-old Sheila Merta. Although only the defendant was apprehended, he acted in concert with others not apprehended.

The thirteen-year-old complaining witness, Sheila Merta, had testified before a Grand Jury and in two separate pretrial hearings, although no spectators were then present. During her testimony at trial, Ms. Merta began to cry. The prosecutor suggested the courtroom be closed because Ms. Merta was afraid of the spectators and embarrassed about having to testify to the details of the assault.

The trial judge held an *in camera* hearing to determine if there were sufficient reasons for removing spectators from the courtroom. When the judge asked Ms. Merta if closure would make it easier for her to testify, she responded in the affirmative. Ms. Merta then stated that she knew that McGee's mother, who had been a family friend and was in the courtroom, hated her. The trial judge then closed the courtroom because Ms. Merta was fearful of testifying before the spectators. The judge concluded that closure would assure Ms. Merta's testimony. The trial court weighed the equities and decided that it would not be an injustice upon the defendant to have the testimony of Ms. Merta taken without spectators being present. Defendant took exception to the ruling.

On January 13, 1987, defendant was convicted of assault with a deadly weapon, but was acquitted on the attempted murder charge. On February 12, 1987, McGee was sentenced to a prison term of five to fifteen years for the assault.

The Intermediate Appellate Court affirmed the trial court's decision that the defendant suffered no sixth amendment violation. The defendant was then given leave to appeal to this court.

Example B

The Appellant, Daniel McGee, is a resident of Kent, who, with other unnamed males, allegedly assaulted Sheila Merta, a young girl from their neighborhood, on June 10, 1986. Only McGee was apprehended and charged with the assault.

On June 15, 1986, the Grand Jury of the County of Kings indicted McGee on two counts: Attempted Murder in the Second Degree and Assault in the First Degree. Prior to the indictment, Merta testified before the Grand Jury and at two pretrial hearings.

At trial, Merta began her testimony, but then paused and started to cry. The prosecutor asked to approach the bench where he suggested the court be closed during Merta's testimony because although she had not been threatened in any way, she was frightened about testifying. The court noted that Merta had already testified before the Grand Jury and at two separate pretrial hearings and indicated that Merta "should be an old pro at testifying."

The defense counsel immediately objected to closure, acknowledging that every witness experienced some fear at the prospect of giving testimony at trial but that this "mild anxiety" was not enough to justify closure of the courtroom.

The trial court held a brief *in camera* hearing with Merta to decide whether to close the courtroom to all spectators during her testimony. The judge asked Merta what was the problem, as she had been a very able witness so far. She answered that she did not know, but felt discomfort at the thought of Daniel's mother and neighbors looking at her as she testified. She did not indicate that she would not testify nor did she express a preference for the courtroom to be closed. The judge asked her if it would help her to testify if McGee's mother and other spectators were not in the courtroom. She replied: "I guess so." The judge then decided to close the courtroom. The defense counsel objected, but the judge interrupted, saying he had made his ruling. Defense counsel's exception was noted for the record, but counsel was not given the opportunity to be heard on the motion for closure. The judge then ordered the courtroom to be closed to all spectators, including defendant's relatives, friends, and the press.

McGee was convicted on the assault charge and acquitted on the murder charge. He was sentenced to an indeterminate sentence of five-to-fifteen years.

On Nov. 13, 1987, the Intermediate Appellate Court affirmed the trial court's decision in all respects and held that there was no sixth amendment violation.

Permission to appeal to this Court was granted to McGee on Dec. 1, 1987. Awaiting appeal, Daniel McGee remains incarcerated pursuant to that judgment of conviction.

2.   In the following exercise, the legal question is whether the testimony of defendant's expert witness on the battered woman's syndrome should have been admitted into evidence because it satisfies the test for relevance in the jurisdiction. Read the excerpts. Then write a Statement of Facts first from the appellant's point of view, then from the appellee's point of view. Assume the procedural history has already been written. Before you begin to write, consider these questions.

    1.   Which facts would form the focus of a Statement of Facts written from the appellant's point of view? from the appellee's point of view?

    2.   Which facts are legally relevant?

Excerpt of Testimony by Joan Brown

Q: (by Defense Counsel William Blake): Please give us your name and address.

A: My name is Joan Brown and I live at 600 Boston Place in Abbottsville.

Q: How old are you?

A: I'm 29 years old.

Q: Were you married to the deceased, John Brown?

A: Yes.

Q: How long were you married?

A: Nine years.

Q: Did you have any children?

A: Yes. We have a son who is 8 and a daughter who is 5.

Q: Do you have a job outside of the home?

A: No, I never finished high school, and since the kids were born, I stopped getting waitressing jobs.

Q: Did your husband ever strike you?

A.D.A. Robert Canon: Objection, your Honor. The deceased is not on trial in this case. I fail to see the relevance of this testimony.

Defense Counsel William Blake: Your Honor, the deceased's violence towards Mrs. Brown is highly relevant to her claim of self-defense.

The Court: Objection overruled. You may proceed, Mr. Blake.

Q: Mrs. Brown, did your husband ever strike you?

A: After my daughter was born, my husband started to beat me up a lot. Before then, he would push me around sometimes, but after Amanda was born, it got much worse and much more frequent.

Q: Can you be more specific?

A: Once John took me outside the house and beat my head against a tree. Another time he stabbed me in the foot with a pencil.

Q: Were there any other episodes?

A: John pushed me down a flight of stairs in the house and I broke my arm and had to go to the hospital to have it set and put in a cast.

Q: Did you go to a hospital on any other occasions?

A: Last February I went to the hospital because I kept vomiting and blacking out after he beat me. There were a lot of times that he would punch me and shove me around. Sometimes he would hit the kids, too. Then other times he would be peaceful for a while.

Q: Were there any other instances in which you went to see a doctor because of your husband's beating you?

A: Two years ago John hit me in the face with a bottle and I went to the doctor to have stitches because my face was all cut up.

Q: Did you ever leave your husband?

A: Yes, last March I left John after one bad night and took the kids to a Women's Shelter on Foster Street. The next day John came to see me and said that he wanted me to come home and that things would be different. I went back with him. He was nice for a week and then he started pushing me and the kids around again.

Q: What happened on the day of April 28, 1985?

A: In the morning on the way out the door, John said he had it with me and that when he got home he was going to really finish me off. He said I humiliated him by going to the shelter. I was petrified all day. I knew he meant it. Whenever he said he would do something to me, he would always do it. Just before I knew John was coming home at six-thirty, I went to the drawer in the bedroom where John kept a gun. I took the gun downstairs, and when John came through the door I shot him.

Q: (By A.D.A. Canon) Mrs. Brown, do you have any family in Abbottsville?

A: Well, my husband's sister lives in Abbottsville, but she and I were never really close.

———

Excerpt of Testimony of Dr. Susan Black

Q: (By Defense Counsel William Blake) Dr. Black, please tell us something about your background.

A: I am a certified psychoanalyst and have spent many years studying the battered woman's syndrome. I have. . . .

A.D.A. Canon: Objection, your Honor. May we approach the bench?

The Court: Yes, you may. The jury is excused. (The members of the jury exit.) Mr. Blake, for what purpose do you intend to introduce expert testimony on the "battered woman's syndrome"?

Mr. Blake: Your Honor, we believe that expert testimony on the battered woman's syndrome is relevant to Joan Brown's claim of self-defense. The testimony would help the jury understand why she reasonably believed that she was in imminent danger on the day of the shooting and why deadly force was necessary to avoid this danger. In addition, this testimony would explain why she did not leave her husband, despite his brutality.

The Court: Mr. Canon?

A.D.A. Canon: I object to any testimony regarding a so-called "battered woman's syndrome." The testimony is irrelevant as it does not explain why, on the particular instant when the shooting took place, Joan Brown reasonably believed that this force was necessary to prevent imminent death or great bodily harm to herself. In addition, the jury has already heard extensive testimony from both Joan Brown and her neighbor on the alleged violence of John Brown. I see no purpose in further discussion of this issue.

The Court: Mr. Blake, do you have a response?

Mr. Blake: Yes, your Honor. Dr. Black is a well-known authority on battered woman's syndrome. Her testimony will describe this syndrome and show how, in her opinion, Joan Brown displayed the classic signs of the syndrome. This testimony will explain Ms. Brown's state of mind and support her claim of self-defense.

The Court: Well, I would like to hear from Dr. Black and then I'll make a decision on whether her expert testimony will be admissible. Could you please describe the battered woman's syndrome?

A: Certainly. The battered woman's syndrome is a three stage form of family "disease". In stage 1, the battering male engages in minor physical abuse and verbal abuse. In this tension-building stage, the woman often attempts to placate the male to avoid more serious violence. Stage 2 is characterized by acute explosions of brutal violence by the battering male. In stage 3, the battering male expresses remorse for his behavior and asks for forgiveness, promising to change. The woman is hopeful during the third stage that her husband will indeed change. This is one reason why she stays with him despite the cycles of abuse. There are other reasons as well. One expert has described the demoralization experienced by some women because they cannot control the violence as "learned helplessness" or "psychological paralysis". They become incapable of taking action to change their situations. Of course, they may also be fearful of what will happen to their children, or fear that their husbands will find them and abuse them even more if they try to get away. And they may not have any money or way of earning a living.

Q: Dr. Black, have you interviewed the defendant, Joan Brown?

A: Yes, I have.

Q: Do you have an opinion on whether Joan Brown is subject to the battered woman's syndrome?

A: Yes, in my opinion, Joan Brown is subject to the battered woman's syndrome.

Q: As a battered woman, how did Joan Brown perceive her situation on the 28th day of April?

A: Joan Brown was terrified that her husband would kill her when he returned from work. He said he would, as he put it, "finish her off," and she believed, knowing him, that he would do it.

Q: I have no further questions. Thank you Dr. Black.

The Court: I have decided not to admit Dr. Black's expert testimony. I do not think it is relevant to the issue of self-defense in this case. In the state of Abbott, the jury applies an objective standard in evaluating a self-defense claim. According to the Abbott statute, which is not being challenged here, the jury must consider how an ordinary, intelligent, and prudent person would have acted under the circumstances existing at the time of the offense.

The jury may return.

IV. *Summary of the Argument*

The Summary of the Argument is a short affirmative statement of the advocate's view of the case. In this section, the neutral tone of the Statement of the Case gives way to open advocacy. You should include only arguments favorable to your case. Generally, you should write the Summary without reference to specific case names and without case citations, although sometimes it is necessary to name and cite to, a crucial case if that decision controls the analysis of the problem. You should always include relevant statutory language and citations, however. The Summary should not be an abstract discussion of the law, but should be specific to the case. You should relate the law to the facts of the case before the court.

Begin the Summary with a conclusory statement that sets out the ultimate claim or claims you want the court to accept, such as "the state of Kent may proscribe an attorney from soliciting clients by mail." You should also make claims about the intermediate steps that make up the arguments, for example, "the good faith exception does not apply." Explain briefly the reasons for each conclusion. Include only the very important points in this Summary section. This section should be a summary and it should be conclusory.

As a rule of thumb, the Summary should not exceed two pages for a ten to fifteen page brief; one page should be sufficient for most briefs.

What follows are sample summaries from briefs on the question of whether the Sioux Falls School District Rules on religious holiday observances comply with the establishment clause of the first amendment.

Petitioner's Summary of the Argument

The Sioux Falls School District violates the neutrality mandated by the establishment clause of the first amendment by adopting a Policy and Rules that permit the observation of religious holidays in public school assemblies. To test the constitutionality of state-authorized rules and statutes under the establishment clause, the Court has developed a three-part test. First, the rules must have a secular purpose. Second, their principal or primary effect can neither advance nor inhibit religion. Third, they must not give rise to excessive entanglement between government and religion. Lemon v. Kurtzman, 403 U.S. 602, 612–13 (1971). The Policy and Rules violate all three parts of this test.

The Court has not hesitated, especially in cases concerning religious exercises in public schools, to look behind the purported purpose of a statute in order to discern the actual motivations giving rise to the enactment. Because the Rules allow the presentation of Christmas carols, religious skits, and nativity scenes, it becomes obvious that the respondent's purpose in adopting these Rules was to allow for the celebration of the religious aspects of Christmas. Because the actual purpose is to advance sectarian ideals, the Rules are unconstitutional.

The Sioux Falls Rules also violate the second part of the Lemon test by having a principal effect that advances religion. Since devotional exercises, which the Rules permit, are inherently religious and their effect is to advance religion, they have no place in the public schools. Due to the devout nature of many Christmas carols, and the undeniably religious impact on a youngster from seeing a nativity scene on the public school stage, the direct and immediate effect of the Rules is the advancement of religion.

Finally, the Rules result in excessive entanglement between the schools and religion because they involve the secular authorities who execute the legislation in surveillance of religious activities. In addition, the Rules foster political divisiveness in the community along religious lines. For example, Assistant Superintendent Nicholas—assigned to monitor the implementation of the Rules—is on the public payroll. Also, both Nicholas and the school board must make discretionary judgments about the religious nature of particular activities. Finally, the amount of time and money devoted to the preparation and presentation of the annual Christmas programs is likely to give rise to divisive issues in local politics.

Respondent's Summary of the Argument

The Sioux Falls School District adopted the Policy and Rules to assist teachers and administrators in fulfilling the duties imposed by the establishment clause to keep religious influences out of the public schools. To test the constitutionality of state-authorized rules and regulations under the establishment clause, the Court has developed a three-part test. First, the rules must have a secular purpose. Then, their principal or primary effect can neither advance nor inhibit religion. Finally, they must not give rise to excessive entanglement between government and religion. <u>Lemon v. Kurtzman</u>, 403 U.S. 602, 612–13 (1971). The Policy and Rules comply with each part of the <u>Lemon</u> test and are constitutional.

The court has consistently accepted the stated legislative purpose of enactments in evaluating the first part of the <u>Lemon</u> test. The stated legislative purpose of the school district—"to foster understanding and mutual respect"—is undoubtedly secular. The Policy and Rules serve no religious purpose. The function of the Rules is to provide guidelines for the school district's teachers in the execution of their constitutional duty to keep purely religious influences out of public schools.

Second, the principal or primary effect of the Policy and Rules neither advances nor inhibits religion. The primary effect is the advancement of a secular program of education. The schools seek to teach the students about the customs and cultural heritage of the world. Thus, there is no constitutional barrier to the inclusion of this material in the schools.

Finally, the Policy and Rules do not excessively entangle government and religion. On the contrary, the Rules seek to limit the introduction of religious material into the classroom. This case presents none of the entanglement concerns which the Court has expressed that arise from government aid to religious institutions. When government aids religious institutions, then the character and purpose of the institution, the form of aid, and the resulting relationship between government and religious authority may entangle the state with religion. These forms of entanglement do not apply to public school cases.

Nor do the Rules provide any potential for political divisiveness that may arise from religious-oriented legislation. The Rules provide no money for religious activity and require no on-going implementation. Thus, the rules preempt ongoing political controversies on the subject and remove the religious issue from the local political sphere.

Exercise 13–C

1. Which of the following two summaries from respondents' briefs on a Parental Kidnapping Prevention Act problem is better? Why?

Example A

The United States District Court for the Northern District of Illinois properly exercised jurisdiction over this dispute under the Parental Kidnapping Prevention Act, 28 U.S.C. § 1738A (1982) (PKPA) because Congress intended that federal courts exercise jurisdiction under the Act to resolve conflicting state court custody decrees under the Act. Consistent with Congressional purpose, the district court used its authority under the PKPA to determine which of the two decrees was enforceable.

In passing the PKPA, Congress addressed itself to problems of precisely this kind: a father defies a valid custody decree, conceals the children from the mother, then wins custody in a distant forum following a hearing based on an incomplete record. Lack of federal jurisdiction to establish the validity of a single state decree in such a case leaves unsolved the very problems of forum shopping and conflicting decrees considered by Congress.

The district court also correctly applied the PKPA to this case to decide that Illinois had continuing jurisdiction over the custody decree because Alaska law itself barred jurisdiction by the Alaska court and gave the Illinois court continuing jurisdiction. The Alaska court was prohibited by Alaska Stat. § 25.30 et seq., and therefore by the PKPA, from taking jurisdiction because Mr. Woody defied the decree of another state court, Illinois. This result strongly supports the goal of the Alaska legislature to prevent child snatching. Moreover, the PKPA § 1738A(d) recognizes continuing jurisdiction in the Illinois court because of the strong ties the children maintain in Illinois, further limiting Alaska state court jurisdiction. Within its limited grant under the PKPA, the federal court was obligated to recognize the continuing validity of the Illinois decree and the insufficiency of the Alaska decree.

Example B

The courts of appeals are split as to whether the Parental Kidnapping Prevention Act (PKPA) creates federal subject matter jurisdiction allowing a parent to bring an action in federal district court to enforce the Act's provisions.

Although the language of the PKPA does not specifically grant federal jurisdiction, it does not state that the Act creates no federal jurisdiction.

An examination of the legislative history and background of the Act, however, suggests that Congress intended to create federal jurisdiction to enforce the Act's provisions. Congress must have intended such an interpretation because if no federal jurisdiction existed under the PKPA, the Act itself would become meaningless.

The domestic relations exception to federal diversity jurisdiction is inapplicable to federal subject matter jurisdiction under the PKPA. The domestic relations exception applies only to diversity actions, and the PKPA creates federal subject matter jurisdiction under 28 U.S.C. § 1331 (1982), which applies to federal questions.

The district court and the Court of Appeals correctly decided that the Alaska court improperly modified the Illinois court's original custody decree. The Alaska court did not have home state jurisdiction to modify the decree. Even if the Alaska court had home state jurisdiction, the court had no authority to modify the original decree because Illinois retained continuing jurisdiction.

2. Father Molloy was convicted in April of willfully transporting firearms across state lines. Last week, he was sentenced to four years in prison. His sentence has been stayed pending his appeal. A summer associate in the firm representing Father Molloy has written the following statement of facts drawn from the trial transcript and a brief summary of the applicable law. Read these materials and then write a

clear and persuasive Summary of the Argument. The only issue is whether Father Molloy was entrapped as a matter of law.

Statement of Facts

Father Molloy runs a soup kitchen and homeless shelter in the parish house of St. Bridget's Church in Brooklyn, New York. A dedicated and outspoken advocate of the poor and oppressed, Father Molloy is much in demand as a speaker at conferences and rallies all over the country. He first came to the attention of the F.B.I. last winter in connection with the arrest near St. Bridget's of suspected terrorist Seamus O'Rourke. No charges have been filed against Father Molloy in New York, but the investigation continues. When Father Molloy (a law school graduate) took a leave from St. Bridget's to teach a course at a law school in Washington ("Faith, Empowerment, and the Law"), he became a target of Prayscam, an F.B.I. "sting" operation.

Calling himself "Kieran Houlihan," Agent William Smith attended a "Housing Now" rally at which the priest spoke ("We cannot rest until all the oppressed are free—Blacks in South Africa, Catholics in Northern Ireland, the poor and homeless everywhere . . . .") and signed up to audit Father Molloy's course.

On February 14, 1990, "Houlihan" approached Father Molloy after class and asked whether he might speak with the priest privately. Smith took Father Molloy to Casey's Pub, where he told Father Molloy that he needed help to save his family in Northern Ireland. Through security leaks, a Protestant terrorist organization had learned the names of all those suspected by British Intelligence of having IRA sympathies. The group was systematically executing everyone on the list. In the town where "Houlihan's" uncles and cousins lived, five people had already been killed, including one of his cousins. His family had begged him to help; the Catholic townspeople needed guns to protect themselves. At that point, Father Molloy said "I can't help you with guns, my son, but my prayers are with you and your people."

After the next class, on February 16, "Houlihan" again sought out Father Molloy. He told the priest that he had been able to obtain two dozen unregistered rifles and had been put in touch with an underground "expediter" who could smuggle them onto a flight from Kennedy Airport to Belfast, where his cousins would pick them up. Now, "Houlihan" said, his problem was to get the guns to New York; he was an illegal immigrant without a driver's license and couldn't take the chance of driving his car 300 miles. "I'm sorry, my son, but I can't drive your cargo to Kennedy for you," Father Molloy replied.

On February 21, "Houlihan" once more took Father Molloy to Casey's. "Houlihan" said he was close to solving his problem: he had arranged to ship the guns to New York on Amtrak, packed in a coffin. At Penn Station, a hearse would pick up the coffin and take it to the "expediter" at Kennedy. But Amtrak would not ship an unaccompanied coffin: would Father Molloy accompany the coffin and see that it was safely delivered to the "expediter"? "This is no easy matter, my son," began Father Molloy. "I know, Father, and I am ready to express my family's gratitude in meaningful terms. We will contribute $5,000 to St. Bridget's shelter if you will help us." Father Molloy stared into his glass without speaking. Finally, he said, "Very well, my son, I'll do it."

Father Molloy was arrested a week later on 33rd Street in Manhattan as he supervised the transfer of a coffin full of Remingtons into a hearse driven by Agent Robert Jones.

At trial, the court refused to find that Father Molloy was entrapped as a matter of law. The question thus became one for the jury. Molloy was convicted. On appeal, the only issue is whether the judge should have found there was entrapment as a matter of law.

Brief Summary of Applicable Law
(Full Citations are Omitted)

A court will find entrapment as a matter of law only when there was "some evidence" of government inducement to commit the crime charged, and the prosecution failed to prove beyond a reasonable doubt that defendant was predisposed to commit that crime. United States v. Kelly.

When the undisputed evidence, with all inferences drawn in favor of the government, indicates to any reasonable mind, "some evidence" of inducement, then the court can determine that there was inducement as a matter of law. Id. Inducement is an objective inquiry measuring whether the government's behavior was such that a law abiding citizen's will to obey the law could be overcome. Id. Although government agents may use "stealth and stratagem" to entrap criminals, they may not attempt to lure law-abiding citizens into the commission of crime. See Sherman v. United States; Sorells v. United States; United States v. Kelly.

Government agents do not entrap if they approach or solicit the defendant to engage in criminal activity. United States v. Burkley. Rather, there must be some undisputed evidence indicating that government agents employed "persuasion, fraudulent representations (beyond offering opportunities to one predisposed to commit a crime), threats, coercive tactics, harassment, promises of reward, or pleas based on the need, sympathy, or "friendship" in order to show inducement as a matter of law. Id. Thus, in Sherman, the Court held that there was inducement as a matter of law when the government informer sought to persuade the defendant to procure narcotics with three repeated pleas based on sympathy and mutual experience as drug addicts. Similarly, in United States v. Owens, because the government agent posed as a fellow drug user and resorted to friendship to convince the defendant to sell the drugs, the court found inducement as a matter of law.

However, the mere promise of money is insufficient to show inducement. In Kelly, the court did not find inducement as a matter of law even though government agents, posing as businessmen, offered Kelly an initial $25,000 to attend a meeting. It should be noted, however, that in Kelly, the defendant did not testify "that his will was overborne by any insistent importunings" by government agents. Id.

Once a defendant shows inducement, the prosecution must introduce evidence beyond a reasonable doubt of the defendant's predisposition to commit the crime charged in order to defeat a claim of entrapment. Burkley. Thus, the prosecution must prove that the defendant had a "state of mind which readily respond[ed] to the opportunity furnished by the officer . . . to commit the forbidden act for which the accused is charged." Id. The defendant's predisposition is determined from the entirety of the events leading up to the commission of the crime. Kelly.

When predisposition is at issue, the major inquiry is thus whether the defendant was "ready and willing to commit the crimes." Kelly. In Kelly, the predisposed defendant was aware of the purpose of the meeting and neither protested nor registered surprise at the initial bribe offer, "coolly" assuring the FBI agents that he would do their bidding, without repeated and insistent government pleas. Id.

Predisposition may also be proven by evidence of a defendant's bad reputation, previous criminal convictions, rumored activities, and response to the inducement. Russell. However, in Owens, although the defendant was a drug user and often in the company of drug sellers, the court found no predisposition to sell narcotics, as district from a predisposition to use narcotics. The court indicated that the facts that Owens had no prior record for selling drugs and did not show up the first time the agent requested the drugs tended to support its finding of no predisposition. Id.

V. Point Headings

Unlike a memorandum, the appellate brief requires headings that divide the Argument section into its main and subordinate components. These headings, called point headings, are more than just topical headings used for easy transition from one topic to another, such as "the first amendment and commercial speech" or "the consent exception." Instead, they are persuasive summaries of the main arguments of the brief arranged in logical order. A point heading should be a conclusory statement about the legal issue which is favorable to your client.

In addition to a heading for each main argument, many writers use subheadings to introduce the subordinate parts of that argument. When read together—as they appear under the Argument section in the Table of Contents, for example—the headings and subheadings should provide a meaningful outline and summary of the entire Argument section. They introduce the court to the scope of the problem and to the direction of your argument.

A. *Organizing Headings in Outline Form*

Point headings provide an outline of the Argument section of a brief. The main point headings should summarize independent, unrelated legal arguments, each of which is an independent ground for relief. These point headings need not be logically

connected to each other, although they should be in the order you
have determined is the best and most logical order for your issues.
Subheadings, however, must relate to the main point heading in a
logical and consistent way because they are the components of a
single argument. An argument that is subdivided is almost always ordered from the general to the specific. The main heading
should state your general contention. The subheadings should
supply specific reasons supporting the general contention. Any
additional divisions should focus on the specific facts supporting
the contention of the sub-heading above it. Thus, the outline
organizes all the parts of your argument by how they relate to
each other.

You need not achieve symmetry of organization among the
major headings of the argument. Even if Section I has two
subdivisions, Section II may have three subdivisions, or none at
all. Where you do have subdivisions, indent and underline the
sub-headings and lay out the divisions in accordance with the
established rules of outlining:

1. Main issues or grounds for relief are introduced by point
   headings which are preceded by roman numerals (e.g., I,
   II, III)

2. Subissues are introduced by subheadings which are preceded by capital letters (e.g., A, B, C)

3. Divisions of subissues are introduced by subheadings
   which are preceded by arabic numerals (e.g., 1, 2, 3) and
   then lower case letters (e.g., a, b, c)

You should not have single subdivisions, that is, a subissue A
without a subissue B, or a subdivision 1 without a subdivision 2.
Because a subdivision indicates that the main issue above it is
divided into more than one point, you should not use a subheading
unless you have at least two entries. If there is only one point to
make about issue I, then incorporate your subissue into your
dominant point heading. This needs to be done in the following
outline of a contempt problem.

A. Paley did not act willfully or intentionally.

   1. Paley did not realize that Spence's trial was scheduled that
      morning.

B. Paley did not act recklessly.

   1. Paley followed standard office practice.

   2. Paley inadvertently did not record the trial date.

The outline should be rewritten.

A. Paley did not act willfully or intentionally because he did not
   realize Spence's trial was scheduled that morning.

B. Paley did not act recklessly.

    1. Paley followed standard office practice.

    2. Paley inadvertently did not record the trial date.

When you use subheadings, be careful not to subdivide the arguments excessively. Too many subdivisions will break up the flow of an argument and result in a choppy product. Thus, when the subject matter is not too different, you should avoid using a new subheading for discussions running only one or two paragraphs in length. Instead, incorporate the material in those paragraphs into the text of the preceding or subsequent subheadings and write those subheadings to include the added material. On the other hand, do not be afraid to subdivide a complex argument that depends on several different types of legal support. Without subdivision, it might be difficult for the reader to understand and differentiate the multiple legal arguments being offered.

Exercise 13–D

Reorder these headings so that those which are logically subordinate to a dominant heading are arranged under that dominant point heading. Correct the outlining of these point headings so that the subordinate points are properly labelled, put in the lower case, underlined, and indented.

    I. DR. BLACK'S TESTIMONY ON THE BATTERED WIFE SYNDROME WOULD AID THE JURY IN ITS SEARCH FOR TRUTH BECAUSE THE SYNDROME IS SO DISTINCTLY RELATED TO SCIENTIFIC AND MEDICAL KNOWLEDGE THAT IT IS BEYOND THE KEN OF THE AVERAGE JUROR.

    II. THE TRIAL COURT ERRED IN EXCLUDING EXPERT TESTIMONY ON THE BATTERED WIFE SYNDROME BECAUSE THAT TESTIMONY SATISFIES THE THREE–PART TEST OF RULE 780 OF THE STATE OF KENT WHICH GOVERNS THE ADMISSIBILITY OF EXPERT TESTIMONY.

    III. DR. BLACK IS A LEADING AUTHORITY ON THE BATTERED WIFE SYNDROME AND HER OPINIONS CAN THEREFORE AID THE TRIER OF FACT.

    IV. THE PROBATIVE VALUE OF DR. BLACK'S TESTIMONY ON THE BATTERED WIFE SYNDROME SUBSTANTIALLY OUTWEIGHS THE DANGER OF UNFAIR PREJUDICE BECAUSE THE JURY NEEDS TO UNDERSTAND JOAN BROWN'S MENTAL STATE AT THE TIME OF THE MURDER TO EVALUATE HER CLAIM OF SELF–DEFENSE.

    V. THE BATTERED WIFE SYNDROME IS GENERALLY ACCEPTED IN THE SCIENTIFIC COMMUNITY AND HAS BEEN THE SUBJECT OF AN INCREASING AMOUNT OF RESEARCH AND PUBLICATION.

B. *Writing Persuasive Headings*

Since point headings provide your reader with an outline and summary of your argument, they should be coherent, logical, and persuasive thesis sentences.   In order for them to exhibit these characteristics, you must provide the reader with several kinds of information: the issue, the pertinent rule of law, the legally significant facts, and your conclusion on the issue.   When you are employing only a single main point heading, all this information must be included in a single, coherent sentence.   When you use subheadings, however, the main point heading need only state your legal contention concerning the application of a rule.   The subheadings will supply the reasons for that contention and show their relevance to your client's situation.

A point heading should be one sentence, not a string of sentences.   To promote ease of comprehension, try to keep each heading and subheading to a readable length so as not to deter the reader from giving attention to its substance.   This is especially important for dominant point headings because they are typed entirely in capital letters, which often make for difficult reading. Although subheadings are printed in ordinary type (and are often underlined), they too should be kept reasonably concise so that their thesis can be easily absorbed.   Other suggestions follow.

1.   Headings should not be abstract statements of the law (unless clearly supported by sub-headings that supply reasoning and relevant facts).   Rather they should combine the law with the relevant facts of the case.   For example, the following heading is only a statement of the law:

> THE FOURTH AMENDMENT GUARANTEES THE RIGHT OF ALL PEOPLE TO BE SECURE IN THEIR HOMES FROM UNREASONABLE SEARCHES AND SEIZURE.

The heading should demonstrate the law's application:

> THE POLICE VIOLATED APPELLANT'S FOURTH AMENDMENT RIGHT TO BE SECURE FROM UNREASONABLE SEARCHES AND SEIZURES BECAUSE THEY SEARCHED HIS HOME WITHOUT A WARRANT AND WITHOUT HIS CONSENT.

Remember, briefs are written to persuade a court to rule in a particular way, for a particular party, in a particular situation; they are not abstract discussions written for the general edification of a judge.   If you have not related the law to the facts, your heading is unpersuasive.

2.   Unless supported by sub-headings that supply your reasoning, headings should not merely state a legal conclusion favorable to your client but should supply supporting reasons.   The following heading states a conclusion only:

THE APPELLANT'S CONSTITUTIONAL RIGHT TO TESTIFY IN HER OWN BEHALF WAS NOT VIOLATED BY THE TRIAL COURT'S EXCLUSION OF APPELLANT'S POST HYPNOTIC TESTIMONY.

The writer should supply some support for this conclusion:

MS. SMITH'S CONSTITUTIONAL RIGHT TO TESTIFY IN HER OWN BEHALF WAS NOT VIOLATED BY THE TRIAL COURT'S EXCLUSION OF HER POST HYPNOTIC TESTIMONY BECAUSE THAT TESTIMONY DID NOT SATISFY THE PROCEDURAL AND EVIDENTIARY RULES THAT ENSURE AN EVEN HANDED ADMINISTRATION OF JUSTICE.

In other words, a heading should be an explanation, not merely an assertion. An assertion can be rejected as easily as it can be accepted; an explanation is more persuasive because it at least provides some basis for the assertion.

3. Headings should clearly articulate relevant legal principles rather than cite cases or statutes. You must not assume your reader knows the rule of law established in a case or statute. For your thesis to be comprehensible, you must supply the rule. The following heading is uninformative:

UNDER THE RULING OF ROSS v. BERHARD, 396 U.S. 531 (1970), THE FEDERAL DISTRICT COURT PROPERLY STRUCK A DEMAND FOR A JURY TRIAL IN AN ACTION FOR DAMAGES AND INJUNCTIVE RELIEF STEMMING FROM A NUCLEAR POWER PLANT ACCIDENT.

The heading should be rewritten so that the legal principle established in Ross is clear.

BECAUSE A JURY DOES NOT PROVIDE AN ADEQUATE REMEDY FOR COMPLEX CASES THAT ARE BEYOND ITS PRACTICAL ABILITIES AND LIMITATIONS, THE DISTRICT COURT PROPERLY STRUCK A DEMAND FOR A JURY TRIAL IN AN ACTION FOR DAMAGES AND INJUNCTIVE RELIEF STEMMING FROM A NUCLEAR POWER PLANT ACCIDENT.

4. Point headings should be easily understood. Because so much information gets packed into point headings, you must work hard to make them intelligible. Two helpful suggestions are to keep the subject of your sentence near the predicate and to put the facts and reasoning at the end of the sentence. In the following heading, the author's reasoning intervenes between the subject and the predicate.

A PARENT–CHILD PRIVILEGE, LACKING CONFIDENTIALITY, AN ELEMENT CENTRAL TO ESTABLISHED PRIVILEGES, IS NOT JUDICIALLY RECOGNIZED, AND THE DISTRICT COURT, THEREFORE, PROPERLY DENIED THE MOTION TO QUASH THE SUBPOENA.

The heading should be rewritten:

> A PARENT–CHILD PRIVILEGE LACKS THE ELEMENT OF CONFIDENTIALITY CENTRAL TO ESTABLISHED PRIVILEGES, AND THUS, THE DISTRICT COURT PROPERLY DENIED THE MOTION TO QUASH THE SUBPOENA.

5. Whenever possible, headings should be written as positive statements, rather than as negative ones. The following is a negative heading:

> PETITIONER MAY NOT SOLICIT CLIENTS BY MAIL UNDER THE GUISE OF EXERCISING HER FIRST AMENDMENT RIGHTS.

Instead, the respondent might have written:

> THE STATE MAY PROSCRIBE PETITIONER'S SOLICITATION OF CLIENTS THROUGH DIRECT MAILINGS BECAUSE SOLICITATION IS INHERENTLY COERCIVE.

Affirmative sentences are clearer and more forceful than negative sentences.

6. You should use active instead of passive voice constructions, unless you want to dissociate the subject of the sentences from the action expressed by the verbs. In the following heading, there is no tactical reason for using the passive voice.

> THE PROSECUTORIAL MISCONDUCT WAS SO PREJUDICIAL THAT THE INHERENT SUPERVISORY POWERS OF THE COURT SHOULD BE INVOKED AND THE GRAND JURY INDICTMENT DISMISSED.

This heading could be rewritten in the active voice.

> THE COURT SHOULD INVOKE ITS INHERENT SUPERVISORY POWERS AND DISMISS THE GRAND JURY INDICTMENT BECAUSE THE PROSECUTORIAL MISCONDUCT WAS PREJUDICIAL.

If a party wants to emphasize prosecutorial misconduct by beginning the sentence with that language, the party could still end the sentence in the active voice.

> THE PROSECUTORIAL MISCONDUCT WAS SO PREJUDICIAL THAT THE COURT SHOULD INVOKE ITS INHERENT SUPERVISORY POWERS AND DISMISS THE GRAND JURY INDICTMENT.

The following point headings illustrate the petitioner's and respondent's arguments on Ms. Bell's claim against her husband for unauthorized eavesdropping and wiretapping of her telephone.

PETITIONER'S POINT HEADINGS

> I. PETITIONER ALICE BELL STATES A CLAIM AGAINST HER HUSBAND UNDER 18 U.S.C. § 2510 BECAUSE HE EAVES-

DROPPED ON AND SECRETLY TAPE RECORDED HER TELE-
PHONE CONVERSATIONS FOR SIX MONTHS.

A. The respondent's secret tape recording of Ms. Bell's telephone
conversations violated the plain language of 18 U.S.C. § 2510,
which prohibits any person from intercepting any wire communication.

B. The legislative history of 18 U.S.C. § 2510 supports the plain
meaning that Congress intended the statute to apply to private
individuals and did not intend to exempt interspousal wire tapping.

II. ALICE BELL STATES A CLAIM UNDER 18 U.S.C. § 2510
BECAUSE THE RESPONDENT'S INTERCEPTION OF MS.
BELL'S TELEPHONE CONVERSATIONS ON HER BUSINESS
LINE DOES NOT FALL WITHIN ANY EXCEPTION TO THE
STATUTE.

A. The respondent's eavesdropping and wiretapping were not conducted in the ordinary course of Ms. Bell's consulting business
and thus were not exempt under 18 U.S.C. § 2510(5)(a).

B. The respondent eavesdropped on his wife's private conversations
without her consent.

RESPONDENT'S POINT HEADINGS

I. THE PETITIONER'S COMPLAINT WAS PROPERLY DIS-
MISSED BECAUSE HER HUSBAND'S INTERCEPTION OF
HER TELEPHONE CONVERSATIONS IS EXPLICITLY EX-
EMPTED FROM THE PROVISIONS OF THE OMNIBUS CRIME
CONTROL AND SAFE STREETS ACT.

A. Mr. Bell used the business extension phone in the ordinary
course of business when he overheard conversations establishing
his wife's infidelity, and thus, his conduct is explicitly exempt
from the statute's provisions.

B. Mr. Bell's original conduct was inadvertent and thus not willful
interception as required by the statute.

II. THE PETITIONER'S COMPLAINT WAS PROPERLY DIS-
MISSED BECAUSE HER HUSBAND'S INTERCEPTION OF
TELEPHONE CALLS WAS WITHIN AN IMPLIED EXCEPTION
FROM THE OMNIBUS CRIME CONTROL AND SAFE
STREETS ACT FOR INTERSPOUSAL WIRETAPS.

A. The entire focus of the Omnibus Crime Control and Safe Streets
Act is on law enforcement personnel and organized crime.

B. Congress did not intend that the Crime Control Act extend to
disputes between spouses because domestic relations is an area
traditionally reserved for state law.

Exercise 13–E

1. Write a point heading on whether Miss Morte's distress was caused
by Gothic Memorial Chapel, first from the appellant's point of view

and then from the appellee's point of view (See the account of Miss Morte in section III, Statement of the Case).

2. One issue raised by the Parental Kidnapping Prevention Act (PKPA) is whether there is federal question jurisdiction under the statute. Which point heading on this issue is best and why? What is wrong with the other headings?

    A. SECTION 1738A LIKE § 1738 MERELY PROVIDES FOR FULL FAITH AND CREDIT TO STATE COURT JUDGMENTS AND UNDER BLUE v. GOLD DOES NOT CREATE FEDERAL JURISDICTION.

    B. THE PARENTAL KIDNAPPING PREVENTION ACT CONFERS SUBJECT MATTER JURISDICTION ON THE FEDERAL COURTS TO DETERMINE WHICH OF TWO CONFLICTING CHILD CUSTODY DECREES IS VALID UNDER THE ACT.

    C. THERE WAS NO INTENT BY CONGRESS TO CREATE FEDERAL JURISDICTION UNDER THE PARENTAL KIDNAPPING PREVENTION ACT. MOREOVER, THIS INTERPRETATION HAS BEEN FOLLOWED BY MOST FEDERAL COURTS.

3. Another issue under the Parental Kidnapping Prevention Act (PKPA) case is which state, Alaska or Illinois, had jurisdiction over the children's custody decision. Which point heading on this issue is best and why? What is wrong with the other point headings?

    A. THE PARENTAL KIDNAPPING PREVENTION ACT PERMITS THE ALASKA COURT TO MODIFY MS. WOODY'S ILLINOIS CUSTODY OVER THE WOODY CHILDREN BECAUSE ALASKA HAS HOME STATE JURISDICTION UNDER ALASKA LAW AND ILLINOIS NO LONGER HAS JURISDICTION UNDER ILLINOIS LAW.

    B. UNDER 28 U.S.C. § 1738(A) AND ALASKA STAT. § 25.30, JURISDICTION TO MODIFY CUSTODY IS IN THE ALASKA COURT.

    C. ALASKA, THE HOME STATE UNDER THE PARENTAL KIDNAPPING PREVENTION ACT BECAUSE THE CHILDREN HAVE LIVED THERE FOR TWO YEARS, HAVE GONE TO SCHOOL AND CAMP THERE, AND HAVE LIVED AS A FAMILY WITH THEIR FATHER THERE, HAS JURISDICTION IN ITS COURTS TO MODIFY THE ORIGINAL CUSTODY DECREE FROM A STATE WHERE THE CHILDREN AND THEIR MOTHER HAVE NOT LIVED FOR YEARS.

VI. *The Argument*

A. *Introduction*

In the Argument section of your brief, you should develop the reasons why your client should prevail in order to convince the court to accept your conclusions. The Argument is divided into sections developing separate claims for relief. These main sections are introduced by dominant point headings, while the legal arguments supporting each claim are often introduced by subheadings when there is more than one argument. Within each section of the Argument, as in the Discussion section of a memorandum, you must thoroughly analyze the legal points and facts relevant to your claim. A thorough analysis requires you to introduce the issue, explain the relevant law, work with the decision from the court below and the most persuasive authorities you can find, argue your facts and compare cases, rebut opposing argument, and conclude. A brief will not be persuasive if the arguments in it are unsupported and insufficiently explained.

You must also organize your analysis carefully. To ensure that the structure of your argument is always apparent, build your analysis in terms of the legal conclusions you want to prevail and announce those conclusions and your reasons for the court to adopt them in headings and subheadings. Begin each paragraph introducing a new topic with a topic sentence that refers to the proposition that paragraph is advancing rather than to the facts of a case.

An analysis in the Argument section of a brief differs from an analysis in the Discussion section of a memorandum mainly in how you frame it. In an argument, the order and focus of your analysis is controlled by your persuasive purpose. Your presentation should be responsive, therefore, to the opinion below, the kind of legal argument you are making, and the degree of support that you have.

Determining the type of legal argument you are making is important in brief-writing because how you structure the argument and what you emphasize will vary with the point you are trying to establish. Some cases lend themselves to particular kinds of arguments. Some arguments may be fact-centered; the rule of law is well established and what alone is at issue is its application to the facts. In this situation, the discussion might focus immediately on the particular facts of the case. The thesis paragraph might key in on the facts in some detail. After discussing the rule of law, you might even decide to marshal your facts before comparing them with analogous precedents.

Other arguments are more doctrinal; the issue is primarily a legal question about which precedent controls the case or how a statute should be interpreted. Here, your thesis paragraph might well lead off with the law you think should control and your authority for so arguing.

Some arguments are more policy-centered; the issue is the purpose of the rule and desirability of its end. In contrast to a fact-centered or doctrinal argument, a policy-centered argument might well treat the facts of the case in a somewhat summary fashion but discuss jurisdictional trends and secondary authorities at length. Thus, the type of argument you are making should influence how much space and emphasis to give to the various steps in your analysis. Be aware, however, that many legal problems, especially those you receive as moot court assignments, may present you with several types of arguments that are not exclusive of each other.

B. Writing a Persuasive Thesis Paragraph

Because the initial paragraph or paragraphs after a point heading are crucial in a brief, they should not simply duplicate the Summary of the Argument. Although you want to forecast the factual and legal points you will be developing, your first task is to get the court's attention. Thus, you may find yourself writing more creative openings than you would in an office memorandum. You might decide, for example, to highlight the facts or to set out your theory of the case.

The thesis paragraph should also be assertive. You want to explain to the court what your client wants and why. You also want to tell the court what it should conclude about the issues in the case and why those conclusions should be favorable to your client. Moreover, you want your points to flow naturally, logically, and inescapably to your conclusion.

For an argument that is broken into subissues introduced by subheadings, the thesis paragraph should be placed after the roman numeral heading and before the subheading A. It should forecast the arguments to be made in each subdivision, and it should relate those arguments to your theory of the case.

Example of a Thesis Paragraph Introducing Subpoints

I. THE SIOUX FALLS RULES REGULATING AND PERMITTING RELIGIOUS HOLIDAY OBSERVANCES IN PUBLIC SCHOOLS COMPLY WITH THE ESTABLISHMENT CLAUSE OF THE FIRST AMENDMENT.

The Sioux Falls Policy and Rules, which regulate permissible observance of religious holidays in the Sioux Falls public schools, are constitutional under the first amendment. The establishment clause of the first amendment has never been interpreted to mean that there can be no connection between government and religion. See Lemon v. Kurtzman, 403 U.S. 602, 612–13 (1971). Rather, the three part test the Court has developed as the standard of analysis in establishment clause cases is intended to clarify the degree and type of connection that is permissible. To satisfy that test, "the statute must [first] have a secular legislative purpose; second, its principal or primary effect must be one that neither advances nor inhibits religion; finally the statute must not foster an excessive government entanglement with religion." Id.

The Sioux Falls Policy and Rules comply with each of these requirements. The purpose of the Rules is to advance secular educational objectives and to foster mutual understanding and respect. Moreover, the Rules have no direct immediate effect on religion. Rather than entangling the schools in religion, the Rules ensure that the schools stay clear of religious matters. Thus, the Policy and Rules are constitutional under the first amendment.

After this thesis paragraph, the writer should go to subheading A and focus on the first prong of the Lemon test, whether the statute has a secular purpose.

An argument which is not subdivided because there is only one basic assertion being made should begin with a thesis paragraph that summarizes the legal and factual contentions you wish to establish. In a doctrinal argument, your thesis paragraph would probably set out the law and the weight of precedent on your side.

Example of Law–Centered Thesis Paragraph

I. THE TRIAL COURT COMMITTED REVERSIBLE ERROR BY ITS FAILURE TO READ BACK A CRUCIAL PORTION OF A COMPLAINING WITNESS'S TESTIMONY THAT WAS REQUESTED BY THE JURY BECAUSE THAT TESTIMONY ADDRESSED A PIVOTAL ISSUE RELATING TO THE APPELLANT'S CONSENT DEFENSE.

The trial court erred in failing to read back a portion of the complainant's testimony requested by the jury pursuant to N.Y. [Penal] Law § 140.20 (McKinney 1975). The Court of Appeals has held that the trial court must, under CPL § 310.30, "give such requested information as the court deems proper," and must "respond meaningfully to the jury's request for further instruction or information." People v. Malloy, 55 N.Y.2d 296, 302, 434 N.E.2d 237, 241, 449 N.Y.S.2d 168, 174 (1982). Failure to provide a meaningful response to a jury's request is reversible error. See, e.g., People v. Lavender, 117 A.D.2d 253, 502 N.Y.S.2d 439 (1st Dept. 1986); People v. Arcarola, 96 A.D.2d 1081, 466 N.Y.S.2d 719 (2d Dept. 1983). Particularly where the jury's question concerned the testimony of the complaining witness about a crucial aspect of appellant's defense, failure to give the jury the requested information requires that the conviction be reversed and a new trial ordered.

You may decide not to begin the thesis paragraph with a conclusion, however, if you have a particularly fact-centered problem, that is, if the facts of the case are particularly interesting or compelling. For example, as the prosecutor of a defendant charged with murder, you might want to emphasize the gruesome facts of the murder. In a fact-centered type of argument, therefore, your thesis paragraph might begin with a parade of facts relevant to the legal issue and end by tying those facts both to the legal principle upon which you are relying and to your conclusion. Be careful that your thesis paragraph is not merely a narrative of background information, however. It must include assertions about the case. Because the rest of the argument is devoted to explaining the reasons for your assertions and conclusions, a narrative which is not tied to your conclusion is confusing and damaging.

Example of a Fact–Centered Thesis Paragraph

I. THE POLICE DID NOT HAVE PROBABLE CAUSE TO ARREST JOSEPH GOLD AND SEIZE HIS PROPERTY MERELY BECAUSE HE PULLED A SHOPPING CART WITH HOUSEHOLD ITEMS DOWN A CITY STREET AT MID–DAY AND REFUSED TO TELL POLICE WHERE THEY WERE OBTAINED.

When two New York police officers saw Joseph Gold pulling a shopping cart down a Brooklyn street at mid-day, they leapt from their car, grabbed him, and demanded to know where he had obtained the items in the cart. The officers' extraordinary behavior had apparently been precipitated by a report from two women that they had seen two suspicious men in the neighborhood, neither of whom fits Gold's description. When Gold's reaction to the police intrusion was to remain silent, the officers then compounded that intrusion with a full scale arrest—frisking, handcuffing, and placing him in the squad car for transportation to the precinct to await a report of a burglary. In the incident just described, Gold's constitutional rights were violated. On the least possible evidence of crime, Gold was subjected to the greatest possible intrusion on his personal privacy even though such an intrusion can be justified by nothing short of probable cause to believe a crime has been committed. Accordingly, the evidence seized from him under these circumstances must be suppressed. U.S. Const. amends. IV, XIV; N.Y. Const. art. I, §§ 6, 12.

Exercise 13–F

1. The following thesis paragraphs introduce the State's arguments that there is no sixth amendment violation when a closure order enables a frightened witness to testify. Which example is better and why? What is wrong with the other example?

Example A

The sixth amendment provides an accused with the right to a speedy and public trial. Nonetheless, a court has the discretion to bar the public when it decides there is an interest sufficiently compelling to justify closure. United States ex rel. Lloyd v. Vincent, 520 F.2d 1272 (2d Cir.), cert. denied, 423 U.S. 937 (1975). Although closure is usually upheld only if the psychological well-being of a sex crime victim is at stake, United States v. Hernandez, 608 F.2d 741 (9th Cir. 1979), and Merta was only the victim of an assault, she is a minor. Moreover, Judiciary Law § 4, which gives a court the discretion to close the courtroom during specifically enumerated crimes (divorce, sex crimes), extends to any victim likely to be embarrassed or humiliated during testimony and Merta falls within that class of witnesses which the statute seeks to protect. Also the order was not too broad because it was the defendant's family which was the source of Merta's embarrassment. Finally, the findings were adequate because the court identified the reason for closure and the interest served. United States v. Brooklier, 685 F.2d 1162 (9th Cir. 1982).

Example B

The trial court properly closed the courtroom during the testimony of Sheila Merta, a thirteen-year-old assault victim who said the spectators frightened her. While the sixth amendment provides that a defendant in a criminal prosecution has the right to a public trial, that right is not absolute when a court concludes that other interests override a defendant's right to an open courtroom. United States ex rel. Lloyd v. Vincent, 520 F.2d 1272 (2d Cir.), cert. denied, 423 U.S. 937 (1975). In determining whether closure was proper, a reviewing court will look to whether: 1) the party advancing closure established an overriding interest; 2) the closure order was no broader than necessary; 3) the court examined reasonable alternatives to closure; and 4) the trial court made adequate findings in the record to support closure. Waller v. Georgia, 467 U.S. 39 (1984). The trial court's order satisfied the Waller test in the case at bar: the psychological well being of a young victim of a brutal assault is an interest sufficiently compelling to justify closure; the closure was limited to Merta's testimony; there were no reasonable alternatives to closure; and the findings made during an *in camera* hearing were sufficient to support closure. Therefore, the intermediate appellate court's order upholding the defendant's conviction should be affirmed.

2.   The following examples introduce the issue of whether a woman's right to privacy under the 14th amendment overrides the state's interest when a woman wants a third trimester abortion and the fetus is, arguably, non-viable. Which is the better thesis paragraph and why?

Example A

The fundamental right to privacy encompasses a woman's decision to terminate her pregnancy. Roe v. Wade, 410 U.S. 113, reh'g denied, 410 U.S. 959 (1973). The state cannot infringe upon Ms. Davis's fundamental right in the absence of a compelling state interest. Id. at 156. Utopia cannot sustain its burden of proving a compelling interest in protecting the life of a fetus that has no brain tissue, no cognizant ability, no chance of sustained survival outside the womb, a defective nervous system and only a partial skull. Thus, the state's interference with Joan Davis's right to an abortion is unconstitutional.

Example B

   Although the district court may have interpreted the Utopia statute correctly, that statute unconstitutionally violates Joan Davis's right to privacy under the fourteenth amendment. The right to privacy, founded in the fourteenth amendment, protects a woman's right to decide whether to terminate her pregnancy. Roe v. Wade, 410 U.S. 113, reh'g denied, 410 U.S. 959 (1973). A woman's decision to terminate her pregnancy may, however, be subject to state regulation when there is a compelling state interest. Id. at 178. The state has two compelling interests. One is in the health of the pregnant woman, and the other is in the protection of the viable fetus. In the interest of protecting the woman's health, the state can regulate the abortion procedure, but cannot restrict the woman's decision whether to terminate her pregnancy. Colautti v. Franklin, 439 U.S. 379, 386 (1979). Nonetheless, the state can prohibit a woman from having an abortion when it has a compelling interest in protecting the potential life of a viable fetus. Id. Even in the third trimester, the severely defective fetus Joan Davis is carrying is not viable. Thus, Joan Davis's right to have an abortion outweighs the state's interest in protecting the potential life of a severely defective non-viable fetus.

3.   What follows is one short and simple argument from an appellate brief submitted to one of New York's appellate courts (full citations are omitted). The thesis paragraph has been omitted. Read the argument carefully and critically. Then,

   1)   determine what kind of argument it is—doctrinal, policy-centered, or fact-centered;

   2)   write the missing thesis paragraph;

   3)   write a point heading.

   The term "dangerous instrument" is defined by the Penal Law as "any instrument, article or substance . . . which, under the circumstances in which it is used . . . is readily capable of causing death or other serious physical injury." P.L. § 10.00(13). It is long settled that the relevant inquiry is not whether an object is inherently dangerous, but whether, as actually wielded by the defendant, it constituted a real threat of grave or even fatal injury. See People v. Carter. Thus, a knife—an inherently dangerous object—has been held not to be a dangerous instrument within the statute when the defendant merely carried it in his hand. See People v. Hirniak. On the other hand, a handkerchief has been held to be a dangerous instrument when used to gag an elderly man. See People v. Ford. Similarly, an ordinarily harmless object used to beat a victim can be a dangerous instrument, because such use created a substantial and obvious threat of grave injury. See, e.g., People v. Carter (rubber boot); People v. Ozarowski (baseball bat); People v. O'Hara (boots); People v. Davis (plaster cast).

However, when an object is put to a non-standard use that *may* cause serious physical injury, but is not very likely to do so, it is not a dangerous instrument—even if it does in fact cause injury. In Matter of Taylor, a teen-ager admitted throwing two rocks at a friend's head, one of which struck the friend, causing physical injury. However, the court dismissed a charge of assault with a dangerous instrument, stating

> [T]he criteria is the circumstance under which they were used. True, such a rock held in the hand and used to repeatedly pound a person on the head or vital organ could cause serious physical injury. Even a thrown rock coming in contact with some part of the body could cause such injury, but this is not to be considered "readily capable". The after effects of an act cannot be used to determine the legality or illegality of the act itself.

Id.

When the evidence at appellant's trial is viewed in the light most favorable to the People and measured against the statutory and case-law criteria detailed above, it is clear that no rational fact-finder could have concluded that the bar glass that injured bartender Bruce Garin was a dangerous instrument. First, the glass that injured Garin was small and thick rather than fragile. Further, the glass was not used as a bludgeon, nor was it broken and used to slash Garin—rather, the glass was aimed at Garin's back after Garin had turned away from Smith. No one heard Smith utter any threats, and when he threw the glass, he acted in an ill-conceived but purely impulsive effort to have the last word or to regain Garin's attention. Unfortunately, Garin turned back to face appellant and the glass struck him in the face. More unfortunately still, the glass broke and cut him.

Although the glass concededly caused physical injury, under the circumstances it was not *readily* capable of causing serious or fatal injury. Like the rock in Taylor, the glass *could* conceivably have caused grave or fatal injury—to a person with an "egg-shell" skull, for instance—but under the circumstances, it was far more likely to miss Garin entirely, to glance unbroken off his back and fall to the floor, or at most, to strike and bruise him. Although Smith may have acted foolishly and immaturely by throwing a small bar glass at the bartender, he did not use the glass as a dangerous instrument. Accordingly, his conviction should be reversed.

C. Summarizing the Law Concisely and Affirmatively

In an argument that is not divided into subissues introduced by subheadings, you should establish more fully the legal context for your argument after the thesis paragraph. Begin by concisely summarizing the principle of law upon which you are relying. Do not assume that judges can instantly recollect the basic law governing your argument; instead, refresh their memories with a description of the law in terms which are both advantageous to your client and responsible to the substance of the law. As the appellant, you will also show how the court below misinterpreted and misapplied that law.

For example, if you were arguing that a state agency must be enjoined from refusing to terminate a pregnancy in the third trimester, do not begin with a recapitulation of the general rule that abortions in the third trimester of pregnancy are usually prohibited. Begin instead with the exception to that rule, that abortions in the third trimester can be performed to preserve the life or health of the mother. If a petitioner is arguing that her right to free speech was infringed, do not begin "commercial speech is subject to some regulation by the state." Write instead, "because commercial speech is constitutionally protected, it may be regulated by the state only in narrowly prescribed instances." In other words, begin with the rule you want the court to adopt and summarize that rule in accurate but favorable language.

Topic sentences in a brief should not therefore be written in the kind of objective, narrative, explanatory style you might use in an office memorandum. In a memo, you might say that "the courts are split on this issue" or that "the courts have not decided how the two statutes relate." In a brief, however, you want to convince the court to accept your interpretation of the two statutes, and thus, you must make your points affirmatively: "five of the courts of appeals have held . . ." or "the statutes are cumulative and each imposes a duty. . . ."

In addition, you should avoid sentences that begin with "I believe." Your analysis should not sound like an assertion of personal opinion, but rather like one that is dictated by the logic of the law.

In a common law problem, your summary of the law may immediately involve you in a discussion of cases (see section D). In a statutory problem, however, your summary of the law may require you to interpret the language of the statute and to examine the legislature's intent in enacting the statute before you move into judicial constructions of the statute. This kind of analysis is presented in the following example. The author argues here that the district court correctly denied appellant's pretrial motion for an order excluding the attorney's fees owed by appellant from forfeiture to the government under § 1963 of The Racketeer Influenced and Corrupt Organizations Act (RICO). The

RICO statute prevents an appellant from transfering criminally obtained assets to third parties in order to prevent forfeiture.

Example

The plain meaning of § 1963 of the Racketeer Influenced and Corrupt Organization Act (RICO), 18 U.S.C. §§ 1961–68 (1982 & Supp. II 1984), is unambiguous and does not exempt attorney's fees from forfeiture. Under § 1963(c), title vests in the government to forfeitable property at the time the criminal act was committed, rather than upon conviction of the defendant. Thus, the government may seek a special verdict of forfeiture of tainted assets which have been subsequently transferred to a third party. § 1963(c). The only way a third party may vacate or modify such an order is to show at a post-conviction hearing that he was "a bona fide purchaser for value" of such property "reasonably without cause to believe it was subject to forfeiture." Id.

Because under the plain meaning of the statute, Congress exempted only two groups of people from the reach of third-party forfeiture, tainted attorney fees are forfeitable. Parties who have acquired title to assets before the commission of a crime are exempt from forfeiture. This group would hardly encompass an attorney in the pretrial stage of a criminal proceeding. In addition, parties who are "bona fide purchasers for value reasonably without cause to believe that tainted assets are subject to forfeiture" are also exempt. § 1963(c). An attorney who "purchased" tainted proceeds in exchange for legal services could not be considered a bona fide purchaser under the statute. An attorney would necessarily be on notice of forfeiture after reading his client's indictment. In re Grand Jury Subpoena Dated Jan. 2, 1985, 605 F. Supp. 839, 849 n.14 (S.D.N.Y.), rev'd on other grounds, 767 F.2d 26 (2d Cir. 1985).

The general legislative purpose behind RICO forfeiture also supports a plain meaning interpretation of § 1963. In Russello v. United States, 464 U.S. 16 (1983), the Court noted that the broad goal of RICO forfeiture provisions was to strip organized crime of its economic base and separate the racketeer from his illegally gotten gains. Id. at 26, 28. The relation-back provision of § 1963(c) furthers that goal by preventing pre-conviction transfers of forfeitable property. See Brickey, Forfeiture of Attorney's Fees: The Impact of RICO and CCE Forfeitures on the Right to Counsel, 72 Va. L. Rev. 493, 496 n.13 (1986). A construction inconsistent with the plain meaning of the statute would undermine this goal by allowing a RICO defendant to utilize what may be the fruits of racketeering activity to finance his criminal defense. See In re Grand Jury Subpoena, 605 F. Supp. at 850 n.14.

Although you should not assume the court will remember every basic principle for each topic in law, do not offer long historical explanations either. The author of the RICO passage establishes the present state of the law as quickly as the topic allows. A general history of the area of law in which your case arises is not effective. Instead, if you have to include some background, try to focus on the development of the particular principles upon which you rely. Make sure that the reader understands the relevance of this introduction to the issue in your case. Remember that the court probably knows more about the importance of the first amendment to a democratic society, for example, than it does about how the law should apply to the facts of your case.

In an argument that has been divided into subissues introduced by subheadings, your first paragraph after the subheading should be a thesis paragraph on the law controlling that subpoint. The following example deals with a subpoint on the first prong of the test that is used to determine establishment clause violations. The author begins with a legal conclusion, follows with an affirmative summary of the controlling law, and moves quickly into a discussion of the case law on that prong.

Example

The purpose of the Sioux Falls Policy and Rules is a secular one: to foster understanding and mutual respect of different religions by exposing students to the various religious cultures and traditions in the world. The court need not inquire behind this statute's stated secular purpose and the lower courts correctly did not do so. Indeed, this Court has consistently accepted a state's avowed purpose. In the recent case of Wolman v. Walter, the Court upheld provisions of an Ohio statute authorizing aid to non-public, primarily parochial schools. The Court's entire inquiry into legislative purpose consisted of a single reference to "Ohio's legitimate interest in protecting the health of its youth." 433 U.S. at 236.

In the last twenty-five years the Court has inquired beyond the stated legislative purpose only twice. In Stone v. Graham, 449 U.S. 39 (1981), the Court held that the state violated the establishment clause by requiring public schools to post the Ten Commandments in each classroom. And in School District v. Schempp, 374 U.S. 203 (1963), the Court held that the state violated the establishment clause by requiring Bible reading every morning in the public schools. The Court found that the purpose of these statutes was "plainly religious" even though each state had justified them on secular grounds.

None of the factors which compelled the Court to look beyond the state legislative purpose in Stone and Schempp exists in the present case. There are four important distinctions. . . .

Exercise 13–G

1. The following paragraphs discuss whether a clothing store's dress code policy for female employees violates § 703(a)(1) of Title VII of the Civil Rights Act. Which paragraph is more persuasive and why?

Example A

Title VII of the Civil Rights Act of 1964 prohibits the dress code implemented by the petitioner. The petitioner forces its female sales clerks to wear an identifiable uniform while it permits its male sales clerks to wear their own business clothing. Section 703(a)(1) of the Act declares that it is unlawful for an employer to "discriminate against any individual with respect to his compensation, terms, conditions, or privileges of employment because of such individual's . . . sex . . . ." 42 U.S.C. § 2000e–2(a)(1) (1982). A dress code which requires women to wear a uniform while men may wear ordinary business attire constitutes discrimination in a term or condition of employment on the basis of sex. Carroll v. Talman Fed. Sav. and Loan Assoc., 604 F.2d 1028 (7th Cir. 1979), cert. denied, 445 U.S. 929 (1980).

Example B

The intent of Congress in enacting Title VII is explained by this Court as being "plain from the language of the statute. [Congress's objective] was to achieve equality of employment opportunities and remove barriers that have operated in the past to favor an identifiable group of white employees over other employees." Griggs v. Duke Power Co., 401 U.S. 424, 429–30 (1971). Although Griggs was concerned with racial discrimination, this language applies with equal force to sex discrimination. Willingham v. Macon Telegraph Publishing Co., 507 F.2d 1084, 1091 (5th Cir. 1975). Indeed, this Court reiterated this point in Phillips v. Martin Marietta Corp., 400 U.S. 542, 544 (1971), by saying that "the Civil Rights Act of 1964 requires that persons of like qualifications be given employment opportunities irrespective of their sex." "It would seem inescapable that Congress was saying that job opportunities must be opened, remain open, and not be denied or terminated because of . . . sex. . . ." Fagan v. National Cash Register Co., 481 F.2d 1115, 1120 (D.C. Cir. 1973). "Consequently, discrimination based on either immutable sex characteristics or constitutionally-protected activities such as marriage or child rearing violate the Act [Title VII] because they present obstacles to employment of one sex that cannot be overcome."

2.   The following paragraphs address the issue of whether the Sioux Falls Policy and Rules have the effect of advancing religion. Which example is more persuasive and why?

Example A

When examining legislation to determine whether its effect advances religion, the Court has usually looked beyond its single most prominent effect and held that although a law had a legitimate primary effect, it was not "immune from further examination to ascertain whether it also has the direct and immediate effect of advancing religion." Nyquist, 413 U.S. at 783. Nquist, however, was a case involving state aid to parochial schools. The Court's refusal to confine its inquiry to principal or primary effect only has come from a long line of parochial school aid cases, see, e.g., Hunt v. McNair, 413 U.S. 734 (1973); Tilton v. Richardson, 403 U.S. 672 (1971). Because of the religious nature of these schools, the Court's analysis must be extensive.

In cases involving the public schools, however, the Court need only examine whether the challenged regulation has a principal or primary effect of advancing religion. The primary effect of school prayer in public schools, for example, is to advance the cause of religion. School District v. Schempp, 374 U.S. at 223; Engel v. Vitale, 370 U.S. at 421. Public school districts thus cannot require a school prayer.

As the court of appeals has held, the primary effect of the Sioux Falls Policy and Rules is neither to advance nor inhibit religion, but to effectuate the school district's secular purposes.

Example B

As long as the principal or primary effect of a regulation neither advances nor inhibits religion, then that regulation is valid under the second part of the Lemon test. "The crucial question is not whether some benefit accrues to an institution as a consequence of the legislative program, but whether its principal or primary effect advances religion." Tilton v. Richardson, 403 U.S. at 679 (emphasis supplied). The primary effect of the Sioux Falls Policy and Rules neither advances nor inhibits religion. Rather its primary effect is to effectuate the school district's secular purpose.

In cases involving public schools, the Court has always looked to the primary effect of a regulation rather than to every effect. For example, in the school prayer cases, because of the unequivocally religious nature of prayer, the primary effect of the required classroom prayer was to advance religion. Engel v. Vitale, 370 U.S. 421, 430 (1961). The cases involving aid to parochial schools provide the exception to the general rule that the Court will invalidate a regulation only if its principal or primary effect advances religion. Because of the character of these institutions, the Court's analysis must be particularly intensive. In those cases only, the Court has invalidated statutes with "any direct and immediate effect of advancing religion," Committee for Public Education v. Nyquist, 413 U.S. at 783. Since the Sioux Falls District Public School has no religious mission, this type of inquiry is unnecessary.

D. *Using Precedent Effectively*

Sometimes your argument will involve an analysis of a statute's language and purpose, and your discussion of cases construing that statute will follow that analysis. Sometimes your argument will immediately involve you in case analysis. Whichever the situation, you should begin your discussion of the precedents with the strongest cases supporting the proposition you need to advance your argument. Because a brief is written to persuade a court of the merits of your position, you must set out your argument first, giving it a prominent position and stating it clearly, thoroughly, and confidently. As a general rule, therefore, you should try to discuss and apply favorable precedents and come to an affirmative legal conclusion before raising and distinguishing unfavorable precedents. Only when the leading precedents are clearly against you, must you deal first with adverse opinions to avoid being misleading. Your task, in other words, is to create and present your own argument, not merely to react defensively to the lower court's decision or to your opponent's arguments by exhibiting their flaws.

Stress the reasoning in cases, as well as the facts. It is important to demonstrate that your case is factually similar to those decisions which you regard as favorable precedents, but factual comparisons are only the beginning of the process of persuasion. Try also to explain and defend the policies behind the favorable precedents, and show how the application of their policies requires a result favorable to your client. To do this, you need to understand what was important to the courts deciding the precedents and why they decided as they did. It is equally important to persuade the court that the true reasoning of those cases which are relied upon by opposing counsel or the court below does not support the decision for which he or she contends or that the adverse decision is factually dissimilar.

If your case involves an unresolved issue, or an application of law to an unusual set of facts, then identify those issues and analogize to ones that have been resolved in a favorable way. The court will be concerned with how the reasoning of those decisions applies to your case. For example, a petitioner might pose an unresolved issue this way:

> Although this Court has not specifically considered whether a letter such as that written by Ms. Fox falls within the protection accorded newspaper advertisements in <u>Bates</u>, a situation similar to the present case came before the Court in <u>In re Primus</u>, 432 U.S. 402 (1978).

You will not be able to discuss every relevant authority that you have found, nor should you try to. You probably want to treat extensively the two or three best cases you have which support your argument. You need to give as much of the facts, reasoning, and holding of a cited case as is necessary for an understanding of its relevance. It is often a good idea to give first the holding of the case you rely on. Then the reader can analyze the facts and the reasons for the decision in light of the outcome.

Several factors must be considered in determining which cases would best promote your argument. You must first consider the weight of authority. Whenever possible, base your argument on previous decisions of the highest court in the jurisdiction of your problem, especially United States Supreme Court decisions if you are analyzing constitutional or federal issues. Even if the highest court has not ruled yet on the particular issue in your assignment, relate your arguments to prior decisions of that court in analogous areas of the law, and to statements that the court has made in dicta. You should also include relevant and favorable lower court cases from the jurisdiction of your problem; show how they are consistent with the higher court's decisions and policy. Although you would discuss first the cases that are most important in your jurisdiction, you may need to use persuasive decisions on the same point by a court that does not bind your court.

Do not mechanically devote a paragraph to each case. You do not want the cases to dictate the argument to you. You want to make your own argument, supporting it with cases readily applicable to your situation. Thus, analyze the precedents in the context of your argument, continually showing their bearing on your case. Although you may need to begin a paragraph with a citation to a new case, avoid beginning a paragraph with a recitation of the facts of a case, for example: "In Millington v. Southeastern Elevator Co., 22 N.Y.2d 498, 503, 239 N.E.2d 897, 899, 293 N.Y.S.2d 305, 308 (1968), the husband had been paralyzed from the waist down." Instead, use the opening sentence to sharpen the point you want to emphasize through that case. The topic sentence below puts historical material and persuasive authorities into an appropriate legal context.

Example

A de facto spouse's right to sue for loss of consortium is the next logical step in the evolution of the doctrine of consortium. Under the early common law, only the husband or father could sue for loss of services of a member of his family. Courts now recognize that wives as well as husbands may bring claims for loss of consortium. In permitting a wife to bring a loss of consortium claim, the New York Court of Appeals identified the wife's loss as arising out of the personal interest she has in the marital relationship. Millington v. Southeastern Elevator Co., 22 N.Y.2d 498, 503, 239 N.E.2d 897, 899, 293 N.Y.S.2d 305, 308 (1968). The husband in Millington had been paralyzed from the waist down as a result of an elevator accident. The court reasoned that the woman's "loss of companionship, emotional support, love, felicity, and sexual relations are real injuries" which altered their relationship "in a tragic way." Id. In coming to a similar conclusion, the California Supreme Court focused on the shattering effect of a husband's disabling accident on the quality of his wife's life when her husband was transformed from partner to invalid. Rodriguez v. Bethlehem Steel Co., 12 Cal. 3d 382, 386, 525 P.2d 669, 670, 115 Cal. Rptr. 765, 766 (1974).

Susan Webster has suffered damage identical to that suffered by a wife whose husband has been injured. Although she was never legally married to John Webster, the stability and significance of their relationship indicates that her emotional suffering will be as great as that of a married woman. Susan Webster's commitment to her relationship is apparent from its nine-year duration and shared parental obligations and demonstrates that her loss was no less real than that of Mary Rodriguez, a bride of only sixteen months. Moreover, she has lived with and cared for John Webster since the accident and likely will continue to do so. The circumstances of Susan Webster's relationship compel a finding that she, like the plaintiff in Millington, has suffered in a "tragic way" as a direct result of the injury sustained by her de facto spouse. See Millington, 22 N.Y.2d at 503, 239 N.E.2d at 899, 293 N.Y.S.2d at 308. Accordingly, her consortium rights should be recognized and protected.

If you want the court to be aware of a number of other cases, group them together with parenthetical explanations—do not merely string cite.

Example

Gold did nothing more than to push a shopping cart on a public street in broad daylight. This innocuous conduct does not even create an "objective credible reason" for the police to request information. People v. DeBour, 40 N.Y.2d 210, 213, 352 N.E.2d 562, 565, 386 N.Y.S.2d 375, 378 (1977). Indeed, it is hard to imagine a less remarkable picture on the urban landscape than a person pushing a shopping cart. Accord People v. Howard, 50 N.Y.2d 583, 408 N.E.2d 908, 430 N.Y.S.2d 578 (1980) (man carrying shopping bag does not justify stop); People v. Lakin, 21 A.D.2d 902, 251 N.Y.S.2d 890 (2d Dept. 1962) (man carrying woman's purse does not justify stop).

Exercise 13–H

1. The following paragraphs, which are addressed to the United States Supreme Court, argue that Fields Brothers' dress code requirements for employees are illegal under Title VII with respect to the "terms and conditions" of employment because different standards apply to men and women employees. Which example uses case law better and why?

Example A

This Court has consistently held that under Title VII, an employer cannot impose one requirement on male employees and a different requirement on female employees. See, e.g., Phillips v. Martin Marietta Corp., 400 U.S. 542 (1971). By imposing the requirement that female employees must wear a store uniform, but that male employees need not, Fields Brothers violates Title VII by discriminating against women in their "terms and conditions of employment." See Carroll v. Talman Savings Ass'n, 604 F.2d 1028 (7th Cir. 1979).

Dress codes that impose burdens on employees of only one sex are suspect because they can be based on offensive sexual stereotypes and thus violate Title VII. In Carroll, the employer had imposed its dress code because it had decided that women tended to follow fashion trends and dressed improperly for work. Id. at 1033. Thus, the employer in

Carroll issued clothing to women employees consisting of a choice of five pieces. The court found the clothing constituted a uniform and held that the defendant's practice of requiring females to wear these uniforms was prohibited by Title VII. Id. at 1029. The court stated that the dress code was based on an improper stereotype that women exercised poor judgment in selecting work attire but men did not. Id. See also EEOC v. Clayton Fed. Savings Ass'n, 25 Fair Empl. Prac. Cas. (BNA) 841 (E.D. Mo. 1981) (requiring only female employees to contribute to and wear uniforms is prima facie evidence of actionable discrimination under § 2000e–2(a)).

Example B

In two cases on point to the case at bar, the courts held that employers who imposed a dress code requirement only on female employees violated Title VII. Carroll v. Talman Savings Ass'n, 604 F.2d 1028 (7th Cir. 1979); EEOC v. Clayton Federal Savings Ass'n, 25 Fair Empl. Prac. Cas. (BNA) 841 (E.D. Mo. 1981). The dress code in Carroll required women to wear a uniform that consisted of choices among five items: skirt or slacks, jacket, tunic or vest. Male employees were required to wear ordinary business attire. Carroll, 604 F.2d at 1029–30.

The United States Court of Appeals for the Seventh Circuit held that the employer's requirement that women but not men wear a uniform violated § 703(a)(1) with respect to "terms and conditions of employment." Id. The court remanded the case for the entry of summary judgment for the female employee plaintiffs. A district court has followed the Seventh Circuit and held that a dress code imposed on female employees only is prima facie evidence of discrimination under § 703(a)(1). Clayton Federal, 25 Fair Empl. Prac. Cas. at 843.

E. *Arguing Your Facts*

Your brief will not be convincing if you fail to argue your facts thoroughly. Regardless of whether you argue your facts before or after you analyze supporting authority, you should always paint your facts in such a way as to elicit a positive application of the law. Stress facts that align your case with favorable precedents. Stress facts that show injustices to your client. After you have dealt with your strong facts, work with damaging evidence. You should not ignore unfavorable evidence, as the opposing counsel will certainly present that evidence, and present it in a worse light. Instead, put that evidence forward, briefly and blandly, and provide an exculpatory explanation if possible. Emphasize both exonerating facts and mitigating facts. Downplay facts that distinguish your case from favorable precedents. Demonstrate the irrelevancy, if at all possible, of facts that may show your client as unworthy.

1. Emphasize Favorable Facts

Treat favorable evidence in depth. Do not describe supportive incidents in broad terms; parade each material detail.

Example (Citations to the record omitted)

The Supreme Court has said that, in the best of circumstances, "[t]he vagaries of eyewitness identification are well-known [and] the annals of criminal law are rife with instances of mistaken identification." United States v. Wade, 388 U.S. 218, 228 (1967). In Moore's case, the conditions made an accurate identification impossible and the court's description of the identification testimony as "highly reliable" is simply unrealistic.

The robbery took place in a parking lot on a dark October night. The complainant never identified Derek Moore as one of the robbers. The most he could say was that Moore "would fit the description" of one of the tall youths. Indeed, the complainant previously testified that Moore was not one of the robbers. Thus, the People's contention that Moore was one of the youths who committed the robbery depended solely upon the testimony of the Smith brothers, Tom and John, who claimed to have seen him at the robbery scene.

Although John Smith asserted that he had seen Moore climb the parking lot fence, this witness admitted on cross-examination that he had been fifty to sixty feet away and had only seen half of the person's face. Tom's identification testimony is also questionable. From a distance of ten to fifteen feet, through the dark, he said he saw Moore's face for a "split second." Although he asserted that this brief view was sufficient for him to recognize Moore, whom he had never seen before, he could not see whether the hood of Moore's light-colored jacket was up or down. Nor was he able to see an identifying mark on Moore's forehead—a two inch keloid scar. In sum, it is hard to imagine a less reliable identification that would still result in a prosecution.

2. Minimize Unfavorable Facts

You should learn to exploit paragraph structure so as to highlight favorable material and subordinate damaging material. Positive information should be advantageously located at the beginning and end of paragraphs. Damaging material should be buried in the middle of paragraphs—and sentences—and described generally. In this way, negative information is framed by the positive and is, to some degree, neutralized by the context.

Example (Citations to the record are omitted)

Upon seeing two white males round a corner armed with tire irons and chains, Derek Moore believed that he was about to become the victim of a racially-motivated assault. Because Derek knew nothing of the robbery these two youths had just witnessed, this assumption on his part was entirely reasonable. So was his decision to run in the opposite direction. The fact that the district court found the Smiths unassailably truthful in asserting that they had a different motive for chasing petitioner is irrelevant to Moore's belief. It is also believable that the Smiths might well have shouted racial epithets at someone they assumed had committed a robbery outside their very window. Thus, there is no significant conflict in these stories, although there is a plausible and exonerating explanation for why Moore took to his heels.

Exercise 13–I

1. The following paragraphs address the question of whether a trial court committed reversible error by failing to respond to the jury's request to have a portion of the testimony reread (Citations to the record are omitted). In which of the following examples are the facts used well? Why?

Example A

A question of fact existed as to whether the defendant and his friend were attempting to steal the complainant's wallet. The defendant testified that the intoxicated complainant initiated the altercation and that the complainant claims to have lost $80.00; yet, the defendant and his friend did not have more than $20.00 at the time they were apprehended. The jury requested this testimony because it was in the process of determining whether the state had proved the elements of the crime charged. The court's failure to provide the jury with this testimony before it reached its verdict was extremely prejudicial. The defendant was denied a fair trial and impartial jury. The possibility that the jury may have returned a different verdict if it had been provided with a read-back of all the requested testimony, and not solely that of the People's witness, cannot be excluded. Thus, the court denied the defendant's right to a fair trial, and its error should be reviewed.

Example B

In the present case, there is neither compelling circumstantial evidence nor eyewitness testimony which discredits defendant's explanation of what happened. We have only the word of the complainant that he lost his wallet. He first testified that he had his wallet when he ran from the scene and later testified that it was returned to him by a police officer (that officer, however, did not testify). He also later testified that he did not know if the defendant took his wallet or if he lost it while he was running. The police officers who did testify did not hear defendant demand the complainant's money, nor did any of them see or retrieve complainant's wallet. In addition, the complainant was admittedly "high" on alcohol at the time.

In light of the questionable nature of the complainant's testimony, the weight of the evidence against the defendant is far from overwhelming. In combination with the taint to the proceedings created by the error of the court below, this court should reverse the judgment of the court below and remand this case for a new trial in the interest of justice.

Example C

The trial court's failure to provide the jury with the requested testimony did not prejudice the defendant's rights and, therefore, does not constitute reversible error. The information which the jury requested and which the court failed to provide did not pertain to a vital point. The jury requested a rereading of the defendant's testimony about what the complainant had said. This testimony amounted to three short lines. The defendant testified that "Hassler got very huffy, saying 'Who are you telling me where to walk?' and 'I'll walk where I damn please'". Later, the defendant testified that the complainant "started saying we'd tried to rob him and all that bull." The substance of this testimony was not vital to the defendant. The testimony revealed only that there was a heated exchange of words between the complainant and the defendant and his friend, that the defendant claimed the complainant was the aggressor, and that the defendant denied trying to rob the complainant. These factors were already known to the jury from other evidence and a rereading of this testimony was not vital to the defendant. Therefore, the court's failure to reread it did not prejudice the defendant's rights.

2. Which example uses facts more persuasively as to whether an employer discriminates on the basis of sex when the store issues business suits to its women clerks only? (Citations to the record are omitted.)

Example A

Fields Brothers' dress regulations distinguish between the sexes but do not discriminate on the basis of sex because the distinctions are not based upon immutable sex characteristics nor do they impinge on a fundamental right. Summary judgment in favor of Fields is consistent with that two-prong test to determine sex discrimination in employment.

Fields Brothers' distinctions between male and female employees is not discriminatory as to conditions of employment because clothing styles are not immutable characteristics of a sex but can be changed at will like hair length. For that reason, a sex-differentiated hair length regulation was held not discriminatory. The employee was able to change his hair length in order to comply with his employer's regulations. The respondent in this case could easily have worn one of the suits issued to her and could have complied with the dress code. Her desire to wear her own choice of suit is not an immutable characteristic. Nor does Fields' code impinge upon an employee's fundamental rights such as marriage and child rearing. In cases in which regulations impinge on female employees' fundamental rights, the employers did not impose any restrictions on male employees. Fields, however, imposes dress regulations, albeit different ones, on its male sales clerks.

Example B

The Fields Brothers adopted a dress code policy for both male and female sales clerks in 1979. The store sells conservative business clothes and its customers are predominantly business people of both sexes. The store's president has explained in his affidavit that the store's management policy is to cater to its customers' preferences for conservatively dressed sales clerks. All members of the store's sales staff are therefore required to wear appropriate business attire.

The court below differentiated between the "uniforms" that the female clerks are required to wear and the "ordinary business" attire required of male clerks. In reality, there is no difference. The male clerks' suits are as much "uniforms" as the female clerks' suits. Male business attire has developed over the years into a recognized uniform of shirt, tie, suitcoat, and suit pants. A male clerk who deviated from this attire would not be appropriately dressed. Design of female business attire, on the other hand, is a relatively new industry, and the same similarity of appearance has not yet developed. The store's decision to supply its female clerks with suits was an attempt to solve the problem created by this difference.

The court also emphasized that female clerks must wear a patch with the store logo on their suits while the men are issued a pin. Yet no real difference exists between a patch and a pin. If a patch makes a business suit a uniform, then so does a pin. All sales clerks wear conservative business suits and the store logo; all are treated alike in the "terms and conditions of employment."

F. Rebutting Opposing Arguments and Authority

Establishing your own argument requires rebutting opposing argument. Yet you do not want to overemphasize those opposing arguments by setting them forth in all their untarnished glory and then scrambling to recoup your losses. Instead, address the argument opposing counsel is likely to make implicitly rather than explicitly, by answering it as you present it. In other words, make your counter-argument affirmatively.

When you rebut your adversary, avoid topic sentences that overemphasize the other party's arguments. Weak introductions frequently include statements like

— It is (has been) argued that . . .

— Respondents assert . . .

— The courts rejecting this claim have said . . .

Such expressions highlight the opposing argument by opening the paragraph with it. For example,

> It has been argued that awarding a child damages for loss of consortium would result in speculative and uncertain damages. However, damages for injuries sustained by the Jones children are no more difficult to ascertain than they are in other classes of injury involving intangible losses where the courts have allowed recovery.

If the author of this example had simply omitted the first sentence, her topic sentence would have focused on the reason why the opposing argument is not sound. She would have suggested the avenue her opponent would take, without giving it undue emphasis.

> Damages for injuries sustained by the children in this case are no more speculative than they are in other classes of injury involving intangible losses where the courts have allowed recovery.

Or again, in arguing that the first amendment's guarantee of freedom of association protects not only activities of an organization but also the activities of attorneys who assist that organization, the petitioner should not say:

> One may argue that Trainmen, Mine Workers, and United Transportation Workers can be distinguished from petitioner's case since in those cases the union was the party charged with violating a statute, while in this case the party charged with violating the statute is the attorney. However, the Court has held that lawyers accepting employment under a constitutionally protected plan of referral have a constitutional protection like that of the union which the state cannot abridge. Trainmen v. Virginia, 377 U.S. at 8.

A more effective advocate might say:

> This Court has long recognized the right of an organization to request an attorney to assist its members in asserting their legal rights. In United Mine Workers and Brotherhood of Railroad Trainmen, the Court held that a state could not proscribe a range of solicitation activities by unions seeking to provide low cost, effective legal representation to their members. Lawyers who accepted employment or acted at the request of these unions were also protected because their actions helped the unions further their members' rights.

In addition, potential weaknesses in your theory of the case should not be discussed at the beginning of an issue or subissue or at the end of such a discussion. Deal with them in the middle of the argument concerning that point. The reader will tend to remember the beginning and ending of a section more than the middle.

Although you should deal with supporting authority first, you must disclose authority in the controlling jurisdiction that goes against you. This is an ethical responsibility imposed by the American Bar Association's Code of Professional Responsibility Disciplinary Rule 7–106(b). In addition, the newer Model Rules of Professional Responsibility, as adopted by each state, also require an attorney to disclose legal authority in the controlling jurisdiction known to be directly adverse to the position of the client if it is not disclosed by opposing counsel.[7] Although it is probable your opponent will find and include these contrary decisions, you

---

7. Model Rules of Professional Conduct 3.3(a)(3) say, in pertinent part, that an attorney must not "fail to disclose to the tribunal legal authority in the controlling jurisdiction known to the lawyer to be directly adverse to the position of the client and not disclosed by opposing counsel."

should address them anyway. Your brief will appear more credible and be more effective if you soften the impact of unfavorable precedents by giving reasonable arguments for distinguishing those cases.

The easiest way to overcome contrary authority is to distinguish the cases on the facts. If you cannot distinguish the cases, however, there are a number of other ways to minimize the significance of an unfavorable precedent and to convince a court that a rule should not be extended to include the circumstances of your case. You could explain, for example, that the reasoning of an unfavorable decision does not apply to your facts and would, therefore, create an injustice unless an exception was made. You could ask a court to overturn a decision because it is no longer sound public policy. Here you might look at persuasive precedents from other jurisdictions which have rules you believe are more indicative of current public policy. You might examine developments in allied fields which support changes in the field of law with which you are concerned. You could also demonstrate that, as a practical matter, a rule is not working well—it is too difficult to administer or too vague.[8] Remember that you might also need to diminish the impact of an unfavorable statute. Here you might try to show that the statute does not control the subject matter of your case, that the language of the statute is ambiguous enough to permit a construction more favorable to your client, or that the statute is unconstitutional.[9]

The following paragraphs are representative examples of arguments attempting to neutralize adverse decisions. The examples are based on the following problem.

Stone v. Eagle

The parents of Juliet Stone, an infant born with severe birth defects, brought a wrongful life action on behalf of the infant against an obstetrician. They allege he negligently failed to inform them that the mother's age made her fetus vulnerable to an increased risk of Down's Syndrome and that amniocentesis, a procedure by which the presence of Down's Syndrome in the fetus can be discovered, was available to her. John and Mary Stone allege that they were deprived of the choice of terminating the pregnancy and that they would have terminated the pregnancy if they had known their child, Juliet, would be born with Down's Syndrome. The suit is for damages to the child. (Wrongful life claims are distinguishable from wrongful birth claims. In a wrongful birth claim, the parents, on their own behalf, sue the physician whose alleged negligence resulted in the birth of an unwanted or deformed child.)

---

8. See Board of Student Advisors Harvard Law School, Introduction to Advocacy, 139–40 (4th ed. 1985).

9. See Handbook of Appellate Advocacy, 44–45 (UCLA 2d ed. 1986).

Defendant moved for summary judgment and dismissal of Juliet Stone's wrongful life action on the grounds that she failed to state a claim upon which relief can be granted. The court granted the motion on the grounds that Juliet Stone had not suffered a legally recognizable injury. It reasoned that no life could not be preferable to an impaired life, that neither the court nor a jury would be able to ascertain an appropriate measure of damages, and that defendant did not cause Juliet Stone's impairment. In fact, she could never have been born a healthy child.

In appealing the dismissal of her wrongful life claim, Juliet Stone must overcome the fact that most courts, like the district court in her case, have rejected actions on behalf of infants who have attempted to sue for wrongful life. Recently, however, a few courts have permitted partial recovery in wrongful life claims, allowing the infant to recover as special damages the extraordinary medical expenses which the infant's condition would require. No court has as yet, however, granted recovery for general damages compensating the infant for being born with birth defects, for pain and suffering, or for an impaired childhood.

Example 1: Precedent is not followed universally

The California Supreme Court has recognized wrongful life as a new cause of action. Turpin v. Sortini, 31 Cal. 3d 220, 643 P.2d 954, 182 Cal. Rptr. 337 (1982). The Turpin court held that a doctor was liable for negligently depriving expectant parents of information that they needed to determine whether birth would be in the best interest of a severely malformed fetus. Id. The court approved of a lower court decision, Curlender v. Bio-Science Laboratories, 106 Cal. App. 3d 811, 165 Cal. Rptr. 477 (1980), recognizing the claim of an infant plaintiff afflicted with Tay–Sachs disease. This child suffered mental retardation, blindness, pseudobulper palsy, convulsions, muscle atrophy, susceptibility to other diseases, and gross physical deformity. The Turpin court recognized that the child in Curlender had a "very limited ability to perceive or enjoy the benefits of life, [and that] we cannot assert with confidence that in every situation there would be a societal consensus that life is preferable to never having been born at all." Id. at 229, 643 P.2d at 963, 182 Cal. Rptr. at 346.

Example 2: Adverse decisions conflict with sound public policy

Two fundamental tenets of tort law are that there should be a remedy for every wrong committed and that future harmful conduct should be deterred. Both these goals are furthered by recognizing a claim for wrongful life. Social interests are advanced when a physician's duty to an unborn child extends to providing expectant parents with the genetic counseling and prenatal testing that enables them to make informed decisions about what is in the best interest of the fetus. The wrongful life claim complements professional practice by requiring all physicians to exercise proper diligence and skill in caring for patients both living and unborn. Curlender v. Bio-Science Laboratories, 106 Cal. App. 3d at 828, 165 Cal. Rptr. at 487. Because physicians have the medical expertise and knowledge to detect fetal abnormalities, they should be responsible for testing for them and counseling parents about them. Neither the state nor the parents should be burdened with the care and maintenance of children suffering from detectable genetic malformations while the physician who failed to exercise diligence and skill remains immune from liability.

Example 3: Precedents are inconsistent with trends in related fields

Many of the issues in a wrongful life action have been recognized in other medical malpractice actions. The prenatal injury cases have established an unborn child's right to sue. The wrongful birth action has found proximate cause and imposed liability on physicians for negligence in counseling and testing for genetic defects. The right to die cases have given the individual a right of self-determination which overrides social assumptions about the sanctity of life. These extensions in tort law reflect its responsiveness to changing social values and establish grounds for recognizing a wrongful life claim.

In a case of first impression or in a case where the application of existing law would produce substantial injustice, or where policy arguments, supported by secondary authorities and persuasive authority, make good sense, they should be pursued. There are and always will be circumstances in which the attorney argues that fairness demands that the court re-examine the law. Be aware, however, that many litigators discourage policy arguments at the intermediate level of the appellate court system. Intermediate court judges may see the highest court as the only policy-making court. In addition, since the courts are overburdened, the judges may prefer to decide cases on the basis of existing law.

Exercise 13–J

1. Identify these writers' techniques for minimizing unfavorable precedents or facts. Evaluate each writer's success.

Example 1   The court below relied heavily on Carroll v. Talman Savings Ass'n, 604 F.2d 1028 (7th Cir. 1979). Yet Carroll is the only decision from a court of appeals that has held a dress code discriminatory. Not only is the case ten years old, but it was decided only by a 2–1 vote over the vigorous dissent of the respected Judge Vest.

Example 2   In Carroll, the court overturned an employer's sex-based dress code policies which required its female employees to wear a uniform but permitted male employees to wear a wide variety of attire, including sport coats and leisure suits. The Carroll dress code is easily distinguishable from the one required by Fields, where both men and women must dress in conservative business suits. In fact, in Carroll, the court said that Title VII does not prohibit uniforms in the workplace but only requires that a "defendant's similarly situated employees be treated in an equal manner." Fields Brothers accomplishes the very thing that the court suggests: it treats its employees equally.

Example 3 Fields Brothers has urged that the proper comparison is to cases involving personal grooming regulations in which the courts have held that grooming standards, such as hair length regulations for male employees that differ from the permitted hair length for females, did not constitute sex discrimination under Title VII. In Knott, for example, the court permitted reasonable grooming standards for its employees that included minor differences for males and females that reflected customary grooming styles.

These grooming codes are markedly different, however, from Fields' dress codes. First, Fields' disparity of treatment between the sexes is more severe. Fields requires female clerks to wear a clearly identified uniform in a limited style and color range while permitting male clerks their own choices. In Knott, each sex was required only to meet a customary standard of good grooming. The limitations on their grooming were minor. Second, grooming regulations merely maintain a standard of conventional grooming for employees to follow. In Knott, men with long hair were unconventional and inappropriately groomed for their employer's business. Fields Brothers, however, fired the plaintiff for wearing her own conventional and entirely appropriate business suit because it was in a different dark color from the one issued. Finally, some courts have justified grooming regulations because they are not based on immutable characteristics. This Court, however, has never limited the reach of Title VII to regulations based on immutable characteristics but has inquired more broadly as to whether the employer imposed disparate treatment on male and female employees.

Example 4 Although several courts have recognized an exception to Title III for interspousal wire tapping, some federal courts have held that a cause of action exists between spouses for violation of the Act. In Jones v. Jones, the court applied Title III to a husband who had tapped a telephone at his estranged wife's residence, and in White v. White, the court held that there is a cause of action for a wife whose husband had hired an investigator to tap her telephone. In these cases, however, the parties had gone beyond a domestic dispute. In Jones, the parties were already estranged. The telephone was located outside of the marital home. In White, a third party to the relationship was the agent of the intrusion. Neither of these cases involved the special nature of an ongoing domestic relationship within a marital home.

Example 5 Those courts that have decided that Title III does not apply to interspousal wiretapping have misinterpreted the policy behind the statute. As the legislative history shows, Congress repeatedly heard testimony about the frequent use of electronic surveillance between spouses in divorce cases. In fact, one committee witness, echoing the testimony of others, said that "private bugging can be divided into two categories: commercial espionage and marital litigation." Several Senators stated in the Congressional Record their understanding that the bill prohibited private surveillance.

2. Rewrite example 2 so that the paragraph begins more persuasively.

3. Rewrite example 3 so that the paragraph begins more persuasively.

4. Rewrite example 4 so that the paragraph begins more persuasively.

Exercise 13–K

A. Read the following background materials so that you are able to edit the argument based on these materials that appears in part B of this exercise.

DEPARTMENT OF INSURANCE v. STALWART

Background

Simeon Stalwart is a partner in a well-known law firm. He is executor of the estate of Martin Met, a former client of the firm. Met died on April 3, 1977. He was president and controlling shareholder of a number of insurance brokerage companies.

Since Met's death, Stalwart has been deluged with suits based on Met's misappropriation of corporate funds. Neither Stalwart nor the other members of his firm have any knowledge of the transactions on which the lawsuits are based.

In August 1977, the Superintendent of the Department of Insurance began to investigate Met's affairs. On September 9, 1977, the Superintendent obtained an Order of Liquidation from the Surrogate's Court (i.e., he was to settle the affairs of Met's companies, and distribute whatever was left over to the remaining shareholders). As liquidator, the Superintendent took control of the books and records of Met's companies.

In February 1978, the Superintendent served a complaint on Stalwart, as executor of Met's estate. The complaint alleged that Met had plundered the assets of the companies, and defrauded the minority shareholders. It sought $2,684,935 in damages.

Stalwart had no idea what the Superintendent was talking about. So he served interrogatories * on the Superintendent. The interrogatories were 30 pages long, and contained 125 separate questions, of which many had several parts. They included numerous questions like the following:

---

* Interrogatories are written questions which one party may serve on another. The party served must give written answers under oath.

Identify the documents on the basis of which the Superintendent claims that Martin Met wrongfully appropriated $16,000 of the assets of National Insurance Company in June and July of 1974.

The Superintendent returned written answers in which he stated, in response to all questions concerning documents,

The answers are contained in the books and records of the various companies involved. Inspection of such records will be available on request.

Stalwart sent his associate, Harry Hopeful, to inspect the documents. Harry was shown to a room with 30 carton boxes of files, and a pile of 17 books of receipts and disbursements from the different companies. No attempt had been made to show which portions of which documents related to which interrogatories.

Stalwart moved for an order to compel discovery. The Superintendent cross-moved for a protective order. The Supreme Court, N.Y. County (Anderson, J.) granted Stalwart's motion and denied the Superintendent's cross-motion. The Superintendent appeals.

———

Statutes

CPLR § 3124 . . . motion to compel disclosure . . .

If a person, without having made timely objection . . . fails to answer . . . interrogatories . . . [the other party] may . . . apply to the court to compel disclosure.

CPLR § 3103 Protective orders

(a) Prevention of abuse. The court may at any time . . . make a protective order . . . limiting . . . the use of any disclosure device. Such order shall be designed to prevent unreasonable annoyance, expense, embarrassment, disadvantage, or other prejudice to any person or the courts.

———

Cases

Schertzer v. Upjohn Co.,
42 A.D.2d 790, 346 N.Y.S.2d 565 (2d Dept.1973)

The court granted the defendant the option of furnishing copies of relevant records instead of providing written answers to interrogatories, as long as the defendant (a) specified which interrogatories were being answered in this manner, and (b) identified each of the copies so supplied to show to which particular interrogatory it related.

Harlem River Consumers Cooperative, Inc. v. Associated Grocers
of Harlem, Inc.,
64 F.R.D. 459 (S.D.N.Y.1974)

A party answering interrogatories could not refer to aggregations of
material, but had to specify the portions on which he relied.

Blasi v. Marine Midland Bank,
59 A.D.2d 932, 399 N.Y.S.2d 445 (2d. Dept.1977)

Motion to strike certain interrogatories granted: The interrogatories,
consisting of 49 pages, are unduly prolix, vexatious, and unreasonably
oppressive.

Commissioners of the State Insurance Fund v. News World
Communication, Inc.,
74 A.D.2d 765, 425 N.Y.S.2d 595 (1st Dept.1980)

Motion to strike interrogatories denied. While "detailed and exhaus-
tive" interrogatories "at first blush" seemed "unduly burdensome and
oppressive," they were necessary to a resolution of defendant's affirmative defense. Having raised this claim, the defendant could not
complain because interrogatories were directed to explore the basis of
the claim. Merely because interrogatories were burdensome was no
reason to strike them, although the court would find differently if
"their use verges on harassment or seeks irrelevant information."

    B. Edit the following argument. Consider whether it is persuasive.
(Is the language persuasive? Are the cases arranged in the most helpful
order? Are opposing arguments handled well?) Correct any spelling or
grammar errors you find. Correct citation errors. If the correct form
requires information you do not have, indicate the missing information
with an underline. If there are places where citations are needed,
indicate with an underline.

Superintendent v. Stalwart

Stalwart's Argument

    Schertzer v. Upjohn Co., 42 A.D.2d 790 (2d. 1973) states that
the Superintendent can furnish copies of relevant documents,
rather than providing written answers to interrogatories. However, we must look further to determine whether the Superintendent
has indeed complied with Schertzer. Schertzer sets forth requirements as to how the documents must be produced. In our case,
the Superintendent failed to identify which interrogatory each
document purported to answer. Therefore, he obviously did not
comply with Schertzer, which requires him to a) specify which
interrogatories are being answered by production of documents

and b) identify each document to show to which particular interrogatory it related. Supra. This is also supported by Harlem River.

Although the Superintendent's answers are definitely inadequate, a motion to strike interrogatories may be granted if they are "unduly prolix, vexatious and unreasonably oppressive". See Blasi, (59 AD 932), in which the interrogatories consist of 49 pages. However, such a motion is clearly not justified in the case at bar, and is a blatant attempt by the Superintendent to avoid compliance with the requirements of the CPLR.

Defendants interrogatories, although 30 pages long and consisting of more than 100 questions, can be easily distinguished from the set of interrogatories referred to in Blasi. Plaintiff's complaint is 26 pages long and charges Martin Met with numerous types of misconduct, including conversion of corporate assets, fraud, and breach of fiduciary duty. Plaintiff seeks $2,684,935 in damages. The interrogatories do no more than track plaintiff's complaint. Defendant is Executor of the Estate of Martin Met. He is therefore a defendant in this case only by virtue of his fiduciary capacity. He has no personal knowledge of the allegations contained in the complaint. Interrogatories seeking further information on each and every allegation in the complaint are therefore essential to allow defendant to defend himself in this case. Compare Commissioner v. News World, 74 A.D.2d 765, 425 N.Y.S.2d 595 (1st Dept.1980). The Court should have no difficulty in finding that the interrogatories are not unduly long; and that the Superintendent's answers were inadequate.

G. *Principles of Style*

The tone of your brief should reflect the serious responsibility that you have assumed as your client's advocate. You are not going to place that client at risk by irritating the court with flippancy, informality, or hysterical overstatement. Nor are you going to lecture the judges by telling them what they must or must not do. Because it is inappropriate to issue commands to a judge, imperative sentences have no place in a brief. You should also avoid being belittling or sarcastic, especially in regard to other judges. You may say that the judge below misapplied the law, or found the facts incorrectly, or reached an incorrect decision, but you should say it respectfully. For similar reasons, heavy irony, hyperbole, exclamation points, or italics are inappropriate in brief-writing. Your readers will more readily believe what you say if you sound reasonable.

To be persuasive, you need to sound objective. You must preserve at least the appearance of calm neutrality about the facts of the case, yet reveal a firm concern and determination that no miscarriage of justice occurs. In other words, you want candor, conviction, and intelligence to serve your persuasive purpose. The writing techniques that follow will help you to be convincing without appearing biased.

1. Achieving Tone

Tone in large measure results from the interplay between diction (word choice) and attitude. Irony is a clear example of this interplay in that the words convey a message belied by the speaker's tone of voice. Lacking tone of voice in the written medium, we must convey tone by skillful use of diction, juxtaposition (or context), and syntax (sentence structure).

a. Tone and Diction

Diction is our most basic means of conveying attitude or tone. Many words have both explicit and implicit meanings. In brief writing, you want to select words on the basis of both their denotation (their explicit meaning or stipulated properties) and their connotation (their implicit meaning or overtones that have evolved from usage). To convey a sense of incredulity, for example, you might tell a jury: "The prosecution's case rests solely on the testimony of a snitch." In labelling the witness as a "snitch," the attorney is able to suggest double-dealing, self-interest, unreliability, unsavoriness. To suggest respectability and credibility, on the other hand, you would probably use a far more neutral label, as in "The allegations against the defendant are supported by the testimony of a reliable police informant."

Unusual words, words that shed a different perspective on the material, are effective tools in establishing tone and attitude. You should, however, select terms carefully because some words not only characterize the subject matter but also reveal something about the user's attitude. If, for example, you were explaining to a court that the defendant struck a person upon learning he was a snitch, your use of the term might be appropriate because it suggests the defendant's sense of his provocation. If you used the term "snitch" throughout your brief, however, a court might infer that the defendant's feelings about informants are largely your own. To suggest the unsavory character of the victim once might be productive; to hammer away at it might needlessly offend the prosecutor or the court and thus be counter-productive.

Often the most effective prose is remarkably simple. Justice Blackmun's dissent in City of Richmond v. J.A. Croson Co., 488 U.S. 469, ___ loses no effectiveness for being written in the vernacular.[10] His sincerity is conveyed by his plain use of language:

> I never thought that I would live to see the day when the city of Richmond, Virginia, the cradle of the Old Confederacy, sought on its own, within a narrow confine, to lessen the stark impact of persistent discrimination. But Richmond, to its great credit, acted. Yet this Court, the supposed bastion of equality, strikes down Richmond's efforts as though discrimination had never existed or was not demonstrated in this particular litigation. History is irrefutable, even though one might sympathize with those who—though possibly innocent in themselves—benefit from the wrongs of past decades.
>
> So the Court today regresses. I am confident, however, that, given time, it one day again will do its best to fulfill the great promises of the Constitution's Preamble and of the guarantees embodied in the Bill of Rights—a fulfillment that would make this Nation very special.

To achieve tone, pay particular attention to verbs. Verbs are helpful in establishing tone because they, without a lot of embellishment, immediately and forcefully characterize an action. "Ogling" connotes a lasciviousness that "looking" does not capture. In the sentence, "The police slammed the suspect against a brick wall," the verb suggests police brutality. This suggestion is absent when you say: "The police pushed the suspect against the wall." To make your prose persuasive and fluid, your verbs should be purposeful and descriptive. Moreover, when you use descriptive verbs, you will not need to rely solely, or even mostly, on adjectives.

Certainly, an adjective or adverb is sometimes in order. In this regard, note that one apt adjective is often preferable to a series of them. It is enough to write: "The victim was accosted by a man screaming racial epithets." To add those epithets were bigoted, insulting and demeaning is unnecessary. If the adjectives do not materially refine the point, they dilute the impact of your description. Understatement is, therefore, often more forceful than overstatement because of its stark concentration on the essential. For similar reasons, you should avoid using qualifiers and intensifiers (very, clearly, possibly, absolutely) since insistence without substance is irritating rather than persuasive.

b. Tone and Figurative Language

Another way to establish tone is to use figurative language. Although extensive use of metaphor is probably inappropriate and distracting in a brief, some metaphors and figures of speech are

---

10. In Croson, the court struck down the Richmond minority set-aside program in the awarding of municipal construction contracts.

simple and effective. A synecdoche, for example, is a figure of speech in which the writer names (1) a part when he means a whole or (2) the whole when he means a part. To add a little jazz to a compliment, for example, you might say, "nice wheels" instead of saying, "I like your car." Justice Holmes used a synecdoche in his dissent to Lochner v. New York, 198 U.S. 45, 75 (1905), when he said, "The Fourteenth Amendment does not enact Mr. Herbert Spencer's Social Statics." To make his point that the 14th Amendment protects no particular economy theory, Justice Holmes uses Spencer's theory of laissez-faire to stand for all economic theories. This synecdoche enables Justice Holmes to make a substantive point effectively while also permitting him to comment ironically on the majority decision. It is, of course, absurd to think the 14th Amendment refers to Spencer, and by extension, the Court is absurd to bend the amendment to Spencer's economic theory.

A related figure of speech is a metonymy, in which the name of something closely associated with the thing is substituted for its name. If we say "the communication came from the oval office" instead of from a particular president, we can invest that communication with all the authority, tradition, and privilege associated with the presidency. Similarly, lawyers often ask the "bench" for a ruling.

Metaphoric language is, on occasion, a useful persuasive tool. In his dissent to Zorach v. Clauson, 343 U.S. 306, 324 (1952),[11] Justice Jackson effectively uses the common reference to Supreme Court justices as "the Brethren" to criticize the majority decision: "My evangelistic brethren confuse an objection to compulsion with an objection to religion."

c. Tone and Context

Context and juxtaposition are other good ways to establish tone. Instead of stridently denouncing testimony as incredible, juxtapose conflicting statements and calmly remark on their discrepancy. Similarly, you can juxtapose an opposing argument with facts or precedents that cast doubt on its validity or applicability. In the following example, the prosecution marshals a series of facts to undermine defense counsel's contention that there was insufficient proof that defendant intended to cause damage to the building, an element of second degree arson.

> In October 1989, Dick Terney ignited five separate fires on a sofa cushion and on the mattress on which Beth Lot's body was lying and then fled from his building, leaving the blaze to consume all of the

11. In Zorach, the majority upheld a New York law allowing schools to release students for religious instruction off school grounds.

mattress, to char Lot's body beyond recognition as a human being, to create an opaque wall of thick, black smoke from floor to ceiling inside the apartment, and to generate heat intense enough to deteriorate the bedroom door. Yet the defense contends the evidence is not legally sufficient to prove beyond a reasonable doubt that Terney intended to damage the building and not simply to destroy his girl friend's body.

d. Tone and Syntax

The length and rhythm of sentences can also establish tone. Short parallel sentences can convey urgency, self-assurance, vigor, as in Churchill's sentence, "We must be united, we must be undaunted, we must be inflexible" or Justice Brennan's, "We Justices are certainly aware that we are not final because we are infallible; we know that we are infallible only because we are final." [12] The similarity or dissimilarity stands out because the parallel sequence highlights the comparisons.

Long sentences often suggest weighty topics, thoughtful explorations of truth, high resolve, responsibility: "The constitutional vision of human dignity rejects the possibility of political orthodoxy imposed from above; it respects the right of each individual to form and to express political judgments, however far they may deviate from the mainstream and however unsettling they might be to the powerful or the elite." [13]

In addition, successive clauses beginning with the same word (a technique called anaphora) can have a cumulative and emphatic effect.[14] Anaphora was successfully used in petitioner's brief in Harper & Row Publishers v. Nation Enters.

> Defendants' trial testimony further demonstrated that defendants sought to, and did, copy Ford's expression. Mr. Navasky testified that he quoted Ford's portrait of Nixon because "this was his [Ford's] own way of saying it." . . . He quoted Ford's evaluation of the reason for granting the pardon "because of the absolute certainty with which he expressed himself." . . . He quoted Ford's account of the negotiations with Ron Ziegler because ". . . when Ford writes about this as a narrator, it was the definitive quality of the statement that made me put it in." . . . And he quoted Ford's account of Nixon's assurances of innocence because it was "a much more powerful statement for the reader."

12. Justice William J. Brennan, Jr., To the Text and Teaching Symposium, Georgetown University, October 12, 1985, Washington D.C., published in *The Great Debate: Interpreting Our Written Constitution*, The Federalist Society, 13–14.

13. *Id.* at 22.

14. Michael Frost brought this point and this quotation to our attention in his article, "Brief Rhetoric—A Note on Classical and Modern Theories of Forensic Discourse," 38 Kan.L.Rev. 429 (1990).

By repeating the same opening words, petitioner underscores his argument that the editor of *The Nation* consciously appropriated substantial portions of Ford's own words.

In brief writing, you must strive for a tone that serves your persuasive purpose. Particularly important in brief-writing are those principles which promote clear and affirmative expression. You must also adhere to the basic principles of good English sentence structure set forth in Chapter Nine.

2. *Quotations*

Whenever you use language that is not your own, you must quote that language exactly. You must place quotation marks around that language and cite the source of the quotation. Failure to do so is plagiarism. You should not use quotation marks for block quotes, however. According to the Bluebook, you block a quotation, that is, indent and single space it, whenever the quotation is fifty words or more. Put the citation as the first nonindented text after the quotation.

Be selective in choosing quotations. Use them principally for statutory language and statements of the rule of a case or cases, or for particularly apt language that you cannot equal yourself. When you do quote an authority, do not immediately repeat its essence in your own words. Instead, tell the reader how the quotation relates to your point.

Do not employ quotations where you can convey that information just as well or better in your own words. It is often difficult to integrate quotations smoothly, and even if this is done successfully, differences in style may be distracting. Moreover, too many quotations will slow the flow of your argument, and a reader may decide to overlook them. A reader might also ignore a lengthy quotation because the quotation is visually oppressive. Try, therefore, to use your own words, but be sure to supply a citation to the source. (See Appendix A, section B for further information on quotation.)

VII. *The Appellee's Brief*

Many attorneys who represent appellees underestimate the importance of the appellee's brief. They reason that because they won in the court below, and because more cases are upheld on appeal than are reversed, all that remains to win again is to explain the lower court's decision to the reviewing court. Indeed, many attorneys believe that because the appellant often turns their arguments against them, the less said the better. Careful attorneys, however, never rest on their laurels. A good appellee's brief requires the same care and creativity as an appellant's brief.

The opinion below is, of course, strong authority in your favor. It is generally advantageous, therefore, to refer to that opinion and to choose quotes from it. Do not, however, rely upon it exclusively, especially if the opinion is poorly reasoned. Because lower court opinions, especially in a moot court problem assignment, often need bolstering, you should argue your case in the way that you think is most effective. You need not confine yourself to the structure of the decision used by the court below.

You should also not confine yourself to the structure used in the appellant's brief. The appellee's Argument section may be organized completely differently from the one in the appellant's brief. If the appellee has stronger arguments for one issue than for another issue, the Argument section should begin with the appellee's strong issue, not the appellant's strong issue. Put your best argument in the most prominent position in the brief.

The Questions Presented, Statement of Facts, Summary of the Argument, and Point Headings should similarly reflect the appellee's orientation rather than the appellant's. As a general rule you should put your side's view of the case first in every section. It is usually more effective to state your view and then refute the appellant's view than it is to put the appellant's viewpoint first and leave your reader waiting to hear your client's arguments. You should also choose those arguments that will create sympathy for your client. While some student advocates are hesitant to do that when representing the government, the effective attorney will find ways to make sympathetic the point of view of her client, regardless of the particulars of the case. In other words, an appellee's brief should not be a negative document that merely argues against the appellant's brief, but should be an affirmative document.

Indeed, as counsel for the party that won below, your style should be positive and assertive. Emphasize your main points; do not be defensive. Nonetheless, be certain to answer every colorable argument that the appellant has raised. Except for clearly frivolous points, you cannot afford to ignore the appellant's weak or strong arguments. Give the judges your side of each point. Dispose of the appellant's weaker arguments quickly; label the frivolous arguments as such. (See section VI, F for suggestions on how to handle opposing arguments.) Be sure to cite to the appellant's brief if you refer to the appellant's argument.

There may be some significant differences between moot court programs and the situation you would face writing the appellee's brief in practice. In an actual appellate case, you would have the benefits of the appellant's brief, the briefs already written for lower courts, and the complete record when you write your own brief. Typically a case that reaches a supreme court has been briefed at least once before. The attorneys know their opponent's arguments and their own weaknesses well. You would know exactly which arguments your opponent relied upon and you could play off your opponent's choice of cases and words.

In moot court programs, however, the parties may not have briefs submitted to lower courts and the appellee may not have the appellant's brief. You may only have the opinion below, the references in that opinion to the arguments raised by each side in the lower courts, and an abbreviated record to help you frame your arguments. You must imagine an appellant's brief written by an opposing counsel. You must decide how you would write the appellant's brief, and, however hard it is to tear apart your own arguments, you must respond in a positive fashion by asserting the appellee's best arguments and rebuttals.

Finally, you should note that in a true case, the appellant may have a parting shot. After the appellee's brief has been filed, the appellant may file a reply brief. The appellee, then, must choose arguments as carefully as the appellant did to avoid giving the opposing counsel an opportunity to tear apart the appellee's arguments unanswered in writing. In moot court, however, the appellee's brief is usually the last written word.

Editing Checklist: Brief

I. Questions Presented

A. Do the questions combine the legal claim and the controlling legal principles with the key facts that raise the issues?

B. Are the questions framed so as to suggest an affirmative answer?

C. Are the questions persuasive without being conclusory?

D. Do the questions read clearly and succinctly?

II. Point Headings

A. Do the Point Headings provide a sound structure for the Argument section of the brief?

B. Do the headings set out legal contentions favorable to your client and support those contentions with reasons and relevant facts?

C. Do the headings have a conclusory tone favorable to your client?

D. Are the headings clearly and concisely written?

E. Is each heading a single sentence?

III. Statement of the Case

A. Are the facts set forth in a narrative that will be easy for a reader unfamiliar with the case to follow?

B. Is the statement complete, accurate, and affirmative?

    1. Are all essential facts included and irrelevant facts omitted?

    2. Are unfavorable facts included without being overemphasized?

    3. Are favorable facts effectively placed in positions of emphasis?

    4. Is the statement accurate?

    5. Are record references included for all facts?

C. Does the statement include any legal conclusions or editorializing that properly belong in the argument section?

IV. Argument

A. Organization

    1. The Thesis Paragraph

        a. Does each point begin with a thesis paragraph setting forth in affirmative (and conclusory) terms the major contentions?

        b. Does the thesis paragraph present an integrated statement of the theory you are putting forth?

        c. Is its length proportionate to the argument?

    2. Large–Scale Organization

        a. Is each ground for relief a separate point heading?

        b. Is the Argument organized around issues and subissues?

        c. Wherever possible, is the first issue the one most likely to succeed? Are all points under it arranged in order of strength?

    3. Small–Scale Organization

        a. Is each issue or subissue introduced by a thesis paragraph or sentence?

        b. Is each issue or subissue developed clearly and logically?

        c. Is your argument made before the opposing argument is countered, i.e., do you make effective use of the positions of emphasis?

        d. If the topic sentences of each paragraph were arranged in an outline would a strong skeleton of the argument emerge?

        e. Does each paragraph advance the argument?

        f. Are there genuine transitions between paragraphs?

        g. Do the sentences within a paragraph coherently relate to each other and the topic?

B. Analysis

1. Are the facts of the case argued effectively?

2. Are the authorities cited appropriately described, explained, and applied?

    a. Are the rules of law stated clearly, accurately, and affirmatively?

    b. Are the facts of cases which are helpful to your client presented as consistent with the facts of your client's case, insofar as this is possible?

    c. Are "harmful" cases adequately distinguished or explained?

    d. Is the decision appealed from either supported or criticized?

3. Are policy arguments effectively made?

4. How have the arguments of the opposition been answered?

    a. Have you made sure that opposing arguments are not treated defensively?

    b. Are affirmative counter-arguments made convincingly?

5. Is the argument logical, internally consistent, and thoroughly developed?

V. Language

Is the language clear, concise, and chosen for persuasive impact?

VI. Grammar, Spelling, and Citation Form

Is an otherwise persuasive brief marred by technical errors?

Chapter Fourteen
Oral Argument

Like most students, you may approach your Moot Court oral argument with some trepidation. For the first time in a short legal career, completely alone and in public, you must face an oral examination of your legal knowledge of a complex problem. However, if you come to the Moot Court well prepared, you will probably enjoy the argument and gain confidence from the experience. For practicing attorneys, oral argument is an opportunity to clarify their case, to clear up any misunderstandings or doubts on the part of the court, and to make an impression that cannot be accomplished through a brief.

I. Preparing the Argument

There is no substitute for solid preparation. You must thoroughly know the Record on Appeal, your arguments, and the facts and reasoning of the relevant cases. Since you have already written a brief on the topic, you will know the strengths and weaknesses of your case. Your aim should be to impress the strong arguments upon the court, to shore up the weak points, and to answer the questions that the court may have. You should not read your argument from notes, so try to prepare a short outline with clear headings that will jog your memory about the points you want to make. You may want to prepare the beginning of your argument in more detail to get you started at the time when you are likely to be the most nervous. Some people advise that you prepare two arguments. One is the outline of the crucial points you must include even if the judges give you little time to make your own presentation. The other is the longer talk to use if your judges ask few questions and you must fill your time with your own presentation.

Anticipate the questions that the court will ask and be prepared for them. The court will probably ask about obvious weaknesses in your case. Therefore, know how to meet those weaknesses. If there are adverse cases, decide in advance how you will distinguish them or diminish their importance. But avoid dropping case names. Concentrate, instead, on the reasoning and analysis which shows why your position is correct and just. Finally, think through your case so that before you give your oral argument, you know which points you can safely concede.

II. Selecting the Arguments

Oral argument is not a spoken version of the written brief. You do not have the time, nor is this the place, to argue every point of your case. Instead, crystallize the issues. Select and make the arguments that you think will probably control the judge's decision for or against you.

Make clear the basic points that you want to establish. Do not try to make complex arguments. Oral argument is a poor time for explaining subtle intricacies of the law or of case analysis. Leave that for your brief. Arguments based on fairness, simplicity, and common sense are often more effective than those based on esoteric complexities.

Choose among the types of arguments you included in your brief, for example, policy arguments, doctrinal arguments, and arguments based on the equities of the facts of your case. Remember, though, that these arguments are not mutually exclusive. You can focus on doctrinal arguments and yet humanize the case by relating these arguments to your client's situation. You should also choose among consequential and persuasive arguments and decide which ones to stress.

Once you have selected your main points, decide which premises and authorities you need to establish those points. Then, plan your outline according to that structure. Present your strongest and most important argument first. Focus the court's attention on your most effective arguments. Attack your opponent's weak points, but do not be defensive and use up your time explaining why your opponent's position is wrong before you make clear why you believe your position is right.

III. *Introduction and Argument*

In an oral argument, the appellant (or petitioner) argues first. Then the appellee (or respondent) argues. In many Moot Courts, the appellant may then have a short rebuttal.

A standard introduction which both appellant and appellee can use is, "Your Honors, my name is _____, counsel for the _____ (appellant/appellee or petitioner/respondent)." In some Moot Court programs, students are advised to preface this statement with "May it please the Court." If your Moot Court rules provide for rebuttal, the appellant should reserve time for rebuttal during this introduction.

After the introduction, the appellant should begin by setting out the context and issues for the court. For example, an appellant might begin, "The issue in this case is whether a clothing store that requires only its female sales employees to wear a prescribed uniform during work hours violates Title VII of the Civil Rights Act of 1964 by discriminating on the basis of sex in the terms and conditions of employment." The appellant might then briefly state the key facts of the case on which this issue of law revolves. Then the appellant could outline the main arguments. "Field Brothers does discriminate on the basis of sex for these three reasons." The brief outline of the argument will provide the judges with a "road map" that will help them follow the development of the argument. Moreover, the outline gives a framework within which to work and to which it is useful to return, especially in the face of interruptions by questioning from the judges. After giving the judges the legal context of the appeal and an outline of the main arguments, the appellant should present the first argument.

The appellee, on the other hand, need not be tied to the same format. The appellee has the opportunity to capture the court's attention with the opening, either by using vivid facts or a persuasive statement of the issues. If the appellee is the prosecutor in a particularly vivid criminal case, the appellee might follow the introduction by saying, "Your Honors, the defendant has been tried and convicted by a jury of the first degree murder of his wife of fifteen years who was pregnant with his third child at the time of her murder." In the Field Brothers case, the appellee might begin, "The Field Brothers Clothing Store requires all its sales personnel, men and women, to wear a business suit at work. The store requires all its sales personnel to wear the store's logo on the suit. The store requires all its sales personnel to wear suits in a dark, conservative color. Thus, Field Brothers does not discriminate on the basis of sex because it treats all of its employees alike."

However, the appellee might also decide to begin as the appellant has by setting out the issues in the case and then outlining the arguments. For example, the appellee might begin, "Your Honors, the issue is whether a clothing store that requires all its sales personnel to wear a conservative business suit and the store's logo during working hours violates Title VII by discriminating on the basis of sex." If the appellant has misstated any facts of the case, the appellee will want to correct them if they are relevant to appellee's case.

In general, the appellee's argument should not be a point by point refutation of the appellant's argument. Instead, appellees should present their arguments in the order that the arguments seem most effective. However, appellees must listen carefully to the appellants' argument and be ready to change their presentation to meet the appellant's points. Flexibility is essential. An appellee should also listen carefully to the questions that the judges ask the appellant. In this way the appellee may learn which aspects of the case particularly concern the court and speak to those issues.

The appellant's rebuttal is the last word in the oral argument. The appellant should not include new information not made during the main presentation. Nor should the appellant use the time to rehash what has been said. Instead, the appellant should use the time to answer important points that the appellee seems to have raised, or to correct significant errors in the appellee's presentation, or to shore up those arguments that were weakened by the appellee or the judges' questioning.

In sum, although oral argument can be quite stylized, there is still a good deal of room for varying the format of the presentation. Your main concern as an advocate should be that the court knows what the issues are and gets the important information it needs to understand your version of the case.

IV. Questions by the Court

An oral argument is a conversation with the court, not a speech or a debate. The purpose of oral argument is to give the judges the opportunity to ask questions. Many first-year students, mainly because of nervousness, however, react to questions as if they were unwarranted interruptions or attacks. Instead of responding this way, you should try to welcome the judges' questions and be receptive and flexible. Use the questioning as an opportunity to find out the judges' thinking on the issues in the case and to resolve any problems the judges may have in deciding the case in your favor. Be sure to respond directly to the question a judge has asked. If it raises a thorny problem that you do not respond to effectively, you may have lost an opportunity to convince the court. Always answer a judge's question, even if, as will often happen, the question takes you away from your prepared outline. In that event, return to the structure of your argument when you have completed your answer so that you can retain control over the argument until the next question.

Expect the court to question you on the weaknesses of your case. Do not evade or misrepresent your case's weak points, but decide how you can limit their importance. You gain the court's confidence by knowing the law and presenting it fairly. If, by evasion or lack of candor, you lose the court's confidence, the judges will look to the other attorney to find out what the case is really about. Your frankness and integrity are essential.

Some questioners will ask you to discuss legal authority, others will be concerned with policy matters, and still others will be concerned simply with clarifying the facts of the case. It is essential that you anticipate every possible area of questioning. Decide how to reply to cases against your position and work out acceptable responses before you go into the argument.

Do not be fooled if, as an appellee, you hear the court rigorously questioning the appellant and believe that the court is on your side and that your own argument will be uninterrupted. The court may do the very same thing to you.

Always remember that you are in an appellate courtroom. Address the judges as "Your Honor" or "Justice." When a judge asks a question, never cut the judge off before the judge has finished. Never indicate that you think the judge's question is unwise or irrelevant. If you disagree with a judge's statement, such as a judge's description of a case holding, do so politely. For example, you can say, "Your Honor, my reading of the case, which seems to differ from yours, is that. . . ." Some lawyers preface their disagreement with a phrase like "With all due respect, Your Honor."

Answer the judge's question directly and immediately. Do not tell a judge you will answer the question later even if the question is about a topic you wanted to put off until later in your presentation. If you can, use your response as a means of returning to the original topic of your argument. Frequently, returning to your argument will not be easy or possible, either because the judge has jumped ahead, or has returned to an earlier point, or because the judge has decided to take you down the slippery slope. Try not to allow yourself to be led too far afield, but do not openly resist a line of questioning. If you must abandon your outline, do so until the line of questioning ends or a subsequent question offers you an avenue of escape. When you have the opportunity, there is nothing wrong in saying "Now, Your Honors, returning to my earlier point . . .," or "Your Honors, the second reason that Field Brothers does not discriminate is. . . ."

Even if you have prepared your argument carefully, you may have difficulty responding to some questions.[1] Respond to a confusing question by requesting a clarification from the court. If you are asked a question and cannot think of an answer, or if the question relates to an area of law with which you are not familiar, first try to give a partial answer that in some way responds to the court's question and gives you a moment to think. If the court is still not satisfied, you would be better off simply saying that you do not know the answer rather than wasting the court's time giving an uninformed response. If you are asked about a case that you did not read or cannot remember, simply say that you are not familiar with the case. The judge may stop the line of questioning there or may explain the case to you and ask how it relates to your case.

Sometimes a judge will pursue a line of questioning that culminates in the request that you concede a point in your argument. Think carefully before conceding. Some points are peripheral and your arguments may be weak. Therefore, you may want to concede that point to maintain your credibility if a concession in no way diminishes your other arguments. Beware of conceding a point that is necessary for your case, however.

V. *Citation of Authority*

You may wish to refer to crucial cases in your argument, but you should limit severely the number of cases you mention. Remember that your brief contains the cases and the citations. Use your time in oral argument to concentrate on facts, reasoning, analysis, and policy. In addition, do not give the reporter citations to cases that you mention unless the court requests them. Reading case citations impedes the conversation with the bench and is awkward.

VI. *Speaking Style*

There is no one single way to present an oral argument. Instead there is a wide range of successful, yet different, styles. Your presentation will depend on your personality, skills, imagination, and your reactions to speaking in public and being questioned by a panel of judges.

---

1. For other suggestions on how to respond to difficult questions, see the Handbook of Appellate Advocacy 96–100 (UCLA 2d ed. 1986).

You should not read your argument. Try to maintain a conversational tone. Speak without notes as much as possible. Look at the judges when you deliver your prepared remarks and when you answer their questions. Do not punctuate your argument with phrases like "I think," "I believe," or "The Appellant would argue". Just state the arguments themselves.

Ideally, you should be poised, confident, and professional. You should speak slowly (nervousness tends to speed up one's speaking style) and clearly. But do not speak in a monotone. Vary your tone to give emphasis to your statements and to maintain the judges' interest. You should also try to stand straight and avoid distracting body movements, like extravagant gestures, or overly casual movements, like slouching over the podium. Do not interrupt the judges, even if they interrupt you. Be polite but not subservient. Above all, try to be relaxed. However, realize that very few law students can accomplish these goals without a good deal of practice and oral argument experience.

Even without much experience, however, you can accomplish the essentials: know your case, look at the judges instead of at your notes, and concentrate on the judges' questions. The best oral arguments are those in which advocates know their case inside out and have a dialogue with the judges in response to their inquiries.

Your speaking style should also convey conviction on behalf of your client's cause. If you are not convinced that your client should win, the court will not be either. As an appellate advocate, your argument may be the last step between your client and imprisonment or a burdensome damage award or fine. Your oral skills and legal ability may win the day.

VII. *Prayer for Relief*

Close your argument with a prayer for relief, such as "For the reasons stated, appellant respectfully requests this court to reverse the judgment of the court below" (or use the specific name of the court below). You may want to briefly remind the court of one central point before you state the prayer for relief, but you must not irritate the court by dragging on the argument once your time has elapsed.

Appendices

Appendix A

Grammar, Punctuation, and Quotation

INDEX

A. Grammar and Punctuation

1. Comma Usage

    a. Put a comma before a coordinating conjunction—and, but, or, nor, for, yet—when the conjunction is connecting two independent clauses (unless the sentences are short).

Example:	A statute must provide fair warning to the public of the nature of the proscribed conduct, and it must provide explicit standards for the application of the statute by the people enforcing it.

    b. Do not put a comma before a coordinating conjunction when that conjunction is forming a compound subject, verb, or object.

Compound Subject Example:	The wrench that flew out of defendant's hand and the box of nails which the wrench dislodged lacerated plaintiff's face (no comma before "and the box of nails").

| Compound Verb Example: | The wrench flew out of his hand and hit plaintiff in the mouth (no comma before "and hit"). |
| Compound Object Example: | Counsel labeled the charges ridiculous and the decision laughable (no comma before "and the decision laughable"). |

c. When a dependent clause follows an independent clause, put a comma before a subordinating conjunction connecting an independent clause to a dependent clause **only** when the dependent clause is nonrestrictive (that is, the dependent clause gives information that is descriptive but not essential to the sentence).

| Non-restrictive Example: | The court upheld the decision, although there was a dissenting vote (comma needed). |
| Restrictive Example: | The plaintiff will agree to settle if the defendant accepts these conditions (no comma—the condition is essential). |

d. When a dependent clause or introductory phrase comes first, put a comma after an introductory phrase or dependent clause to separate it from the independent clause. You may omit the comma only if the introductory phrase is short and cannot be misread.

Introductory Clause Example:	If a court finds a contract is unconscionable, it may refuse to enforce it.
Introductory Phrase Example:	To establish economic duress, plaintiff must show three elements.
Comma for Clarity Example:	To clarify, the element requires a showing of involuntary submission to a person in authority. (Without the comma after "clarify," a misreading is possible.)

e. Do not use a comma to separate a complex or compound subject from its verb. You may want to avoid long, complex subjects by rephrasing your sentence.

| Example: | Relying on the employee-at-will doctrine may prove to be a mistake (no comma after the complex subject "relying on the employee-at-will doctrine"). |

f. Surround nonrestrictive, interrupting words, phrases, or clauses with commas. A nonrestrictive element contributes information to the sentence but does not limit or define the meaning of the word/s it modifies. A nonrestrictive modifier can be omitted without altering the meaning of the sentence. (See Chapter Nine, #8.)

Example: Jessica Stone and Michael Asch, while in their senior years at college, met and fell in love.

g.   Do not surround restrictive phrases or clauses with commas. A restrictive modifier identifies or limits the word it modifies and is essential to the sentence. ("That" always introduces restrictive modifiers; "which" and "who" can be restrictive or nonrestrictive; "which" cannot refer to persons.)

Example: One jurisdiction that does not award pecuniary damages for loss of consortium is Kent.

h.   Separate the elements of a series with commas. Although a comma before the conjunction joining the last element is optional, most grammar and usage books encourage its use because a comma before the conjunction connecting the last element can clarify the number of units you have in the series and their proper division.

Example: Since then, Mrs. Pascal has been suffering from depression, insomnia, recurring nightmares, and severe weight loss.

Example of an Ambiguous Series: He wrote to several department stores, including Macy's, Bloomingdales and Abraham and Strauss. (Do we have a series of two—Macy's, Bloomingdales & Abraham & Strauss—or a series of three—Macy's, Bloomingdales, Abraham & Strauss? What are the proper divisions—Macy's, Bloomingdales, and Abraham & Strauss? Macy's, Bloomingdales & Abraham, and Strauss? To avoid this ambiguity, put a comma before the conjunction introducing the last element.)

i.   You may put a comma before a phrase or a word you wish to highlight.

Example: The vice-president had called for the meeting, then missed it.

j.   Commas (and periods) are put inside quotation marks but outside parenthesis and brackets. (If the parenthetical material is a complete sentence, however, the period goes inside the parenthesis.)

Example: **Quotation Marks**	Once we recognize that "designed for use" means "intended by the manufacturer," the court's application seems reasonable.
Example: **Parenthesis**	Given the limitation on length (20 pages), we dropped that discussion.
Example: **Complete Parenthetical** **Sentence**	Given the limitation on length, we dropped that discussion. (The brief could not be longer than twenty pages.)

2. Semicolon Usage

a. Connect two independent clauses with a semicolon when they are not linked by a conjunction.

Example:	Her moods wavered between depression and hostility; she often expressed a wish to die.

b. When a conjunctive adverb (however, hence, therefore, etc.) or other transitional expression links two independent clauses, put a semicolon before the conjunctive adverb and a comma after it.

Conjunctive **Adverb:**	Bills are admissible if they comply with CPLR § 4533a; however, judges can relax those standards.
Transitional **Phrases:**	A formal defect may be waived by a guilty plea or by a failure to object at trial or on appeal; on the other hand, a fatal defect may always be challenged by a writ of habeas corpus.

c. When elements in a series are long or contain internal punctuation, use a semicolon to separate the elements.

Example:	There are three steps outlined in this section of the statute: first, the jury must decide the full value of the injured party's damages; second, they must decide the extent, in form of a percentage, of each party's negligence, with a total of all percentages of negligence of all parties equal to 100; third, the judge must mold the judgment from the jury's findings of facts.

d.   Semicolons and colons go outside quotation marks.

> **Example:**   In 1981, Andrea received an Academy Award for her supporting performance in "The Mouse in the Microwave"; in celebration, Dirk converted the basement into a screening room.

3. Colon Usage

a.   Colons are used to introduce enumerations or lists.

> **Example:**   The contractor made three demands: first, Charo must fire Smith; second, Charo must enter an exclusive distributorship agreement with Champlow; third, Charo must fly to N.Y. to sign a contract to this effect.

b.   Colons may be used to introduce and highlight a formal statement or example.

> **Example:**   The jury had been out for twelve hours: this may account for the defendant's edginess.

c.   Colons are used to introduce a long quotation.

4. Sentence Fragments and Run–Ons

a.   Sentence Fragments

A sentence must have a subject and a predicate. Most sentence fragments do not result from the absence of a subject and a predicate; rather they are the result of punctuating a dependent clause as a sentence. A dependent clause does not express a complete thought and must, therefore, be combined with an independent clause.

> **Example:**   Even though his contributory negligence may diminish damages.

You must either add a comma and finish the sentence with an independent clause or omit "even though."

> **Rewrite:**   Even though his contributory negligence may diminish damages, he will recover.

b.   Run–On Sentences

There are two kinds of run-on sentences. First, there are those in which two complete sentences are written as one, i.e., with no punctuation (fused sentence). Second, there are those run-on sentences in which two complete sentences are joined by a comma instead of a semicolon (comma splice.)

Fused Sentence Example:	Personal service upon Multitech Associates was not proper and Village Realty's suit will therefore be dismissed.
Rewrite:	Personal service upon Multitech Associates was not proper, and Village Realty's suit will therefore be dismissed.
Comma Splice Example:	Multitech had not designated Sue Johnson to accept summons, she had neither express nor implied authority.
Rewrite:	Multitech had not designated Sue Johnson to accept summons; she had neither express nor implied authority.

5. Apostrophe Usage

Apostrophes are used to indicate possession or contraction.

a. Singular possessive nouns are formed with **'s.**

(The court's decision)

b. If a singular possessive noun ends in **s,** add an **'s.** (Some writers use an apostrophe only.)

(James's plea)

c. Plurals not ending in **s** take an **'s.**

(Women's rights)

d. Plurals ending in **s** take an apostrophe.

(The associates' employment handbook)

e. The possessive case of two closely linked nouns is formed by the addition of a single **'s** if, and only if, one thing is possessed by both. (The brother and sister's treehouse but the brother's and sister's workbooks).

f. *Note an important exception: possessive pronouns are not formed with apostrophes.*

"It's" is the contraction of "it is."

The possessive form of "it" is "its."

"Who's" means "who is." "Whose" is the possessive form.

6. Agreement Between Subjects and Verbs

A verb must agree in number with its subject.

a. If the subject is singular, the verb must be singular. (Everyone, everybody, each, either, nobody, one, and anyone are singular.)

b. If the subject is plural, the verb must be plural.

c. If the subject is third person and singular (he, she, it), the present tense verb ends in **s.**

d. If 2 singular subjects are connected by an **or** or **nor,** the verb is singular. (Either John or Jane <u>is willing</u> to speak to the professor.)

e. If 2 plural subjects are connected by **or** or **nor,** the verb is plural. (Either 1st-year or 2nd-year students <u>are</u> registering on Friday.)

f. If one singular and one plural subject are connected by **or** or **nor,** the verb agrees with the nearer form. (Neither Joan nor her classmates <u>want</u> to rewrite the memorandum.)

g. If the subject is a collective noun, like jury, the verb is plural if the writer is thinking of the individuals and singular if the writer is thinking of the group. (The jury [individuals] were [plural] fighting over the verdict. The jury [group] has rendered [singular] a guilty verdict.)

7. Agreement Between Pronouns and Their Antecedents

Just as subject and verb must agree in number, so subjects and pronouns must agree in number and person.

This line, for example, was the lead into an ad for a well-known Chicago store:

EVERYONE HAS THEIR PRICE

"Everyone" is singular, and "has" is singular. But "their" is plural and does not agree with the subject to which it refers. Of course, in correcting the "their," the copy writer should try to rewrite the ad without using sexist language. The writer could try "his or her" or could look for some other construction that attracts less attention. You could try an article, for example:

EVERYONE HAS A PRICE

The following rules govern subject-pronoun agreement.

a. If the antecedent is singular, the pronoun is singular.

b. If the antecedent is plural, the pronoun is plural.

c. If the antecedent is **everyone, everybody, each, either, neither, nobody, one or anyone,** the pronoun is singular.

d. If the antecedent is two nouns joined by **and,** the pronoun is plural.

e. If the antecedent is two singular nouns joined by **or** or **nor,** the pronoun is singular.

f. If the antecedent is two plural nouns joined by **or** or **nor,** the pronoun is plural.

g. If the antecedent is singular and neuter (neither masculine nor feminine), the pronoun is it or its.

> **Example:** The court recessed for lunch. It returned at 1:00 P.M.

8. Pronoun Reference

a. Avoid Vague Referents. If the pronoun is **this, that, it, such,** or **which** and refers to a preceding noun or statement, the relationship between the pronoun and the noun should be clear.

— "This" is best used in combination with a noun so that it is absolutely clear what the "this" refers to.

> **Example:** The defendant travelled west on Main Street at fifty miles per hour. This violates the law.

Since the "this" could refer to travelling west as well as to the rate of speed, the word "this" needs a noun.

> **Rewrite:** "This rate of speed violates the law."

— If the pronoun can refer to two preceding nouns, make it clear which noun the pronoun refers to.

> **Example I:** The parent corporation and the subsidiary, which places great emphasis on loyalty, have a singularly responsive relationship.
>
> **Rewrite:** The parent corporation, which places great emphasis on loyalty, has a singularly responsive relationship with its subsidiary.
>
> **Example II:** Jim talked to John while he waited for the elevator.
>
> **Rewrite:** While Jim waited for the elevator, he talked to John.

b. The referent or antecedent for every pronoun should be present in the sentence or, at least, in the preceding sentence.

B. Use of Quotations

Keep quotes short. But if you do use a long passage of fifty words or more, you must set out the quote in block form, that is, indented and single spaced. You do not use quotation marks when you set out a quote in block form. Put the citation as the first nonindented text after the quotation.

When you do use quotations, it is important to use them accurately. You must quote material exactly as it appears in the source from which you quote. You may alter the quote, but if you do, you must indicate the alterations. Use these devices:

1. Indicate omissions with an ellipsis (three periods). Do not indicate omissions from the beginning of the quote. When an omission indicated by ellipsis points occurs at the end of the sentence, you must add a fourth dot which is the period for the sentence.

    Examples: "and so . . . ask not what your country can do for you, ask what you can do for your country."

    And

    "ask not what your country can do for you, ask what you can do. . . ."

    But Not

    John F. Kennedy said, ". . . ask not what your country can do for you."

2. Indicate explanations and changes, such as changing a letter from upper to lower case, with brackets. Put your own version inside the brackets.

    Examples: "[A]sk not what your country can do for you."

    Or

    The court said, "he [the defendant] must have known the gun was loaded."

    In the first sentence, the writer used "Ask" to begin a sentence. The writer had to capitalize the "a." The writer of the second sentence decided to clarify the referent for the pronoun "he."

3. You may underline to add emphasis but you must explain your additions after the citation. Use this device sparingly.

    Example: "The statute applies to tort actions only." Jones v. Smith, 510 S.E.2d 53 (Fla. 1980) (emphasis supplied).

    If the underlining is part of the original quotation, put in parenthesis (emphasis in the original).

4. Use "[sic]" to indicate that you have quoted accurately and that the original contains a mistake.

Example: "The statue [sic] applies to tort actions only."

5. Begin a quotation with a capital letter if it is introduced by a colon or if the quotation is syntactically independent of the rest of the sentence. If the quotation is a syntactical part of the sentence, do not capitalize the first letter.

Example: As the judge said, "The motion is denied."

Example: He said that the cross-examination was "almost finished."

Example: The testimony of the plaintiff was explicit: "At all times, I was free to leave the site of the polygraph examination."

Exercise A–1: Grammar and Punctuation

Correct the grammar and punctuation errors in the following sentences.

1. Every decision concerning the children were made jointly.

2. It is unlawful in N.Y. to confine a person against their will.

3. The filing fee violates Doone's right to be heard in court, therefore, this fee requirement should be invalid.

4. The aerial surveillance was a concentrated search undertaken for the express purpose of observing defendants activities.

5. Olympia Department Store denied they had committed outrageous acts.

6. As a general rule the court will refuse to enforce that part of the contract that is unconscionable.

7. The District Court following a hearing denied defendant's suppression motion.

8. A sufficient connection between the litigation and the forum state exist; therefore, the court possesses jurisdiction over the defendant, and they should hear the case.

9. Based on aerial surveillance, the police entered the premises seized certain evidence and arrested the three defendants.

10. The requirement, that interrogatories be answered by the production of the relevant documents, was not met.

11. CPLR § 3124 requires disclosure "if a person, without having made timely objection, fails to answer interrogatories".

12. The superintendent's answer was insufficient and the protective order was unjustified.

13. Neither defendants nor plaintiff contest the facts.

14. Its reasonable to take inflation into account.

15. When Mr. Lattimore refused to answer Mr. Smith, he upset a salad tray.

16. We needed to edit (given the twenty-page limitation.)

17. The court said that "the actor disregarded the probability that severe distress would follow . . ."

18. Once we recognized that "designed for use" means "intended by the manufacturer", the court's application seems reasonable.

19. The court denied the defendant's motion because they had not filed in time.

20. Given the limitation on length (twenty pages) we dropped that discussion.

21. There is no reason to strike burdensome interrogatories if they are ". . . necessary to a resolution of defendant's affirmative defense."

Exercise A–2: Review Exercise—Coherence, Grammar, and Style

Diagnose errors and revise.

(1) "First, the conduct must be extreme and outrageous". (2) In Davis the court argued that if the tactics' used by the creditors have involved the use of abusive language, repeated threats of ruination of credit and threats to the debtor's employer to endanger his job, recovery could be sustained, citing authorities and previous cases in other jurisdictions. Id., at p. 407. (3) It is clear that based on these tests liability could be established by the various tactics used by the Department store. (4) Disregarding, for now, the fact that Augusta the plaintiff herein didn't actually owe money, the employee of the credit department used abusive language such as "four-flushing bitch," sent letters with statements threatening to report Augusta's delinquency to the credit rating bureau which, if done, would substantially hurt her credit rating and, in addition, on numerous occasions threatened to report her "refusal" to pay to her employer which might be construed by a reasonable person as a serious impairment to her continued employment. (5) An argument that could be made by Olympia, at this juncture, is that some meaningless speech from a collection department employee would hardly be considered oppressive or outrageous. (6) One only has to look at the aforementioned decisions to see that the store's position is weak at best. (7) In finding only one instance of outrageous conduct in Davis, the number of extreme actions here are clearly distinguishable. (8) The second factor involves the foreseeability by the store that the severe emotional distress will occur. (9) "Liability extends to

situations in which there is a high degree of probability that the severe distress will follow and the actor goes ahead in conscious disregard of it" is a direct extraction from the courts opinion. <u>Davis</u>, *supra*. (10) This standard can be used as a basis for the instant situation, thus, the letter written by Augusta to the store's president is evidence that the store knew of the situation in April, and the harassment was not stopped nor correcting the billing error. (11) If a letter to the store's president is not sufficient information, establishing foreseeability, and consequences that might result from the store's continued actions then what is?

Appendix B

Introduction to Citation Form

INDEX

I. INTRODUCTION

A Uniform System of Citation, commonly known as the Bluebook, is the generally accepted authority for citation form for legal writing, although other citation forms exist.[1] A citation is used to identify the authority for a statement and to tell the reader where to find that authority. Citations also provide other information, such as the kind of support that the cited source supplies for your statement.

Most of the types of writing you do in your first year of law school probably are legal memoranda and trial or appellate briefs. In these forms of writing, you cite authority within the text rather than in footnotes, and you put the citation right after the text that you are citing to. In other forms of writing, such as law review articles, you cite authority in footnotes. The information in this Appendix is about citing in text. Because most of the authorities

---

1. See, e.g., The University of Chicago Manual of Legal Citation (the Maroon Book 1989).

you will use for first-year memoranda and briefs are cases, statutes, constitutions, law review pieces, and books, only the rules for
citing these authorities are included.

A citation can be in the form of either a sentence or a clause.
A citation sentence comes after the sentence of text that it is the
authority for. It is punctuated as a separate sentence. You use a
citation sentence if the authority you cite supports the entire
sentence in your text. If the citation supports only part of your
sentence of text, then use a citation clause following that part of
the sentence it is an authority for. Set off the citation with
commas.

Example: (A case name represents the citation)

Parents may be immune from a tort suit by their children.
Jones v. Day. However, parents are not immune from suits for
intentional torts, Red v. Green, or from suits brought by emancipated
children, Fred v. Frank.

In this example, Jones v. Day is the case authority for the
information in the sentence about parental immunity that precedes it. Jones v. Day is written as a separate citation sentence.
There are two citation clauses in the next sentence. Each citation
provides authority for a part of the sentence. The writer has cited
Red v. Green for its holding that there is no immunity from
intentional torts, and cited Fred v. Frank for its holding that there
is no immunity from suits brought by emancipated minors.

II. CASE CITATIONS

A case citation identifies the case and gives the reader the
information necessary to find the published form of that case.
The first time you cite a case, you must include the name of the
case, the reporter in which it is published (or, if not yet in a
reporter, its place of publication, which may be a looseleaf service
or computer data base), the page on which the case begins, the
date the case was decided, and, if necessary, the court that decided
the case. The date and court information are enclosed in parentheses. The examples in these materials are for citations of cases
from the United States published in official and West Publishing
Company case reporters.

Table H in the Bluebook lists each jurisdiction in the United
States. It tells you the names of the courts in that jurisdiction,
the case reporters that publish each court's decisions, and the
abbreviations for the jurisdiction, its courts, and the reporters.

Below is an example and explanation of a citation to a case
reported in a West regional reporter, the Pacific Reporter, Second
Series, abbreviated P.2d. (The supernumerals are not part of the
citation, but are keyed to explanations below.)

1   2   3   4 5   6

<u>Jones v. Day</u>,   25   P.2d   100   (Okla. 1955)

1. Name of case, italicized, achieved by underlining if typed or written. Use the last names of the parties, if the parties are individuals, and use only the first named of each party. Use the complete name of a business entity, but abbreviate as permitted in the Bluebook. For example, if "Day" were the Day & Smith Steel Company, Incorporated, write as <u>Day & Smith Steel Co.</u>[2]

2. Comma after the case name.

3. Volume number of the case reporter and name of the reporter, abbreviated. Put a space between volume number and name of reporter.

Do not put a space between P. and 2d because there should be no space between adjacent single capitals, and the Bluebook considers "2d" a single capital. If the reporter were the South Eastern Reporter, Second Series, you would write as S.E.2d. If the reporter were the Southern Reporter, Second Series, however, you would write as So. 2d because "So." is not a single capital and thus requires a space before the numeral.

4. Page number at which the case begins.

5. No punctuation.

6. Parenthetical that identifies the jurisdiction and court, and the year the case was decided. Because the Pacific Reporter includes cases from many states, you must identify the jurisdiction of the case. Identification by the abbreviation of the state means that the case was decided by the highest court in that state. If the case was not decided by the highest court, then identify the court if it is not otherwise identified (by the name of the reporter, see below). For example, if a case was decided by the Minnesota Court of Appeals in 1978, cite as (Minn. Ct. App. 1978). If the reporter publishes cases from only one jurisdiction, you do not need to include the jurisdiction in parenthesis.

A. Citation to State Court Cases

State court decisions are reported in one of three ways:

1. An official and a regional (West) case reporter.

Cite both reporters, citing the official reporter first. Citing the same decision in more than one reporter is called a parallel citation.

<u>Blue v. Green</u>, 85 Wis. 2d 768, 270 N.W.2d 390 (1980).

---

2. Bluebook rule 10.2.1(h) instructs that abbreviations such as "Inc." or "Ltd." be omitted if a party's name contains words such as "R.R.," "Co.," "Bros.," or "Ass'n," which indicate that the party is a business firm.

Blue v. Green, 85 Ill. App. 2d 768, 270 N.E.2d 390 (1980). [This case is from the Illinois Appellate Court, which is not the highest court in the state. However, the reporter identifies the court so that it need not be identified in the parentheses.]

or

2. An official and two regional reporters.

West publishes an additional reporter for New York cases, the New York Supplement, and for California cases, the California Reporter. Cases reported in all three reporters are cited:

Blue v. Green, 46 N.Y.2d 401, 386 N.E.2d 807, 413 N.Y.S.2d 895 (1978).

or

3. A regional reporter only.

Some states no longer publish an official reporter. You will find this information in Table H of the Bluebook. For these states, cite only to the regional reporter and identify the jurisdiction in the parentheses.

Smith v. Jones, 310 S.W.2d 500 (Mo. 1978).

B. Citation to Federal Court Cases

1. The Supreme Court of the United States.

Supreme Court cases are cited to the official reporter, United States Reports, abbreviated U.S.

Nathanson v. Victor, 300 U.S. 52 (1980).

If the case is not yet reported in United States Reports, cite to West's Supreme Court Reports or United States Law Week in that order of preference. Do not give parallel citations.

2. United States District Courts and Courts of Appeals.

There are no official reporters for decisions from these courts; cases are cited only to West reporters. Federal Supplement (F. Supp.) reports cases from the district courts, Federal Reports (F. or F.2d) reports cases from the courts of appeals, and Federal Rules Decisions (F.R.D.) reports cases concerning federal procedural issues.

Because the citation does not identify the court in which the cited case was decided, you must always identify the court, by district or by circuit, in the parentheses.

John v. Marshall, 400 F. Supp. 12 (W.D. Va. 1976). [This case is from the United States District Court for the Western District of Virginia.]

John v. Marshall, 400 F. Supp. 12 (D.R.I. 1976). [This case is from the United States District Court for the District of Rhode Island. Rhode Island comprises one federal district.]

John v. Marshall, 400 F.2d 12 (2d Cir. 1976). [This case is from the United States Court of Appeals for the Second Circuit.]

John v. Marshall, 400 F.2d 12 (D.C. Cir. 1976). [This case is from the United States Court of Appeals for the District of Columbia Circuit.]

C. Unreported Cases

To cite cases that are not reported or are reported only in slip opinions, cite by the case's docket number, the court, and the full date of the decision. If the case is available in a computerized research data base, identify that source in parentheses.

> Silver v. Gold, No. 90–45 (N.D. Ill. June 5, 1988) (LEXIS, Genfed Library, Dist. file).

D. Case History

Because parties to litigation may appeal losing decisions, many cases build up a litigation "history." This history may include a decision on a motion or trial, one or more appeals, and one or more rehearings. Some or all of this prior or subsequent history of a case may be relevant authority for your analysis and should be cited.

Give the prior history (usually the trial court decision) only if significant to the point for which you cite the case. The entire subsequent history (usually appellate decisions or denials of further review) should be included, unless the cite is for a denial of rehearing or the case history on remand if these are not relevant to your analysis.

Subsequent history citations should be preceded by a word or phrase that explains the history, such as aff'd, which means that the higher court affirmed the decision below, or rev'd, which means that the higher court reversed. These explanatory words and phrases are quite stylized and are explained in the Bluebook. Note that the explanatory phrases are underlined and some are followed by a comma.

> Blue v. Green, 100 F.2d 25 (7th Cir. 1962), cert. denied, 312 U.S. 420 (1963).

This citation means that the Supreme Court of the United States denied review of the case that had been submitted by a petition for a writ of certiorari. If the date of the two decisions were the same, both 1963, then omit the date in the citation to the earlier decision.

The Maroon Book does not require prior or subsequent history unless the citation shows the strength of that case as an authority or shows if the case is continuing. Thus, you would use cert. denied only for a recent case to show finality.

III. CONSTITUTIONAL AND STATUTORY CITATIONS

A. Constitutions

Cite constitutions by country or state and abbreviate constitution as "Const." Do not include a date unless the constitution you are citing has been superseded.

U.S. Const. art. III, § 1, cl. 2.

N.M. Const. art. IV, § 7.

B. Statutes

1. Codes

Statutes are published in codes and are cited to the current official code volumes. The basic citation form includes the abbreviated name and volume of the code in which the statute appears, the section number (or whichever identification is used) of the statute, and the year the code was published. Statutes are also published by private publishing companies in unofficial codes which are usually annotated. Cite to this code only if there is no official code cite; do not use parallel citations. You will find the title of each jurisdiction's codes and their abbreviations in Table H of the Bluebook.

Example:

42 U.S.C. § 1985(3) (1982).

The cited statute is found in Title 42 of The United States Code as section 1985(3). The date is the year the code was published, not the year the statute was passed.

If the statute is published entirely in the supplement because it was enacted after the code was published in hardcover, then cite to the supplement:

42 U.S.C. §§ 2000f(a-b) (Supp. I 1983).

If you are citing to an amended statute where the original version appears in the code and the amendment is in the supplement, cite

42 U.S.C. §§ 2000e(k-m) (1982 & Supp. I 1983).

2. Session laws

If a statute has not yet been published in the code, then cite it as an act in the session laws. Give its name and public law number, the volume and name of the session laws (for state laws, begin with the name of the state) and page.

Public Debt Act, Pub.L. No. 86–74, 73 Stat. 156 (1959).

Also cite to the act if you are using material, such as the statement of legislative purpose, that is not published in the code.

Some statutes that have been codified are commonly still cited by the name and identification from their original passage as a public act, in addition to their current code citation.

The Omnibus Crime Control and Safe Streets Act of 1968, Title III, 18 U.S.C. § 2510 et seq. (1982).

IV. PERIODICALS

Your most common citations to periodicals will be to law reviews. To cite law review material in your text, cite by author's last name (if required, see below), the title of the material, underlined to italicize, the abbreviated name of the periodical in roman type (not large and small capitals), the page on which the piece begins, and the year of publication in parentheses. See the Bluebook for the appropriate abbreviations for periodicals.

A. Lead Material

Lead articles, usually written by faculty and attorneys, are cited by the author's last name. The Maroon Book requires the author's full name.

Friday, Just the Facts, 50 J. Crim. L. & Criminology 78 (1980).

B. Student Material

Student material is not usually cited by author's name, although the Bluebook now permits the author's last name in parentheses. For longer pieces, cite to the type of piece as designated in the periodical.

Comment, Will Thanksgiving Never Come?, 50 Nw. U.L. Rev. 5 (1704).

Short commentary, such as on recent developments, may be cited by designation alone.

Recent Case, 10 J. Int'l. L. & Bus. 357 (1982).

V. BOOKS

Cite books by the author's first initial and last name. The Bluebook permits, and the Maroon Book requires, the full first name. Then cite the title of the book (underlined), as it appears on the title page, the page, section, or paragraph from which the material is taken, and, in parentheses, the year of publication and edition, if more than one edition. If the book is known by the name of its editor or translator, include the name in the parenthetical.

B. Cardozo, The Growth of the Law 16 (1924).

or

Benjamin Cardozo, The Growth of the Law 16 (1924).

G. Gunther, <u>Cases and Materials on Constitutional Law</u> 375 (10th ed. 1980).

VI. GENERAL CITATION INFORMATION

A. Citation to a Particular Page

If you quote from a source or discuss material on a particular page or pages in the source, you must cite to the page or pages on which the quotation or material is found. If you are citing the source for the first time, put the page citation after you cite the page at which the material begins. This page citation is often called a jump cite; the Bluebook calls it a pinpoint citation.

<u>Blue v. Green</u>, 50 Ala. 100, 103, 200 So. 2d 108, 109 (1975).

In this example, the quotation from <u>Blue</u> is on page 103 of the Alabama Reports and page 109 of the Southern Reporter. The Maroon Book requires the jump cite for one reporter only.

In the following example, the material cited appears from page 161 through page 164 of the A.L.R. annotation.

Annotation, <u>Patentability of Computer Programs</u>, 6 A.L.R. Fed. 156, 161–64 (1971).

Examples of the jump cite in citations after the first full citation are given below.

B. Short Citation Form

Once you have cited an authority with a complete citation, you may use a short citation form for subsequent citations, as long as the short form is not confusing to the reader.

1. <u>Id</u>.

<u>Id</u>. is a citation form that refers to the immediately preceding cited authority, and can be used to refer to any kind of authority. If the second citation is to material on the same page as the preceding cite, use just <u>id</u>.

Citation one: <u>Green v. Blue</u>, 426 Pa. 464, 233 A.2d 562 (1967).

Citation two: <u>Id</u>.

If the citation is to a different page, use "<u>id</u>. at" the page number.

Citation one: B. Cardozo, <u>The Growth of the Law</u> 16 (1924).

Citation two: <u>Id</u>. at 25.

If the citation is to a case that requires a parallel citation, use "<u>id</u>. at" the page number for the first reporter cited and then the parallel citation.

Citation one: <u>Blue v. Green,</u> 426 Pa. 464, 233 A.2d 562 (1967).

Citation two: <u>Id</u>. at 473, 233 A.2d at 581.

Do not capitalize <u>id</u>. if you use it within a sentence as a citation clause.

Because the thirteenth amendment does not require state action, id. at 104, the court should hold that a private conspiracy violates that amendment.

2. Supra

Supra is used as a short citation when the authority has been cited previously but is not the immediately preceding citation. Do not use supra to cite to cases, statutes, or constitutions. For these, use id. where appropriate or the form discussed below.

B. Cardozo, supra, at 10. [This refers to Cardozo's previously cited book, cited for material at page 10.]

3. Short Form for Cases, Statutes, and Constitutions

a. Cases: The necessary short form consists of the case reporter volume and page for each reporter. The Bluebook provides a choice as to how much of the case name to include. You may omit the case name and cite to reporter and page when it is perfectly clear which case you are referring to, or you may shorten the case name to the name of one party, or you may provide the full case name. If in doubt, use at least one party's name.

Grey v. Pink, 85 Wis. 2d at 768, 270 N.W.2d at 390.

or

Grey, 85 Wis. 2d at 768, 270 N.W.2d at 390.

or

85 Wis. 2d at 768, 270 N.W.2d at 390.

When you discuss a case in text, as opposed to citing the case, you may always refer to the case by the name of a party if you have already cited the case. Do not identify a case only by the governmental party, such as "In United States. . . ."

To invalidate an agreement, one court has required actual fraud. Blue v. Green, 35 P. 220 (Okla. 1910). Later courts have limited Blue to its specific facts, however.

b. Statutes: You may use a short form to cite a statute in the same general discussion in which you have cited the statute in full as long as the citation is clear to the reader. For example, if you are discussing the Civil Rights Act, 42 U.S.C. § 1983, you may cite it as § 1983 in that discussion, or as the Civil Rights Act, or as 42 U.S.C. § 1983. When you discuss a statute in text, you may also use the short designation. Most people probably use the section designations.

c. Constitutions: Do not use a short form citation except id. where appropriate.

4. Hereinafter.

You may devise your own short form for particularly cumbersome citations to any kind of material. After you cite the material in full, follow with "hereinafter" and the form you will use. Enclose this information in brackets.

> P. Bator, P. Mishken, D. Shapiro & H. Wechsler, Hart and Wechsler's The Federal Courts and the The Federal System 300 (2d ed. 1973) [hereinafter Hart and Wechsler].

C. String Citation

A list of citations to several authorities for a particular point is called a string citation. You will see string cites used in judicial opinions and in memoranda and briefs, but you should use them sparingly. Unless your purpose is to actually list every case or other authority on point, or to literally show overwhelming authority, a string cite is usually not necessary and is difficult to read. The reader will tend to avoid it.

A citation of just a few authorities is fairly common, however, and the Bluebook prescribes a correct order. For case law, the order is federal cases, state cases, listed alphabetically by state, and foreign cases. Within each jurisdiction (all federal courts are one jurisdiction), cite cases from highest court to lowest court, and within each court level, most recent to least recent. Use the same order of jurisdictions to cite constitutions and statutes.

Separate the citations with a semicolon.

> Dawson v. Ryno, 350 F. Supp. 80 (N.D. Ill. 1987); Gant v. Justice, 150 Ga. 25, 400 S.E.2d 10 (1986); Smith v. Tudor, 200 Mo. 10, 430 S.W.2d 85 (1986); Gooden v. Hojo, 42 N.Y.2d 60, 500 N.E.2d 3, 25 N.Y.S.2d (1985); Murphy v. Dykstra, 80 Pa. Super. 51, 420 A.2d 10 (1990).

Remember, however, that not all authorities are equal in weight. A string cite obscures the differences in the importance of the authorities listed. A case or statute from the jurisdiction of your assignment, for example, should be more important than those from other jurisdictions, and these citations should precede the others. Use an introductory signal (see below) to cite the cases from other jurisdictions, as is done in this example from an Illinois problem:

> A parent is not immune from suit brought by an emancipated minor. Smith v. Jones, 400 Ill. 2d 32, 350 N.E.2d 10 (1971). See also Roosevelt v. Franklin, 142 N.J. 63, 390 A.2d 50 (1965); Kit v. Carson, 41 N.W.2d 200 (N.D. 1962); Black v. Hills, 460 N.W.2d 80 (S.D. 1964).

D. Introductory Signals

Introductory signals are the italicized underlined words that often precede citations to authority. Signals are used to show what type of support the citation supplies for the author's statement.

1. Direct citation without a signal.

    Use no signal before a citation if the authority

    a. is the source of a quotation, or

    b. provides direct support for the statement in the text, or

    c. identifies an authority in the text.

2. Introductory signals.

    a. See is the signal most often used. It means that the cited authority is a basic source material for the proposition in the text. See is used if the proposition is not stated in the cited authority (use no signal if it is) but follows directly from it.

    See also is used to give additional support, especially after other supporting authorities have been cited and discussed.

> Because Jones did not act intentionally or recklessly, she is not guilty of criminal contempt. See Yellow v. Orange, 100 F. Supp. 58 (S.D. N.Y. 1951).

> Because Jones did not act intentionally or recklessly, she is not guilty of criminal contempt under the rule of Yellow v. Orange, id. See also Gold v. Brass, 394 F.2d 42 (D.C. Cir. 1971); Silver v. Copper, 285 F.2d 512 (D.C. Cir. 1968).

    b. E.g. means "for example." Use it to give one or more examples of support for the proposition in the text. E.g. may be combined with other signals.

> Most state statutes require that the defendant act intentionally or recklessly. E.g., N.Y. Penal Law § 50 (McKinney 1980); Or. Rev. Stat. § 32 (1985); Utah Code Ann. § 12 (1981).

> A defendant, therefore, should not be guilty if he acted negligently. See, e.g., Blue v. Green, 400 F.2d 12 (7th Cir. 1972); Gold v. Brass, 394 F.2d 42 (D.C. Cir. 1971); Yellow v. Orange, 100 F. Supp. 58 (S.D. N.Y. 1951).

    c. Cf. means that the proposition in the cited authority is different from, but analogous to, the proposition in the text. Cf. can show comparisons, as does the signal "compare."

    d. Show authority in contradiction to your proposition with the signal "contra," or signals introduced by "but," such as "but see."

> Either intentional or reckless disregard of a court order constitutes criminal contempt. Gold v. Brass, 394 F.2d 42 (D.C. Cir. 1971). Contra Lead v. Pipe, 512 F.2d 65 (12th Cir. 1980) (criminal contempt requires intentional conduct).

A signal may be used with an explanatory parenthetical as in the example above. Provide some parenthetical information about the case or other authority if it is helpful to the reader. The information should relate to the material discussed in your text. You may also supply other parenthetical information, such as information that explains the weight of the cited authority.

Gold v. Brass, 394 F.2d 42 (D.C. Cir. 1971) (Bork, J., dissenting).

Lead v. Pipe, 512 U.S. 65 (1980) (per curiam).

BLUE BOOK EXERCISES

Rewrite these citations correctly. If the correct form requires information that you do not have, such as a page number, indicate the information with an underline.

1. Cleary v. Cardullo's, Inc., 198 N.E.2d 281, 347 Mass. 337 (Mass. 1964).

2. Haskell Lemon Construction Company v. Indep. School Distr., 589 P.2d 677 (Okla. 1979).

3. Rogers v. Okin, 478 F.Sup. 1342 (Mass. 1979).

4. Deppe v. Lufkin, 116 F.2d 483 (CA 1 1940).

5. Udall v. Tallman, 380 U.S. 1, 410 S.Ct. 25 (1964).

6. Desmarais v. Wachusett Regional School Dist., 276 N.E.2d 691 (Mass. 1971), certiorari den. 414 U.S. 859 (1973).

7. Brite Lite Co., Incorporated v. Alice Smith et al., 25 Ill.App.2d 723, 150 N. E.2d 556 (Ill. App. 1962).

8. U.S. v. Simpkins, 313 F. Supp. 1045, quoted on page 1048 (E.D. Tex. 1970).

9. The appellee has distinguished Illinois law from the cases cited by the appellant. The appellee has relied on Pioneer Steel Inc. v. Jones, 9 Ill.2d 522, 300 N.E.2d 260 (1978) for the proposition that Illinois law is unique. (a) The Structural Work Act, Chap. 11, Ill.Ann.Stat. 35 (1968), which is the statute at issue in Pioneer Steel, however, is different from the one at issue here. The court limited its discussion to that statute. (b) Pioneer supra 524 (1978).

   [Correct only the citations at (a) and (b)]

10. The statute requires that three witnesses sign the will. § 15 Miss. Code Ann. Only two witnesses signed the decedent's will, and the will is invalid. See, Macabre v. Macabre, 150 So. 2d 35 (Miss. 1972), Rigor v. Mortis, 182 So. 2d 10 (Miss. 1979). This court has said, "It is more important that the statute be enforced than the will be valid," Macabre, at 37.

11. By some bizarre occurrence, you have a statement from a book by Tom Clark, "The Rise and Fall of Finley's A's" in your memorandum. It was published in 1976 by Crown Publishers, Inc., which is located in New York City. The statement is in footnote 10, on page 143. Cite this source.

12. You have just read a law review article "Videotaping Wills: a new frontier in estate planning." The author is Alfred W. Buckley. It appeared in volume 11 of Ohio Northern University's law review in 1984 on pages 271–287. Cite it.

Appendix C

Sample Office Memorandum

TO: Senior Attorney

FROM: Law Clerk

DATE: November 21, 1988

RE: Emily West Contract Litigation

QUESTION PRESENTED: Can a buyer of wheat successfully defend a breach of contract suit on the grounds that both express and implied warranties under the Kansas Commercial Code were breached when 15–20% of the wheat the seller delivered was blighted and unusable?

CONCLUSION: The buyer has a strong defense based on breach of implied warranty of merchantability, Kan. Stat. Ann. § 2–314 (1983), since the goods sold to her were neither of fair average quality nor fit for the ordinary purpose of baking bread. She can also prove a breach of the implied warranty of fitness for a particular purpose, Kan. Stat. Ann. § 2–315 (1983), since she informed the seller of her particular use for his goods, that of baking breads without additives or preservatives, and he knew she was relying on his judgment to select suitable goods. However, she probably cannot successfully use breach of express warranty, Kan. Stat. Ann. § 2–313 (1983), because the seller's statement to her was an opinion and not an affirmation of fact.

FACTS: Emily West is president of the newly formed Aunt Em's Natural Heartland Bake Company, a producer of goods baked without additives or preservatives. While searching for a source of very high quality wheat, West was referred to Abel Prentice, an experienced wheat farmer with an excellent reputation as a knowledgeable grower and dealer. Prentice grows wheat on a 3,000 acre farm he owns and operates in this state. For over thirteen years he has been selling his own wheat and wheat grown by other farmers to manufacturers.

West visited Prentice in May 1988 and described the kind of bread she wished to produce. Prentice assured West that he knew a great deal about the bread business. In fact, Prentice told her that he probably knew more about her business than she did. After thinking it over, West signed a contract to buy wheat from Prentice. The written contract contained the terms of quantity, price, delivery, and payment schedules. No description or warranty as to the quality of the wheat, however, was included. After signing the contract, Prentice said: "You won't be sorry. I grow the finest wheat money can buy."

When the wheat was delivered in July, West found that 15–20% of it was blighted and unusable. West rejected the wheat and refused to pay Prentice. On August 5, 1988, Prentice filed suit against West's company for breach of contract.

APPLICABLE STATUTES:

Kan. Stat. Ann. § 84–2–104. Definitions: "Merchant"; "Between Merchants"; "Financing Agency"

(1) "Merchant" means a person who deals in goods of the kind or otherwise by his occupation holds himself out as having knowledge or skill peculiar to the practices or goods involved in the transaction or to whom such knowledge or skill may be attributed by his employment of an agent or broker or other intermediary who by his occupation holds himself out as having such knowledge or skill.

. . . .

Kan. Stat. Ann. § 84–2–313. Express Warranties by Affirmation, Promise, Description, Sample

(1) Express warranties by the seller are created as follows:

(a) Any affirmation of fact or promise made by the seller to the buyer which relates to the goods and becomes part of the basis of the bargain creates an express warranty that the goods shall conform to the affirmation or promise.

(b) Any description of the goods which is made part of the basis of the bargain creates an express warranty that the goods shall conform to the description.

. . . .

(2) It is not necessary to the creation of an express warranty that the seller use formal words such as "warrant" or "guarantee" or that he have a specific intention to make a warranty, but an affirmation merely of the value of the goods or a statement purporting to be merely the seller's opinion or commendation of the goods does not create a warranty.

Kan. Stat. Ann. § 84–2–314. Implied Warranty: Merchantability; Usage of Trade

(1) Unless excluded or modified (Section 2–316), a warranty that the goods shall be merchantable is implied in a contract for their sale if the seller is a merchant with respect to goods of that kind.

. . . .

(2) Goods to be merchantable must be at least such as

(a) pass without objection in the trade under the contract description; and

(b) in the case of fungible goods, are of fair average quality within the description; and

(c) are fit for the ordinary purposes for which such goods are
used;

. . . .

Kan. Stat. Ann. § 84–2–315. Implied Warranty: Fitness for Particular Purpose

Where the seller at the time of contracting has reason to know
any particular purpose for which the goods are required and that the
buyer is relying on the seller's skill or judgment to select or furnish
suitable goods, there is unless excluded or modified under the next
section an implied warranty that the goods shall be fit for such
purpose.

DISCUSSION: Abel Prentice's breach of contract claim is based
on Emily West's wrongful rejection of the goods. However, if
Prentice breached any of the three warranties under the Kansas
Commercial Code, then West rightfully rejected the goods and has
a successful defense. The Kansas Commercial Code provides three
possible defenses based on breach of warranty: breach of implied
warranty of merchantability, § 2–314; breach of implied warranty
of fitness for a particular purpose, § 2–315; and breach of express
warranty, § 2–313. West has a strong defense based on breach of
implied warranty of merchantability. Moreover, she has a good
defense based on implied warranty of fitness for a particular
purpose. However, she cannot successfully defend the suit by
claiming breach of express warranty.

The best defense against Prentice's suit is under § 2–314, the
implied warranty of merchantability. This section provides that if
the seller is a merchant, a warranty of merchantability is implied
in a contract. <u>Id</u>. (1). Section 2–314(2) sets out minimum standards which goods must meet to be merchantable. Under these
standards, goods must, *inter alia*, "pass without objection in the
trade under the contract description," § 2–314(2)(a); and, in the
case of fungible goods, be "of fair average quality within the
description," § 2–314(2)(b); and be "fit for the ordinary purposes
for which such goods are used," § 2–314(2)(c). Prentice is a
merchant and the goods did not meet any of these standards.
Therefore, Prentice breached the implied warranty of
merchantability.

The statute itself defines merchant, in pertinent part, as "a
person who deals in goods of the kind or otherwise by his occupation holds himself out as having knowledge or skill peculiar to the
practices or goods involved in the transaction." Kan. Stat. Ann.
§ 2–104(1) (1983). One court in Kansas has addressed the question of whether a farmer is a merchant in a case involving the sale
of hogs between hog farmers. <u>Musil v. Hendrich</u>, 6 Kan. App. 2d
196, 627 P.2d 367 (1981). The court concluded that the defendant

farmer in the hog transaction was a merchant under either definition in the statute. First, as someone who had been in the hog business for thirty years and was selling 50–100 hogs per month, he was a dealer in hogs. Second, he held himself out as having knowledge or skill relating to the goods, since he had equipment and buildings related to hog farming and sold hogs to private individuals, as well as to a slaughterhouse. Id. at 202, 627 P.2d at 373. Prentice, like the hog farmer in Musil, is a merchant under either definition. Prentice is a dealer because he is a wheat farmer who sold manufacturers not only his own wheat, but also the wheat of other farmers. He also held himself out as having knowledge relating to the goods, since he has been a wheat farmer for thirteen years, runs a 3,000 acre farm, and stated to West that he knew more about her business than she did. Prentice is therefore a merchant, and it is appropriate to apply § 2–314.

Under the standards of merchantability provided in § 2–314, the warranty was breached first because the 15–20% blighted wheat was of lesser quality than would "pass without objection in the trade" and was not of "fair average quality." § 2–314(2)(a)(b). Fair average is described as "the middle belt of quality . . . not the least or the worst . . . but such as can pass without objection." § 2–314 Comment 7. According to regulations from the Kansas Department of Agriculture, to be of fair average quality, a wheat shipment can contain no more than 10% of a blighted or inferior product. Kan. Admin. Regs. 397.41 (1981). Since the wheat Prentice shipped was 15–20% blighted, it did not meet this standard.

The implied warranty of merchantability was also breached because the wheat was not fit for its ordinary purposes. Under Kansas law, the buyer must show the ordinary purpose of the goods involved and show that the goods are not fit for that purpose. Black v. Don Schmidt Motor, Inc., 232 Kan. 456, 460, 657 P.2d 517, 525 (1983). The ordinary purpose for wheat is to make flour for bread. Since wheat that is 15–20% blighted would not make acceptable flour, the wheat is not fit for its ordinary purpose. Accordingly, Prentice breached the implied warranty of merchantability.

Prentice has also breached the implied warranty of fitness for a particular purpose. A warranty of fitness for a particular purpose is implied "when the seller, at the time of contracting, [knows] any particular purpose for which the goods are required, and [knows] that the buyer is relying on the seller's skill or judgment to select or furnish suitable goods." § 2–315. At the time the contract was made, Prentice knew that West required a high quality wheat for her all-natural bread, and that she was relying on his judgment to select and provide suitable wheat.

Since the making of all-natural bread is a particular purpose, and since wheat that is 15–20% blighted is not fit for this purpose, Prentice has breached an implied warranty of fitness.

The first requirement is that the goods are to be used for a particular, as opposed to an ordinary purpose. In International Petroleum Services, Inc. v. S & N Well Service, Inc., 230 Kan. 452, 461, 639 P.2d 29, 37 (1982), the court described a particular purpose as more specific, narrow, and precise than an ordinary purpose. Id. The court also stated that a particular purpose meant a use peculiar to the nature of the buyer's business. Id. West intended to use the wheat to make all-natural bread and cakes using no preservatives. She would, therefore, need especially high quality wheat, not a product that could be used in making ordinary baked goods which could rely on preservatives for freshness.

In addition, Prentice had reason to know of the particular purpose she intended for the wheat. Prior to signing the contract, West described her business to Prentice and told him the kind of bread she wanted to produce.

Finally, West relied on Prentice's skill and judgment to select the appropriate goods. See Addis v. Bernadin, Inc., 226 Kan. 241, 597 P.2d 250 (1979). In Addis, the plaintiff buyer, a manufacturer of salad dressings, informed the defendant seller that he needed jar lids for dressings containing vinegar and salt. Although the seller knew that the lids the buyer had ordered were incompatible with their intended use, he did not tell the buyer. Id. at 246, 517 P.2d at 254. The court held the seller, who had superior knowledge, had breached the implied warranty of fitness for a particular purpose. The buyer had relied on the seller's knowledge of his product and on his judgment to select appropriate goods in conformity with the use the buyer described. Id. West, too, relied on Prentice's judgment to provide appropriate goods. She was just starting her business, but Prentice had been selling his own wheat for over thirteen years. Moreover, Prentice not only said he knew all about the wheat business, he boasted that he knew more about her business than she did. Therefore, a court would probably hold that Prentice breached an implied warranty of fitness for a particular purpose.

It is not likely, however, that an express warranty had been created. An express warranty is created by a seller's "affirmation of fact" about the goods, or a description, sample, or model of the goods given to the buyer, any of which is "made part of the basis of the bargain." § 2–313(1)(a)(b)(c). The seller need not use formal words of guarantee, or intend to create a warranty. § 2–313(2). However, a statement which is merely the seller's opinion of the goods does not create a warranty. Id. The written Prentice–West contract made no mention of any express warranty. It could only have been created in Prentice's statement to West that he grows "the finest wheat money can buy". However, as this statement is more opinion than an affirmation of fact, Prentice did not create an express warranty.

Kansas courts have held that express warranties can be created by oral statements if these statements are affirmations of fact and not opinions. Formal words of guarantee are not necessary, but an affirmation merely of the value of the goods is not sufficient to create an express warranty. Young & Cooper, Inc. v. Vestring, 214 Kan. 311, 521 P.2d 281 (1974); Brunner v. Jensen, 215 Kan. 416, 524 P.2d 1175 (1974). In Young, the defendant buyer purchased cattle from the plaintiff seller who told him that the cattle were "a good reputable herd . . . clean cows." 214 Kan. at 315, 521 P.2d at 285. The court held that such statements are taken by cattlemen to mean that cattle are free of brucellosis. The seller thereby created an express warranty, which was breached when the cattle were found to have the disease. Id. at 327, 521 P.2d at 293. The court classified these statements as affirmations of fact and not opinion, since they were representations of fact "capable of determination" or "susceptible of exact knowledge." Id. at 318, 521 P.2d at 290. Similarly, in Brunner, another case concerning cattle, the seller's oral statement to the buyer that cows would calve by a certain date was not, the court said, an opinion. The court held that the seller's statements created an express warranty which was breached when the cows did not calve on time. 215 Kan. at 418, 524 P.2d at 1186.

The facts in West, however, are distinguishable from those in Young and Brunner. A court would probably classify Prentice's statements about his wheat as opinion, rather than fact because his statement is neither "capable of determination" nor "susceptible of exact knowledge." The statement more resembles sales talk, and therefore, did not create an express warranty.

Appendix D

Sample Appellate Brief

In the

APPELLATE COURT OF ILLINOIS
SECOND DISTRICT

Spring Term, 1987

No. 86–45

JONATHAN FINE,

Appellant

vs.

ELLEN FINE,

Appellee

On an order granting motion
for leave to appeal from the
Circuit Court of Lake County

BRIEF FOR THE APPELLEE

Northwestern University
School of Law
357 East Chicago Avenue
Chicago, Illinois 60611

Attorney for the Appellee
[E8577]

QUESTIONS PRESENTED FOR REVIEW

1. Should an Illinois court recognize a claim for custodial inter-ference and award a parent who shares custody of his child damages against the other jointly custodial parent?

2. If the court does recognize this claim, is a parent immune from a suit for damages arising from the alleged custodial interference if the parent believes that her child would be subject to physical harm if returned to the other parent's custody?

i

TABLE OF CONTENTS

TABLE OF AUTHORITIES
Cases

Statutes

Texts

Miscellaneous Authorities

OPINION BELOW

The Circuit Court of Lake County granted summary judgment against Jonathan Fine. The court's opinion is attached.

JURISDICTION

The Appellate Court of Illinois for the Second District has jurisdiction to hear this appeal on order granting motion for leave to appeal pursuant to Ill. Rev. Stat. ch. 110, § 2–101 (1986).

STATUTES INVOLVED

Illinois Marriage and Dissolution Act, Ill. Rev. Stat. ch. 40, § 602 (1986)

Best Interest of Child

(a) The court shall determine custody in accordance with the best interest of the child. . . .

(c) The court shall presume that the maximum involvement and cooperation of both parents regarding the physical, mental, moral, and emotional well-being of their child is in the best interest of the child. However, such presumption shall not be construed as a presumption that an order awarding joint custody is in the best interests of the child.

Illinois Criminal Code, Ill. Rev. Stat. ch. 38, § 10–5 (1986)

Child Abduction

. . .

(b) A person commits child abduction when he or she:

(1) Intentionally violates any terms of a valid court order granting sole or joint custody, care or possession to another, by concealing or detaining the child or removing the child from the jurisdiction of the court;

. . .

(c) It shall be an affirmative defense that:

. . .

(3) The person was fleeing an incidence or pattern of domestic violence.

STATEMENT OF FACTS

The appellant, Jonathan Fine, brought this action to recover compensatory and punitive damages from Ms. Ellen Fine, his former wife. (R. 1) He alleged that Ms. Fine, in protectively assuming custody of their daughter, had tortiously interfered with his right to the child's society and companionship. (R. 1) The

Circuit Court of Lake County granted summary judgment for Ellen Fine.

Ellen Fine was married to Jonathan Fine in Lake County, Illinois, on December 24, 1976. (R. 1) She gave birth to a daughter, Lisa Joy Fine, on April 6, 1981. (R. 1) Ms. Fine's marriage was dissolved by the Circuit Court of Lake County on April 22, 1983. (R. 1) Evincing a desire to confer upon her daughter the benefit of a father's as well as a mother's love, Ms. Fine agreed to share custody of Lisa Joy with Jonathan Fine. Under the court's decree, Ms. Fine entered into a joint-custody arrangement whereby she and Jonathan Fine would alternately assume custody of Lisa Joy for two-month periods. (R. 1, 3) In order to preserve continuity of environment for Lisa Joy as she moved between her mother's and her father's home, Ms. Fine remained in the same neighborhood as her former husband for more than two years.

Ms. Fine has stated in her affidavit that on July 2, 1985, one day after Ms. Fine had assumed custody of her daughter for a customary two-month period, Lisa Joy, then four years old, told her mother that her father had been making her "feel bad" and pointed to bruises on her arms and legs. (R. 5) Trusting her former husband, Ms. Fine calmly allowed the matter to rest. On July 6th, however, Lisa Joy told her mother that she did not want to leave her. Ms. Fine asked her daughter why, and Lisa Joy said, "Daddy's mean to me. He tells me he loves me, but then he hurts me." (R. 7) When Ms. Fine asked her daughter how her father had hurt her, the four-year-old began to cry hysterically and would not elaborate.

The next day, Ms. Fine took her daughter to see Dr. Elizabeth Andrews, a pediatrician in Waukegan, Illinois. In the course of this July 7th visit, Dr. Andrews examined Lisa Joy and questioned her about her relationship with her father. Lisa Joy told Dr. Andrews that she was afraid of her father and no longer wanted to live with him. (R. 5, 6) According to Dr. Andrews, the difficulty with child abuse cases is that the abuse a child has suffered is difficult or even impossible to confirm, even when it has occurred. (R. 5)

Lisa Joy became increasingly anxious as the time approached for her return to her father's custody. She reacted to Ms. Fine's occasional reminders with tears and repeated pleas that she be allowed to remain with her mother. Driven by evidence of Jonathan Fine's abuse, her daughter's extreme anxieties, and her own fears that further harm would befall Lisa Joy upon return to her father, Ms. Fine moved from her former apartment to an undisclosed location on August 31st. She has, however, remained in Lake County, where her former husband may contact her through her attorney. (R. 5) She also stands willing to return Lisa Joy to her father's custody when the child no longer fears him.

Jonathan Fine responded to his daughter's fears and misery by suing Ms. Fine for $100,000 in punitive damages and $100,000 in compensatory damages on December 1, 1985. He has alleged that his former wife acted solely to deprive him of his custodial rights. (R. 1, 6) Ms. Fine filed an answer to the complaint, an affirmative defense, and supporting affidavits. She also moved for summary judgment.

The Circuit Court of Lake County granted judgment for Ms. Fine. The court refused to recognize Jonathan Fine's claim as one upon which relief could be granted. (R. 8) The court also stated that even if it recognized a cause of action for custodial interference, that claim might not be appropriate in this case because Mr. and Ms. Fine share custody of Lisa Joy, and in addition, Ms. Fine had raised the affirmative defense that she feared harm to her child from her former husband's custody.

This court subsequently granted Jonathan Fine's motion for leave to appeal to consider whether he should be permitted to pursue a civil action against his daughter's jointly custodial mother, even though circumstances indicate that he may subject the child to physical harm if she is returned to his custody.

SUMMARY OF THE ARGUMENT

Jonathan Fine's action for damages arising from Ellen Fine's alleged interference with his custodial rights falls far outside the limited scope of actions for loss of a child's society and companionship that has been recognized by Illinois courts. His action also lacks legislative approval. Even if Ms. Fine had abducted her child, the Illinois legislature has chosen to impose criminal, not civil sanctions for such actions. A suit for damages, like the one Jonathan Fine proposes, should be carefully considered by the Illinois legislature before it is condoned by the courts because of its potential ramifications and abuses.

Moreover, Jonathan Fine is not entitled to recover damages from Ms. Fine for her alleged interference with his rights to the child's society and companionship because he shares custody of his daughter with Ms. Fine. The Restatement of Torts prohibits actions for custodial interference where both parents share custody. Restatement (Second) of Torts § 700 (1977). No court has permitted a parent with less than sole custody of a child to recover damages for tortious interference from a parent who shares custodial rights to the child.

Illinois' policy of promoting maximum cooperation between jointly-custodial parents also militates against permitting Jonathan Fine to recover damages from Ms. Fine for interference with his custodial rights. This policy is intended to serve the best interests of the child. The action he proposes is detrimental to his child's best interests and inimical to future cooperation between himself and his former wife. It will serve no meaningful purpose in deterring child abductions, and is otherwise unsound.

Finally, Ms. Fine's belief that her former husband might subject their daughter to physical harm provides her with immunity to any suit for custodial interference. The circumstances of Ms. Fine's case fall within the privilege accorded by the Restatement of Torts § 700. Ms. Fine's justified concerns also provide her with an affirmative defense that is consistent with other Illinois law. Jonathan Fine, therefore, may not subject Ms. Fine to liability.

ARGUMENT

I. JONATHAN FINE IS NOT ENTITLED TO COMPENSATO-
RY OR PUNITIVE DAMAGES FOR CUSTODIAL INTER-
FERENCE BECAUSE THIS CLAIM GOES BEYOND ANY
THAT IS RECOGNIZED BY ILLINOIS LAW AND IS INIMI-
CAL TO THE BEST INTERESTS OF HIS CHILD.

This court should not permit Jonathan Fine to subject his
former wife to liability for the measures she has taken to protect
their frightened daughter from his possible abuse. The claim that
Mr. Fine advances lacks legislative approval. He also asks this
court to condone an action that falls far outside the scope of civil
actions for loss of a child's society and companionship that have
been recognized by the Illinois courts. Moreover, even if this
court recognized a claim for custodial interference, that action is
not available to one parent against a parent with joint custody of
their child. Permitting a cause of action against a custodial
parent would subvert this state's policy of ensuring the best
interests of the child through maximum cooperation of the divorced parents. For these reasons, the ruling of the lower court
granting judgment against Jonathan Fine should be affirmed.

A. Ms. Fine is not liable for assuming protective custody of
her daughter because Jonathan Fine's claim falls outside
the scope of both civil actions for loss of a child's society
and existing statutory sanctions.

Illinois law provides no precedent to sustain this claim. Recently faced with the issue of whether to permit an action for
custodial interference akin to that proposed by Jonathan Fine,
Illinois' Fourth Appellate District held that a father had no claim
based upon tortious interference with his rights to his daughter's
care and companionship against schoolteachers and others who
removed and kept her from his custody. Whitehorse v. Critchfield, 144 Ill. App. 3d 192, 494 N.E.2d 743 (1986). The Whitehorse
court expressed its reluctance to unleash increased litigation in
the sensitive area of family rights absent clear legislative approval. Id. The court rejected the Restatement of Torts position,
which, under certain circumstances, condones a parent's suit
against another who abducts or otherwise removes a child from
the parent's custody. Id. at 194, 494 N.E.2d at 744; Restatement
(Second) of Torts § 700 (1977). The Fourth Appellate District
declined to recognize a tort as yet unrecognized by the Illinois
legislature, emphasizing its "multiple ramifications and potential
for abuse." Whitehorse, 144 Ill. App. 3d at 194, 494 N.E.2d at
744.

5

In this holding, the court followed the Appellate Court of Illinois for the First District. That court emphasized that actions based on familial rights to society and companionship are best left to the legislature's discretion "so that all aspects are considered and protected." Koskela v. Martin, 91 Ill. App. 3d 568, 570, 414 N.E.2d 1148, 1150 (1980). The court upheld the dismissal of a child's action to recover damages for loss of the society and companionship of her injured father.

This court should likewise affirm the lower court's judgment against Jonathan Fine's action for custodial interference for its absence of legislative support. In essence the same action as that advanced by the Whitehorse appellant, Jonathan Fine's suit carries with it the same docket-filling ramifications. Condoning suits for mere interference with custodial rights may logically spawn a multitude of actions brought not only by parents, but also by children, grandparents, and other interested parties. See Wood v. Wood, 388 N.W.2d 123, 128 (Iowa 1983) (Wolle, J., dissenting). Mr. Fine's action for custodial interference involves the complex interests of his emotionally distressed daughter, of her solicitous mother, and of others who may in the future find themselves similarly subjected to the financial and emotional burdens of litigation. These interests must, in the words of the First Appellate District, be legislatively "considered and protected" before being subjected to the potential abuses of litigation.

Indeed, the legislature already has considered the matter and has chosen to adopt criminal rather than civil sanctions against a person who unlawfully abducts a child. Ill. Rev. Stat. ch. 38 § 10–5 (1986). That statute provides no authority for the remedy Jonathan Fine seeks. The statutory remedy is directed toward obtaining the child's return from wrongful detention. In asking for compensatory and punitive damages, Mr. Fine, on the other hand, seeks a remedy motivated by malice toward his former wife, rather than by a desire for Lisa Joy's return.

Illinois courts have for good reason limited the actions that may be brought by a parent based on rights to a child's society and companionship within a narrow scope that excludes Jonathan Fine's suit. Parents may bring a wrongful death action to recover damages for the complete and irrevocable loss of their child's society. Bullard v. Barnes, 102 Ill. 2d 505, 468 N.E.2d 1228 (1984). A parent may bring an action for loss of his child's society and companionship under the limited circumstance of a psychiatrist's unauthorized and allegedly prejudicial treatment of the child at the behest of his noncustodial parent. Dymek v. Nyquist, 128 Ill. App. 3d 859, 469 N.E.2d 659 (1984). Parents may also bring an

action to recover damages for loss of the society and companionship of a child born with birth defects allegedly caused by negligently prescribed or defectively packaged drugs. Dralle v. Ruder,
148 Ill. App. 3d 961, 500 N.E.2d 514 (1986).

The operative and essential word in the holdings of the
Bullard, Dymek, and Dralle courts is "loss": loss of a child's life,
loss of a child's healthy mental state prior to detrimental psychiatric intervention, loss of a child's normal physical and mental
development. In contrast, the court below described Jonathan
Fine's claim as one, like the impermissible action of the Whitehorse plaintiff, based on "interference" with his rights to his child's
society and companionship (emphasis supplied). (R. 8) In Bullard,
Dymek, and Dralle, the defendants allegedly caused losses both
substantial and largely or wholly irrevocable. Ms. Fine, however,
has sought to preserve her child's mental health and physical
wellbeing. She stands ready to return her daughter to her former
husband's custody, moreover, when Lisa Joy no longer fears him.

B. Jonathan Fine fails to state a claim for custodial interference because he shares custody of his daughter with Ellen
Fine.

Jonathan Fine has failed to state a claim for custodial interference because he shares custody of his daughter with Ms. Fine.
The Restatement of Torts prohibits one jointly custodial parent
from bringing an action for custodial interference against another.
Restatement (Second) of Torts § 700 comment c. Where a parent
possesses less than sole custody of a child, moreover, the common
law rule is clear. That parent may not bring an action for
custodial interference against another parent who also has rights
to custody.

Even the relatively expansive Restatement formulation of the
tort of custodial interference bars one parent from suing another
"where the parents are by law jointly entitled to the custody and
earnings of the child." Id. No court has permitted one jointly
custodial parent to recover tort damages from another based on
custodial interference. Because the essence of the tort is the
deprivation to the parent of the child's society, only a parent who
possesses superior rights to the child's society can sue the other
parent. Moreover, a suit against the other custodial parent does
not vindicate the best interests of the child. A parent who has
been awarded joint custody of a child has been recognized by the
court as a fit parent who will act in the child's best interests.

It is impossible to imagine a more complete joint custody
arrangement than that provided for Mr. and Ms. Fine in the
Circuit Court of Lake County's dissolution decree. Under this

7

decree, each parent is entitled to physical custody of Lisa Joy for periods of time totalling one half of each year. (R. 1, 8) Under this decree, therefore, Lisa Joy's parents are jointly entitled to her "earnings" or, in the more modern words, her "society and companionship." (R. 2) The Restatement's joint-custody exception to tort liability for custodial interference, coupled with the absence of any precedent to support his action, must bar Jonathan Fine's claim against Ms. Fine.

The Restatement further requires that a parent have "sole custody" of a child to be entitled to sue for custodial interference. Id. Moreover, where a suing parent, such as Jonathan Fine, has less than sole custody of his child, courts nationwide have refused to recognize any action he might bring for custodial interference.

Two recent Missouri cases exemplify the hard-and-fast nature of this "sole custody" rule. In Politte v. Politte, 727 S.W.2d 198 (Mo. Ct. App. 1987), for example, the plaintiff father had temporary rights to full custody of his children and had also been accorded permanent visitation rights. The court in Politte affirmed a lower court's ruling that the father had no claim against his former wife because his custody right to the child was not superior to that of his former wife. Id. The court concluded that the Restatement rule and public policy prohibited the appellant's action. Id. at 199–200.

In the view of the Politte court, the tort may vindicate one parent against the other, but it does not necessarily serve the best interests of the child. Id. at 200–01. The child's best interests are served by prompt return to the parent the court has determined is the more qualified custodian, rather than by assessing damages against one parent.

In a case in which the court had awarded custody to the mother and then temporary custody to the father, another Missouri court affirmed dismissal of the father's suit to recover damages from his former wife for harboring the children. Kipper v. Vokolek, 546 S.W.2d 521 (Mo. Ct. App. 1977). This court held that in the absence of a clear showing that the appellant was entitled to sole custody of his children, he had stated no claim upon which relief could be granted. Id. at 527.

In contrast to the Kipper appellant, Jonathan Fine can raise no possible entitlement to full custody of his daughter. Like the Politte appellant, Jonathan Fine has, in a sense, temporary rights to full custody of his daughter for six months out of the year. Application of the sole custody requirement to his case therefore yields the clear result that he is not entitled to sue Ms. Fine for her alleged interference with his custodial rights. Jonathan Fine seeks to vindicate his own interests, rather than those of Lisa Joy, by seeking damages from Ms. Fine.

A survey of remaining cases in which courts that have decided the issue of whether a parent with less than sole custody of a child may sue for custodial interference further compels the conclusion that Mr. Fine has no grounds on which to press his action. A parent with custodial rights to visitation may not bring an action for custodial interference against another parent who also has rights to custody. See, e.g., Owens v. Owens, 471 So. 2d 920 (La. Ct. App. 1985) (parent with partial custody of children held to have no claim for alleged tortious interference by parent with possessory custody); Friedman v. Friedman, 79 Misc. 2d 646, 361 N.Y.S.2d 108 (Sup. Ct. 1974) (father's claim for damages for mental anguish arising from interference with visitation rights held not actionable against former spouse awarded physical custody of children). In only one reported case has a parent with less than sole custody of her child been permitted to recover damages for custodial interference. Ruffalo v. United States, 590 F. Supp. 706 (W.D. Mo. 1984). This case, however, involved an action against the government, as opposed to another parent, for its failure adequately to protect the parent's visitation rights when it included her son in the Witness Protection Program. Id.

Jonathan Fine essentially asks this court to condone an action for custodial interference that the courts of our state have rejected. Even if this claim were recognized, he asks the court to ignore its inapplicability to his case. He asks this court to ignore the Restatement's prohibition of actions for custodial interference in joint custody cases. He asks this court to set aside the rule, established in case after case, that a parent must have sole custody of a child to be entitled to bring the action he proposes. Ms. Fine respectfully requests that this court reject an action so perverse and unprecedented.

C. Jonathan Fine should not be permitted to seek damages from Ms. Fine because his action is detrimental to his daughter's best interests, and his suit subverts this state's overriding policy of promoting cooperation between divorced parents.

A policy of deterring strife between divorced parents who must cooperate in sharing custody of their children is implicit in the rules prohibiting one parent from bringing an action for custodial interference against another, unless he has sole custody of his child. In this state, however, such a policy is explicit. In order to implement Illinois' legislative policy of promoting divorced parents' maximum cooperation and involvement in the

9

lives of their children, this court must hold Jonathan Fine's monetary attack against his former wife unactionable.

The Illinois legislature has recently declared a policy that places the ongoing welfare of children above the sad, if all too common, tendency of a divorced parent to seek self-interested vindication against a former spouse through adversarial proceedings involving custody. The legislature has amended the Illinois Marriage and Dissolution Act's custody provisions to include the presumption that a child's best interests are served by "the maximum involvement and cooperation of both parents." Ill. Rev. Stat. ch. 40, § 602 (1986). This amendment and accompanying amendments formulate a legislative policy that favors mediated settlements over adversary judicial proceedings in the interests of a child's stability. Abraham, An Interpretation of Illinois' New Joint Custody Amendments, 75 Ill. B.J. 332, 333 (1987).

Permitting one parent to attempt to levy heavy civil damages for custodial interference against another contravenes this state's child-oriented, litigation-discouraging policy. Civil actions alleging custodial interference, especially those brought by one jointly custodial parent against another, can only harm the children involved. Jonathan Fine accomplishes nothing in the way of assuaging his daughter's fear of him by suing for $200,000 in damages to visit punishment on his former wife and to redress his own sense of personal injury. Indeed, the "Daddy" whom Lisa Joy says has already hurt her must grow into a yet more fearful character for inflicting the pain, expense, and time-consuming worries of litigation upon her mother. Through pursuing this litigation, moreover, he must effectively destroy future channels of communication and cooperation between himself and the former wife who supported his relationship with his daughter until the child's fears compelled her to assume her exclusive custody. The Illinois legislature surely rejected any such traumatic scenario in the policy it enunciated in amending the Illinois Marriage and Dissolution Act.

In deferring to the legislature on the advisability of civil actions for interference with familial rights to society and companionship, the First and Fourth Appellate Districts have implicitly recognized the potentially detrimental effects such actions may have on the parent and children involved. Koskela v. Martin, 91 Ill. App. 3d 508, 414 N.E.2d 1148; Whitehorse v. Critchfield, 144 Ill. App. 3d 192, 494 N.E.2d 743. In the Politte case, a Missouri appellate court addressed these detrimental effects directly. In dismissing an action for custodial interference, the court reasoned that the primary goal of this tort was "the vindication of one parent against the other" to the potential detriment of the child involved. Politte v. Politte, 727 S.W.2d at 200. "Disarmament is needed to limit post-marital warfare," the Politte court declared, "not additional armament to increase it." Id. at 201.

This court should refuse to arm Jonathan Fine with a weapon so inimical to healing his family's wounds when his future cooperation with Ms. Fine is needed to promote the best interests of their daughter. This court may remand this case to the court below for court-supervised counseling and mediation. The Circuit Court of Lake County, which has overseen the Fines' family situation from the outset of dissolution proceedings, will be able to create a far better solution to their problems than the appellant can provide through this destructive action.

   D. Because Ms. Fine holds her daughter in protective custo-
       dy in good faith, her conduct provides no basis for
       Jonathan Fine's claim for damages.

Ms. Fine has protectively withheld her daughter from her former husband's custody, but contrary to his false accusations, she has not engaged in child abduction. Child abduction has been defined in joint hearings before the Congress as occurring when a parent, with little attention to the child's best interests, undertakes an abduction chiefly for retaliatory reasons and for fear of losing control of the child. Proposed Federal Prevention Kidnapping Act: Addendum to Joint Hearings on S. 105 Before the Subcomm. on Criminal Justice of the House Committee of the Judiciary and the Subcomm. on Child and Human Development of the Senate Comm. on Labor and Human Resources (Submission of Children's Rights Inc.), 96th Cong., 2d Sess. 27 (1980). Child abduction frequently involves a relative's possessive acts toward the child, and a child's transport to a distant jurisdiction, with the object of completely depriving a custodial parent of his or her rights. Note, The Tort of Custodial Interference—Toward a More Complete Remedy to Parental Kidnappings, 1983 U. Ill. L. Rev. 229, 233.

Thus, in a particularly aggravated case such as that of Kunz v. Deitch, in which maternal grandparents prevented a father from regaining custody of his daughter after her mother's death, and even put the child up for adoption, a court may permit a tort action for custodial interference for reasons of deterrence. 660 F. Supp. 679 (N.D. Ill. 1987). See also Kajtazi v. Kajtazi, 488 F. Supp. 15 (E.D.N.Y. 1978) (custodial mother permitted to recover from father and paternal relatives who abducted child to Yugoslavia).

Ms. Fine is clearly not a self-interested "child snatcher." She supported Jonathan Fine's custodial relationship with his daugh-

11

ter for two years, until Lisa Joy revealed her fears of her father to both her mother and a pediatrician. She assumed custody of her daughter for justified protective reasons, and she is willing to permit her former husband to resume custody of Lisa Joy when her daughter no longer fears him. Ms. Fine, moreover, has remained within the jurisdiction of the courts of this state, has kept her child in familiar surroundings in Lake County, and has provided a residence for her daughter where Jonathan Fine may reach her through counsel. Therefore, this case presents no policy considerations regarding child abduction which permits this court to recognize a tort action for custodial interference. Even if child abduction had occurred in this case, other more effective remedies are available to ensure the child's return, such as contempt, habeas corpus, and civil actions under the Uniform Child Custody Act. See Politte, 727 S.W.2d at 201.

Jonathan Fine's claim for $100,000 in compensatory damages and $100,000 in punitive damages, unjustified for policy reasons, is also unsupported by the circumstances of this case. Courts that have awarded compensatory damages for custodial interference have usually awarded damages only in cases in which suing parents have had to launch extensive searches for their children. See, e.g., Fenslage v. Dawkins, 629 F.2d 1107 (5th Cir. 1980) (plaintiff mother permitted to recover $65,000 in compensatory damages for extensive efforts to locate children concealed in Canada); Kajtazi v. Kajtazi, 488 F. Supp. 15 (custodial mother permitted to recover $20,400 in actual compensation for living expenses, legal costs, and loss of society incumbent on lengthy search for child abducted to Yugoslavia). Even setting aside the many policy reasons that militate against permitting Mr. Fine to seek recovery of compensatory damages, it is difficult to see how he could have accumulated $100,000 in losses when Ms. Fine has kept her daughter within Lake County, has remained open to contact through her attorney, and has not launched him on an extensive search. Furthermore, the reasonable fears for her daughter's safety that have led Ms. Fine to withhold Lisa Joy from her former husband's custody forestall his claim for punitive damages. Such damages, only justified by a defendant's particularly aggravated misconduct coupled with bad faith, are hardly justified in Ms. Fine's case. See D. Dobbs, Handbook of the Law of Remedies 204–05 (1973).

Jonathan Fine's action is detrimental to his child's best interests. His attempts to recover damages from Ms. Fine are also inimical to this state's policy of promoting cooperation between divorced parents in order to maximize their involvement in their child's life. Ms. Fine's good reasons for withholding her daughter from his custody, along with the local residence she has maintained for her daughter, provide this court with no reason to permit the appellant to proceed with his action as a means of deterring child abduction. Because Jonathan Fine's claim for damages is also otherwise unjustified, this court should not permit him to proceed with his action.

II. BECAUSE MS. FINE REASONABLY BELIEVES THAT HER DAUGHTER WOULD BE SUBJECTED TO PHYSICAL HARM IF RETURNED TO JONATHAN FINE'S CUSTODY, SHE IS IMMUNE FROM HIS SUIT FOR DAMAGES ARISING FROM HER ALLEGED INTERFERENCE WITH HIS CUSTODIAL RIGHTS.

Ms. Fine's belief that her former husband may subject their daughter to physical harm if she is returned to his custody is eminently reasonable and justifies her protective assumption of her daughter's custody. Under the formulation of the tort of custodial interference in the Restatement of Torts, she is immune from Jonathan Fine's suit and cannot be subject to liability for damages. See Restatement (Second) of Torts § 700. Ms. Fine's fears for her daughter's safety, moreover, constitute an affirmative defense to Illinois' statutory offense of child abduction. By implication, she also possesses an affirmative defense to a civil action for interference with custodial rights.

The measures Ms. Fine has taken to protect her daughter fall clearly within the exception to liability for custodial interference in the Restatement's formulation of this tort. Restatement (Second) of Torts § 700 comment e. The Restatement provides that one who rescues a child from physical violence by a parent is immune from liability for custodial interference. Id. Under the Restatement, Ms. Fine is immune from suit because it appeared "reasonably probable" that Lisa Joy would suffer "immediate harm" if she returned to Jonathan Fine's home, id., and because Ms. Fine acted only for the purpose of saving her daughter from danger at his hands. Her motives for doing so cannot be questioned. For two years prior to receiving Lisa Joy's alarming indications that her father was harming her, Ms. Fine supported and furthered the joint custody arrangement. She can now have only protective reasons for withholding Lisa Joy from her father's custody.

Furthermore, Lisa Joy's hysteria upon being asked how her father had hurt her, her repeated, tearful pleas to be allowed to remain with her mother, and her bruises certainly justified Ms. Fine's conclusion that Jonathan Fine either had or would physically harm her daughter. Lisa Joy fulfills the psychological profile of an abused child. An abused child exhibits intense distrust of the adult who has abused her, has great need for nurturance, and often has difficulty telling others about what she has experienced. Halperin, <u>Abused and Non–Abused Children's Perceptions of Their Mothers, Fathers, and Siblings: Implications for a Comprehensive Family Treatment Plan</u>, 30 Fam. Relat. 89, 91 (1981).

Lisa Joy's bruises and fears certainly show a reasonable probability that she would suffer immediate harm upon return to her father's custody. As Dr. Andrews has indicated, actual abuse can be difficult to confirm. A child should not have to receive severe injuries before she is protected, however. The author of an article on child welfare malpractice describes a tragic case in which a social worker dismissed a parent's report, based on his children's bruises, that they were possibly being subjected to abuse by their custodial mother. Ten days later, one of the children died of abuse. Basharov, <u>Child Welfare Malpractice</u>, 20 Trial 56, 57 (1984).

Ms. Fine's affirmative defense to the action gains strong support from this state's criminal statute on child abduction. Ill. Rev. Stat. ch. 38, § 10–5(c)(1) (1986). This statute provides that flight from an incidence of domestic violence constitutes an affirmative defense to the offense of concealing a child from a custodial parent. <u>Id</u>. Lisa Joy's statement that her father inflicted her bruises, coupled with the fear she has expressed toward him, indicates that her father had subjected her to some form of violence. Ms. Fine is therefore justified in protectively concealing her daughter's whereabouts from her former husband. Since she may be relieved of any criminal liability for these actions, she should be similarly freed from any civil liability for them.

Lisa Joy's bruises and fears justify Ms. Fine's belief that her daughter might be subjected to physical harm upon her return to Jonathan Fine's custody. Since Ms. Fine is entitled to remove her daughter from a potentially dangerous environment and did so for protective purposes, she possesses a privilege that relieves her from liability for custodial interference as formulated in the Restatement of Torts. Because Ms. Fine could have successfully raised an affirmative defense to the Illinois offense of child abduction, she implicitly possesses the same defense to a civil action for custodial interference. Ms. Fine, therefore, is free from any civil liability to Jonathan Fine.

14

CONCLUSION

For the foregoing reasons, the decision of the Circuit Court of Lake County granting summary judgment to the appellee, Ellen Fine, should be affirmed.

Appendix E

Sample Memorandum in Support of a Motion

IN THE CIRCUIT COURT OF COOK COUNTY,
ILLINOIS COUNTY DEPARTMENT, LAW DIVISION

PARK, INC., et al.,
               Plaintiffs,

    v.

DAVID RYAN, et al.,
               Defendants.

No. 86 L 22939
N.W.

MEMORANDUM IN SUPPORT OF MOTION TO DISMISS COMPLAINT AS TO WRIGLEY HOUSING, INC., JOE SAYERS, ANN CHRISTIE, AND MARGARET JAMES

INTRODUCTION

Plaintiffs PARK, INC. ("Park"), a real estate management company, and its President, Earl Marple ("Marple"), have sued more than thirty individuals and organizations active in the tenants' rights movement in the West Park section of Chicago. Plaintiffs' four-count complaint purports to state claims for libel and slander. On December 22, 1986, defendants Wrigley Housing, Inc. ("Wrigley"), Joe Sayers ("Sayers"), Ann Christie ("Christie") and Margaret James ("James"), filed a motion to dismiss the complaint as to those defendants pursuant to Rule 2–615 of the Illinois Rules of Civil Procedure. This memorandum is submitted in support of those defendants' motion to dismiss.

STATEMENT OF FACTS

Plaintiff Park is a corporation engaged in the business of managing and developing real estate. (Complaint ¶ 1.) Park has developed and manages more than 500 rental units in the West Park area of Chicago. (Complaint ¶ 12.) Plaintiff Marple is President of Park, and has been in the real estate business since 1969. (Complaint ¶¶ 1, 9.) This case arises out of a dispute between Park and Marple, on the one hand, and the West Park Tenants' Committee ("WPTC"), the Professionals for Better Housing ("PBH"), and Alderman David Ryan, on the other hand, concerning Park's real estate management practices. (Complaint ¶¶ 16–22.)

In April 1986, WPTC convened a meeting of tenants and former tenants of Park and of representatives of other tenants' rights organizations and block clubs, in response to complaints about Park's rental policies and practices. (Complaint ¶ 22; Exhibit A.) Park's tenants continued to meet, to distribute literature to Park tenants, and to picket at Park's rental office and at Marple's home. (Complaint ¶ 22.)

Plaintiffs allege that the communications thus published by WPTC and PBH were defamatory. (Counts I and II.) Specifically, in Count I, they allege that a newsletter attached as Exhibit A to the complaint contains the following defamatory statements:

> That in August 1985 (or on or about said time) there were complaints regarding Park as to "giant rent increases"; "failure to refund security deposits and pay interest"; "chronic heat and hot water problems"; "intimidation of tenants"; and "outrageous set of move-out policies."

(Complaint ¶ 30.)

Plaintiffs allege that a leaflet attached as Exhibit B to the complaint contains the allegedly defamatory statement "that the WPTC wanted to meet with Park 'to discuss the state investigation of Park.' " (Complaint ¶ 28.) They also allege that leaflets attached to the complaint as Exhibits C and D libel Park and Marple by stating, inter alia, that Park's tenants want to meet with Marple to discuss "problems relating to his mismanagement of ten buildings in West Park with nearly 500 apartments" and, specifically, "lack of water," "lack of heat," "poor building security," "unfair security deposit deductions," "lack of smoke detectors," "unresponsiveness to requests for repairs," "failure to pay security deposit interest," "electrical problems," "roaches," "intimidation and harassment of tenants," "infrequent garbage pickup," and "outrageous move-out policies." (Exhibits C–D; Complaint ¶ 31.) Plaintiffs allege that Exhibits A, B, C and D were authored by WPTC and PBH and that the authors "were one or more of the following Defendants," with Christie included on a list of thirteen names. (Complaint ¶ 25.)

In Count II, plaintiffs allege that various defendants, including Christie, picketed the offices of Park's rental agent. (Complaint ¶¶ 47–48.) Plaintiffs claim that various picket signs and oral communications included defamatory statements that Park and Marple were "in housing court," did not supply heat in their buildings, had a policy "not to return security deposits," "made bogus deductions" from security deposits, and that the buildings managed by Park had roaches. (Complaint ¶ 49.)

Counts III and IV concern a letter sent to the limited partners of Park on or about October 1, 1986. (Complaint ¶ 64.) The letter indicates that it was endorsed by Alderman Ryan and a number of tenants' and housing rights groups, including Wrigley Housing. (Exhibit E.) Plaintiffs allege in Count III that the letter contains the following allegedly defamatory statements:

A.   Evidence exists documenting continuous complaints by tenants about maintenance problems and the indifferent handling of these complaints by Park, Inc.

B.   City inspection reports detail numerous instances of housing code violations in Park, Inc. properties.

C.   Park is not repairing housing code violations and is not making repairs in a workmanlike manner.

D.   Numerous outgoing tenants have complained about not receiving proper disbursement of their security deposits.

E.   Most tenants have not received the requisite interest on their security deposit interests.

F.   The buildings show serious signs of mismanagement and distress.

G.   Many tenants are not renewing their leases with Park, Inc. because they cannot deal with habitually poor management.

H.   The buildings are developing high vacancy rates and falling into disrepair.

ARGUMENT

The plaintiffs' complaint must be dismissed because the communications complained of in Counts I, II, III, and IV are not defamatory *per se* under Illinois law. Even assuming that the statements are defamatory, Illinois law grants them a qualified privilege. Furthermore, plaintiffs' prayer for punitive damages is unsupported and must be stricken from the complaint. Finally, the complaint contains no allegations concerning defendants Sayers and James and should be dismissed as to those defendants.

I.   ALL COUNTS MUST BE DISMISSED BECAUSE THE COMMUNICATIONS COMPLAINED OF ARE NOT DEFAMATORY PER SE.

Under Illinois law, the defendants' statements are not defamatory *per se*. To be considered defamatory *per se*, the language must be so obviously and naturally harmful to the person to whom it refers that damage is a necessary consequence and need not be specially shown. Owen v. Carr, 113 Ill. 2d 273, 274, 497 N.E.2d 1145, 1147 (1986); Sloan v. Hatton, 66 Ill. App. 3d 41, 42, 383 N.E.2d 259, 260 (4th Dist. 1978). Four classes of words, if falsely communicated, give rise to an action for defamation without a showing of special damages:

>   1. Those imputing the commission of a criminal offense

>   2. Those imputing infection with a communicable disease

>   3. Those imputing inability to perform or want of integrity in the discharge of duties of office or employment, and

>   4. Those prejudicing a particular party in his profession or trade.

Fried v. Jacobson, 99 Ill. 2d 24, 26, 457 N.E.2d 392, 394 (1983). With respect to corporate plaintiffs, moreover, the alleged libel must assail the corporation's financial or business methods or accuse it of fraud or mismanagement. American International Hospital v. Chicago Tribune Co., 136 Ill. App. 3d 1019, 1022, 483 N.E.2d 965, 969 (1st Dist. 1985); Audition Division, Ltd. v. Better Business Bureau, 120 Ill. App. 3d 254, 256, 458 N.E.2d 115, 118 (1st Dist. 1983).

In determining whether particular language constitutes libel *per se,* Illinois courts apply the rule of innocent construction:

>   a written or oral statement is to be considered in context, with the words and the implications therefrom given their natural and obvious meaning; if, as so construed, the statement may reasonably be innocently interpreted as referring to someone other than the plaintiff it cannot be actionable *per se.* This preliminary determination is properly a question of law to be resolved by the court in the first instance.

Chapski v. Copley Press, 92 Ill. 2d 344, 347, 442 N.E.2d 195, 199 (1982). Thus, the court must examine the statements here within the context of the surrounding circumstances and events, and judge the words accordingly. Id.; Sloan v. Hatton, 66 Ill. App. 3d at 43, 383 N.E.2d at 261. Moreover, the trial court is required to make this determination in the context of the entire publication. Chapski, 92 Ill. 2d at 345, 442 N.E.2d at 199.

The following emerges clearly from an examination, in context, of Exhibits A through E to the complaint: As Exhibit A shows, tenants of buildings owned and managed by Park were meeting and organizing in early 1986. It is clear from Exhibits B through E that the tenants' goal was to meet with Park and Marple to discuss various problems the tenants perceived:

>   "To plan other direct action to get Park to meet with us" (Exhibit B)

"We want to meet with Earl Marple to discuss and get action on these problems" (Exhibit C)

"Quite simply we want Park to meet with us and begin to address our legitimate concerns" (Exhibit D);

"Therefore, we are asking that (1) you attend a special meeting of the West Park Housing Forum. . .and (2) that you encourage Mr. Marple to attend this meeting also" (Exhibit E, at 3).

Thus, the context of the communications here was clearly a dispute between tenants and a landlord about the manner in which he was managing his buildings.

Chapski requires that, in ruling on a motion to dismiss, the trial court must review the allegedly libelous documents to determine, as a matter of law, whether they are subject to a reasonable *non-defamatory* construction; if so, the documents are not actionable even if they may also be subject to a reasonable *defamatory* construction and even if the party receiving the communications understood them in a defamatory sense. Chapski, 92 Ill. 2d at 345, 442 N.E.2d at 199. Following this mandate, Illinois courts have repeatedly dismissed libel cases after finding that the statements complained of were susceptible of a reasonable innocent construction. See, e.g., Meyer v. Allen, 127 Ill. App. 3d 163, 165, 468 N.E.2d 198, 200 (4th Dist. 1984); Audition Division, Ltd. v. Better Business Bureau, 120 Ill. App. 3d at 257, 458 N.E.2d at 119; Cartwright v. Garrison, 113 Ill. App. 3d 536, 537–40, 447 N.E.2d 446, 447–50 (2d Dist. 1983).

Rasky v. CBS, Inc., 103 Ill. App. 3d 577, 431 N.E.2d 1055 (1st Dist.), cert. denied, 459 U.S. 864 (1982), is particularly relevant to this case. The Rasky plaintiff was a landlord whose building maintenance and business practices were criticized by a number of tenants' groups and a state representative, among others; CBS News then broadcast a news program describing the controversy and interviewing tenants. The appellate court, affirming dismissal of the case, found that the derogatory remarks by the news media and community groups could be interpreted innocently:

The overall thrust of the CBS news telecast was that citizens in the community were bitterly opposed to the way in which they perceived that plaintiff managed his buildings and that, through their representatives, they intended to explore available legal remedies for redress. In that context, the report noted that Edgewater citizens: have accused plaintiff of being a "slumlord"; have previously taken legal action against him; claim he does not make repairs. In our opinion, the CBS news telecast, taken as a whole, is capable of an innocent construction and cannot be considered defamatory as a matter of law.

103 Ill. App. 3d at 577, 431 N.E.2d at 1059.

The communications complained of in this case, read as a whole and in context, amount to no more than the statements found to be non-defamatory in Rasky. The thrust of Exhibits A through E is that numbers of citizens were "bitterly opposed to the way in which they perceived that plaintiff[s] managed [their] buildings and . . . intended to explore available legal remedies for redress." Id. In that context, Exhibits A through E may reasonably be construed innocently and thus may not sustain an action for defamation.

Furthermore, it is not libel *per se* to state that complaints have been filed about a business. See, e.g., Audition Division, Ltd. v. Better Business Bureau, 120 Ill. App. 3d at 254, 458 N.E.2d at 119; American Pet Motels, Inc. v. Chicago Veterinary Medical Ass'n, 106 Ill. App. 3d 626, 628, 435 N.E.2d 1297, 1300 (1st Dist. 1982). Illinois courts have reasoned that a statement that customers have complained about a business is not equivalent to a statement that the business is incompetent, fraudulent, or dishonest. Thus, the statements complained of in Exhibit A—that in August 1985 there were a variety of complaints regarding Park (Complaint ¶ 30)—are not defamatory, as a matter of law.

Under Illinois law, it is also not libel *per se* to state that a plaintiff's business activities are under investigation. Cartwright v. Garrison, 113 Ill. App. 3d 536, 539, 447 N.E.2d 446, 450 (2d Dist. 1983); see also Spelson v. CBS, Inc., 581 F. Supp. 1195, 1205 (N.D. Ill. 1984), aff'd mem., 757 F.2d 1291 (7th Cir.1985). Thus, the statement complained of in paragraph 28 of the complaint (that the WPTC wanted to meet with Park "to discuss the state investigation of Park") is not defamatory *per se*, as a matter of law.

In short, when considered as a whole and in context, the statements in Exhibits A through E are susceptible of a reasonable innocent construction, and do not constitute libel *per se*.

II.   THE COMMUNICATIONS COMPLAINED OF ARE ENTITLED TO A QUALIFIED PRIVILEGE UNDER ILLINOIS LAW.

Even assuming, *arguendo*, that this Court finds the statements complained of defamatory, they are nonetheless not actionable, because they are privileged under Illinois law. Certain communications, even if false and defamatory, are afforded special protection—a qualified privilege—because the law recognizes their social importance. The elements of this qualified privilege are: (1) good faith by the defendant, (2) a legitimate interest or duty to be upheld, (3) publication limited in scope to that purpose, and (4) publication in a proper manner to proper parties. See, e.g., Edwards by Phillips v. University of Chicago Hospitals, 137 Ill. App. 3d 485, 488, 484 N.E.2d 1100, 1104 (1st Dist. 1985); American Pet Motels, Inc. v. Chicago Veterinary Medical Ass'n, 106 Ill. App. 3d at 630, 435 N.E.2d at 1301.

The face of plaintiffs' complaint demonstrates that the privilege applies here. First, the defendants had a good faith, legitimate purpose for the communications challenged: to address a matter of shared concern—the availability of decent, affordable, safe housing in the West Park community—and to assist one another in dealing with problems they perceived in the management practices of one large landlord. The documents themselves, a newsletter and leaflets, show that defendants' purpose was entirely legitimate, i.e., to meet with Park to discuss those problems.

Moreover, the statements in Exhibits A through E were limited in scope to furthering these common concerns. The newsletter describes community efforts to improve housing conditions. (Exhibit A.) The leaflets and letter to Park's limited partners are directed at the goal of meeting with plaintiffs to discuss certain perceived problems in Park's rental units. (Exhibits B, C, D, E, at 3.)

Finally, the statements here were communicated in a proper manner and to proper parties. The newsletter and leaflets were distributed to Park's tenants and to other residents of the West Park community interested in improving their housing conditions. (Complaint ¶¶ 31, 54B.) Exhibit E was addressed only to the limited partners of Park. (Complaint ¶ 64.)

Similarly, the statements complained of in Count II, which concern the picketing of Park's rental agent, are privileged under Illinois law. The persons making these statements spoke in good faith and in the interest of promoting good rental housing; they limited their statements to Park tenants and prospective tenants; and they made the statements in furtherance of their purpose to persuade plaintiff to meet with them to discuss their perceived problems and complaints. (See Exhibit D: "Why we're picketing Park/Rental Express" . . . "Quite simply, we want Park to meet with us and begin to address our legitimate concerns . . . .")

Under these circumstances, the qualified privilege clearly applies to all the communications complained of in plaintiffs' complaint, requiring dismissal as a matter of law, absent factual allegations that defendants abused the privilege. See, e.g., American Pet Motels, 106 Ill. App. 3d at 626, 435 N.E.2d at 1302.

III. PLAINTIFFS FAIL TO STATE A CLAIM FOR PUNITIVE DAMAGES.

Punitive damages may not be recovered without a showing of actual malice. Gertz v. Robert Welch, Inc., 418 U.S. 323, 349–50 (1974). Plaintiffs here seek an award of punitive damages based solely upon the bald assertion that defendants acted "maliciously, willfully, and with a conscious disregard for the rights of Plaintiffs." (Complaint ¶¶ 32, 52, 55, 60, 67, 71.) Bare allegations of actual malice in a complaint, however, do not suffice; "rather, conclusions of malice and intent must be clothed with factual allegations from which the actual malice might reasonably be said to exist." L.R. Davis v. Keystone Printing Service, Inc., 111 Ill. App. 3d 427, 433, 444 N.E.2d 253, 262 (2d Dist. 1982). Because plaintiffs do not adequately plead actual malice, their prayers for punitive damages should be stricken from the complaint.

IV. THE COMPLAINT DOES NOT CONTAIN THE NECESSARY FACTUAL ALLEGATIONS CONCERNING CERTAIN INDIVIDUAL DEFENDANTS AND SHOULD THEREFORE BE DISMISSED AS TO THOSE DEFENDANTS.

Finally, the complaint should be dismissed as to certain of the individual defendants, because it contains no allegations of wrongdoing on their part. The complaint contains no factual allegations whatsoever concerning the conduct of defendants Sayers and James, and should therefore be dismissed in its entirety as to them. Counts III and IV, which concern the letter to Park's limited partners, contain absolutely no allegations that defendants James, Sayers, or Christie participated in the composition or publication of that letter, and should therefore be dismissed as to those defendants. Additionally, Count II, alleging defamation based on picketing the office of Park's rental agent, is devoid of any allegations concerning the conduct of defendants James or Sayers, and should therefore be stricken as to those defendants.

Finally, plaintiffs fail throughout to allege defamation with sufficient particularity. In actions for libel and slander, a plaintiff is held to a high standard of specificity in pleading. Altman v. Amoco Oil Co., 85 Ill. App. 3d 104, 106, 406 N.E.2d 142, 145 (1st Dist. 1980). By contrast, plaintiffs here allege, for example, that the authors of Exhibits B, C and D "were one or more of the following Defendants," including defendant Christie in a list of thirteen names. (Complaint ¶ 25.) Unless plaintiffs can amend to specify the personal involvement of each named individual, the complaint should be dismissed as to those individual defendants.

CONCLUSION

For the foregoing reasons, defendants Wrigley Housing, Inc., Joe Sayers, Ann Christie and Margaret James respectfully request that this Court enter an order dismissing the complaint with costs, or, in the alternative, dismissing them as defendants in this case.

WRIGLEY HOUSING, INC.,
JOE SAYERS, ANN CHRISTIE
AND MARGARET JAMES

By: _____
Their Attorney

Cynthia G. Bowman
Northwestern University
  School of Law
357 E. Chicago Avenue
Chicago, IL 60611
(312) 503–8576

INDEX

INDEX
References are to Pages

†